Cook 'em Horns

This picture of the West Wing of the Old Main Building was taken from Nineteenth Street (now Martin Luther King Blvd.) at University Avenue in the summer of 1883 by Paul McCombs. It is the oldest photograph of the campus.

Cook 'em Horns

Texas Exes' Cookbook Celebrating The University of Texas Centennial

The Ex-Students' Association
of The University of Texas

Bebe Canales Inkley, Cookbook Committee Chairman, '57
Gladys Bravenec Howard, Recipe Editor, BS '55
Dr. Margaret C. Berry, Historical Editor, BA '37
Nell Jones Herndon, Testing Chairman, BA '30
Loraine McNeil Jackson, ESA Staff Coordinator, '46

Additional copies may be obtained by sending $16.95 plus $2.00
for postage and handling to the address below. Texas residents
add 5% sales tax.

The Ex-Students' Association
The University of Texas
P.O. Box 7278
Austin, Texas 78712

First Edition   1981   8,000 copies

Library of Congress Catalogue Card Number 81-68280

Design by
John Franzetti
Smitherman Graphic Design

Cover photo by
Sherwood Inkley

Printed in the United States
by Hart Graphics, Inc.

Foreword

*C*ompiling *Cook 'em Horns* has been like preparing a gourmet meal: careful planning, the right combination of ingredients and the expertise and talent of putting everything together and serving it in an appealing way. And the result will be especially satisfying to The University of Texas students who will benefit from scholarship funds generated by the book.

From its inception in 1979, the project has been charged with the kind of contagious enthusiasm that is characteristic of Texans everywhere. It is seasoned with the affection for The University of Texas, felt by nearly 10 generations of ex-students.

Cook 'em Horns is a blend of the tradition of alumni involvement combined with the accomplishment of a new idea . . . of old friends and new volunteers who have never been involved before . . . of the top leadership of The Ex-Students' Association and folks like the Texas Ex from San Angelo who tested 91 recipes and at the end of the project wrote, "I really don't know what I am going to do when the testing is over. My family wants to know what's new for dinner every day."

But the preparation is just the beginning. Whether you whet your appetite by browsing through the beautiful photographs, reading the fascinating historical commentary, or by preparing one of the carefully selected and tested recipes for your family and friends, we hope that you will find *Cook 'em Horns* spiced with the key ingredients of pride and loyalty which typify Texas Exes and their University.

John Stuart, BBA '58
Immediate Past President
The UT Ex-Students' Association

Jean Welhausen Kaspar, BA '52
President
The UT Ex-Students' Association

Contents

Introduction

$\mathcal{F}$ood interests most of us and provides for us not only the nourishment our bodies need but also an opportunity to escape from the reality of the routine, a nostalgic interlude, a euphoric plateau of momentary pleasure. On the occasion of the centennial anniversary of the founding of the University of Texas, this book of favorite recipes of hundreds of alumni and friends recognizes these two functions of good food. It even enhances the second by interspersing among the select recipes vignettes of student life for each decade of the University's history. These portraits are not intended to relate to the recipes of the various sections of the book; rather they are provided to give its users an opportunity to become reminiscent, nostalgic, even euphoric about their own student days.

These vignettes also show how the student culture changed during the past 100 years as the University grew from an enrollment of 221 to more than 46,000 and from 40 acres to more than 300. The introduction to each section provides the reader with information about student life styles, favorite haunts, interests, changing value structures, and collegiate high jinks, and thus provides an opportunity to reflect briefly on a particular part of our history that helped make the University what it is today. The student culture is a microcosm of the greater Texas society. Invention and diffusion have provided an interesting diversity of life styles among the growing student population, and professors and students from all over the world have injected ideas from society's cutting edge.

Enjoy these excellent tested recipes as you lose yourself in thoughts about your own student days. Celebrate the Centennial! Bake a cake and light a candle!

Margaret Berry
Historical Editor

8

And now a word about the recipes . . .

Because of the overwhelming response to recipe requests, and because Longhorns have a common heritage, many duplicate and similar recipes were received. The variations included on the recipes reflect these similarities and are given with the hope that if your larder does not yield the initial ingredients, you might persevere. For the tireless kitchen engineer, may the variations be a challenge to determine whose recipe is the tastiest! The notations under the recipe titles were gleaned from the testers' reports and voice the comments of the cook, the guests, the unwilling dieter, the clamoring children and their crumb-snatching friends, the unsuspecting Aggie, the hungry husband, the next-door neighbors, the pot-luck diners—all of whom have now tasted the glories and vagaries of Longhorn cuisine.

The selected recipes were reworded to make them as concise as possible; therefore, it is not necessary to sift flour, grease pans, cover casseroles, or whatever, unless specified in the directions. The word "divided" following an ingredient indicates this ingredient will be used more than once in the recipe but not in more than the amount given. Oven temperature is always preheated to the temperature designated in directions unless otherwise specified.

The diversity of these recipes reflects the lives of Texas Exes. During these past 100 years as Longhorns have departed the academic community to venture forth to various areas of the world, their cooking has been influenced by adaptation to assorted regional traditions and origins. Some of the recipes, having been handed down through the generations, arouse certain nostalgia. Occasionally, following a recipe, a contributor's quote or explanation has been included and offers its own verbal history. As the cuisine and decades unfold, and to further inspire readers, eaters and cooks to savor the full benefits of a collection cookbook, we have arranged suggested menus at the outset of each section. In addition, following the tradition of the big-hearted Texan, we have interspersed other menu ideas where whimsy dictated.

Soooooo, round 'em up and commence to cookin'! The stampede is on! Cook 'em Horns!

Gladys Howard
Recipe Editor

9

The 1880s

Breads, Game
Food Preservation

On November 17, 1882, the cornerstone of the Old Main Building was laid in the presence of an assemblage of over three thousand spectators, who heard speeches by Governor Oran M. Roberts, Colonel Ashbel Smith, and the Honorable J. H. McLeary.

$\mathcal{A}$ legislative act to establish The University of Texas was approved on March 30, 1881, and went into effect on August 1. An election to decide the location of the University was held on the first Tuesday in September; following votes counted on October 17 showed that the Main Branch would be in Austin and the Medical Branch in Galveston. The elevated terrain on which the University was to be located, embracing forty acres of land, was selected when the City of Austin was surveyed for the state capital and was for many years called "College Hill." Eight regents, appointed by Governor O.M. Roberts, convened on November 15 in Austin. A year later, on November 17, 1882, the cornerstone of the Main Building was laid. Finally, on September 15, 1883, the University formally opened in the incomplete wing of the old Main Building. Class work, however, was conducted in the old temporary Capitol on the corner of Congress and Twelfth until January 1, 1884.

The campus was covered with mesquite trees and a few live oaks when the University opened its doors. Here and there a cactus appeared. In the spring, bluebonnets and other wild flowers covered the Forty Acres. At the end of the first year, the proctor recommended the purchase of a wagon, a pair of mules, and an iron roller to use on campus roads and walks, and a plank fence was built around the campus to keep out cows and other stray animals.

In 1883, there were eight faculty members in addition to the proctor. The next year a lady assistant was added and a few additional faculty members were employed. A president was not chosen until 1895. Only 221 students—58 women and 163 men—enrolled that first year. By 1890, enrollment reached 300. Student life was far from exciting. It was unorganized, slow-paced, and often tiresome in its rural, pastoral setting. Buggy rides along trails that later became busy thoroughfares; conversations in beer gardens around the campus; afternoons spent along the banks of Waller Creek where low tree branches tangled the high coiffures of the girls and the tall grass swished against their long full-gored skirts; and pecan hunts, hikes to Mount Bonnell, and class excursions to San Antonio, Marble Falls and Barton's Creek all provided social and educational experiences. Students complained of their boredom both in and out of class. Time honored traditions were established with class day and commencement exercises.

During the 1885-1886 session, groups of young men formed "mess clubs" to cut expenses. These clubs were a distinctive feature of student life during the first decade of University operation. A letter from the president of one of the clubs indicated a lack of variety in the menus. For instance, he pointed out that "biscuits, rice, and syrup were served at every meal; coffee and oatmeal were served at breakfast and supper, and light-bread only at dinner." Sweet potatoes were fried for breakfast and baked for dinner. Steak was on the table for breakfast, while bacon was served for dinner and supper. Dinner at twelve o'clock was the big meal of the day, for besides the items already mentioned, one found Irish potatoes, cabbage, turnips, onions, prunes, and cornbread were served. Butter, usually a whole pound, was always on the table. "Dessert is very occasional," the student added, "though we do have something of the kind at times, when it appears in the shape of sliced potato pie, or like dishes." Twenty members composed his club, whose expenses for two months averaged $9.20 each per month.

Organizations appeared only gradually but once established they proliferated rapidly. Simple in structure at first, their purposes were not always compatible with faculty expectations. A certain amount of sterility of the early curriculum, combined with the impersonality of the relations between faculty and students, helped to produce an extracurriculum. The faculty did not organize out-of-class activities.

Before the University was ten days old, two literary societies, the Athenaeum and the Rusk, were organized. A local paper editorialized that the University "must be accorded the honor of having youths who joined a literary society before organizing a baseball or boat club." By 1885 students had a baseball club. When the team went to Georgetown to play Southwestern University that year, a group of students distributed orange and white ribbons. This was the first occasion at which these colors, years later made official, were used.

Scholz's Garten, with its adjacent Saengerrunde Halle, had been in operation since 1866. Students liked to spend afternoons sipping beer at tables under the big trees at this East Austin establishment. A big green parrot spoke freely of the morals of prominent students and faculty members, as well as the state's political leaders. Lamme's Candies began operation on Congress Avenue in 1885 and has continued as a family business since that time. Generations of University students have bought Lamme's sugar stick candy, kisses, chewy pralines, and divinity. In the early years, Lamme's also served "Gem," a cross between ice cream and sherbet, in such wonderful flavors as fig, apricot, pineapple, and cherry.

Also in 1886, the University Drug Store, operated by P. W. McFadden and Claude E. Hill, became the first business establishment on The Drag. The Driskill Hotel, built in 1886, was officially opened at Christmas that year. The cost, complete with furniture, was $400,000. The hotel had an electric bell system and a billiards and barroom with a made-to-order sideboard. Rooms had marbletop bureaus and washstands, carved walnut furniture, and some rooms had balconies. The Driskill became the site of numerous student dances and celebrations.

On Commencement Day, June 17, 1885, The University of Texas Alumni Association was organized. Twenty lawyers and one "academ" of the class of 1885 joined the three graduates of the class of 1884 to form the organization. John S. Stone was elected its first president.

Sunday in the Country

Breakfast

Beulah's Cush - p. 22
Country Ham With Red-Eye Gravy - p. 437
Coffee

Dinner

Venison Steak - p. 48
Country Potatoes - p. 258
My Mama's Purple Hull Peas - p. 258
Sally Lunn Bread - p. 21
Pickled Okra - p. 49
Bread and Butter Pickles - p. 50
Pickled Peppers - p. 50
Mommom's Peach Cobbler - p. 140
Mint Ice Tea - p. 163

Supper

Baked Acorn Squash
With Homemade Pork Sausage - p. 266
Homemade White Bread - p. 17
Fig Preserves - p. 53
Milk

Bauer House is the official residence of the Chancellor of The University of Texas System. Mrs. E. D. Walker, through a selective program of borrowing items from collections of The University of Texas at Austin, has enriched the decor of the public rooms at Bauer House. The portion of the formal dining room shown contains an antique Sheraton mahogany, three-part dining table, c. 1810; a breakfront from the Sheraton period, c. 1790; Royal Crown Derby china in breakfront as well as some pieces on the table, along with Steuben glasses. The chandelier is Bacarat crystal. Most of the items shown are from the Hoblitzelle Collection.

photo by Sherwood Inkley

Homemade White Bread
Never fails, a meal in itself, terrific hot with butter and honey

3 tablespoons shortening
½ cup sugar
1 cup milk
2 packets dry yeast
¼ cup warm water
1 egg, beaten until light
1 teaspoon salt
4½ to 5 cups sifted flour

In large bowl, using egg beater, cream shortening and sugar. Scald milk and pour over creamed mixture. Cool. Dissolve yeast in warm water. Cool. Combine mixtures, add egg, salt and flour, 1 cup at a time. Add only enough flour until dough can be kneaded with hands. Put dough in large greased bowl, turn to grease top part of dough. Cover with hot damp cloth, refreshing several times while dough rises. Set in warm place to rise until double in bulk, about 2 hours. Toss the dough on pastry board with enough flour to prevent sticking. Knead 5 minutes, working outside toward inside with balls of hand, repeating until light and "bubbly." Divide into 2 equal-sized greased glass bread pans or 4 small pans. Let rise until doubled in bulk. Bake 10 minutes at 450°. Reduce heat to 350° and bake 30 minutes more until bread is completely brown and shrinks from sides of pans. Yield: 2 loaves.

Eloise Engle Thornberry, BA '42
Austin

Honey Whole Wheat Bread

1 cup milk
2 tablespoons sugar
1 tablespoon salt
¼ cup (½ stick) butter
  or margarine
½ cup honey
2 packets dry yeast
1½ cups warm water
2½ cups flour
5 cups whole wheat
  flour

Scald milk; add sugar, salt, butter and honey. Stir until butter melts. Cool to lukewarm. In large-sized mixing bowl, sprinkle yeast over warm water, stirring until dissolved. Stir in cooled milk mixture. Add flour and half the whole wheat flour; beat with wooden spoon until smooth. Gradually add remaining wheat flour to make a dough. Turn out dough onto lightly floured board. Cover with bowl. Let rest 10 minutes. Knead until smooth and elastic, about 10 minutes. Place in lightly greased bowl, turning over to grease top. Cover with towel, let rise in warm place until doubled, about 1¼ hours. Punch down, divide in half and shape each into a ball. Cover with towel, let rest 10 minutes. Shape each ball into a loaf, placing in greased bread pans. Cover with towel, let rise in warm place until doubled, about 1¼ hours. Bake 40 to 50 minutes at 400°. Yield: 2 loaves.

John T. Ryder, BA '68
San Antonio

Icebox Rolls
Yum, yum, more! Please!

1 cup boiling water
⅓ cup sugar
1½ teaspoons salt
¼ cup shortening
1 packet dry yeast
¼ cup warm water
½ teaspoon sugar
1 egg
4 cups flour, sifted

Combine boiling water, sugar, salt and shortening; stir to melt shortening. Cool to lukewarm. Dissolve yeast in warm water and sugar; proof 5 minutes. Add yeast to cooled mixture. Add egg, mix well. Add flour, 2 cups at a time, and beat well. Cover tightly, refrigerate 24 hours. On floured board roll dough to ½-inch thickness. Cut rolls with biscuit cutter, dip in cooled melted butter, and fold over. Let rise 4 hours in a warm place. Bake 15 to 20 minutes at 400°. Yield: 40 to 50 small rolls.

Amy Purcell Powell, BS '55
Navasota

Dark Pumpernickel Bread

3 packets dry yeast
1½ cups warm water
    (110°)
½ cup dark molasses
4 teaspoons salt
2 tablespoons caraway
    seeds
2 tablespoons shortening
2¾ to 3 cups rye flour
¼ cup cocoa
2½ to 3 cups unbleached
    flour
Cornmeal

Dissolve yeast in warm water in large mixing bowl and proof 5 minutes. Stir in molasses, salt, caraway seeds, shortening, rye flour and cocoa. Beat until smooth. Stir in enough unbleached flour to make dough easy to handle. Turn dough onto lightly floured surface. Cover and let rise 10 to 15 minutes. Place in greased bowl (large enough for bread to rise). Turn greased side of bread to top. Cover and let rise in warm place until double in bulk, about 1 hour. (Dough has risen when an indentation remains when top of dough is touched.) When doubled, punch dough down, fold sides into middle, shape into round. Let rise again until doubled, about 40 minutes. Grease baking sheet, sprinkle with cornmeal. Punch dough down. Divide in half. Shape each half into a round, slightly flat loaf. Place loaves in opposite corners of baking sheet. Let rise 1 hour. Bake 30 to 35 minutes at 375°. Bake until loaves sound hollow when tapped. Remove from baking sheet. Cool on wire racks. Yield: 2 loaves.

Variation: *For light pumpernickel bread, substitute light molasses for dark molasses. Omit cocoa and increase white flour from 2¾ to 3¼ cups. For rolls: after second rising, divide dough into 12 equal parts. Shape into balls. Let rise. Bake 20 to 30 minutes. Yield: 2 loaves or 12 Texas-sized rolls.*

Theresa Velten Thompson, BS '78
Enid, Oklahoma

DILLY CASSEROLE BREAD. Dissolve 1 packet dry yeast in ¼ cup warm water. Heat 1 cup creamed small curd cottage cheese to lukewarm. Add 1 tablespoon sugar, 1 tablespoon dried onion flakes, 2 tablespoons butter, 2 tablespoons dill seed, 1 teaspoon salt, ¼ teaspoon baking soda, and 1 egg. Mix well and add yeast. Add 2½ cups flour and mix. (This is a stiff dough.) Let rise until double in bulk. Punch down, place in a well greased 8-inch casserole. Let rise again, about 40 minutes. Bake 40 to 50 minutes at 350°. When baked, butter top and sprinkle with salt. Yield: 8 wedges.

Maurine Redfearn Bartos, BS '57
Waco

Irish Soda Bread
A bread as crusty as its trusty tradition

1 cup buttermilk
2 tablespoons butter or margarine
3 tablespoons sugar
½ teaspoon baking soda
1 packet dry yeast
½ teaspoon salt
2¼ cups flour

Heat buttermilk and butter until lukewarm (110°). Combine with sugar, baking soda, yeast and salt. Mix well, add ¼ cup flour and beat 2 minutes. Add enough flour to make a soft dough. Place in oiled bowl and turn dough to coat with oil. Cover, let rise 50 minutes or until double in bulk. Punch dough down. Divide dough in half. On floured board knead each half 20 times, making smooth round balls. Place on greased baking sheet, press down to form 8-inch circles, score an X design across tops with back of knife. Cover, let rise until double in bulk, about 50 minutes. Bake 30 minutes at 350°. Serve warm with butter and cranberry jelly. Yield: 2 (8-inch) round loaves.

Dorothy Hudson Burr, BBA '26
Corpus Christi

Champion Egg Bread

½ cup warm water
1 packet dry yeast
    Pinch sugar
1½ cups milk
6 tablespoons (¾ stick) butter
2 or 3 tablespoons wild honey or ¼ cup sugar
3 eggs, beaten
1 tablespoon salt
6 to 8 cups unbleached flour

Dissolve yeast in warm water with sugar and proof 5 minutes. Scald milk, remove from heat, add butter. When lukewarm, add honey and eggs. In large mixing bowl, combine yeast and milk mixtures. Add 3 cups flour, 1 cup at a time, beating until smooth. Set aside, covered, 10 minutes. Add remaining flour, 1 cup at a time, until a soft sticky dough. Remove to floured board or marble and knead adding more flour as needed to make smooth and satiny dough. Knead at least 5 minutes. Cover and let rise in warm place until double in bulk, about 1½ hours. Punch down and divide dough into 2 portions. Braid 1 portion into long loaf and place on greased cookie sheet that has been dusted with cornmeal. Roll out remaining portion and shape into loaf, place in greased loaf pan. Cover, let rise in warm place until double in bulk, about 45 minutes to 1 hour. Bake 30 minutes at 350°. Yield: 2 loaves.

Peter Agnew Bickel, BA '66
Pert

Sally Lunn Bread
Circa 1890 recipe of contributor's grandmother

1 tablespoon butter
1 cup sugar
2 eggs, beaten
1 cup milk
2 cups flour
2 teaspoons baking
    powder
Pinch salt

Cream butter and sugar. Add eggs, milk, flour, baking powder and salt. Bake 20 minutes at 400° in a greased 10 x 15-inch sheet pan. Serve hot with butter. Serves 12.

G. P. Herndon, Jr., BBA '28
Bastrop

Beer Bread

3 cups self-rising flour
2 tablespoons sugar
1 teaspoon dill weed
1 can (12 oz.) beer
Sesame seeds

Combine dry ingredients, add beer, stir to soft dough. Heavily grease bottom and sides of 2 (7½ x 3½-inch) loaf pans. Divide mixture into pans. Sprinkle with sesame seeds. Set aside dough in pans 15 minutes. Bake 30 minutes at 350° or until brown on top and bread springs back when lightly touched. Yield: 2 loaves.

Carol A. Crabtree, BS '77
Beaumont

Pull-Apart Vegetable Bread

1 cup chopped green
    pepper
1 cup chopped onion
½ cup chopped chives
1 cup (2 sticks) butter or
    margarine
3 cans buttermilk
    biscuits
½ pound fried bacon,
    crumbled
½ cup Parmesan cheese

Saute pepper, onion and chives in butter. Quarter biscuits. Combine all ingredients. (Be sure biscuits are well-coated with butter.) Pour into ungreased bundt pan. Bake 30 minutes at 350°. To serve, simply pull apart and eat. Serves 12.

Peggy Jetton, wife of Bobby R. Jetton, BS '72
Spring

Cheesy Jalapeño Cornbread

1 cup cornmeal
1 cup milk
1 teaspoon salt
½ teaspoon baking soda
¼ cup bacon grease
½ pound sharp Cheddar
  cheese, grated
2 eggs, slightly beaten
1 cup yellow cream-
  style corn
1 large-sized onion,
  grated
3 jalapeño peppers,
  finely chopped

Combine all ingredients and mix well. Pour into greased muffin tins. Bake 25 to 30 minutes at 400°. Yield: 18 muffins.

Brenda Wilson Barber, BS '68
Palestine

Beulah's Cush With Egg Cornbread

CORNBREAD:
1½ cups white cornmeal
3 tablespoons flour
1 teaspoon salt
1 teaspoon baking soda
2 cups buttermilk
2 eggs
2 tablespoons bacon
  grease
CUSH:
  Left-over cornbread
  Water
½ small-sized onion,
  chopped
2 tablespoons butter or
  margarine
2 strips bacon
  Poached eggs

Mix dry ingredients in a mixing bowl. Add buttermilk and eggs and beat until well combined. Put bacon grease in an iron skillet and heat. Swirl grease to cover pan. Add drippings to mixture, and pour mixture into skillet. Bake 20 to 25 minutes at 450°. Crust should be golden brown.

Since we usually have about a half recipe of cornbread leftover from the evening meal, we save it for breakfast CUSH: Break cornbread into pea-sized pieces. Moisten with water and set aside. Saute onion in butter in a covered skillet. Drain when clear. For each serving, fry 2 strips bacon until crisp. Remove and drain grease. Add moistened cornbread. Usually enough grease remains in skillet to prevent sticking, but add butter if needed. Stir lightly. When cornbread begins to brown slightly, add onion and crumbled crisp bacon bits. Make a "cush"-ion of the cornbread on a hot plate. Top with poached egg or soft-fried egg. Serves 6 to 8.

Wales Madden, Jr., BA '50 LLB '52
Amarillo

Tolbert's Cornbread

1½ cups white cornmeal
3 tablespoons flour
1 teaspoon salt
2½ tablespoons sugar
2 tablespoons baking
  powder
2 eggs
2 cups sweet milk and
  no baking soda or
  2 cups buttermilk
  and 1 teaspoon
  baking soda
3 tablespoons bacon
  grease

Sift dry ingredients in a mixing bowl. Add eggs, milk and bacon grease. Stir until well mixed. Pour into a greased pan (preferably an iron skillet) that has been heated to "sizzling." Bake 20 to 25 minutes at 450°. Serves 6 to 8.

"This recipe appeared in the column Frank Tolbert wrote for many years in The Dallas Morning News. *He got the recipe from a cook in Sulphur Springs, Texas."*

Carol Gallman, wife of James Scott Gallman, BS '74
Richardson

Spoon Corn Bread

2 cups water
1 cup white cornmeal
1 cup milk
1 tablespoon shortening
1 teaspoon salt
2 eggs, beaten

In saucepan mix water and cornmeal and bring slowly to boil. Cook 5 minutes. Add milk, shortening, salt and eggs. Beat thoroughly. Bake in well-greased 8-inch square pan 30 minutes at 400°. Use a spoon and serve from the baking pan. Serves 8 to 10.

Jane Weinert Blumberg, BA '37
Seguin

Variation: *Use 3 eggs and 2 tablespoons shortening. Bake 50 minutes at 400°.*

Charles Inge Francis, BA '15 LLB '17 Deceased
Submitted by Martha F. Singleton, '42
Houston

Variation: *Omit water, increase milk to 4 cups, add 3 teaspoons baking powder. Use 3 tablespoons butter for shortening.*

Louise Buckner Milburn, BBA '48
Odessa

Variation: *Omit water, increase milk to 2 cups, decrease cornmeal to ⅔ cup. Use 3 eggs, separated. Beat egg whites until stiff, fold into mixture with 2 tablespoons baking powder.*

Nell Jones Herndon, BA '30
Bastrop

Creamy Spoon Bread
Delicious, a great combination of crusty outside and custardy inside

2 teaspoons shortening
2 eggs
1 cup cornmeal
½ cup flour
¼ cup sugar
½ teaspoon baking soda
1 teaspoon baking
   powder
1 teaspoon salt
1 cup buttermilk
1 cup milk

Preheat oven to 375°. Put shortening into heavy 9-inch metal pan or cast iron skillet. Set in oven. Beat eggs; combine dry ingredients and add, alternating with buttermilk, to eggs. Mix well. Pour into the very hot greased skillet. Pour milk into center of batter. Bake 25 to 30 minutes at 375°. Serves 4 to 6.

Aline Calhoun, '23
Austin

CRACKLING BREAD CIRCA 1915. Put 1 cup cracklings in a shallow pan. Bake at 350° until crisp. Break into small pieces. Mix together 2 cups yellow cornmeal, ½ teaspoon salt and enough boiling water for cornbread consistency. Add cracklings. Drop from a spoon onto baking pan. Bake at 350° until done.

Katie Lewis Cheatham, '15
Cuero

CRACKLING BREAD CIRCA 1951. "First, catch your pig. Then ship it to the Abattoir (see dictionary) nearest you. Bake what they send back. Remove the solid fat and throw the rest away. Fry fat, drain off liquid grease, and combine the residue (called "cracklings") with: 1½ cups water-ground white cornmeal sifted with 1 teaspoon salt and 1 teaspoon baking powder; add 1 egg (beaten); add 1 cup milk. Bake in very hot oven until brown, about 15 minutes. Result: 1 pan crackling bread serving 6. Total cost: about $250, depending on size of pig. Some historians say by this recipe alone fell the Confederacy."

Nita Hixon Galloway, BJ '51
Wilmington, Delaware

Alabama Hush Puppies

1¾ cups cornmeal
4 tablespoons flour
1 teaspoon baking
  powder
1 teaspoon salt
6 tablespoons chopped
  onion
1 egg, beaten
2 cups boiling water
  Garlic powder
  Oil for deep-fryer

Sift together dry ingredients. Add onion and egg. Combine well. Add boiling water slowly, stirring constantly until smooth. Add a sprinkle of garlic powder. Drop from a spoon into deep-fryer and fry until browned. Yield: 3 dozen Southern traditions.

Sheila M. Gray, BBA '78
Houston

CORN PONE. "Melt a dab of bacon grease in a big iron skillet in an oven heated at 350°. While bacon grease is heating, mix 1½ cups of yellow or white cornmeal with 1 teaspoon baking powder, ½ teaspoon salt, 1 egg, and about 1 cup buttermilk in a mixing bowl. Don't mix too much . . . and use enough buttermilk to give the stuff a pretty good consistency . . . not too loose . . . not too firm. Pour bacon grease into mix . . . but again, don't mix too much. Then pour mix into the same skillet in which the bacon grease was heated. Bake in a 350° oven for about 25 minutes. Serve with surenuff country butter. Serves 8 Capital rustlers."

Cactus Pryor, '41
Austin

Mama's Biscuits
Remember Pappy O'Daniel's "Pass the biscuits!"

2 cups flour
3 teaspoons baking
  powder
1 teaspoon salt
⅓ cup shortening
¾ cup milk

Mix together all ingredients. Roll out to ¼-inch thickness. Cut with biscuit cutter. Place on ungreased cookie sheet. Bake 15 minutes at 450°. Yield: 12 biscuits.

Louise Buckner Milburn, BBA '48
Odessa

Variation: *Reduce baking powder to 2 teaspoons, add ½ teaspoon baking soda. Use 1 cup buttermilk for milk. Bake 20 minutes at 400°.*

Joyce Kocurek Brooks, BS '69
Burleson

Cheese Biscuits

½ cup (1 stick) butter
   or margarine
½ pound (2 cups) cheese,
   grated
1¼ cups flour
¼ teaspoon red pepper
½ teaspoon salt

Bring butter and cheese to room temperature, then cream together. Add dry ingredients. Roll out between sheets of waxed paper. Use small round cutter (tradition seems to be to use a snuff can lid as a cutter). Prick each biscuit with a fork. Bake 10 to 15 minutes at 350°. Store in tightly covered container or freeze. Yield: 24 biscuits.

Halley Bailey Porter, '09 Deceased
Submitted by Walter L. Geyer, BM '61
Dallas

Sausage Biscuits

1 cup flour
1 teaspoon baking
   powder
¼ teaspoon baking soda
¼ teaspoon salt
2 tablespoons
   shortening, divided
½ cup sausage,
   uncooked
Buttermilk

Sift together dry ingredients. Cut in 1 tablespoon shortening and the sausage. Add buttermilk, a small amount at a time, until dough is of soft consistency. Drop walnut-sized bits of dough into a pan containing 1 tablespoon melted shortening. Bake at 450° until nicely browned. Serve hot from the oven. Yield: 18 shadows.

"I have always used them at Ground Hog time to carry out the theme for that day."

Lena Pettit Hickman, BA '15
Austin

Yeast Waffles
Make night before, no fuss in morning; just pour, bake, eat!

1 packet dry yeast
¼ cup warm water
2 cups milk
2 cups flour
1 teaspoon salt
2 tablespoons sugar
3 eggs, beaten
¼ cup salad oil

Dissolve yeast in warm water. Scald milk, cool. Sift dry ingredients, add milk and yeast. Add eggs and oil, beat until batter is smooth. Keep covered in refrigerator. Stir before using. The batter is better if used after 2 or 3 days. Bake in hot waffle iron. Serve immediately. Yield: 6 to 8 waffles.

Wayne Ferguson, BBA '59 MBA '60
Oklahoma City, Oklahoma

French Toast
Santa Fe Railroad Diners' Special

3 slices bread, 1-inch
    thick ("Texas toast")
3 eggs
  Dash nutmeg
  Dash salt
½ cup milk
2 cups shortening

Trim crusts from bread slices, round corners and edges, and cut diagonally. Beat eggs, add nutmeg and salt. Add milk and thoroughly beat mixture. Dip bread slices into this batter. Soak bread, then take bread between hands and press batter out of the bread. Soak again to be sure bread is saturated. Stroke each slice lightly, reducing the slice to about half its height to remove batter drippings. Fry in moderately hot shortening until golden brown. Drain on paper towel. Place toast on cookie sheet with a paper towel under each slice. Bake 5 to 6 minutes per side at 400°. Dust generously with powdered sugar. Serve hot with jam, marmalade, syrup or honey. Serves 3.

"This was a recipe that the Santa Fe Railroad served on its diners in the days when many people rode trains. Of all the items served, the French Toast was the most popular. People would actually get on the Santa Fe in Houston and get off in Rosenberg, or get on in Chicago and get off in Joliet, just so they could have French Toast!"

Henry Renfert, Jr., Friend of UT
Austin

Cottage Cheese Pancakes

4 eggs, separated
4 tablespoons flour
1 cup small curd cottage
    cheese
  Fluffy Vanilla Sauce
    (See Index)
1 can (14 oz.) wild
    blueberries

Beat egg whites until stiff. Combine egg yolks, flour and cottage cheese. Fold in egg whites. Cook on lightly greased griddle. Serve with a large dollop of Fluffy Vanilla Sauce. Top with 1 tablespoon drained, canned wild blueberries. Serves 4.

Carol Reeb Nietenhoefer, BS '66
Boerne

Lumberjack Flapjacks
Voilà . . . Backwoods Crepes Suzettes!

2 cups flour
1 tablespoon baking
   soda
1 teaspoon salt
1 tablespoon sugar
1 quart buttermilk
2 eggs
3 tablespoons salad oil

Mix dry ingredients and add buttermilk while stirring. Put eggs and oil in cocktail shaker and shake well; add to mixture; stir until well mixed but no more. Pour onto fairly hot griddle (375°) and cook until bubbles appear in the center. Turn and cook until light brown on underside. Refrigerate any leftover batter. Cook later in large diameter cakes. After cooking, lay a dab of your favorite ice cream along the equator and roll edges to form a banana shaped cake. Top with powdered sugar or syrup and eat while hot. Serves 4 to 6.

M.L. "Bud" Felker, '43
Longview

Dutch Baby
A single giant popover-pancake to serve plain or fancy

2 eggs
½ cup flour
½ teaspoon salt
½ cup milk
2 tablespoons melted
   butter
1 tablespoon lemon
   juice
   Powdered sugar
TOPPING
OPTIONS:

1½ pints fresh straw-
   berries
1 package (10 oz.)
   frozen sliced
   peaches
   Sour cream
   Brown sugar
   Cinnamon

Beat eggs. Combine flour and salt, add with milk to eggs and beat until smooth. Stir in butter. Pour into buttered 9-inch skillet or pie pan. Bake 20 minutes at 450°. Reduce heat to 350°, prick shell, bake 10 minutes more. Sprinkle with lemon juice, dust with powdered sugar. Cut into wedges and serve topped with your choice of fruit, a dollop of sour cream mixed with brown sugar and cinnamon. Serves 4 plain or 6 fancy.

Pauline McAnelly Wilson, BS '40
San Antonio

Lady Bird's Popovers

1 cup flour
¼ teaspoon salt
2 eggs, beaten
1 cup milk
2 tablespoons
   shortening, melted

Sift together flour and salt. Combine eggs, milk and shortening. Gradually add to flour mixture, beating 1 minute or until batter is smooth. Fill greased, sizzling hot popover pans ¾ full. Bake 20 minutes at 450°, reduce heat to 350° and bake 15 or 20 minutes more. Yield: 5 or 6 popovers.

"This is one of our favorite 'house dishes.' Our friends know they're sure to have popovers for one meal during a houseparty."

Claudia Taylor (Lady Bird) Johnson, BA '33 BJ '34
Stonewall

Variation: *Use 4 (6 oz. size) glass custard cups. Substitute 1 teaspoon butter for shortening. Put ¼ teaspoon butter in bottom of each cup, place cups in oven until very hot. Fill heated cups ¾ full. Bake 30 minutes at 400°; reduce oven to 300° and bake 20 to 30 minutes more (depending upon how dry you prefer centers).*

Bonita Granville Wrather, wife of Jack Wrather, BA '39
Los Angeles, California

Charlotte's Bran Muffins
A return to nature with an old-time favorite

1 cup oil
3 eggs
¾ cup honey
1 teaspoon vanilla
3 cups whole wheat
   flour
3 teaspoons baking soda
2 teaspoons salt
3 teaspoons baking
   powder
1 teaspoon cinnamon
3 cups natural raw bran
1 cup white raisins
3 cups buttermilk

In mixer at high speed, combine oil, eggs, honey and vanilla. Sift together dry ingredients. Mix bran and raisins with buttermilk. Add to honey mixture alternately with dry ingredients. Mix quickly. Set aside 10 minutes before baking. Bake 20 to 25 minutes at 350° in paper-lined muffin tins. Yield: 5 dozen.

Charlotte Thornton, BA '78 MA '81
Tulsa, Oklahoma

Kolaches

1 packet dry yeast
¼ cup warm water
   (110°)
1 teaspoon sugar
1 cup lukewarm milk
½ cup sugar
1 teaspoon salt
8 tablespoons (1 stick)
   unsalted butter,
   melted
1 egg
3½ to 4 cups flour
   FILLINGS:
1 cup blueberries
8 ounces cottage cheese,
   drained
2 tart apples, peeled and
   cored   .
   STREUSEL TOPPING:
8 tablespoons (1 stick)
   unsalted butter
1 cup sugar
1 cup flour
   Heavy cream

Proof yeast in water with 1 teaspoon sugar until bubbly. In large mixing bowl, combine milk, sugar, salt and butter. Add proofed yeast. Add egg and mix to creamy texture. Add flour, ½ cup at a time. Dough will be soft. Butter a clean bowl and place dough in bowl to rise. Cover with plastic wrap and let rise until double in bulk (about 1½ to 2 hours). Punch down. Divide dough into 3 equal pieces. Pat into buttered 9-inch glass pie pans.

FILLINGS: Top one pan of dough with blueberries, the second with drained cottage cheese, and the third with apples sliced like match sticks.

STREUSEL: Combine ingredients until coarsely crumbled. Cover each filling with Streusel Topping. Let rise 30 to 40 minutes. Bake 20 to 25 minutes at 375° or until color is golden. Brush with heavy cream as kolaches cool. Serves 12 to 15.

Variations: *Spread ½ cup drained cottage cheese thinly on dough, top with 1 cup blueberries and ⅓ cup Streusel Topping. This variation won first prize in foreign breads at the Texas State Fair. To make the old-time favorite BUCHTA, after dough rises, roll out on floured board to 14 x 16 inches as for cinnamon rolls. Spread dough with 1 can Solo Poppyseed Filling. Roll up dough as for cinnamon rolls. Cut into ½-inch slices. Butter a bundt pan, and place slices alternately horizontal and vertical in the pan. Let rise until dough fills the pan, about 1 hour. Bake 30 to 35 minutes at 375°. Remove from oven, brush top with softened unsalted butter, and unmold onto cake rack. Turn over so buttered surface is topside.*

Dolores Simmons Snyder, BS '54
Irving

Bertie's Cinnamon Rolls

1 cup milk
½ cup shortening
2 teaspoons salt
¾ cup sugar
2 cakes compressed
  yeast
2 eggs, beaten
5 cups flour
6 tablespoons butter,
  melted
2 teaspoons cinnamon
½ cup sugar
½ cup raisins (optional)
½ cup nuts (optional)

Scald milk, add shortening, salt and sugar. Stir until dissolved. Cool to lukewarm. Add crumbled yeast cakes. Stir until dissolved. Add eggs. Add flour and knead to a smooth dough. Cover and set in warm place; let rise until doubled in bulk, about 2 hours. Punch dough down and roll to ¼-inch thick. Spread with melted butter, sprinkle with cinnamon, sugar, raisins and nuts. Roll as for jellyroll, press edges firmly together. Slice into ½- to ¾-inch rolls. Place in greased pan. Let rise until very light. Bake 15 to 20 minutes at 375°. Serves 36.

Charles Schreiner, III, BA '47
Mountain Home

Maple Nut Cinnamon Rolls

1 packet dry yeast
¼ cup warm water (110°)
2 eggs
1 cup quick-cooking
  oats
¾ cup milk, scalded
½ cup shortening
⅓ cup brown sugar
1½ teaspoons salt
3½ to 4 cups flour

TOPPING:

½ cup maple syrup
¼ cup brown sugar
¼ cup butter
1 tablespoon water
¼ teaspoon maple
  flavoring
⅔ cup (3 oz. pkg.) nuts

FILLING:

¼ cup butter, softened
⅔ cup brown sugar
1 tablespoon grated
  orange rind
1 teaspoon cinnamon

Proof yeast in warm water. Add unbeaten eggs. Combine oats, milk, shortening, brown sugar and salt. Add yeast mixture. Beat well. Gradually add enough flour to form a stiff dough. Beat well. Cover and let rise in warm place until double, about 1½ hours.
TOPPING: Combine in 9 x 13-inch pan the syrup, brown sugar, butter, water, flavoring and nuts. Heat mixture until butter melts. Knead dough 3 to 5 minutes on floured surface. Roll out to 12 x 24-inch rectangle.

FILLING: Spread with softened butter. Combine remaining ingredients and sprinkle across buttered dough. Roll up dough from the 24-inch side. Cut into 1-inch slices. Place in pan on topping mixture. Let rise until light and double in bulk. Bake 30 to 35 minutes at 350°. Cool 1 minute. Invert immediately. May be frozen and reheated. Yield: 24.

Agnes Warren Barnes, BS '57
Waco

Applesauce Nut Bread With Apple-Cream Cheese Spread

1 cup sugar
1 jar (8 oz.) applesauce
⅓ cup salad oil
2 eggs
3 tablespoons milk
2 cups flour
1 teaspoon baking soda
½ teaspoon baking
    powder
¼ teaspoon salt
½ teaspoon cinnamon
¼ teaspoon nutmeg
1 cup chopped nuts,
    divided
¼ cup brown sugar
½ teaspoon cinnamon

APPLE-CREAM
CHEESE SPREAD:
3 ounces cream cheese,
    softened
1 tablespoon orange
    juice
2 teaspoons powdered
    sugar
½ cup peeled, grated
    apple

Combine sugar, applesauce, oil, eggs and milk; mix well. Combine flour, baking soda, baking powder, salt, cinnamon and nutmeg. Add to sugar mixture. Stir in ¾ cup nuts. Spoon batter into greased 5¼ x 9¼-inch loaf pan. Combine brown sugar, cinnamon and ¼ cup nuts; sprinkle over batter. Bake 1 hour at 350°. Cover loosely with foil during last 30 minutes. Cool on rack. Slice and serve with APPLE-CREAM CHEESE SPREAD: Combine cream cheese, orange juice and powdered sugar. Mix until smooth. Stir in apple. Chill. Use as a spread for banana bread or Applesauce Nut Bread. Yield: 1 loaf bread and 1 cup spread.

Elizabeth Howrey Gray, '76
Austin

Boston Brown Bread

3 cups raisins or dates
    or both
3 cups boiling water
2 tablespoons shortening
1½ cups sugar
2 eggs
4 cups sifted flour
4 teaspoons baking soda
1 teaspoon salt
2 tablespoons dark
    molasses
2 cups 40% Bran Flakes

Pour water over fruit and set aside to cool. Cream together shortening and sugar. Add eggs. Combine dry ingredients, add to creamed mixture alternately with raisin-date mixture. Add molasses and bran flakes. Mix well (batter will look thin). Grease and flour four 1-pound coffee cans and fill two-thirds full with batter. Bake 1 hour at 350°. Yield: 4 loaves.

Theresa Velten Thompson, BS '78
Enid, Oklahoma

Banana Honey Bread
Bran lends pioneer texture

2 cups unbleached flour
½ teaspoon baking soda
1 teaspoon baking
  powder
½ teaspoon salt
1½ cups mashed fully
  ripened bananas
1½ cups wheat bran
  cereal or raw bran
½ cup butter or
  margarine, softened
⅔ cup honey
2 eggs
½ cup chopped nuts

Sift together flour, baking soda, baking powder and salt. Set aside. Combine mashed bananas and bran. Set aside 2 or 3 minutes or until bran is softened. Cream butter and honey, add eggs, and mix well. Stir in bran mixture, dry ingredients, and nuts. Spread batter in buttered 5 x 9-inch loaf pan. Bake 1 hour at 350° or until toothpick inserted near center comes out clean. Cool 10 minutes before removing from pan. Cool before slicing. Yield: 1 loaf.

Kathleen Kenny Reily, BS '77
Vaihingen, Germany

Banana Nut Bread

2¼ cups cake flour
1⅔ cups sugar
1¼ teaspoons baking
  powder
1¼ teaspoons baking soda
1 teaspoon salt
1 teaspoon cinnamon
½ teaspoon nutmeg
4 eggs, beaten
⅔ cup oil
5 medium-sized
  bananas, mashed
1 teaspoon vanilla
⅔ cup buttermilk
¾ cup chopped pecans

Combine dry ingredients. Mix eggs, oil, bananas and vanilla. Add dry ingredients alternating with buttermilk. Fold in pecans. Bake in 2 greased and floured 3½ x 8½-inch pans. Bake 45 minutes to 1 hour at 350°. Serves 12.

Pam Farley, BS '79
Corpus Christi

Banana breads are generally more flavorful when over-ripe bananas are used. Editor.

Carrot-Apple-Raisin Bread

exc. get good carrots

1¾ cups sugar
⅓ cup brown sugar
1½ cups oil
3 eggs
2 teaspoons vanilla
3 cups flour
1 teaspoon baking soda
1 teaspoon baking powder
1 teaspoon salt

a lot apple spice

2 teaspoons cinnamon
2 cups grated carrots
2 cups peeled and diced apples
¾ cup raisins
1 cup chopped walnuts

In large mixing bowl with electric mixer at medium speed, combine sugars, oil, eggs and vanilla. Sift together dry ingredients and add to mixture ½ cup at a time, beating after each addition. With spoon gently stir in carrots, apples, raisins and walnuts. Divide batter evenly between 2 greased and floured 5 x 9-inch loaf pans. Bake 1 hour at 350° or until top of bread springs back when lightly touched. Yield: 2 loaves.

Roseanne Paul Elling, BS '75
San Antonio

Cranberry Bread

1 orange, juice and rind
2 tablespoons salad oil
Boiling water
1 egg, beaten
2 cups flour
1 cup sugar
1½ teaspoons baking powder
½ teaspoon baking soda
1 teaspoon salt
1 cup chopped pecans
1 cup raw cranberries

Combine juice, rind, oil and enough boiling water to make ¾ cup. Add egg. Sift together dry ingredients and add to liquid ingredients. Stir only until flour is moistened. Add nuts and cranberries. Pour into 2 buttered 4 x 8-inch loaf pans leaving center slightly hollow. Set aside batter in pans 20 minutes before baking. Bake 45 to 50 minutes at 350°. Cool. Bread also can be baked in 4 soup cans, buttered and floured. Bake 35 to 40 minutes at 350°. Yield: 2 loaves.

John T. Ryder, BA '68
San Antonio

Variation: *Substitute ½ cup concentrated frozen orange juice and ¼ cup water for the fresh orange juice. Substitute ¼ cup shortening for the salad oil. Increase sugar to 1½ cups and cream with shortening.*

Sara Avant, BS '78
New Orleans, Louisiana

Easy Eggnog Bread

3 cups flour
¾ cup sugar
1 tablespoon baking
   powder
1 teaspoon salt
½ teaspoon nutmeg
1 egg, beaten
¼ cup butter,
   melted
1½ cups eggnog
¾ cup chopped walnuts
   or pecans
¾ cup candied fruits

In large mixing bowl, sift together flour, sugar, baking powder, salt and nutmeg. Combine egg, butter and eggnog. Add to dry ingredients, stir until thoroughly mixed. Add nuts and fruits. Bake in loaf pan 60 to 70 minutes at 350°. Cool on wire rack. Yield: 1 loaf.

"This bread is wonderful with Swiss, Cheddar, or brick cheeses and cold meats . . . especially for a quick supper during Christmas season."

Susan Weber Munson, BFA '67
Denison

Lemon Bread

½ cup shortening
1 cup sugar
2 eggs
1½ cups flour
1 teaspoon baking
   powder
Pinch salt
½ cup milk
1 teaspoon lemon
   extract
Rind of 2 lemons
   grated
½ cup pecans or
   walnuts
GLAZE:
Juice of 2 lemons
¼ cup sugar

Cream shortening and sugar, add eggs and beat thoroughly. Sift flour, baking powder and salt. Add alternately with milk to creamed mixture. Add lemon extract and grated lemon rind (yellow zest only). Fold in chopped nuts. Line 2 (3½ x 7½-inch) loaf pans or 1 (5 x 9-inch loaf pan with waxed paper. Bake 45 minutes at 350°; bake larger loaf 1 hour. GLAZE: Combine lemon juice and sugar, pour over bread while still hot. Use toothpick to pierce bread so juice will run into loaf. This bread is better tasting the second day. Yield: 1 large or 2 small loaves.

Janis Dechman Modrall, BA '53
Houston

Maine Blueberry Nut Bread

2 eggs
1 cup sugar
1 cup milk
3 tablespoons salad oil
¼ teaspoon butter
    flavoring
3 cups flour
1 teaspoon salt
4 teaspoons baking
    powder
1 cup blueberries, fresh
    or frozen
½ cup chopped walnuts

Beat eggs until light. Add sugar and mix *Bla* thoroughly. Add milk, oil and butter flavoring. Sift together dry ingredients. Add to egg mixture. Stir only until moistened. Fold in blueberries and nuts. Bake in greased 5 x 9-inch loaf pan 1 hour 15 minutes at 350°. Yield: 1 loaf.

Merle Tooke Lewis, BA '53 MLS '70
Waterville, Maine

Orange Nut Bread

A very special delight for Christmas morning breakfast

2 eggs
1 cup sugar
2½ cups flour, divided
1 cup chopped nuts
3 teaspoons baking
    powder
½ teaspoon salt
1 tablespoon butter,
    melted
1 cup milk
CANDIED
ORANGE PEEL:
6 oranges
1 teaspoon baking soda
1⅓ cups sugar
¾ cup water

Combine eggs and sugar until light and creamy. Sprinkle nuts with ¼ cup flour. Combine remaining flour with dry ingredients and add to egg mixture alternately with milk-butter mixture. Fold in floured nuts and candied orange peel. Pour batter into 2 buttered 4½ x 8½-inch loaf pans. Bake 1 hour at 325°.
CANDIED ORANGE PEEL: Thinly peel the oranges, colored zest only. (A potato peeler works best for this.) Cover peel with hot water and baking soda. Boil 5 minutes or until tender. Drain and rinse peel. Shred peel into small pieces. Return to saucepan, add sugar and water, and cook 15 minutes or until consistency of maple syrup. Keep mixture refrigerated, or freeze for use as needed. Yield: 2 loaves.

Sunshine Neely Thurmond, BA '37
Tyler

Fresh Sweet Potato Bread
The fresh sweet potatoes do make a difference!

2 cups flour
¾ cup soy flour
½ cup raw bran
¼ cup wheat germ
1 teaspoon salt
1 teaspoon cinnamon
½ teaspoon allspice
2½ teaspoons baking soda
2 teaspoons double-
   acting baking
   powder
⅔ cup honey
⅔ cup cooking oil *-apple sauce*
4 eggs, beaten
1 teaspoon vanilla
2 cups cooked, mashed
   sweet potatoes or
   pumpkin
¾ cup raisins (optional)
¾ cup chopped nuts
   (optional)

Combine dry ingredients. Beat together remaining ingredients except raisins and nuts. Add dry ingredients, beat until just moistened. (Add ⅓ cup water or milk if batter is too stiff.) Pour batter into 2 greased, floured 5 x 9-inch loaf pans or 4 medium-sized loaf pans. Bake 1 hour at 325° or until toothpick inserted near center comes out clean. Crack in top is characteristic. Yield: 2 large or 4 medium-sized loaves.

NOTE: *"All of the flour can be all-purpose. However, the mixture of flours adds to the healthfulness and flavor. The fresh cooked sweet potatoes can be mashed and frozen until ready for use. The flavor of fresh cooked sweet potato or pumpkin will make you never want to use canned products again!"*

Sharon Wehner, BA '67
Houston

Oatmeal Raisin Muffins
A nice, quick breakfast delight

1 cup instant oats
½ cup raisins
¾ cup milk
½ cup oil
⅓ cup brown sugar
1 egg, beaten
1 cup sifted flour
3 teaspoons baking
   powder
1 teaspoon salt
½ teaspoon cinnamon
¼ teaspoon nutmeg
TOPPING:
6 tablespoons flour
3 tablespoons brown
   sugar
1½ teaspoons cinnamon
3 tablespoons butter

Combine oats, raisins, milk, oil, brown sugar and egg. Mix thoroughly. Sift together flour, baking powder, salt, cinnamon and nutmeg. Add to oat mixture until moistened. Spoon into greased muffin tins.

TOPPING: Combine flour, brown sugar and cinnamon. Cut in butter. Sprinkle 1 tablespoon mixture on each muffin. Bake 20 minutes at 400°. Yield 1 dozen.

Ruth Ann Neves Powell, BS '72
Alvin

Pumpkin Bread Revisited

3 cups sugar
3½ cups flour
2 teaspoons baking soda
½ teaspoon salt
2 teaspoons nutmeg
2 teaspoons allspice
2 teaspoons cloves
2 teaspoons cinnamon
4 eggs
2 cups fresh or canned
    pumpkin
1 cup oil
1 cup water or ½ cup
    water and ½ cup
    rum, brandy or
    Cherry Herring
1 cup chopped pecans
1 cup raisins

Combine dry ingredients. Mix eggs, pumpkin, oil and water; combine with dry ingredients mixing well. Fold in pecans and raisins. Bake in greased bundt pan 1 hour 15 minutes at 325° or bake in 4 greased 1-pound coffee cans 45 minutes at 325°. Serves 18 to 20.

Ann Barber Brinkerhoff, BA '49
Houston

Zucchini Bread

3 eggs
1 cup salad oil
1 cup brown sugar
1 cup sugar
3 teaspoons maple
    flavoring
2 cups shredded
    zucchini, unpeeled
    (about 3 medium-
    sized)
2½ cups flour
2 teaspoons salt
2 teaspoons baking soda
½ teaspoon baking
    powder
½ cup wheat germ
1 cup finely chopped
    walnuts or pecans
⅓ cup sesame seed

Beat eggs until light. Add oil, sugars and flavoring. Continue beating until thick and foamy. Fold in shredded zucchini. Combine flour, salt, baking soda, baking powder, wheat germ and nuts. Stir gently into zucchini mixture only until combined. Divide batter equally between 2 greased and floured 5 x 9-inch loaf pans. Sprinkle sesame seeds evenly over top of each loaf. Bake 1 hour at 350° or until wooden toothpick inserted in center comes out clean. Cool in pan 10 minutes. Turn out onto wire rack to cool completely. NOTE: For holiday gifts, bake in 5 mini-loaf pans for 40 minutes. Yield: 2 large loaves or 5 mini-loaves.

Rosemary Fanning Pinson,
wife of Robert M. Pinson, BA '41
Dallas

Strawberry Bread
Hooray!

3 cups flour
2 cups sugar
1 teaspoon baking soda
1 teaspoon cinnamon
½ teaspoon salt
1 package (10 oz.)
    frozen strawberries,
    thawed
1 cup salad oil
4 eggs, well beaten

Combine and mix thoroughly all dry ingredients. Make a well in center of mixture, pour in all liquid ingredients. Mix by hand. Pour mixture into 2 greased, floured 4 x 8-inch loaf pans. Bake 1 hour at 350° or until toothpick inserted in center comes out clean. This bread may be frozen. Slice thinly before completely thawed. Yield: 2 delicious loaves.

Lynn Rosenfeld, BJ '72
Houston

Kinsolving Coffee Cake

2 cups biscuit mix
⅓ cup sugar
½ cup milk
1 egg
3 tablespoons butter,
    melted
TOPPING:
¾ cup flour
¾ cup sugar
6 tablespoons butter
4 teaspoons cinnamon

Combine dry ingredients. Add milk, egg and butter. This makes a thick dough. Pour into greased 7 x 11-inch pan.
TOPPING: Combine ingredients to consistency of coarse crumbs. Sprinkle over dough. Topping ingredients may be doubled for more sweetness and flavor. Bake 25 minutes at 375°. Serves 6 to 8.

Phyllis Horn Rozen, BS '68
Corpus Christi

St. James Coffee Cake

3 cups flour
2 cups sugar
½ teaspoon cinnamon
½ teaspoon cloves
½ teaspoon nutmeg
¾ cup shortening
2 cups buttermilk
1 teaspoon baking soda
1 cup seedless raisins
1 cup nuts, chopped

Sift together flour, sugar and spices, cut in shortening until the texture of cornmeal. Reserve ½ cup of shortening mixture. Combine buttermilk and baking soda. Add to dry ingredients in halves, beating well after each addition. Stir in raisins and nuts. Spread in greased and floured 9 x 13 x 2-inch pan. Sprinkle reserved mixture over top. Bake 35 minutes at 350°, or bake in 2 (9-inch) layer pans. This recipe freezes well. Serves 12.

Roberta Caffarelli Rife, BA '35
San Antonio

Merk's Coffee Cake

½ cup shortening
¾ cup sugar
1 teaspoon vanilla
3 eggs
2 cups flour
1 teaspoon baking
    powder
1 teaspoon baking soda
1 cup sour cream
6 tablespoons butter or
    margarine, softened
1 cup brown sugar,
    firmly packed
2 teaspoons cinnamon
1 cup chopped nuts

Cream shortening, sugar and vanilla. Add eggs, 1 at a time, beating well after each addition. Sift together flour, baking powder and baking soda. Add to creamed mixture alternately with sour cream, mixing thoroughly after each addition. Spread half of batter into greased and lined 10-inch tube pan. Cream together butter, brown sugar and cinnamon. Add nuts. Spoon half the mixture over batter in pan. Add remaining batter, top with other half of nut mixture. Bake 50 minutes at 350°. Cool cake 10 minutes before removing from pan. Yield: 24 coffee-break yummies!

Susan J. Allen, BJ '78
Austin

Blueberry Kuchen
Very light, delicious dessert . . . more like a cobbler than a coffee cake

1 cup flour
¼ teaspoon salt
2 tablespoons sugar
½ cup butter
1 tablespoon vinegar
FILLING:
1 cup sugar
2 tablespoons flour
½ teaspoon cinnamon
2 cups blueberries
TOPPING:
1 cup fresh blueberries
    Powdered sugar

Combine flour, salt and sugar. Cut in butter. Mix in vinegar. In a 9-inch spring-form pan, spread the pastry on bottom and thinly up the sides to about 1 inch high.
FILLING: Combine sugar, flour, cinnamon and 2 cups blueberries. Pour into pastry shell. Bake 1 hour at 400°. Remove from oven, cover kuchen with blueberries and dust with powdered sugar. Serves 8.

Brenda Wilson Barber, BS '68
Palestine

Sour Cream Coffee Cake
Looks good enough to enter in a county fair

1 cup (2 sticks) butter
1 cup sugar
3 eggs
2 cups flour
2 teaspoons baking
    powder
1 teaspoon baking soda
½ teaspoon salt
1 carton (8 oz.) sour
    cream
1 teaspoon vanilla
1 can (16 oz.)
    blueberries, drained
FROSTING:
½ cup (1 stick) butter,
    softened
2½ cups powdered sugar
1 teaspoon vanilla
    Milk
1 can (16 oz.)
    blueberries, drained

Cream butter and sugar, add eggs. Combine dry ingredients, add to creamed mixture. Fold in sour cream. Add blueberries, fold in lightly. Pour batter into greased 9 x 13-inch ovenproof pan. Bake 30 to 40 minutes at 325°.
FROSTING: Combine butter, powdered sugar, vanilla and enough milk to moisten. Frost cake in pan, cover with blueberries. Serves 16.

Bobbie Rainey Sublett, '31
Dallas

Variation: *Omit blueberries, pour half the batter into greased, floured tube pan. Top with mixture of ½ cup brown sugar, ½ cup nuts, 1 tablespoon cinnamon. Pour in remaining batter. Bake 1 hour at 350°.*

Cynthia Henneberger Babel, BS' 74
Austin
Mary Zapalac Edwards, BFA '73
Dallas

Finnish Coffee Cake

1 cup brown sugar
¾ cup sugar
2½ cups flour
¾ cup oil
1 teaspoon salt
1 tablespoon nutmeg
1 egg, beaten
1 cup buttermilk
1 teaspoon baking soda
1 teaspoon baking
    powder
TOPPING:
1 teaspoon cinnamon
1 cup chopped walnuts

Combine sugars, flour, oil, salt and nutmeg. Reserve ¾ cup mixture for topping. Add egg and buttermilk mixed with baking soda to dry ingredients, beat well. Add baking powder. Pour into greased, floured 8¾ x 13½-inch pan.
TOPPING: Combine reserved ¾ cup mixture with cinnamon and walnuts. Sprinkle over batter. Bake 30 to 35 minutes at 350°. Serve warm. Serves 12 to 15 generous portions.

Carolyn Fonken,
wife of UT Vice President Gerhard Fonken
Austin

Pheasant Amarillo

1 pheasant
¼ cup butter
1 cup sour cream
½ cup Bleu cheese,
   crumbled
1 clove garlic, mashed
   Salt to taste
   Pepper to taste
   Pinch of Mei Yen
   seasoning
½ cup white wine

Skin pheasant, cut into serving pieces. Saute pheasant in butter until lightly browned. Arrange pieces in casserole. Combine sour cream, Bleu cheese, garlic and seasonings with butter in skillet. Pour over pheasant, cover, bake 1½ hours at 350° or until tender. During last 30 minutes of cooking, pour wine over pheasant. Serves 4.

Hudson Moyer, BBA '54 LLB '57
Nancy Gilmore Moyer, '53
Amarillo

MENU SUGGESTION: Serve with Fried Apples, wild rice, Mincemeat Salad, and Alicia's Lemon Ice with Shortbread Perfect for dessert. Don't forget a bottle of chilled white wine, especially a French wine, perhaps Loire Sancerre.

7C Wild Duck

6 Teal ducks, halved, or
4 large ducks, quartered
   or deboned
MARINADE:
½ cup Soy Sauce
½ cup dry white wine
GRAVY:
1½ cups flour
1 teaspoon salt
1 teaspoon pepper
½ teaspoon paprika
½ teaspoon Beau Monde
   seasoning
   Oil for frying
1 can (5.33 oz.)
   evaporated milk
1 cup water or more
   as needed

Marinate ducks in wine and soy sauce in covered glass (do not use metal) dish in refrigerator 4 hours.
GRAVY: Combine flour with salt, pepper and seasoning. Remove ducks from marinade, dip in seasoned flour. Heat oil in heavy frying pan. Fry ducks slowly until golden brown. Set aside and keep warm. Drain excess oil, add some of the remaining seasoned flour to drippings and simmer until lightly browned. Combine milk and water and gradually add to flour, whisking constantly until thickened. Serves 6.

Mary Canales Jary, '56
San Antonio

Dove Rice Casserole

6 or 7 doves
2 strips bacon, cubed
2 tablespoons butter or
    margarine
¼ cup chopped onion
¼ cup chopped celery
    Salt and pepper to
    taste
1 cup chicken stock
⅔ cup uncooked brown
    rice or wild rice
¼ cup grated carrots
1½ teaspoons dried
    parsley flakes
1 can (12 oz.) beer
¼ cup chopped mush-
    rooms (optional)

Remove skins from doves, clean and wash, remove as many shots as possible. In large-sized skillet, fry bacon pieces; add butter, dove, onion and celery. While browning this mixture sprinkle with salt and pepper. Pour chicken stock into 2-quart casserole, add skillet mixture. Cover, bake 1½ hours at 350°. Remove from oven, add uncooked rice, carrots, parsley, beer and mushrooms if using. Return to oven, cover, cook 40 minutes. If using wild rice, cook only 30 minutes. Serves 3.

Carol Hall Wood, BS '54
Fort Worth

BARBECUED DOVES. Salt, pepper and garlic salt 24 dove breasts. Quarter 6 jalapeños and put a slice on the inside of each breast. Wrap with bacon. Lay in shallow pan and cover with barbecue sauce of your choice. Cover pan with foil and cook on barbecue grill until the bacon is well done, about 45 minutes. Serves 6 to 8.

Steve Rivers, '68
Bastrop

Quail With Sour Cream

10 to 12 quail
    Lemon juice
    Salt
    Pepper
½ cup (1 stick) butter,
    divided
1 pound mushrooms,
    sliced
1 onion, chopped
1 cup chicken stock
1 cup white wine
1 cup sour cream
    Dash Tabasco

Rub quail with lemon juice, salt and pepper. In skillet, brown quail in ¼ cup butter. Remove quail and place in baking dish. In additional ¼ cup butter, saute mushrooms and onion. Cover quail with mushrooms and onion. Add chicken stock and wine. Cover and bake 1 hour at 350°. Baste quail every 10 minutes. Cover quail with sour cream, bake 10 minutes more. Add dash Tabasco to each bird and serve. Serves 5 or 6.

William P. Fitch, III, BA '64
San Antonio

Quail In Wine Sauce

Salt
Pepper
8 quail
1 medium-sized onion,
   chopped
1 tablespoon butter
1 can (4 oz.) sliced
   mushrooms, drained
1 can (10¾ oz.) cream
   of chicken soup
½ cup dry white wine

Salt and pepper quail, inside and outside. Saute onion in butter, add mushrooms. Fill cavities of quail with this mixture. Place in baking pan. Combine soup and wine, pour over quail. Cover, bake 3 hours at 275°, basting occasionally. Serves 4.

Becky Barlow Rivers, BS '71
Steve Rivers, '68
Bastrop

Quail In Beer

2 cups flour
Seasoned salt
Pepper
½ cup (1 stick) butter
   or margarine
10 quail
1 clove garlic, minced
½ cup chopped celery
1 cup chopped onion
1 can (12 oz.) beer

Mix flour with salt and pepper, heat butter until bubbly. Dredge quail in flour and saute in butter until lightly browned. Arrange quail in baking dish. Using butter left in pan, saute garlic, celery and onion. Add beer, cook until liquid is reduced by one-fourth. Pour over quail, cover and bake 1 hour at 350°.
Serves 4.

Louise Stromberg Bates, BS '34
Alice

Quail Véronique

8 quail
Salt and pepper
½ cup (1 stick) butter
1 onion, chopped
1 cup chopped fresh
   mushrooms
1 cup white wine
1 cup green grapes

Rub quail with salt and pepper, saute in butter. Remove and place in roasting pan. In same frying pan, saute onion and mushrooms in remaining butter; add wine. Pour sauce over birds, bake at 350° until tender. Remove quail to platter. Add green grapes to sauce. Heat 5 minutes. Pour sauce over quail and serve with wild rice. Serves 4.

John P. Harbin, BBA '39
Dallas

Sensational Sauce
For Game Birds

1½ cups Worcestershire
 sauce
½ cup fresh lemon juice
 Lemon rinds with
 pulp (reserved after
 squeezing for juice)
½ cup (1 stick) butter
 Lemon pepper
 marinade
 Salt
 Dove, quail or duck

Combine Worcestershire sauce, lemon juice, lemon rinds and butter. Cook sauce until butter is melted, discard lemon rinds. Clean and wash game thoroughly. Birds are best skinned. Salt and pepper each piece. Arrange breast down in a deep baking dish; add sauce. At least half of each bird should be submerged in sauce. Cover dish tightly with foil, bake at 350° for 45 minutes to 1 hour or until tender. Turn birds several times during cooking. Yield: 2½ cups.

John Hudnall, BA '58 MD '61
Tyler

MENU SUGGESTION: Serve with Fiesta Pilaf, Spinach-Stuffed Zucchini, Purple Plum Salad, and Unusual Pound Cake with Bay Leaf Sauce.

Rabbit Casserole

1 rabbit, skinned and
 deboned
1 tablespoon Worcester-
 shire sauce
1 cup soy sauce
 Juice of 1 lemon
½ teaspoon garlic salt
1 cup uncooked rice
1 can (10¾ oz.) cream
 of mushroom soup
1 soup can milk
1 can (6 oz.) sliced
 mushrooms
 Paprika

Combine Worcestershire sauce, soy sauce, lemon juice and garlic salt for marinade. Place rabbit pieces in marinade for 1 hour. Combine remaining ingredients in bottom of buttered 2-quart casserole and place rabbit pieces on top. Cover with foil and bake 1 hour at 350°. Remove from oven, turn rabbit over, sprinkle with paprika, return to oven 10 minutes more. Serves 4.

Terry Green, wife of Leonard F. Green, BA '79
Houston

MENU SUGGESTION: Serve with Parsleyed Carrot Vichy, Head Lettuce with Italian Dressing, and Holee Pudding for dessert, and Mint Iced Tea.

Venison With Fitch's Marchand De Vin Sauce

2 pounds venison backstrap, thinly sliced
Salt and pepper to taste
1 cup (2 sticks) butter, divided
⅓ cup finely chopped mushrooms
½ cup minced ham
⅓ cup finely chopped shallots
½ cup finely chopped onion
2 tablespoons minced garlic
2 tablespoons flour
Salt to taste
Pepper to taste
Dash red pepper
½ cup red wine
¾ cup beef stock

Salt and pepper venison and saute in ½ cup butter. Set aside venison in warm oven. Melt remaining butter and saute mushrooms, ham, shallots, onion and garlic. When onion is golden brown, add flour, salt, pepper and red pepper. Brown thoroughly 7 to 10 minutes. Stir in wine and stock, simmer at low heat 45 minutes. Spoon sauce over venison and serve. Serves 6 to 8.

William P. Fitch, III, BA '64
San Antonio

Venison Swiss Steak

¾ cup flour
½ teaspoon pepper
1 tablespoon salt
3 pounds venison steak, cut 2-inches thick
½ cup bacon grease or oil
2 medium-sized onions, sliced
1 cup sliced celery
1 large-sized green pepper, sliced
1 can (20 oz.) tomatoes
1 cup water
1 tablespoon soy sauce

Combine flour, salt and pepper. Pound venison with mallet, then dredge with flour mixture. Heat fat in deep, heavy skillet. When hot, slowly brown venison. Drain fat. Add remaining ingredients. Cover, bring to boil. Reduce heat, simmer 2½ hours. Serves 6 to 8.

Charles D. Mathews, LLB '37
Austin

Venison Mulligan

A hearty camp stew to serve 8 Mustangs with mania or 4 hungry Longhorns

2 pounds venison
Coarsely ground pepper
Salt
Paprika
Flour
½ cup vegetable oil
1 large-sized green pepper, cut into rings
1 large-sized white onion, cut into rings
1 large stalk celery, sliced
1 can (20 oz.) stewed tomatoes
Dash red pepper
6 carrots
2 large-sized Idaho potatoes
1 can (12 oz.) beer
2 cans water
1 can (16 oz.) whole kernel corn

Cut venison into bite-sized pieces. Combine pepper, salt and paprika to taste; season venison about twice as much as you would domestic meat. Flour lightly but thoroughly. Brown in oil, do not drain as venison is dry. When meat begins to brown (which takes about 10 minutes), add green pepper and onion. As these soften, add celery, tomatoes and red pepper. Simmer slowly 5 minutes. (The browning is most important. Be certain not to add the other ingredients until meat is thoroughly browned.) Cut carrots and potatoes into bite-sized pieces, add to meat mixture and add beer. Simmer in open pot 5 minutes more. Add 2 beer cans full of water and simmer, covered, 1½ to 2 hours. Add corn, simmer in open pot 10 or 15 minutes more to cook down a bit. Serve with garlic bread and a fruit salad.

Margaret Macha Kiefer, BA '69
Austin

DEER PARMESAN. "Cook 1 medium-sized eggplant (weighing about 1¾ pounds) until tender. Peel and slice. Layer in bottom of 1½-quart casserole. Cook 1½ pounds deer meat seasoned with Greek seasoning in skillet or microwave until tender. Layer meat on top of eggplant. Pour 2 cups spaghetti sauce over the meat and top with generous amount of Parmesan cheese. Bake 30 minutes at 350°." Serves 4 to 6.

Irene Reeb Meitzen, BA '65
San Angelo

TEXAS VENISON FILLETS: Thinly slice venison backstrap, soak in milk 2 to 3 hours. Dip in seasoned flour (salt, pepper, garlic powder), then in beaten egg, then again in flour. Fry in ½ oil, ½ butter mixture until golden brown, turning once. Remove, drain on paper towels. Squeeze lemon juice onto venison immediately after removing from skillet if desired. Salt and pepper to taste.

Sarah Ragle Weddington, LLB '67
Washington, D.C.

Venison Barbecue

3 bay leaves
1 cup water
  Salt and pepper to
    taste
2 quarts bone stock
  Venison roast, 4 to
    6 pounds
2 tablespoons oil

MOP:

1½ teaspoons salt
1½ teaspoons dry mustard
1 teaspoon garlic
  powder
1 bay leaf, crushed
1 teaspoon chili powder
1½ teaspoons paprika
1 teaspoon Louisiana
  hot sauce
¾ cup Worcester-
  shire sauce
⅓ cup vinegar
3 cups bone stock
⅓ cup oil
1½ teaspoons mono-
  sodium glutamate

Put bay leaves in 1 cup water, bring to boil. Simmer 10 minutes; remove leaves, add salt, pepper and bone stock (bone stock may be prepared with bouillon cubes). Thoroughly coat meat with oil, place in Dutch oven, add liquid to cover up to about one-fourth of the roast. Cook covered, at low heat, turning often until roast is tender.

MOP: Combine all ingredients and bring to boil. Set aside in refrigerator overnight. Roast may be cooked ahead, refrigerated overnight, and reheated on grill 1 hour, brushing frequently with Mop. If grilling immediately after removing from Dutch oven, allow 30 to 45 minutes, brushing frequently with Mop. Serves 10 to 12.

Maurine Redfearn Bartos, BS '57
Waco

BAKED VENISON. Backstrap, tenders, round steak or chops may be used; however, I prefer to use backstrap or tenders. Slice venison ¼ to ½-inch thick. Marinate in dry red wine and soy sauce for at least 2 hours. Remove from marinade and coat with flour. Quickly brown both sides in hot fat. Place in shallow baking pan and splash soy sauce over all. Cover tightly with foil and bake 1 hour at 325°.

Charles D. Mathews, LLB '37
Austin

VENISON STEAK. Use backstrap or round steak, cut into serving portions. Trim fat. If wild taste is too strong for your palate, soak venison in vinegar water at least 1 or 2 hours or refrigerate overnight. Salt and pepper and brown in a heavy skillet with garlic and onions; a can of tomato sauce may be used for moisture. Cover and cook until tender.

Arno Nowotny, BA '22 LLB '25 MA '32
Austin

Crunchy Cucumber Pickles
A sweet treat from Tennessee

7 pounds large-sized
    cucumbers
5 tablespoons calcium
    hydroxide (available
    in drug stores)
4 ounces powdered
    alum
2½ quarts white vinegar
2½ quarts water
14 cups sugar
1 teaspoon pickling salt
1 tablespoon celery seed
3 tablespoons pickling
    spice

Peel, remove seeds, and slice cucumbers into sticks. Mix calcium hydroxide thoroughly in sufficient water to cover pickles. Soak cucumbers 24 hours. Remove pickles and rinse thoroughly. Mix powdered alum with sufficient water to cover pickles. Soak 6 hours. Drain, rinse well. Soak in plain water 6 hours. Mix together vinegar, water, sugar, salt, celery seed and pickling spice. Soak pickles 24 hours in this mixture. Cook until transparent. Put into jars and seal. Yield: 3 quarts.

Myrtle Ligon, wife of Jack A. Ligon, BA '50
San Antonio

CHRISTMAS PICKLES. *(A festive, tasty addition to holiday relish trays).* "Peel and slice into ½-inch rounds 7 large-sized cucumbers. Mix 1 cup lime and 1 gallon water and soak cucumbers overnight. Drain, soak in clear water 4 hours. To make pretty pickles use canape cutter to remove seeds making donut-shaped rings. Mix 1 cup white vinegar, a small bottle red food coloring, 1 tablespoon alum, and enough water to cover pickles. Simmer 2 hours, drain. Bring to boil 2 cups white vinegar, 2 cups water, 10 cups sugar, 2 cinnamon sticks, 1 package (2¾ oz.) red hot candies. Pour over pickles. Cover, set aside 3 days. Drain into sauce pan, reheat and pour heated mixture over pickles. Set aside 3 days more. Reheat syrup to boil. Pack pickles in sterilized jars. Pour syrup over pickles in jars, seal. Yield: 3 to 5 pints.
"This recipe is well worth the time involved. Really, however, not much time is involved on any given day—just lots of days."

Louise Harrell Mulkey, BA '61
Panhandle

PICKLED OKRA: Wash 5 or 6 pounds medium- to small-sized pods of okra. Scrub lightly with a piece of nylon net or brush to remove 'fuzz.' Trim okra stems without cutting into pod. Sterilize 6 pint jars. Into each jar put ¾ teaspoon dill seed (or sprig and heads of fresh dill, if available), 2 to 4 red and green small-sized hot peppers, and 1 clove garlic (crushed). Pack okra into jars in 2 vertical layers, the first layer with stems down and the second layer with stems up. Pack as firmly as possible without crushing pods. Combine 1 quart white vinegar, 1 cup water and ½ cup pickling salt; bring to a rolling boil and pour over okra. Seal. Set aside to age 3 weeks, if you can wait that long! Shelf life: 1 year. Yield: 6 pints.

Crockett English, '42
Leander

Country Bread and Butter Pickles

6 quarts sliced
    cucumbers
12 medium-sized onions,
    sliced
2 green peppers,
    chopped (optional)
1 can (4 oz.) pimientos,
    sliced
¾ cup salt
1 teaspoon turmeric
½ cup mustard seed
6 cups vinegar
6 cups sugar

Layer cucumbers, onions, peppers and pimientos salting each layer. Set aside 3 hours. Drain juice, add remaining ingredients. Mix well, bring mixture to boil. Remove from heat, seal in sterilized jars while hot. Yield: 8 pints.

Jean Welhausen Kaspar, BA '52
Shiner

Lake Caddo Relish

1 quart cider vinegar
2 cups sugar
½ tablespoon pepper
⅓ cup salt
1½ gallons chopped green
    tomatoes
1 quart chopped green
    and red peppers
1 quart chopped onion
½ cup chopped fresh
    jalapeños

In large enamel pot, combine vinegar, sugar, pepper and salt. Heat until sugar dissolves, add remaining ingredients, and bring to boil. Cook 5 minutes. Pack in sterilized jars and seal. Yield: 16 pints.

Zuleika Stranger Griffin, BA '43
Lufkin

PAPA'S PICKLED PEPPERS. Clean bell peppers and cut into wedges. (Size of the wedges will depend on size of the peppers. A small pepper can usually be cut into 4 wedges; a large pepper can usually be cut into 6 or 8 wedges. Follow the pepper's natural grooves from top to bottom when cutting.) Put wedges into sterilized Mason jars. Fill jars with either equal amounts pickling vinegar and distilled water or with apple cider vinegar (5% acidity or stronger) and no water. Make sure the vinegar covers all of the peppers and that there are no air bubbles. Add 1 rounded teaspoon Kosher salt. Screw on sterilized lids. Put in pantry. Pull out about 3 to 4 months later and enjoy! NOTE: A warning to novices—pickled peppers are *very* sour.

Mary Barnes James, BA '75 BJ '75
Houston

Chow Chow

3 quarts cabbage
6 quarts tomatoes
2 quarts onion
1 dozen red sweet
    peppers
2 tablespoons salt
2 pounds (4 cups) sugar
4 tablespoons mustard
2 tablespoons pepper
2 tablespoons cinnamon
½ teaspoon red pepper
1 tablespoon allspice
1 teaspoon cloves
1 quart vinegar
½ cup flour

Chop all vegetables coarsely. Layer vegetables in crock, sprinkling each layer lightly with salt. Repeat until all vegetables are used. Set aside a few hours. Drain, mix in remaining ingredients except the flour and vinegar. Boil the vegetable mixture 30 minutes. Mix flour into smooth paste with 1 cup vinegar, add to vegetable mixture and add remaining vinegar. Boil 10 minutes. Seal hot. Yield: 6 quarts.

Aline Calhoun, '23
Austin

EDITH GLAZEBROOK'S HOT STUFF. *"My brother and I always enjoyed hot refried beans. In order to serve refried beans, Mother would take her refrigerated ½ pint jar, with corroded lid and full of 'hot stuff,' and using just the tip of a teaspoon would remove enough 'stuff' to flavor a whole skillet of refried beans. Even to smell the 'stuff' in the jar was hot! When the 'hot stuff' jar needed refilling, my brother and I would gather little red and green chile peppers, which grew abundantly in our yard, for our Mother to make another batch of the 'stuff.'*

"Like many old recipes, the amounts are not given. I have added, in parenthesis, the amounts I have used. I would advise: adjust to taste; yet, after just a taste, one's taste buds are seared. So, I would suggest tasting the 'stuff' mixed in another dish, such as refried beans.

"The recipe was given to Mother by our neighbor, Mrs. Edith Glazebrook, who was a Kenedy of the famed Kenedy Ranch near Corpus Christi. I remember Mrs. Glazebrook as a little old lady with a house full of interesting glass and things we could not touch. Now, when I drive through the ranch, which is presently a wild-life preserve as well as a working ranch, I always think of Mrs. Glazebrook and her 'HOT STUFF:' Grind together: green chile pequins (1 cup), garlic cloves (2 or 3), white onions (2 small-sized), and peppercorns (1 tablespoon). Soak overnight in enough vinegar to cover; use glass container. Next day, bring mixture to boil. Drain excess vinegar. Add salt (1 teaspoon), comino seed (1 cup), Worcestershire sauce (1 teaspoon), olive oil (1 tablespoon), and Heinz chili sauce (enough to make a thin sauce of spreading consistency.)

"Always store in glass container, refrigerated. This 'hot stuff' will corrode metal and soak into plastic."

Mary Ann Maley, BA '54
Smithville

Francis Nalle's
Hot Pepper Jelly

4 large-sized green
    peppers, seeded and
    coarsely chopped
4 jalapeños, seeded
    and coarsely
    chopped
1½ cups cider vinegar
6 cups sugar
1 bottle or 2 pouches
    Certo

Pile peppers into blender with ½ cup of the vinegar. Puree at high speed until well blended. Pour pepper mixture into saucepan. Rinse blender with remaining (1 cup) vinegar, add to peppers. Add sugar. Bring to rolling boil and, stirring constantly, cook 5 minutes. Remove from heat, skim if necessary. Add Certo. Return to heat and boil 2 to 5 minutes after the mixture comes to a hard boil (all bubbles). Pour into sterilized jars and seal. NOTE: Use either red or green peppers. Food coloring can be used for a clearer color. Yield: 5 or 6 half-pints.

Suzanne Williams Nash, BA '67
Dallas

Variation: *Use 2 cups finely ground green peppers and 1½ cups white vinegar.*

Rosemary Fanning Pinson,
wife of Robert M. Pinson, BA '41
Dallas

Variation: *Use 3 green peppers and 6 jalapeños.*

Trudy Iverson Kokernot, BS '71
Boerne

Cantaloupe Conserve

8 cups cubed cantaloupe
1 can (20 oz.) crushed
    pineapple
    Juice of 2 oranges
    Juice of 2 lemons
8 cups sugar
1 jar (10 oz.)
    maraschino cherries,
    halved
1 package (3½ oz.)
    slivered almonds

Combine first 5 ingredients, bring to full boil. Reduce heat, simmer 2 hours or until mixture thickens. Remove from heat, add cherries and almonds. Pour into dry sterilized jars and seal. Yield: 7 to 9 half-pints.

Myrtle Ligon, wife of Jack A. Ligon, BA '50
San Antonio

Fig Preserves

6 cups sugar
3 cups water
4 pounds figs, washed
1 lemon, thinly sliced

Cook sugar and water about 5 minutes. Add figs and sliced lemon, cook until syrup is thickened, about 1½ to 2 hours. Skim the mixture as the figs cook. Store in refrigerator. Yield: 3½ to 4 pints.

Helen Dixon Brown, MA '34
San Antonio

Mock Strawberry Preserves (Figs)

6 cups sugar
2 boxes (6 oz. each) strawberry-flavored gelatin
8 cups peeled and sliced figs
1 bottle Certo

Combine sugar, gelatin and figs. Boil slowly 20 minutes, carefully watching that mixture does not boil over or burn. Add Certo, boil 2 minutes more. Put into sterilized jars and seal. Yield: 4 pints.

Myrtle Ligon, wife of Jack A. Ligon, BA '50
San Antonio

FRESH PUMPKIN PUREE. Don't let that uncut Halloween pumpkin sit around too long. Cut 3 to 4 pound pumpkin in eighths, scoop out and discard seeds and fiber. Place pieces in vegetable steamer. Cover and steam over boiling water for 20 to 25 minutes or until flesh is tender. Or place pieces in large baking pan (do not stack pieces), add ½ cup water, cover with foil. Bake 40 minutes to 1 hour at 325°. Remove, cool. When cool, scrape flesh from outer peel, puree in food processor or blender. This puree will keep indefinitely in the freezer. Yield: 1 pound fresh equals 1 cup cooked pumpkin. *Editor.*

Louise Appleman, wife of Gordon Appleman, BA '59
Fort Worth

HOMEMADE CRANBERRY JELLY. Put 1 quart washed cranberries in 1 cup boiling water. Cook 5 minutes or until berries burst. Remove from heat and press through sieve. Add 2 cups sugar, stir until dissolved. Pour into mold, chill until firm. Serves 6 to 8

Louise Appleman, wife of Gordon Appleman, BA '59
Fort Worth

The 1890s

Cakes, Ice Creams
Sweet Sauces

In April 1892, an Athletic Association was formed; it fielded The University's first football team that autumn. This is a picture of the 1894 team.

$\mathcal{T}$he University of Texas did not always have an easy time in
the 1890s. Economic conditions caused financial difficulties for students and for
the institution. Although student fees remained stable at low rates, faculty
salaries often dropped $1,000 or more in a year's time. Issues included the need
for increased space, smaller classes, curriculum changes, new grading systems,
and library expansion. Difficulties with collecting taxes and a need for increased
appropriations, plus an increasing enrollment, worried administrators.

By 1899 the forty-acre campus had four buildings: B Hall, the
Chemical Laboratory, the power house, and the recently completed Main
Building. The Library contained 34,000 books, compared to only 6,000 in 1890.
The Regents decided in 1895 that the University should have a president and
appointed Leslie Waggener to be president *ad interim.* He died at the end of the
first year after his appointment and was followed by George Tayloe Winston.

Money worries plagued students as much in those days as now.
Even though the University charged no tuition, and fees totaled only $15 to $20
in the Academic and Law Departments, students always sought ways to cut
expenses. In 1891 the University began awarding fellowships to deserving
graduate students. In return for $300 a year, a student might assist professors
while pursuing a graduate degree. In 1893 the Academic Department exempted
from all fees the valedictorians of "affiliated" high schools, those schools that
met University qualifications. Texas had 21 affiliated schools in 1890; 93 by
1899.

A major step toward reducing costs and promoting closer
relations among male students came with the opening of B Hall on December 1,
1890. Just east of the Main Building, it was built with a donation from Regent
George W. Brackenridge. It had rooms for 58 at first and a dining room for at
least 150. At the end of the decade, two wings were added. Rent at the
beginning was $2.50 per month per student, but it was increased to $3 the
following year. A "bill of fare" for February 1892, published in the University

Catalogue, would jolt a present day restaurateur. Breakfast items included oatmeal and milk, 3¢; tenderloin steak, 3¢; two eggs, 3¢; hot biscuits, 2¢; sweet milk, 2¢ per glass; buttermilk, 1¢ per glass; and 4¢ for service. The menu for dinner (served from noon to 2:15 p.m.) included oxtail soup with crackers, 2¢; and mince pie, 3¢. At supper (served from 6 p.m. to 7 p.m.) one might select grits and milk, 3¢; cold roast or beef hash, 2¢; broiled steak, 4¢; cheese and crackers, 2¢; butter and syrup, 2¢ each; prune or apple pie or lemon wafers, 2¢ each.

The need for residence halls for women on campus was recognized slowly. Early leaders for education in the state believed that provision of living quarters was not an essential function of an educational institution. Before the turn of the century, however, attitudes began to change. The Episcopal Church opened the Young Ladies Church Institute in 1895 and offered a church home in Grace Hall in the fall of 1897 to a limited number of girls who attended the University. Teaching in Grace Hall included music, art, and other cultural subjects not offered at the University.

For a number of years after the erection of the hall, its residents led an isolated life. Telephones were not installed because the "matron" thought the ringing of the bell would disturb girls who were studying. Callers were discouraged during the week, and parlor dates were not permitted. The women could go out on Saturday and Sunday nights but had to be in by 10 p.m. They could attend productions at the Hancock Opera House or Saturday night "germans." Hall lights were turned out at 11 p.m. The "Colonial Ball," with only girls in attendance, was the big annual event. In the spring, routine was relieved by an outing on the Colorado River. Students also had entertainments such as soda-pop parties on the lawn, fudge parties, tacky parties, and geographical charades parties. Going to see a fortune teller or administering "mild hazing" to freshmen were also dormitory pastimes for the girls.

Football started in 1892. Students formed an athletic association in April, and organized a football team the following fall. Four games were played in 1893, and the University had an undefeated season. Years away were pre-game cocktail parties, tail-gate luncheons, post-game barbecues, half-time snacks, and other social events that have become traditional. Years away also were football scholarships, competitive recruiting, and ticket scalping.

The *Cactus* appeared in 1894. Thus began a documentation of the University student culture that is marked by changes closely related to those of the outer society. In December 1895, students initiated publication of a newspaper, the *Alcalde*. Another newspaper, the *Calendar*, merged with the *Alcalde* in 1900 to become *The Texan*, a weekly at first and semi-weekly by 1907.

The Final Ball, usually held in June at the Driskill Hotel, climaxed the extracurricular activities of the year. All classes spent time, money, and effort preparing for the occasion, and students vied for chairmanship of the ball, the most prestigious social position one could attain. During the late 1890's, excursions to Dallas for the big football game during the Dallas Fair became popular. The football game in 1899 turned into a fight, but students had a good time on the train to and from Dallas.

In the early years of the University, the administration discouraged student groups from participating in politics. Nevertheless, a Bryan Club and a Gold Club appeared in 1896. When the *Galveston-Dallas News* criticized the appearance of a "16 to 1" Club, the *Alcalde* came to the defense of students by saying, "The students of this institution are perfectly at liberty to think on political questions exactly as they please . . . . It is not the business of the University to meddle with the politics of the students."

One day in the spring of 1896, students met in a quiet and dignified way to adopt resolutions concerning the failure on the part of University Regents to re-elect a physics professor. Approximately a year later, on March 2, a boisterous group of students, led by the senior law class, left their books to celebrate Texas Independence Day. Students fired a cannon "borrowed" from the Capitol grounds and made numerous speeches before they finally were joined by faculty members for a celebration that ended that evening.

Freshman and junior law students also had their annual battles. "Cane rushes," common on East Coast campuses, were not tolerated at the University, but unorganized horseplay served similar ends. The class of 1892 began a practice, followed for a number of years, of burning their hated Latin texts. The first such bonfire on record was in a backyard on Whitis Avenue.

A student survey in 1898 indicated that pool was not popular among University students; its unpopularity was attributed to "the Dingley Bill price of billiard cloth." The "bones," however, were quite popular. The survey further indicated that XXX and soda pop were favorite drinks and that political party affiliation was "overwhelmingly Democrat."

Outbreak of the Spanish-American War during the last weeks of the term of 1898 and epidemics of dengue and yellow fever aroused mild excitement among students. As the century closed, student life as students viewed it was still often dull.

Victorian Ice Cream Socials

Texas Chocolate Cake
All-time favorite—our most popular cake

1 cup (2 sticks) butter or
 margarine
4 tablespoons cocoa
1 cup water
2 cups flour
2 cups sugar
1 teaspoon baking soda
1 teaspoon cinnamon
½ cup buttermilk
2 eggs, slightly beaten
1 teaspoon vanilla

ICING:

½ cup (1 stick) butter or
 margarine
4 tablespoons cocoa
6 tablespoons milk
1 box (16 oz.) powdered
 sugar
1 teaspoon vanilla
1½ cups pecans

Boil together butter, cocoa and water. Sift together dry ingredients. Pour boiling mixture over dry ingredients, beating constantly. Stir in buttermilk, eggs and vanilla; mix well. Pour into greased and floured 9 x 13-inch pan. Bake 30 minutes at 400°.

ICING: Boil together butter, cocoa and milk. Remove from heat; add powdered sugar, vanilla and pecans. Beat until thick and spread over hot cake. Serves 20.

Rex Baker, Jr., BA '41 LLB '47
Houston

Variation: *Substitute 1 cup shortening for 1 cup margarine. Reduce pecans to 1 cup.*

Burt C. Hooten, '68
Yorbalinda, California

Variation: *Reduce butter to ½ cup. Substitute 3 squares (1 oz. each) unsweetened chocolate for cocoa. Increase vanilla to 2 tablespoons. Omit cinnamon. For icing, melt together 1 cup butter and 4 squares (1 oz. each) unsweetened chocolate; add 2 eggs, 3 cups powdered sugar, 2 teaspoons lemon juice and 2 teaspoons vanilla. Spread on cake and sprinkle with 2 cups chopped nuts.*

Johnnye Jean Weinert Lovett, BA '48
Seguin

Variation: *Use ½ cup margarine and ½ cup shortening. Decrease cocoa to 3 tablespoons. In icing, decrease cocoa to 3 tablespoons and pecans to 1 cup.*

Anna Pearl Alexander, BA '38
Swannanoa, North Carolina

Apple Spice Cake

3 eggs
2 cups sugar
2 cups flour
2 teaspoons cinnamon
2 teaspoons baking soda
¼ teaspoon salt
½ cup salad oil
1 teaspoon vanilla
¾ cup chopped nuts
4 cups unpeeled, finely
    chopped apples
Powdered sugar
or
FROSTING:
2 tablespoons butter or
    margarine, softened
3 ounces cream cheese,
    softened
1½ cups powdered sugar
1 teaspoon vanilla
⅛ teaspoon salt

Beat eggs until light and creamy. Gradually add sugar. Sift together dry ingredients and add alternately with oil and vanilla mixture to egg batter. Add flour mixture last. Fold in nuts and apples. Spread in greased and floured 9 x 13-inch pan. Bake 45 minutes at 350°. Cool. Dust with powdered sugar or FROSTING: Combine all ingredients. Spread onto top and sides of cake. Serves 12.

Patricia Lind Derx, '62
Austin

Banana Split Cake
Simple to make—colorful, delicious, and extremely rich!

1½ cups flour
2 tablespoons sugar
3¾ sticks butter or
    margarine, divided
1 cup chopped pecans
1 box (16 oz.) powdered
    sugar
2 eggs
2 teaspoons vanilla
1 can (20 oz.) crushed
    pineapple, drained
3 or 4 bananas, sliced
1 can (5½ oz.) chocolate
    syrup
1 carton (8 oz.) Cool
    Whip
Chopped cherries
Chopped pecans

Combine flour, sugar and 1¾ sticks butter. Add pecans. Press into 9 x 15-inch pan and bake 20 minutes at 350°. Cool. Combine powdered sugar, eggs, vanilla and 2 sticks butter. Mix well, spread over cooled cake. Next, spread crushed pineapple, cover with banana slices. Drizzle chocolate syrup over bananas. Top with Cool Whip. Garnish with chopped cherries and pecans. Serves 20.

Don Chandler, BS '78
Houston

Madge's Apricot Cake

Perfect orange and white after-game or victory cake

2 cups sugar
1 cup oil
3 eggs
2 jars (4½ oz. each)
   strained apricot-
   tapioca baby food
2 cups flour
2 teaspoons baking
   powder
1 teaspoon cinnamon
1 cup chopped nuts

ICING:

1 cup finely cut fresh
   apricots
4 tablespoons orange
   juice
½ cup butter
2 egg yolks
2 teaspoons grated
   orange rind
1 teaspoon vanilla
4 cups powdered sugar

Beat together sugar, oil and eggs. Add baby food. Sift dry ingredients, add to creamed mixture. Fold in nuts. Pour into greased, floured 10-inch bundt or tube pan. Bake 1½ hours at 325°, begin baking in cold oven.

ICING: If unable to obtain fresh apricots, use well drained canned apricots and decrease orange juice to 2 tablespoons. If using dried apricots, soak fruit in the orange juice until softened. Cream butter, add egg yolks, rind and vanilla. Add powdered sugar alternating with orange juice. Fold in cut apricots. Serves 16 to 20.

Nancy Krause Nibling, BA '73
Lakewood, Colorado

Quick Banana Cake

2 cups self-rising flour
1½ cups sugar
1 teaspoon vanilla
½ cup shortening or
   butter
⅓ cup buttermilk
3 ripe bananas, sliced
2 eggs
⅓ cup chopped pecans

Combine all ingredients except nuts with mixer at low speed until moistened; then mix 3 minutes at medium speed, scraping bowl occasionally. Add nuts. Pour into 9 x 13-inch baking dish with only bottom of the dish buttered. Bake 30 to 35 minutes at 350°. Cool, cut into squares. Serves 12 to 15.

Elizabeth Lynn Rosen, BBA '80
New Orleans, Louisiana

Banana Cake

½ cup (1 stick) butter
1½ cups sugar
2 eggs
2¼ cups cake flour
½ teaspoon baking
   powder
¾ teaspoon baking soda
½ teaspoon salt
1 cup bananas, pureed
1 teaspoon vanilla
¼ cup sour milk
ICING:
2 cups sugar
1 cup water
2 egg whites
⅛ teaspoon salt
⅛ teaspoon cream of
   tartar
1 teaspoon vanilla
2 bananas, sliced

Cream butter. Gradually add sugar and beat until light and creamy. Beat in eggs, 1 at a time. Sift together dry ingredients. Combine bananas, vanilla and milk. Add dry ingredients to butter mixture in 3 portions alternating with banana mixture. Beat batter until smooth after each addition. Pour batter into 2 greased 9-inch layer pans. Bake 30 minutes at 350°.

ICING: In saucepan over direct heat combine sugar and water. Cook mixture without stirring until medium firm ball stage (238 to 240°). Combine egg whites, salt and cream of tartar. Beat egg whites until soft peaks form. Add the syrup mixture in a thin stream, whipping constantly. Add vanilla. After cake has baked and cooled, place bottom layer on cake plate, spread with thin layer of icing and top with sliced bananas. Spread with more icing, top with second layer. Spread remaining icing on top and sides of cake. Icing may be omitted and cake dusted with powdered sugar or served with whipped cream. Serves 12 to 15.

June Barrett, BS '54
Houston

Farmers Cake

2 cups sugar
1 cup (2 sticks) butter
   or margarine
2 eggs
3 cups flour
2 teaspoons baking soda
1½ teaspoons cinnamon
1 teaspoon cloves
3 tablespoons cocoa
1 cup cold coffee
1 teaspoon vanilla
2 cups peeled and
   chopped apples
1 cup raisins

Cream together sugar and butter; add eggs. Combine flour, baking soda, cinnamon, cloves and cocoa. Add to creamed mixture alternating with coffee. Add vanilla. Mix well. Add apples and raisins. Bake in ungreased tube pan or 9 x 12-inch cake pan. Bake 1 hour at 350°. Frost with butter cream or caramel icing. Serves 15 to 20.

Jacqueline B. Davis, MLS '78
Austin

Gone With The Wind — two original costume renderings by Walter Plunkett for Miss Pittypat from the Selznick Archive of the Hoblitzelle Theatre Arts Library. Giving support to the colorful Plunkett drawings are various items from the Humanities Research Center, including: a Waterford Crystal wine decanter and two wine glasses (from the Stark Young Collection); a black lace fan, an oriental pearl necklace, and bracelet (from the John Foster and Janet Dulles Collection).

The shawl belonged to Queen Victoria and was presented to Natalie Krassovska, ballerina of Ballet Russe de Monte Carlo, by Princess Marie Louis, granddaughter of Queen Victoria, when Ms. Krassovska danced at a command performance in London in 1950.

photo by Sherwood Inkley

Black Forest Torte

Tall and gorgeous like a Texas woman

1¾ cups flour
1¾ cups sugar
1¼ teaspoons baking soda
½ teaspoon salt
1½ cups water
¼ teaspoon baking
    powder
⅔ cup soft-type
    margarine
4 squares (1 oz. each)
    unsweetened
    chocolate, melted
    and cooled
1 teaspoon vanilla
3 eggs

CHOCOLATE FILLNG:

1½ bars (4 oz. each)
    German's sweet
    chocolate
¾ cup soft-type
    margarine
½ cup chopped almonds

CREAM FILLING:

2 cups whipping cream
1 tablespoon sugar
1 teaspoon vanilla

CAKE: Combine all ingredients except eggs. Stir to moisten, then beat 2 minutes at medium speed. Add eggs, beat until smooth. Bake in 4 buttered 9-inch cake pans 15 minutes at 350°. Cool. Remove from pan.

CHOCOLATE FILLING: Melt chocolate over hot water. Cool. Blend in margarine and almonds. Set aside.

CREAM FILLING: Whip cream. Add sugar and vanilla.

FINISH: Place 1 layer of cake on serving plate. Spread with one half of chocolate filling. Add a second cake layer. Spread with one half of cream filling. Repeat layers, ending with cream filling on top. Do not frost sides. Make chocolate curls with the remaining sweet chocolate bar to decorate top of cake. Keep refrigerated. Serves 15 to 20.

Nina Cook Segler, BBA '79
Dallas
Irene Reeb Meitzen, BA '65
San Angelo

German Peach Cake

2 cups flour
1 teaspoon baking soda
½ teaspoon cinnamon
1½ cups sugar
¼ teaspoon salt
2 eggs, beaten
¾ cup oil
1⅓ cups mashed fresh
    peaches (3 or 4
    large-sized)
1 cup chopped nuts

Combine dry ingredients. Add eggs, oil and peaches. Mix thoroughly; add nuts. Bake in greased bundt pan 1 hour at 350°. Serves 20.

Nancy Milburn Granaghan, '70
San Angelo

Frosted Carrot Cake

Best carrot cake I've ever eaten, and I thought I didn't like carrot cake.

1½ cups salad oil
2 cups sugar
4 eggs
2½ cups flour
2 teaspoons baking soda
1 tablespoon cinnamon
1 teaspoon salt
3 cups peeled, grated carrots
1 can (8 oz.) crushed pineapple, drained
1 cup chopped pecans

FROSTING:

8 ounces cream cheese, softened
6 tablespoons butter, softened
2 tablespoons vanilla
2 tablespoons grated orange rind
1 box (16 oz.) powdered sugar

Combine oil and sugar. Add eggs, 1 at a time, beating well after each addition. Sift together flour, baking soda, cinnamon and salt. Add dry ingredients to oil mixture, stirring thoroughly. Add carrots and pineapple, fold in pecans. Pour into well-greased tube pan. Bake 1¼ hours at 325°. Frost when cool.

FROSTING: Beat cream cheese and butter until creamy and fluffy. Add remaining ingredients. Spread evenly onto cake. Serves 16 to 20.

Charlotte Plemmons Warren, BJ '76
Austin

Variation: ORANGE QUICKIE. *Substitute 3 small baby food jars of strained carrots, use 1 teaspoon cinnamon, add 1 cup raisins.*

Susan Marie Palousek Harding, BA '69
Norristown, Pennsylvania

Variation: *Omit pineapple and pecans in cake. Add 2 teaspoons allspice to batter. Add ½ cup chopped pecans, ½ cup chopped raisins, ½ cup coconut to frosting.*

Penny Porter Helms, BFA '66
Austin

Whipped Cream Cake

1½ cups whipping cream
3 eggs, beaten
1½ teaspoons vanilla
2¼ cups cake flour
1½ cups sugar
2 teaspoons baking powder
½ teaspoon salt

Whip cream until stiff. Fold in eggs and vanilla. Sift dry ingredients and with rubber spatula fold into cream mixture. Pour into 2 greased and floured 8- or 9-inch cake pans or 9 x 13-inch pan. Bake layers 30 to 35 minutes; bake oblong 35 to 40 minutes at 350°. This cake freezes well. A seven-minute frosting is a nice touch. Serves 8 to 10.

Louise Harrell Mulkey, BA '61
Panhandle

Chocolate Cherry Nut Cake
Velvety texture, great flavor!

½ cup (1 stick) butter
  or margarine
1 cup sugar
1 egg, beaten
1½ cups all-purpose flour
  or 1¾ cups cake
  flour
1 teaspoon baking soda
¼ teaspoon salt
1 jar (8 oz.) maraschino
  cherries, chopped
  (reserve juice)
1 square (1 oz.)
  chocolate
Cherry juice
1 cup sour milk
½ cup chopped walnuts

Thoroughly cream butter and sugar, add egg and beat well. Sift flour with baking soda and salt. Drain cherries, reserving juice. Melt chocolate with 3 tablespoons cherry juice. Add flour and liquids alternately to creamed mixture. Fold in cherries and nuts. Pour into 2 greased, floured 8-inch cake pans. Bake 35 minutes at 350°. When cool, frost with any chocolate cream cheese frosting of your choice. Serves 10 to 12.

Jeanette Anne Fleming, BS '76
Pearland

Surprise Devil's Food Cake

1 cup (2 sticks) butter
2 cups sugar
½ cup cocoa, sifted
1 teaspoon vanilla
3 eggs
1 jar (10 oz.) plum jelly
3 cups flour
2 teaspoons baking
  powder
1 cup milk

MOCHA FROSTING:

½ cup (1 stick) butter
1 teaspoon vanilla
1 box (16 oz.) powdered
  sugar
½ cup cocoa
¼ cup strong coffee

Cream butter and sugar. Add cocoa and vanilla, mix well. Add eggs, 1 at a time, beating after each addition. Add jelly (the secret ingredient), mix well. Add flour and baking powder alternately with milk. Bake in 3 greased, floured 9-inch cake pans 18 to 20 minutes at 400°.

FROSTING: Cream butter, add vanilla. Sift powdered sugar and cocoa and add alternately with coffee (may be necessary to add more coffee). Spread between layers and frost top and sides of cooled cake. Serves 20 to 24.

Mary Fletcher White, BA '40
Oro Valley, Arizona

Cakes

Waldorf Cheesecake

This is a real cheesecake, like you pay $2.50 a slice for!

CRUST:
1¾ cups graham cracker crumbs
2 tablespoons sugar
1½ teaspoons cinnamon
½ cup (1 stick) butter, melted

FILLING:
24 ounces cream cheese, softened
3 eggs
1 cup sugar
1 teaspoon vanilla
½ teaspoon almond extract or juice of 1 lemon

TOPPING:
1 pint (16 oz.) sour cream
3 tablespoons sugar
½ teaspoon vanilla

GLAZE:
½ cup sugar
3 tablespoons flour
Pinch salt
½ cup tart cherry juice
2 tablespoons butter
2 cups cherries, drained
Red food coloring

Combine crumbs, sugar, cinnamon and butter. Pat into bottom and up sides of 10-inch springform pan. Set aside.

FILLING: Combine cream cheese, eggs, sugar and flavorings. Beat until creamy and fluffy. Pour into prepared crust. Bake 30 minutes at 350°. Remove from oven. Reset oven to 500°.

TOPPING: Combine sour cream with sugar and vanilla. Spread on top of cake, return to oven, bake 5 minutes at 500°. Refrigerate until well chilled.

GLAZE: Combine sugar, flour and salt. Add cherry juice slowly, cooking at low heat, until mixture has thickened. Remove from heat, add butter, cherries and food coloring. Refrigerate glaze until chilled. Pour over cake. Keep refrigerated at all times. Serves 16 to 20 non-dieters.

Beth Miller Clegg, '50
Dallas

Variation: *Substitute 1 can (14 oz.) sweetened condensed milk for sugar and use only 16 ounces cream cheese. Omit glaze.*

Judith Morrison Martin, BA '77 BJ '77
Houston

Variation: *Reduce cream cheese to 16 ounces and combine with 16 ounces sour cream. Bake 40 minutes at 350°. Turn off oven, leave cake in oven 1 hour more. Omit topping and glaze.*

Jo Shropshire Hannon, BBA '47
Austin

Variation: *Omit crust. Generously butter springform pan, sprinkle with graham cracker crumbs. Substitute 1 can pie filling of your choice for cooked glaze.*

Nancy Mitchell Meyers, BS '75
Midland

Kinsolving Peanut Butter Cheesecake

3 ounces cream cheese, softened
1 cup sifted powdered sugar
6 tablespoons creamy peanut butter
½ cup milk
1 cup plus 3 table- spoons frozen whipped topping, thawed
1 unbaked 9-inch graham cracker pie shell
¼ cup peanuts, finely chopped

Whip cream cheese until soft and fluffy. Beat in sugar and peanut butter. Slowly add milk. Fold topping into mixture. Pour into pie shell. Sprinkle chopped peanuts across top. Freeze until firm. Remove from freezer 30 minutes before slicing and serving. Serves 8 coeds.

Merle Tooke Lewis, BA '53 MLS '70
Waterville, Maine

STRAWBERRY GLAZE FOR CHEESECAKE. Arrange large, hulled strawberries (approximately 2 cartons) on cheesecake top. Crush and strain 1 cup imperfect berries. Combine with ⅓ cup sugar, 1 tablespoon lemon juice, 1 tablespoon cornstarch and a few drops red food coloring. Heat until thick and transparent. Cool. Spoon over arranged berries. *Editor.*

Mocha Cheesecake

Silken chocolate consistency with the accent of coffee

24 ounces cream cheese, softened
1 cup sugar
2 eggs
1 package (8 oz.) semisweet chocolate
½ cup double-strength cold coffee
1 teaspoon vanilla
1 cup sour cream, divided
Graham cracker crust

In blender or food processor, combine cream cheese, sugar and eggs; blend until smooth. Melt chocolate over boiling water, add 2 tablespoons sour cream. Cool. Add to cream cheese mixture. Add coffee and vanilla. Fold in remaining sour cream. Pour mixture into 10-inch graham cracker crust-lined springform pan. Bake 45 minutes at 350°. The cake will be soft in center. Cool, refrigerate several hours, or freeze. Stores well. Serves 10 to 12.

Elaine Martini Dove, MA '72
Hamden, Connecticut

Cheesecake For Pumpkin Lovers

CRUST:
- ¼ cup butter, softened
- ⅓ cup sugar
- 1 egg
- 1¼ cups flour

FILLING:
- 16 ounces cream cheese, softened
- ¾ cup sugar
- 2 eggs
- 2 cups cooked, mashed pumpkin
- 1 teaspoon ground cinnamon
- ¼ teaspoon ground ginger
- ¼ teaspoon ground nutmeg
- ⅛ teaspoon salt
- Whipped cream (optional)

Cream butter and sugar. Add egg. Add flour and mix to cookie dough consistency. Spread and pat dough on bottom and up sides of 9-inch springform pan. Bake 7 minutes at 400°. Remove from oven. Reduce oven to 350°.

FILLING: Combine cream cheese and sugar, beating until smooth. Add eggs, 1 at a time, beating after each addition. Mix in pumpkin, spices and salt. Pour into crust, bake 50 minutes at 350°. Cool cheesecake, refrigerate overnight. Garnish with whipped cream, if desired, before serving. Serves 12 to 15.

"This gets better after a couple of days if it lasts that long. Great to make ahead for a fall dinner party."

Irene Reeb Meitzen, BA '65
San Angelo

Texas Style Fruit Cake
Rated Four Star!

- 1 cup sugar
- 4 eggs
- 1 teaspoon vanilla
- 1 package (14 oz.) dates, halved
- 1 pound candied pineapple, chopped
- 1 pound candied cherries, halved
- 2 pounds (8 cups) pecans
- 1¾ cups flours
- 2 teaspoons baking powder
- ¼ teaspoon salt
- B & B liqueur (optional)

Beat together eggs, sugar and vanilla until light and creamy. Dredge fruits and nuts in flour. Mix remaining flour with dry ingredients. Add to creamed mixture and beat well. Fold in fruits and nuts. Line loaf pans with foil. Press dough firmly into pans leaving no spaces but allowing 2-inch head space. Cover securely with foil. Bake 2½ hours at 275°. Lift foil from top of pans during last 20 minutes. Cool. Lightly moisten with B & B liqueur to hasten age. Serves 18 to 20.

Erika Reeb, Friend of UT
Corpus Christi

Hummingbird Cake

Colorful as its namesake and disappears as readily

3 cups flour
2 cups sugar
1 teaspoon salt
1 teaspoon cinnamon
1 teaspoon baking soda
3 eggs, beaten
1 cup salad oil
1½ teaspoons vanilla
1 can (8 oz.) crushed
    pineapple
1 cup chopped pecans
2 bananas, chopped
FROSTING:
4½ ounces cream cheese,
    softened
1 cup butter or
    margarine, softened
1½ pounds powdered
    sugar
2 teaspoons vanilla

Combine flour, sugar, salt, cinnamon and baking soda. Add eggs and salad oil, stir until dry ingredients are moistened. Do not overbeat. Stir in vanilla, crushed pineapple, pecans and bananas. Pour batter into 3 well-greased, floured cake pans. Bake 25 to 30 minutes at 350° or until cake tests done. Cool in pans 10 minutes, remove from pans and cool thoroughly before frosting.

FROSTING: Combine cream cheese and butter and cream until smooth. Add powdered sugar slowly, beat until light and fluffy. Stir in vanilla. Spread between layers and on top and sides of cake. Serves 16.

Samuel L. Kone, CE '12
San Antonio

Lazy Day Cake

2 eggs
1 cup sugar
1 teaspoon vanilla
¼ teaspoon salt
1 teaspoon baking
    powder
1 cup flour
1 cup milk
1 teaspoon butter
FROSTING:
5 tablespoons butter
½ cup brown sugar
½ cup cream
1 cup coconut

Beat eggs. Add sugar, vanilla, salt, baking powder and flour. Heat milk until scalded, add butter. Add to flour mixture, beating only enough to mix thoroughly. Bake in a buttered 8-inch square pan 25 minutes at 350°.

FROSTING: Combine all ingredients. Pour over cake while cake is still in pan. Place under broiler until golden brown. Serves 8 to 10.

Nancy DeGraffenreid Barnes, BA '51
Brownwood

Texas Jam Cake

1 cup (2 sticks) butter
   or margarine
2 cups brown sugar
3 eggs, separated
1 cup seedless
   blackberry jam
1 teaspoon cocoa
1 teaspoon cinnamon
1 teaspoon cloves
3½ cups flour
2 teaspoons baking soda
2 cups buttermilk
1 cup seedless raisins
¾ cup chopped pecans
¼ cup flour

FROSTING:

¾ cup (1½ sticks) butter
   or margarine
1½ cups brown sugar
¼ cup plus 2
   tablespoons milk
3 cups powdered
   sugar
1 teaspoon vanilla

Cream butter and brown sugar. Add egg yolks and beat well. Fold in jam. Combine cocoa, cinnamon, cloves and flour. Dissolve baking soda in buttermilk. Beginning and ending with flour, add buttermilk and flour mixture alternately to creamed ingredients. Dredge raisins and nuts in ¼ cup flour. Add to batter. Beat egg whites until stiff, fold into cake mixture. Pour into greased bundt or tube pan. Bake 1½ hours at 350°.

FROSTING: Melt butter, add brown sugar. Beat mixture until smooth, add milk and bring to boil. Remove from heat, cool 5 minutes. Add powdered sugar and vanilla. Beat until creamy. Serves 16 to 20.

Everett Tucker, BA '58
Poquoson, Virginia

Lemon Christmas Cake

1 pound (4 sticks)
   butter
2½ cups sugar
6 eggs
3 ounces lemon extract
4 cups flour, sifted
1½ teaspoons baking
   powder
½ teaspoon salt
1 pound pitted chopped
   dates
4 cups pecans (whole or
   chopped)

Cream butter and sugar. Add eggs, 1 at a time, and beat well. Add extract. Sift together dry ingredients, add dates and pecans and toss thoroughly to coat fruit and nuts. Add to creamed mixture. Pour into 2 greased 5 x 9-inch loaf pans. Bake 1½ to 2 hours at 300°, or bake in 5 small loaf pans 1½ hours at 300°. Yield: 2 large or 5 small loaves.

Margaret Johnson Frazier, BM '42
Houston

Spirited Marble Cake
Serve after the Horns tame the supposedly spirited Mustangs!

3 cups cake flour
3¼ teaspoons baking powder
½ teaspoon salt
1 cup (2 sticks) butter or margarine
2 cups sugar
4 eggs, separated
2 teaspoons vanilla
1 cup milk
¾ cup canned chocolate syrup
¼ cup creme de cacao liqueur

CHOCOLATE FROSTING:
¾ cup butter or margarine
2 eggs
2 squares (1 oz. each) unsweetened chocolate
1 tablespoon creme de cacao liqueur
2 teaspoons vanilla
¼ teaspoon salt
3 cups powdered sugar

Sift together flour, baking powder, salt and set aside. Cream butter until soft and beat in sugar until light and fluffy. Add egg yolks, 1 at a time, beating well. Stir in vanilla. Stir in flour mixture alternately with milk, just until combined. Beat egg whites until stiff, but not dry. Fold whites gently into batter. Divide batter; add chocolate syrup and creme de cacao to one half. Spoon both batters into greased, floured 10-inch bundt or tube pan, alternating layers of white and dark. Draw a knife or spatula through batter several times to spin marble effect. Bake 1 hour at 350° or until center springs back when lightly pressed. Cool 10 minutes on wire rack, then remove from pan onto rack to cool thoroughly.

FROSTING: Beat butter until soft, beat in eggs, 1 at a time. Continue beating until mixture is creamy and smooth (mixture will look curdled at first). Add melted chocolate, liqueur, vanilla and salt. Gradually add sugar, beating until smooth and fluffy. Frost top and sides of cooled cake. Serves 20 to 25.

Gail Hayes Cromeens, BS '70
Mineral Wells

Mother Barber's Nut Cake

1 cup (2 sticks) butter
2 cups sugar
4 cups flour
3 teaspoons baking powder
1½ cups milk
1 tablespoon vanilla
1 cup pecans, chopped
7 egg whites

Cream butter and sugar. Dredge nuts with a little flour. Sift baking powder into remaining flour and add alternately with milk and vanilla. Beat well. Add nuts. Whip egg whites until stiff peaks form. Fold egg whites into batter. Bake in buttered and floured bundt pan 1 hour at 350°. Do not invert or empty cake from pan until completely cool. Sift powdered sugar over cake after removing from pan. Serves 20.

Carolyn Row Barber, BS '46
Colorado Springs, Colorado

Cakes

Mrs. Carruth's Meringue Cake

5 egg whites
5 tablespoons sugar
½ teaspoon vinegar
Pinch salt
½ teaspoon vanilla
TOPPING:
½ box (12 oz. size) vanilla wafers
1 cup whipping cream
Maraschino cherries (optional)
Chopped nuts (optional)

Combine egg whites, sugar, vinegar, salt and vanilla; beat until stiff. Grease a square-cornered pan, then line with waxed paper so that paper extends on all sides. Grease sides and bottom of waxed paper. Spread meringue mixture into pan and bake 20 to 25 minutes at 275° or until browned. Cool in pan. Repeat recipe again, pouring second meringue mixture into a second pan, bake as directed.

TOPPING: While cakes cool, finely crush vanilla wafers. Whip cream. Sprinkle a platter with some crumbs, remove first layer of meringue by grasping sides of waxed paper. Put meringue over crumbs, spread with whipped cream. Add more crumbs, stack second meringue layer, top with whipped cream and cover with crumbs. Refrigerate until ready to serve. Garnish, if desired, with maraschino cherries or nuts. Serves 10 to 12.

Marialice Shivers, wife of Allan Shivers, BA '31 LLB '33
Austin

Mother's Orange Cake
Bake in large flat pan for party cake squares

½ cup shortening
1 cup sugar
Rind of 2 oranges
2 eggs, separated
1½ cups flour
1 teaspoon baking soda
¼ teaspoon salt
1 cup buttermilk
½ cup chopped pecans
ICING:
1 box (16 oz.) powdered sugar
Juice from 2 oranges

Cream shortening and sugar; add grated orange rind and 2 egg yolks; beat well. Sift together dry ingredients. Add dry ingredients alternately with buttermilk, ending with dry mixture, and beat at medium speed. Fold in nuts and 2 stiffly beaten egg whites. Pour into greased, floured 10 x 15-inch jellyroll pan. Bake 20-25 minutes at 325°.

ICING: Combine powdered sugar with orange juice until smooth consistency and not runny. Spread over cake while warm. Serves 12 to 15.

Sara May McCampbell Meriwether, BA '51
Austin

Orange Date Cake

Grandmother's Imperial Valley Cake,
circa 1920

½ cup shortening
1 cup sugar
2 eggs
2 cups flour
1 teaspoon baking soda
¼ teaspoon salt
1 cup sour milk
1 teaspoon vanilla
1 package (8 oz.)
   chopped dates

GLAZE:
½ cup sugar
½ cup fresh orange juice

Cream shortening. Add sugar and eggs, beating well. Combine dry ingredients and add to creamed mixture, alternating with milk and vanilla mixture. Important to begin and end with flour. Fold in dates. Bake in greased and floured 9 x 13-inch pan 45 minutes at 350°.

GLAZE: Combine sugar and orange juice. Pour over cake while hot. Cool before serving. Serves 12 to 16.

Pat Howard, wife of Henry Howard, BS '59
Danbury

Variation: *Omit vanilla. Add grated rind of 2 oranges to milk before combining with dry ingredients. Add 1 cup chopped pecans. Do not use orange glaze.*

Bernice Milburn Moore, BJ '24 MA '32
Austin

Pineapple Nut Cake

2 cups flour
2 cups sugar
2 teaspoons baking soda
2 eggs, beaten
1 can (20 oz.) crushed
   pineapple
1 teaspoon vanilla
1 cup chopped nuts

ICING:
6 ounces cream cheese,
   softened
2 tablespoons butter,
   softened
2½ cups sifted powdered
   sugar
1 teaspoon vanilla

Sift together dry ingredients, add eggs, beat well. Add pineapple, vanilla and nuts. Pour into 9 x 13-inch cake pan. Bake 40 to 45 minutes at 325°. Cool.

ICING: Combine all ingredients and spread over cooled cake. This cake freezes well. Serves 16 to 20.

Jerry Wilke English, '39
Leander

Praline Pineapple Coconut Cake

A special cake that travels well in its own pan for outings

2 eggs
2 cups flour
1¾ cups sugar
1 teaspoon baking soda
½ teaspoon salt
2½ cups crushed pine-
apple and juice
1 teaspoon vanilla
1 cup coconut
1 cup brown sugar

FROSTING:

½ cup (1 stick) butter
¾ cup sugar
¼ cup evaporated milk
1 cup chopped pecans

Beat eggs. In order listed, combine all other ingredients except coconut and brown sugar. Stir ingredients until smooth. Pour batter into greased 9 x 13-inch pan. Mix coconut and brown sugar, sprinkle across top of cake. Bake 30 to 40 minutes at 350°. Cool in pan.

FROSTING: Melt butter, add sugar and milk. Boil 2 minutes. Add pecans, spread onto cake. Serves 20 to 25.

Mary Lu Ryan Haase, BS '57
Taylor

Poppyseed Cake

¾ cup poppyseed
¾ cup milk
¾ cup (1½ sticks) butter
1½ cups sugar
2 cups flour
2 teaspoons baking
powder
1 tablespoon rum
4 egg whites, stiffly
beaten

FILLING:

4 egg yolks, beaten
2 cups milk
3 tablespoons cornstarch
1 cup sugar
½ teaspoon salt
2 tablespoons rum
1 cup broken nuts

Soak poppyseeds in milk at least 5 hours or overnight. Cream butter and gradually add sugar. Beat in poppyseeds, milk and rum. Combine baking powder and flour and add ½ cup at a time. Fold in egg whites. Bake in 2 greased and floured 9-inch pans 20 minutes at 375°. Cool completely before preparing layers for filling.

FILLING: Combine yolks with ½ cup milk. Combine cornstarch, sugar and salt; add to eggs. Stir in remaining milk and rum. Bring to boil at low heat, stirring constantly. Cook 5 minutes or until mixture has thickened. Remove from heat, add nuts. Cool. Holding a long, sharp knife parallel to bottom of cake layer, slice the cake layers in half. Place generous portions of filling between layers. A rich chocolate or orange buttercream frosting is ideal. Serves 16 to 20.

Rose Marie Sharp, BJ '73
Pert

Buttermilk Pound Cake

½ cup (1 stick) butter
1 cup shortening
2½ cups sugar
4 eggs
1 teaspoon vanilla or
    almond extract
½ teaspoon baking soda
1 tablespoon hot water
3½ cups flour
1 cup buttermilk

Cream butter, shortening and sugar until smooth and creamy. Add 1 egg at a time, beating 1 minute after each addition. Add flavoring. Mix baking soda with hot water, add buttermilk. Add flour and buttermilk mixture alternately to creamed ingredients, beginning and ending with flour. Bake in greased, floured 10-inch bundt pan 1 hour 15 minutes at 325°. Serves 20.

Fred Parks, BBA '59
Euless

Unusual Pound Cake

1 pound butter,
    softened
3 cups sugar, divided
8 eggs, separated
3 cups flour, sifted
2 teaspoons vanilla
2 teaspoons almond
    extract
⅓ cup whiskey
1 cup finely chopped
    pecans

Cream butter and sugar ⅓ cup at a time, beating until fluffy. Add egg yolks, 1 at a time, beating well after each addition. Add flour, ⅓ cup at a time, at low speed. Add flavoring and whiskey. Beat egg whites until stiff but not dry. Add 1 cup sugar slowly to egg whites, beat briefly. Stir ⅓ of the egg whites into mixture to lighten the batter. Gently fold in remaining egg whites. Pour batter into greased 10-inch bundt pan, sprinkle with chopped nuts. Bake 1½ hours at 350°. Serves 20 to 24.

Mary Fletcher White, BA '40
Oro Valley, Arizona

OLD-FASHIONED POUND CAKE. Cream 1 cup (2 sticks) butter until pale yellow. Add 1¾ cups sugar and again cream well. Add 1 egg, beat well. Add ½ cup flour, beat well. Continue adding egg and flour alternately until you have used 5 eggs total and 2 cups flour total for this recipe. When all ingredients have been combined, beat some more. This recipe was given to Mrs. Kone by an elderly lady who did not have an electric mixer. The last sentence in her recipe read, 'Beat until exhausted.' Bake in buttered and floured 5 x 9-inch loaf pan 1 hour 10 minutes at 300°. Serves 12.

Samuel L. Kone, CE '12
San Antonio

Chocolate Pound Cake
Moist, needs no glaze, keeps fresh a long time

1 cup (2 sticks) butter
1 cup shortening
3 cups sugar
5 eggs
3 cups flour
1½ teaspoons baking
 powder
½ teaspoon salt
4 tablespoons cocoa
¼ cup hot coffee
1 cup milk
1 tablespoon vanilla

Cream butter, shortening and sugar. Add eggs, 1 at a time; cream well. Sift together dry ingredients except cocoa. Dissolve cocoa in hot coffee, cool. Add dissolved cocoa and milk to creamed mixture. Add dry ingredients, a little at a time, to the creamed mixture. Add vanilla. Bake in greased, floured 10-inch tube pan 1 hour 20 minutes at 325°, reduce to 300° for last 30 minutes of baking. Serves 10 to 12.

Marjorie Price, wife of Meredith Wayne Price, BBA '70
Eden

Prune Cake
Everyone loved it, even the non-prune lovers

½ cup shortening
1½ cups sugar
3 large-sized eggs,
 beaten
2¼ cups flour
½ teaspoon salt
1 teaspoon baking soda
1 teaspoon baking
 powder
1 teaspoon nutmeg
1 teaspoon cinnamon
1 teaspoon allspice
1 cup buttermilk
1 cup stewed prunes,
 drained and
 chopped
ICING:
6 tablespoons butter
1 egg yolk
3 cups powdered sugar
1½ tablespoons cocoa
 Hot coffee

Cream shortening and sugar. Add eggs. Sift together dry ingredients and add to creamed mixture alternately with buttermilk. Add prunes. Bake in 2 greased and floured 9-inch layer pans. Bake 30 to 35 minutes at 350°. This recipe may be easily doubled and baked in 4 layer pans.

ICING: Cream butter. Add egg yolk. Sift together powdered sugar and cocoa. Add to egg mixture. Add enough hot coffee to make icing smooth and easy to spread. Serves 12 to 16.

Louise Harrell Mulkey, BA '61
Panhandle

Variation: *Omit buttermilk, substitute ½ cup more prunes and ⅔ cups prune juice from stewed prunes. Substitute cloves for allspice.*

Denise Jaroszewski Chandler, BS '76
Houston

Red River Mud Cake
Sinfully rich—good enough to eat with a spoon!

1 cup oil
4 eggs, beaten
⅓ cup cocoa
1½ cups sugar
1½ cups self-rising flour
1 tablespoon vanilla
1 cup finely chopped
    pecans
1 jar (7 oz.)
    marshmallow creme
    or 1 package (8 oz.)
    miniature
    marshmallows

ICING:
1 box (16 oz.) powdered
    sugar
¾ cup (1½ sticks)
    butter, melted
¼ cup evaporated milk
⅓ cup cocoa
1 teaspoon vanilla
1 cup chopped pecans

Combine all ingredients except marshmallow. Pour into greased 9 x 13-inch pan. Bake 30 minutes at 375° or until mixture tests done with a toothpick.

ICING: Prepare icing while cake is baking. Combine all ingredients. Remove cake from oven, spread with marshmallow. Top warm cake with icing. Allow icing to harden before cutting. Serves 12 to 15.

Edward F. Manning, JD '72
Fairfax, Virginia

Variation: *Add 1 cup coconut to cake batter.*

Nina Cook Segler, BBA '79
Dallas

Butter Rum Cake

1 cup (2 sticks) butter
1¾ cups sugar
5 eggs
1 teaspoon vanilla
1 teaspoon butter
    flavoring
1 teaspoon rum
2 cups flour
ICING:
1 cup sugar
½ cup water
1 teaspoon rum or rum
    flavor

Cream butter, add sugar. Add eggs, 1 at a time. Add vanilla, butter flavoring, rum and flour. Mix well. Bake in a bundt pan 50 to 60 minutes at 325°.

FROSTING: Bring sugar and water to boil. Cool, add rum. Use pastry brush to apply to warm cake.

Frances Stanhiser Von Bieberstein, '31
Austin

Sherry Cake
A fabulous dessert, let's have it again!

4 egg yolks
½ cup sherry, dry or cream
½ cup sugar
1 packet unflavored gelatin
⅓ cup milk
4 egg whites
2 cups heavy whipping cream
1 cup sugar
1 small-sized angel food cake
1 cup whipped cream
Toasted sliced almonds and/or toasted coconut (optional)

Beat egg yolks, sherry and sugar. Cook at medium heat, stirring with whisk, until like custard. Soak gelatin in milk, stir into hot sherry custard. Cool. Whip egg whites until stiff. Whip cream with sugar, fold into cooled custard. Crumble angel food cake and place a layer of crumbs in bottom of greased 9-inch springform pan. Make several layers, alternating crumbs and mixture. If using toasted almonds and coconut, sprinkle between each layer. Set aside in refrigerator 12 hours. Remove to serving platter, frost cake with whipped cream, sprinkle toasted almonds on top of cake. Serves 12.

Joyce Jennings Hudnall, BS '57
Tyler

Old-Fashioned Sugar Cake
Just right for morning coffee, with ingredients from pantry.

1 cup butter
2½ cups sugar
5 eggs, beaten
2½ cups flour
1 teaspoon baking powder
1½ teaspoons mace
½ cup milk
Powdered sugar

Cream butter and beat in sugar. Add eggs, beat well. Sift together flour, baking powder and mace. Add dry ingredients alternately with milk, beat well. Pour batter into greased, floured 10 x 15-inch jellyroll pan. Bake 30 to 35 minutes at 325°. Sift powdered sugar over hot cake until sugar makes a thick layer, about ¼ inch. Cool. Serves 20.

Pat Biel Holley, BBA '50
Fort Worth

CHOCOLATE SOUR CREAM FROSTING: Melt 3 packages (6 oz. each) semisweet chocolate chips in top of double boiler. With a whisk, stir in ¼ teaspoon salt and 1½ cups sour cream. Frost cake while frosting is still slightly warm.

Sylvia Cook, BA '65
Santa Fe, New Mexico

Yellow Cake
Very moist, quick and easy

1 cup shortening
3 cups sugar
6 eggs
3⅓ cups flour
2 teaspoons baking
    powder
1 teaspoon salt
1¼ cups milk
1 teaspoon vanilla or
    orange or almond
    extract

Cream shortening and sugar. Add eggs, 1 at a time. Sift together dry ingredients. Combine milk and vanilla. Alternating with dry ingredients, add milk to creamed mixture. Mix ingredients 3 minutes. Bake in greased and floured bundt or tube pan 1 hour 15 minutes at 300°. Serves 16.

Joan Ortloff Steinhoff, BS '70
Houston

Magic White Frosting
Mock Seven-Minute Frosting, only better; a recipe for the microwave

1 cup sugar
¼ teaspoon salt
¼ teaspoon cream of
    tartar
5 tablespoons cold
    water
2 egg whites
1 teaspoon almond
    extract

MICROWAVE: Combine sugar, salt, cream of tartar and water in 2-cup measuring cup. Cook 1 minute at highest setting, stir. Cook 2 minutes more at same setting, stir. Cook 1 minute more at highest setting.

STOVE: Combine first four ingredients in saucepan and cook at medium heat, stirring often until sugar dissolves. Beat egg whites until stiff; slowly add sugar syrup, constantly beating. Add extract and beat until spreading consistency. Yield: enough frosting for 2-layer cake.

Joyce Kocurek Brooks, BS '69
Burleson

White Joy Icing

3 tablespoons shortening
3 tablespoons butter
1 egg yolk
3 cups sifted powdered
    sugar
4 to 6 tablespoons
    hot water

Cream shortening and butter. Stir in egg yolk. Add sifted powdered sugar alternately with enough hot water to make icing smooth and easy to spread. Yield: frosting for 1 cake.

Joan Ortloff Steinhoff, BS '70
Houston

Cakes

Chocolate Chip Cupcakes

4 squares (1 oz. each) semisweet chocolate
1 cup (2 sticks) butter or margarine
1¾ cups sugar
4 eggs
1½ cups chocolate chips
1 cup flour
1 teaspoon vanilla
1 cup chopped pecans

Melt chocolate and butter at low heat. Add remaining ingredients, mix well. Pour batter into muffin tins lined with paper cupcake liners, almost filling each as there is minimal rising. Bake 35 minutes at 325°. Cool. Yield: 1 dozen cupcakes.

Penny Porter Helms, BFA '66
Austin

Suzanne's Cupcakes
Different, consistency of a brownie

2 squares (1 oz. each) baking chocolate
1 cup (2 sticks) butter or margarine
1½ cups flour
1¾ cups sugar
4 eggs, slightly beaten
1 teaspoon vanilla

Melt chocolate and butter in microwave or in double boiler. Cool. Combine flour, sugar, eggs, vanilla and chocolate mixture. Stir by hand; *do not* use mixer. Mix only until dry ingredients are thoroughly combined into chocolate mixture. Pour into well-greased muffin tins, filling about half full. Bake 15 to 20 minutes at 350°. Yield: 20 cupcakes.

Bobbie Fly, wife of UT Regent Sterling Fly, '43
Uvalde

Lemon Peel Ice Cream
Great after a heavy meal!

Juice of 7 lemons
1 tablespoon grated lemon rind
4 cups sugar
1 pint heavy cream
Milk

Combine lemon juice, rind and sugar. Set aside overnight. Put into 1-gallon ice cream freezer, add cream and milk to fill container. The original recipe used very thinly sliced lemon peel added to the ice cream. Yield: 1 gallon.

"The original recipe included very thinly sliced lemon peel in the ice cream."

Diane Davis Cravens, BS '61
Tom Cravens, BBA '64
Arlington

Variation: *Omit rind. Add 1 teaspoon lemon extract.*

Janette McIntyre Morrow, BA '45
Alpine

French Lemon Ice Cream

2 cups whipping cream
¾ to 1 cup sugar
　Juice of 2 small-sized
　　lemons
　Zest of 1 lemon
3 tablespoons Kirsch
　Kiwi
　Fresh mint leaves

Whip cream, gradually adding sugar. Add lemon juice, zest and Kirsch. Whip until cream peaks. Pour into 1 quart mold and freeze 3 or 4 hours. Unmold, decorate with kiwi fruit and fresh mint leaves. Serves 4 to 6.

Roger E. Joseph, '54
Austin

MOTHER'S BUTTERMILK ICE CREAM. Combine 2 quarts buttermilk, 1 pint half and half cream. Add 1 cup sugar (or more to taste), 1 teaspoon vanilla, pinch of baking soda. Pour into 1-gallon ice cream freezer and freeze until firm.

Sara May McCampbell Meriwether, BA '51
Austin

Peaches And Cream Ice Cream
Microwave cooking at its finest!

3 cans (13 oz. each)
　　evaporated milk
2½ cups sugar
2½ tablespoons flour
¼ teaspoon salt
7 eggs, beaten
½ tablespoon almond
　　extract
¼ tablespoon vanilla
　　extract
4 cups freshly cut and
　　sugared peaches
2 cups whipping cream
　Milk

In a large glass container, scald milk in microwave 5 minutes. Using a wire whip add sugar, flour and salt to scalded milk. Cook in microwave, stirring between each break, for the following minutes: 3 - 3 - 3 - 2. Place eggs in a second glass bowl, add hot milk mixture gradually, stirring constantly. Do not add too rapidly or lumps of cooked egg may result. Microwave in 30 second intervals, up to 3 total minutes, until mixture thickens. Refrigerate 2 hours. Add extracts, peaches and whipping cream (unwhipped). Place in freezer container, add enough milk to fill container. Freeze. Yield: 6 quarts.

Variation: *To make vanilla ice cream, omit almond extract and use ½ tablespoon more vanilla extract.*

Sue A. Lebel Shirley, BS '64
Charles W. Shirley, BBA '63
Houston

Picosa Fresh Peach Ice Cream

6 eggs
1 cup sugar
1 can (14 oz.)
    sweetened
    condensed milk
2 to 4 cups mashed
    fresh peaches
2 teaspoons vanilla
Milk

Beat eggs until thick and creamy. Add sugar and condensed milk and continue beating until smooth. Add peaches and vanilla. Pour into 1-gallon freezer. Add enough milk to fill freezer, allowing 2-inch top margin. Yield: 1 gallon.

Idanell Brill Connally, '40
Houston

Variation: *Substitute 1 can (13 oz.) evaporated milk and 18 large-sized marshmallows for sweetened condensed milk. Cook in double boiler with the eggs, sugar and 2 cups milk until marshmallows melt. Cool, put into freezer, add 4 cups peaches and milk to fill.*

Myrtle Ligon, wife of Jack A. Ligon, BA '50
San Antonio

Polka Dot Ice Cream

1 cup small-sized red
    cinnamon candies
    ("Red Hots")
½ cup water
1¾ cups sugar, divided
6 eggs
½ teaspoon salt
1 tablespoon lemon
    juice
1 cup half and half
    cream
1 cup whipping cream
Milk

Combine candies, water and ¼ cup sugar in a saucepan. Over low heat, melt candies and sugar, stirring frequently. Cool. Beat eggs until light and creamy. Gradually add remaining sugar, salt and lemon juice. Beat 5 minutes in blender or with electric mixer. Add cream, milk and cinnamon candies and mix thoroughly. Pour into 1-gallon freezer and add enough milk to fill freezer, allowing 2 inches at top for cream expansion. Freeze until firm. Yield: 1 gallon or 16 servings.

Glynda Harrell Eschle, BS '63
Groom

ALICIA'S LEMON ICE. Combine 1 cup sugar with ¾ cup lemon juice and grated rind of 2 lemons. Beat with whisk, add 1½ cups white corn syrup and 4 cups milk, whisking until smooth. Pour into shallow pan and freeze. Stir occasionally during freezing time to allow a smooth texture. Serve with Texas Tea Cookies. Serves 8 to 10.

Alicia Hudnall, '81
Tyler

Peppermint Ice Cream

Tastes like the old-fashioned peppermint ice cream we used to buy at the pharmacy.

3 cups milk
39 marshmallows, halved
2¼ cups peppermint
    candy, crushed
½ pint (8 oz.)
    whipping cream or
    half and half cream

Scald milk. Add marshmallows and candy, stirring until melted. Cool. Add cream and any extra milk needed to fill freezer container. Freeze in an ice cream freezer. Yield: ½ gallon.

Edwin Argyle Bailey, '64
Dallas

Mock Pistachio Ice Cream

2½ quarts half and half
    cream
3 teaspoons vanilla
3 cups sugar
    Green food coloring
4½ teaspoons almond
    extract
1 cup chopped almonds
1 package (4 oz.)
    German's sweet
    chocolate, grated

Mix together all ingredients except chopped almonds and grated chocolate. Freeze in ice cream freezer. Add almonds and chocolate when mixture is partially frozen. Yield: 1 gallon.

Verna Sykes Farris, BS '74
Hurst

Sour Cream Strawberry Ice Cream

Perfect dessert for ladies luncheon

2 cans (14 oz. each)
    sweetened
    condensed milk
2 cups sour cream
2 cartons (10 oz. each)
    frozen strawberries
Milk

Combine condensed milk, sour cream and strawberries. Pour into 1-gallon freezer. Add enough milk to fill ⅔ full. Freeze. Remove dasher and harden in deep freezer. Yield: 1 gallon.

Louise Harrell Mulkey, BA '61
Panhandle

Vanilla Ice Cream
Fred Akers' favorite! And the players', too!

4 eggs
2¼ cups sugar
10 cups milk
1 can (13 oz.)
    evaporated milk
½ teaspoon salt
2 tablespoons vanilla

No cooking! Beat eggs until light and creamy. Add sugar gradually. Add remaining ingredients, mixing thoroughly. Pour into freezer. Serves the coach and 3 hungry players or 16 spectators. Yield: 1 gallon.

Diane Akers, wife of UT Football Coach Fred Akers
Austin

Variation: *Substitute 2 cans (14 oz. each) sweetened condensed milk for evaporated milk and reduce sugar to 1 cup. Add milk to 6 cups.*

Kimberly Fojtik, BBA '79
Greenwood, South Carolina

Variation: *Reduce sugar to 1½ cups. Substitute 1 can (14 oz.) sweetened condensed milk for evaporated milk.*

Jane Cornick Jamison, BS '66
Austin

AFTER THE GAME DESSERT. The old orange and white can be a festive dessert for serving if you scoop 1 gallon vanilla ice cream into round balls, place on cookie sheet and freeze. Do the same with 1 gallon orange sherbet. Freeze hard. Mix together in a silver bowl and you have dessert for about 20 folks.

Liz Carpenter, BJ '42
Austin

Lime Buttermilk Sherbet
A 3rd-generation family favorite

1 box (3 oz.) lime-
    flavored gelatin
½ cup water
¾ cup sugar
Rind of 2 lemons
Juice of 3 lemons
1 quart buttermilk

Dissolve gelatin in boiling water. Add sugar and grated rind. Mix well until dissolved. Add lemon juice and buttermilk. Freeze in ice cream freezer. Delicious served with fresh blueberries. Yield: 2 quarts.

Lowell Lebermann, Jr., '57
Austin

Classic Tortoni

15 crisp macaroons
½ cup powdered
   sugar
Pinch of salt
⅓ cup dark rum
1½ teaspoons vanilla
½ cup slivered almonds,
   toasted
12 maraschino cherries
2 cups whipping cream,
   chilled
3 egg whites

Chill mixing bowls and beaters. Place 12 paper liners in muffin tin. Crush macaroons into fine crumbs, combine with sugar and salt. Stir well, add rum and vanilla and mix well. Refrigerate while preparing cream and egg whites. Beat cream until thickened and set aside in refrigerator. Whip egg whites until stiff but not dry. Add crumb mixture to egg whites, fold in almonds and whipped cream. Fill liners with mixture. Freeze at least 4 hours, overnight is better. Will keep frozen for several weeks if covered. Serve straight from freezer, do not thaw; top each serving with a cherry. Serves 12.

Virginia Stanberry Williams, '35
Austin

Ice Cream Tortoni

3 tablespoons butter,
   melted
1 teaspoon almond
   extract
⅓ cup chopped almonds,
   toasted
1¼ cups vanilla wafers,
   finely crushed
½ gallon vanilla ice
   cream, softened
1 jar (12 oz.) apricot
   preserves

Combine butter, extract, almonds and crumbs. Mix well and set aside ¼ cup of the mixture. In 9-inch square pan, layer half the crumb mixture, half the ice cream and half the preserves. Repeat layers. Sprinkle reserved crumb mixture across top. Freeze. Cut into squares to serve. Serves 8.

Charlotte Curtis Henderson, BS '37
Baytown

LEMON ICE MILK. Soften ½ gallon vanilla ice milk, add ½ can (6 oz. size) frozen lemonade (undiluted), and juice and grated rind of 1 lemon. Keep frozen in deep freezer.

Rosemary Fanning Pinson, wife of
Robert M. Pinson, BA '41
Dallas

HOMEMADE ORANGE SHERBET. Combine 5 cans (12 oz. each) orange crush, 1 can (15 oz.) crushed pineapple and 1 can (14 oz.) sweetened condensed milk in ice cream freezer. Freeze to make 1 gallon.

Nina Cook Segler, BBA '78
Dallas

Spoom

1 cup sugar
½ cup water
4 egg whites, room
    temperature
2 pints lemon sherbet,
    softened
    Rosé, white wine, or
    champagne

In saucepan over medium heat, cook sugar and water until 238° on candy thermometer. While sugar syrup boils, beat egg whites until soft peaks form. Continue beating, pouring hot syrup in thin threads into the whites. Fold in lemon sherbet. Spoon into 12 freezer-proof dessert glasses. Fill ¾ full. Freeze. To serve, top each portion with your choice of wine. This recipe can be served not only as a dessert, but also as a palate cleanser between courses. Serves 10 to 12.

Carol Pirrung Mann, MA '75 MLS '77
Mesquite

PEACHY ICE CREAM TOPPING. Peel 6 large-sized freestone peaches and cut in half. Boil 1 cup water, 2 cups sugar and 2 teaspoons vanilla for 2 minutes. Add peaches, cook at low heat 10 minutes or until peaches are soft but firm. Chill. Delicious with vanilla ice cream. Yield: 2 cups.

Shirley Coin Kleiman, BBA '48
Victoria

Bay Leaf Sauce

¾ cup brown sugar
1 tablespoon flour
    Juice of 1 lemon
6 bay leaves
1 cup water

Combine ingredients and cook slowly 15 minutes. Strain. Use as a sauce for gingerbread, pound cake or with turkey, chicken or ham. Yield: 1 cup.

Gladys Bravenec Howard, BS '55
Tyler

Hot Fudge Sauce
Make your own sundae special

1 can (14 oz.)
    sweetened
    condensed milk
1 cup sugar
3 squares (1 oz. each)
    unsweetened
    chocolate
¼ cup butter or
    margarine
1 teaspoon vanilla

Combine milk, sugar and chocolate in top of double boiler. Stir until chocolate melts. Add butter and vanilla. Stir until butter melts. Serve over vanilla ice cream and top with chopped pecans. Yield: 2 cups.

Carolyn Braselton Townsend, BA '66
Dallas

Super Fudge Sauce

4 squares (1 oz. each)
    unsweetened
    chocolate
½ cup (1 stick) butter
3 cups sugar
    Dash salt
1 can (13 oz.)
    evaporated milk

Melt chocolate and butter in double boiler. Stir in sugar and salt. Add milk slowly. Cook 1 minute. Serve over homemade ice cream. Yield: 2 cups.

Diane Akers, wife of UT Football Coach Fred Akers
Austin

Variation: *Reduce chocolate to 2 squares, sugar to 2 cups, and omit butter.*

John D. Ryder, BBA '65
Seguin

Variation: *Substitute ⅓ cup cocoa for squares of chocolate and reduce sugar to 1 cup. Use small can of milk (5.33 oz.).*

Dorothy Burwitz Doss, BA '40
Austin

Chocolate Sauce
For real chocolate freaks!

1 cup cocoa
1½ cups sugar
¼ teaspoon salt
1 cup boiling water
1 teaspoon vanilla

In heavy saucepan, combine cocoa, sugar and salt. Gradually stir in boiling water. Cook at medium heat 8 minutes or until smooth, shiny and slightly thickened. Do not boil. Remove from heat. Stir in vanilla. Keep in covered jar in refrigerator. Yield: A little dab will do you.

Mary Boyles, wife of Jimmy G. Boyles, BBA '59
Dallas

Fluffy Vanilla Sauce
Tastes like homemade vanilla ice cream! Forget the cake and ice cream, just serve the sauce!

3 tablespoons butter
4 tablespoons flour
2 cups milk
¾ cups sugar
2 teaspoons vanilla
1 cup whipping cream

Melt butter and stir in flour. Add milk and sugar and bring slowly to a boil. Remove from heat. Add vanilla. Cover with plastic wrap and chill. Before serving, stir in whipped cream. Serves 10.

Fred Leisering, BBA '42
Lima, Peru

The 1900s

Cookies, Candies
Confections

Three co-eds were sunning in a field of bluebonnets on the campus early in the century. In the background are the Woman's Building and the Chemical Laboratory.

On campuses across the country during the Progressive era, attempts were made to shift some of the disciplinary and regulatory burden from faculty and administration to the students themselves. The new century, therefore, marked renewed interest in student government on the UT campus. It is not clear whether the movement was completely spontaneous on the part of students or was given some inspiration and encouragement by the administration. B Hall already had tried student government at one time, and in the 1900-1901 fall session the boys in B Hall again took over its management. What was called the "golden age" of the dormitory began. The manager was backed by the hall committee and was loved for years by men who lived there.

At a mass meeting of the student body on January 10, 1901, a resolution called for organization of a students' council and asked that a committee of seven be appointed to form a constitution and a set of by-laws. President William L. Prather, who held office from 1899 until he died in 1905, envisioned an organization that could help with practical problems, such as hack hire and laundry bills. Noise in the corridors and library, excessive absences from classes, and promiscuous cheating, despite the honor system, were other problems that bothered the president and the faculty. On Saturday, May 24, 1902, a constitution was finally adopted at a mass meeting in the auditorium, and a students' council became a reality.

The council gradually assumed control of student publications, the annual March 2 celebration, and the annual all-students' outing on April 21 to Landa Park in New Braunfels, 60 miles from Austin. More than 350 students bought round-trip tickets for 75¢ each in 1904 (when enrollment was only 800) for the special train trip to the park. The band gave a concert at noon, then played for dancing until the big picnic dinner was served under the trees by the B Hall management, which chartered a railroad car and transported cooks, utensils and food to feed the crowd.

Mess clubs still were being organized after the turn of the century. The Capitol Boarding Club, formed on January 3, 1900, reduced living expenses of 100 young male members over a five-year period. This club finally became affiliated with a national fraternity in 1913.

The first two fraternity houses were erected in 1902 and soon became centers of social life for those who joined. Action of the fraternities was praised by University officials as "a move in the right direction."

Charlie's Confectionery, owned and operated by Charles G. Wukasch, opened at 24th and Guadalupe in 1902. It was the third business in the University area. It was moved two years later to 23rd and Guadalupe. For more than a quarter of a century, Charlie's was a favorite hangout of University students. More than a business, it was a study hall, a meeting place, and a social center. Charlie knew most of the students who attended the University from 1902 until 1929; many worked their way through school by waiting tables at his place. In the University neighborhood, other Wukasches established businesses. Martha and Louise started a bake shop, Joe opened a grocery store, and August and Otto had a cafe. Another Charlie had a liquor store in later years. Generations of students became friends of the Wukasches.

A reception marked the official opening of the Woman's Building at the beginning of the 1903-1904 session. The rich red "art square" rugs in the parlor, drawn shades and "mellow light from the many electric globes," and palms, ferns, and cut flowers enhanced the decor of the fashionable new building. No provision was made for closets when it was first built because Colonel George W. Brackenridge, one of the contributors, believed that a girl needed only two dresses at a time while in school, the one she wore and the other in a bureau drawer. When the building was made fireproof, however, Colonel Brackenridge gave money for installation of closets. The first housekeeper was a graduate of the University of Chicago and of the Boston Cooking School. Through her everyday duties, she was to provide the young women residing in the building an opportunity "to get practical notions of domestic duties."

President and Mrs. Prather, to encourage classes to get together socially and to get to know students themselves, had "at homes" honoring class groups. At one reception for freshmen in January 1901, refreshments were "ice cream, dainty little 'kisses' and ladyfingers." Saturday night "germans," dances sponsored by the German Club, were popular. On Sunday nights, residents of the new Woman's Building held receptions. They wore long dresses and had a receiving line. The boys in B Hall would stay in their dining room for after-dinner oratory, would play practical jokes, and would hold midnight initiations for membership in secret organizations.

Fraternities and sororities provided a major element of social life. Sororities did not come to the campus until 1902 because of objections by Helen Marr Kirby, dean of women. By 1904, four groups were established, three of which had houses. Dances, banquets, at homes, teas, excursions, and picnics were popular. The Tri Sigmas, a group later chartered by a national sorority, gave a party in 1900 that was described in *The Texan* as follows: "Pink and white roses and green ferns were used for a center piece. Platters of molasses candy, steaming hot and ready to pull, were brought in, and the delightful sticky pulling contest began."

A trolley party was always fun and inexpensive. On one occasion a sorority had a trolley party, decorated the car in sorority colors, traversed all the tracks in the city, and bought popcorn at Scarbrough's corner (6th and Congress) for refreshments. Big parties at which euchre and progressive flinch were played were popular.

Austin residents often entertained groups of University students. Arrangements for a small dinner party for eight freshmen girls at an Austin home were described by a guest: "The cloth was pastel blue silk with exquisite Battenberg doilies under each plate, and the center piece was a handsome square of Mexican drawn work on which sat a bowl of blue plumbago."

In 1905 senior girls gave junior girls a trolley ride. They made a round of all the tracks and ended at the Prather home for refreshments. A banquet for seniors was held at the Woman's Building, and the University Ladies' Club gave a reception for freshman girls at the president's home, where refreshments were served from a table on the lawn. Decorations included "art squares" and numerous pillows.

The alumni banquet was a prominent feature of Commencement Week at the turn of the century, but one who attended the banquet in 1902 complained of the heat: "It is impossible to avoid giving utterance to the hope for electric fans at the next banquet and of a more strenuous effort after brevity in the speeches, or else fewer of them."

The Final Ball continued to be the "grand climax of social events attendant upon University commencement week." In March 1902 the faculty passed a resolution limiting the extent of Commencement Week social activities. They had become too numerous and expensive and the faculty thought they were detrimental to the interests of the University.

New buildings constructed during this decade included the Engineering Building (now Student Services Building), the Law Building (later called Pearce Hall), and a new Power House (later used for radio and television). In addition to Dr. Prather, two other men—David Franklin Houston and Sidney Edward Mezes—served as president before 1910.

At~Homes

Crisp Ginger Cookies
Grandmother Herndon's 1890 recipe

2 cups molasses
1 cup lard or shortening
1 tablespoon ground
    ginger
½ teaspoon salt
1 teaspoon baking soda
    dissolved in 1
    tablespoon hot
    water
7½ to 8 cups flour
2 cups finely chopped
    pecans (optional)

Bring molasses to boil, add lard or shortening. Add ginger, salt and soda dissolved in water. Cool, add flour to make a stiff dough. Add pecans if desired. Roll thin, cut into squares. Bake on greased baking sheet 8 to 10 minutes at 350°. Yield: enough cookies for all your friends.

G. P. Herndon, Jr., BBA '28
Bastrop

Poppop's Ginger Cookies

¾ cup shortening
1 cup white sugar or
    brown sugar, firmly
    packed
1 egg
¼ cup dark molasses
2 cups flour
2 teaspoons baking soda
1 teaspoon cinnamon
1 teaspoon ginger
1 teaspoon ground
    cloves
Granulated sugar

Cream shortening, sugar, egg and molasses. Mix in remaining ingredients. Cover, chill 1 hour. Form into walnut-sized balls, dip into granulated sugar. Place sugar side up, 3 inches apart, on lightly greased cookie sheet (balls will flatten). Bake 10 to 12 minutes at 350°. Immediately remove cookies to cool. Yield: 2½ dozen.

Mary Barnes James, BA '75 BJ '75
Houston

Grandmother's Tea Cakes

2 cups sugar
1 cup (2 sticks) butter
1 teaspoon baking soda
½ cup buttermilk
2 eggs, beaten
3 teaspoons baking
    powder
5 cups flour
1 teaspoon salt
    Ground or freshly
       grated nutmeg

Beat sugar and butter until creamy. Mix baking soda and buttermilk and add with eggs to sugar mixture. Sift together baking powder, flour and salt. Add to liquid mixture and mix well. Roll out and cut into squares. Dust with nutmeg. Bake 10 to 15 minutes at 350°. Yield: 6 to 8 dozen.

Bob R. Dorsey, BS '40
Houston

1830s Texas Teacakes

1 cup butter
1¼ cups sugar
3 eggs
2 tablespoons buttermilk
½ teaspoon baking soda
2 teaspoons vanilla
    Dash salt
3¼ to 4 cups flour

Cream butter, sugar and eggs. Add buttermilk mixed with baking soda. Add vanilla, salt and enough flour to make a soft dough. Adapt one or more of variations: #1: Put marble-sized balls of dough on greased cookie sheet. Press flat with bottom of glass that has been greased and dipped in cinnamon and sugar mixture.
#2: Add chopped nuts and/or chopped dates or raisins.
#3: Add nutmeg to part of dough.
#4: Roll out dough, use cookie cutter for shape variation.
#5: Vary trim with pecan halves, raisins, chocolate drops, or commercial trims.
Bake 8 to 10 minutes at 375° or until lightly browned. Yield: 5 dozen.

"This is a basic sugar cookie recipe. Variations developed when a trip to the 'grocery' from the Williamson-Lee counties' ranches was usually made once yearly."

Jonelle Thornberry Jordan, BM '48
Dallas

Best-Ever Sugar Cookies
More, more! The cookie jar is empty!

2½ cups flour
1 teaspoon baking soda
1 teaspoon cream of
tartar
¼ teaspoon salt
1 cup butter or
margarine
1 teaspoon vanilla
2 cups sugar
3 egg yolks

Sift together first 4 ingredients and set aside. Cream butter and vanilla until butter softens. Add sugar gradually, beating until fluffy. Add egg yolks, 1 at a time, beating well after each addition. Add dry ingredients in fourths, beating after each addition until well mixed. Form dough into balls about 1-inch diameter. Roll each ball in sugar. Place 2 inches apart on ungreased baking sheet. Bake 8 to 10 minutes at 350°. Yield: 10 dozen.

Lynne Prater, wife of Harold G. Prater, BBA '55
Arlington

SHORTBREAD PERFECT. Cream 1 pound (4 sticks) butter with 1¼ cups sugar. Add 6 cups flour, 1 cup at a time. Press into ungreased 9 x 15-inch jellyroll pan. Use rolling pin to flatten dough neatly. The dough may be stamped with a decorative cookie stamp. Bake 35 to 45 minutes at 325°. While hot, cut into squares or fingers. Cool in pan. Keeps well if tightly covered. Do not freeze. Yield: 25 to 30 cookies for tea or with a parfait dessert after dinner.

Joyce Jennings Hudnall, BS '57
Tyler

Chocolate Covered Cookies

½ cup (1 stick) butter
½ cup brown sugar
1 egg yolk
½ teaspoon vanilla
1 cup flour
TOPPING:
1 bar (10 oz.) Hershey's
semisweet chocolate
or 2 packages (6 oz.
each) semisweet
chocolate chips
1 bar (4 oz.) German's
sweet chocolate
½ cup chopped pecans

Cream butter and sugar. Add egg yolk and vanilla. Stir in flour. Spread very thinly on ungreased 12 x 15-inch pan. Bake 15 minutes at 350° until very light brown.

TOPPING: Melt chocolate over hot water. Spread chocolate on cookie top while both are still hot. Sprinkle generously with nuts. Refrigerate cookie sheet until well chilled. Break dough into pieces like toffee. Keep refrigerated. This cookie dough recipe can be tripled, and the frosting doubled as there will be plenty of icing. Yield: 36 to 48 pieces.

Edith Mae Sanders Livingston, BBA '41
Austin

Chocolate Mint Wafers
Blue Ribbon winners at Delaware State Fair

⅔ cup butter
1 cup sugar
1 egg
2 cups flour
¾ cup cocoa
1 teaspoon baking
    powder
½ teaspoon salt
½ teaspoon baking
    soda
¼ cup milk
1 teaspoon vanilla
FILLING:
½ cup sifted powdered
    sugar
  Dash salt
2 drops peppermint
    extract
3 to 4 teaspoons light
    cream

Cream butter and sugar thoroughly. Add egg. Sift dry ingredients. Add alternately with milk. Add vanilla and mix well. Chill. Roll ⅛-inch thick. Cut with 2½-inch floured cutter. Bake on greased cookie sheet 8 minutes at 350°. Cool. FILLING: Combine ingredients and beat until spreading consistency. Spread onto one cookie, top with second cookie. Yield: 2 dozen sandwich cookies.

Nita Hixson Galloway, BJ '51
Wilmington, Delaware

Nancy Wilson's Chocolate Goodies
Heavenly treat for chocolate lovers!

½ cup (1 stick) butter or
    margarine
1 can (14 oz.) sweetened
    condensed milk
1½ packages (6 oz. size)
    chocolate chips
1 cup flour
1 cup chopped nuts

Combine butter, milk and chocolate chips in glass mixing bowl. Melt in microwave or in double boiler. Stir in flour and nuts. Drop from a teaspoon onto cookie sheet. Bake 16 minutes at 350°. Yield: 48 cookies.

Mary Lou Hopson Nuhn, '44
Austin

"Forgotten" Kisses
Do not be tempted to open oven door

2 egg whites
Pinch of salt
⅔ cup sugar
1 teaspoon vanilla
1 cup chocolate chips
1 cup finely chopped
    pecans

Line cookie sheets with foil or butter heavily. Preheat oven to 350°. Beat egg whites with salt. until foamy, add sugar gradually and beat until extremely stiff. Add vanilla, fold in chips and nuts quickly. Drop from teaspoon onto prepared cookie sheets. Place in oven, *turn off heat!* Keep overnight in oven. Do not peek! Yield: 5 dozen.

Phyllis Horn Rozen, BS '68
Corpus Christi

LOUISE'S LUCIOUS LEMON LAYERS. Melt ½ cup (1 stick) butter in a 9 x 13-inch pan. Add 1 box lemon cake mix and 1 egg. Mix and spread evenly. In a bowl mix most of 1 box powdered sugar, 3 ounces softened cream cheese, 2 beaten eggs, and 1 teaspoon lemon extract. Spread over cake mix. Bake 35 to 40 minutes at 350°. Sprinkle with remaining powdered sugar. Cut into 1 x 2-inch bars. Yield: about 4 dozen squares.

Louise Harrell Mulkey, BA '61
Panhandle

Quick Texas Pecan Sheath Cookies

24 graham crackers
1 cup (2 sticks) butter
1 cup brown sugar
1 cup finely chopped
    pecans

Line a 10½ x 15½ x 1-inch pan with foil. Cover entire surface with graham crackers. Combine butter and sugar over medium heat, stirring constantly until mixture bubbles. Do not boil. Add pecans and stir until all pecans are coated. Pour mixture over graham crackers. Bake 8 minutes at 350°. Remove when bubbly. Cool. Cut into 24 squares.

Tommy Nobis, '62
Marietta, Georgia

Variation: *Boil mixture exactly 2 minutes. Remove from stove, stir in nuts.*

Doris Weldon Stokes, '29
Duncan, Oklahoma

Whoopie Pies
Large, homemade Oreo-type cookies

1 cup sugar
½ cup shortening
2 egg yolks
1 cup milk
1 teaspoon vanilla
⅓ cup cocoa
2 cups flour
1 teaspoon baking
    powder
1 teaspoon baking soda
½ teaspoon salt

FILLING:
½ cup shortening
2 cups powdered sugar
    Dash salt
2 egg whites
1 teaspoon vanilla
2 tablespoons
    marshmallow creme
    (optional)

Cream sugar and shortening, beat in egg yolks, milk and vanilla. Sift together dry ingredients, add to creamed mixture, stir and beat well. Drop from a spoon onto ungreased cookie sheet. Bake 15 minutes at 350°. Cool. Then prepare "sandwiches" with filling.

FILLING: Combine shortening and sugar with salt. Add egg whites, marshmallow creme and beat until fluffy. Add vanilla. Spread on half of cooled cookies, top with remaining cookies. Yield: 16 sandwich cookies.

Kathryn Lewis Colon, BBA '77
Corpus Christi

Fruit Nut Cookies

1 cup (2 sticks) butter or
    margarine
2 cups brown sugar
2 eggs
3½ cups flour
½ teaspoon salt
1 teaspoon baking soda
½ cup buttermilk
1½ cups chopped nuts
2 cups candied
    cherries, chopped
2 cups chopped dates

Cream butter and sugar. Add eggs. Combine flour and salt. Dissolve baking soda in buttermilk. Add to creamed mixture, alternately with dry ingredients.
Add nuts and fruits. Chill 1 hour. Drop from a tablespoon onto greased cookie sheet. Bake 10 minutes at 375°. Yield: 10 dozen.

Cissy McDaniel Parker, BS '44
Tulsa, Oklahoma

Christmas Rocks

Make ahead for holidays, and age to improve flavor!

1 cup light brown sugar
½ cup (1 stick) butter or
    margarine
4 eggs, beaten
3 cups flour, divided
½ pound candied
    cherries, chopped
½ pound candied
    pineapple, chopped
½ box (15 oz. size)
    raisins
3 teaspoons baking soda
1 teaspoon nutmeg
1 teaspoon cinnamon
1 teaspoon cloves
1½ pounds (6 cups)
    pecan halves
3 tablespoons milk
2 ounces Bourbon

Cream brown sugar and butter. Add eggs and beat well. Dredge chopped fruit with flour, and sift remaining flour with all other dry ingredients. Add to creamed mixture. Add pecans, milk, Bourbon and floured fruit. Mix well. Drop from a spoon onto greased cookie sheet. Bake 20 minutes at 325° or until brown. Yield: 130 cookies.

Ruth Sterling, wife of Walter G. Sterling, LLB '25
Houston

Variation: *Omit nutmeg and cloves. Add ½ teaspoon allspice, ½ pound dates, chopped, and an additional ½ pound pineapple (1 pound total), chopped. Use ⅓ cup Bourbon for all liquid.*

Louise Farmer Boyer, BS '30
Austin

Honey Cookies

1 pound (1⅓ cups)
    honey, heated to
    thin consistency
1 pound (2 cups) sugar
3 eggs
1 teaspoon cloves
1 teaspoon cinnamon
8 ounces citron, finely
    chopped
 Pinch salt
 Pinch baking
    powder
3 cups chopped pecans
5 cups flour

Beat, beat, beat the honey, sugar and eggs. Add remaining ingredients. Roll out on floured board, with not too much flour. Using a knife, cut into variety of shapes, none too large. Bake 10 or 12 minutes at 400° or until lightly browned. Yield: 6 to 8 dozen.

"This recipe was handed down to me by my mother who received it from her grandmother. It is a German recipe."

Nannette Avant Borden, BM '76
Corpus Christi

Tweety's Famous Oatmeal Cookies
A chewy, tasty basic cookie with many variations.

1 cup (2 sticks) butter or margarine
1 cup sugar
1 cup brown sugar
2 eggs
2 cups flour
1 teaspoon baking soda
½ teaspoon baking powder
½ teaspoon salt
1 teaspoon cinnamon
2 cups non-instant oats
1 teaspoon vanilla
1 package (6 oz.) chocolate chips

Cream butter, add sugar, then add eggs. Add dry ingredients, except oats; mix well. Add oats and vanilla, fold in chocolate chips. Drop from a spoon onto ungreased cookie sheet. Bake 8 to 10 minutes at 350°. Do not over-cook, remove from cookie sheet immediately. Yield: 6 dozen.

Willetta Albritton Eastland, BS '76
Hunt

Variation: *Omit chocolate chips and cinnamon. Add 2 cups coconut.*

Carol Pirrung Mann, MA '75 MLS '77
Mesquite

Variation: *Use only 1½ cups flour, increase oats to 3 cups. Omit chocolate chips, add ½ cup nuts. Form into long rolls, chill, then cut into ¼-inch slices before baking.*

Harriet Williams Peavy, BA '63
San Antonio

Monster Cookies
Kids love their huge size

12 eggs, beaten
2 pounds brown sugar
1 tablespoon vanilla
1 tablespoon corn syrup
8 teaspoons baking soda
3 pounds peanut butter
1 pound (4 sticks) butter
18 cups (43 oz.) Quick Oats
1 package (16 oz.) chocolate chips
1 package (14 oz.) coconut
1 package (16 oz.) plain M & M's

Mix together all ingredients in a large bowl. Use ice cream scoop to spoon onto greased cookie sheet. Flatten cookies before baking. Bake 12 minutes at 350°. This dough can be frozen and used as needed. Yield: 8½ dozen 4-inch cookies.

Sheila M. Gray, BBA '78
Houston

Barefoot Cookies

Barefoot Sanders' mother baked 95,000 of these for his US Senate campaign in 1972.

3 eggs
1 cup white sugar
1 cup brown sugar
1½ cups (3 sticks) butter
1 teaspoon baking
    soda
1 teaspoon cinnamon
5 cups flour

Combine all ingredients and mix thoroughly. Chill. Roll dough to ⅛-inch thickness on floured board. Cut into 4-toed, 2-inch long barefoot-shaped cookies. Bake at 300° until brown. Yield: 100 footprints.

Barefoot Sanders, BA '49 LLB '50
Dallas

Almond Cookies

Add orange food coloring; use Longhorn, armadillo, or UT cookie cutter!

1½ cups sugar
1 cup (2 sticks) butter
2 eggs
1 teaspoon almond
    extract
3 cups flour
½ teaspoon baking
    powder
½ teaspoon salt

Cream sugar and butter until light and fluffy. Add eggs and almond extract. Combine flour, baking powder and salt; gradually add to creamed ingredients. Put dough through cookie press or roll out on lightly floured pastry cloth, cut cookies with cookie cutter. Bake on ungreased cookie sheet 12 to 15 minutes at 375°. Yield: 6 to 8 dozen.

David M. Gould, BA '76
Houston

Peanut Blossoms

½ cup (1 stick) butter
½ cup peanut butter
½ cup white sugar
½ cup brown sugar
1 egg, beaten
1 teaspoon vanilla
1¾ cups flour
1 teaspoon baking soda
½ teaspoon salt
85 chocolate candy
    kisses

Cream together butter and peanut butter. Add sugars. Add egg and vanilla. Mix well. Sift dry ingredients, add to creamed mixture. Using a rounded teaspoon, shape dough into balls. Place on ungreased cookie sheet. Bake 8 minutes at 375°. While cookies bake, remove foil from chocolate kisses. Remove cookies from oven, press a chocolate kiss on each cookie so cookie cracks around edges. Return to oven and bake 2 to 3 minutes more. Yield: 7 dozen.

Nina Cook Segler, BBA '79
Dallas

Half Moons
Traditional recipe from Alsace

3 pounds brown sugar
1 pint water
1 pound (2 cups)
   shortening
1 sifter (4 cups) flour
2 teaspoons salt
2 tablespoons cinnamon
2 tablespoons allspice
3 teaspoons baking soda
1 pound (4¼ cups)
   pecans

Combine brown sugar and water, bring to boil. Remove from heat, add shortening to melt while mixture cools. Sift together dry ingredients. When sugar mixture is lukewarm, add dry ingredients and chopped pecans. Add enough flour to roll. Keep dough warm. Cut into shape of half moons. Bake 10 to 15 minutes at 375°. Tops should wrinkle. Yield: enough moons to serve at the teahouse until August.

"This recipe was given to my grandmother by a neighbor who was a native of Castroville, Texas, and the two vied to see who baked the best. The recipe is well over 150 years old and originated in Alsace, to my knowledge. Christmas isn't complete without Half Moons!"

Walther John Ives, MA '51
San Antonio

Pecan Macaroons

1 cup shortening
2 cups sugar
4 eggs
  Grated rind of 1
   orange
3 ounces candied
   pineapple, finely
   chopped
2 cups chopped
   pecans
4 cups flour
2 teaspoons baking
   powder
½ teaspoon salt
1 tablespoon cinnamon
1 teaspoon cloves
1 teaspoon nutmeg

Cream shortening and sugar; add eggs, beating until light and creamy. Add orange rind. Using part of the flour, dredge pineapple and pecans. Sift remaining flour with dry ingredients. Add to egg mixture. Mix well. Drop from a teaspoon onto lightly greased cookie sheet. Bake 12 to 15 minutes at 375°. Yield: 8 dozen.

Walther John Ives, MA '51
San Antonio

Sand Dainties

A consolation for Texas Tech Raiders after a round-up by the Horns

½ cup (1 stick) butter
½ cup (1 stick) margarine
⅓ cup sugar
2 teaspoons water
2 teaspoons vanilla
2 cups flour
½ cup chopped walnuts
    or pecans
    Powdered sugar

Cream butter and margarine to soften, then cream with sugar. Mix in water, vanilla, flour and nuts. Chill 3 or 4 hours. Form dough into long rolls, ½ inch across. Cut into 3-inch lengths and shape to look like Longhorns! Bake on ungreased cookie sheet 15 minutes at 325°, do not brown cookies. Remove from sheet, cool slightly and dip in powdered sugar. Yield: 4 dozen.

Evelyn Brown Squyres, BA '51
Tyler

Potato Chip Cookies

1 pound (4 sticks) butter
    or margarine
1½ cups sugar
1 teaspoon vanilla
3 cups flour
⅛ teaspoon salt
1½ cups crushed potato
    chips
1 cup chopped pecans

Cream butter and sugar. Add vanilla. Add flour and salt and stir well. Stir in potato chips and pecans. Drop from a spoon onto ungreased cookie sheet. With spoon dipped in water, flatten each cookie. Bake 15 minutes at 325°. Yield: 5 dozen.

Peter S. Solito, '42
Houston

Variation: *Reduce sugar to 1 cup. Use less expensive, old-fashioned greasy potato chips for best cookies.*

Patricia Doney Holt, '45
Fort Worth

Variation: *Omit sugar and pecans. Substitute 1 package (6 oz.) butterscotch morsels, 1 teaspoon baking soda and 1 cup brown sugar. Use ½ cup less flour.*

Lawana Geren, '71
Houston

Cheesecake Cookies
These cookies are absolutely wonderful!

½ cup (1 stick) butter,
  softened
3 ounces cream cheese
9 tablespoons sugar
1 cup flour, sifted
  Milk
¾ cup finely chopped
  pecans

Combine butter and cream cheese. Add sugar, then flour. Mix well. Use 1 teaspoon dough, dip fingers in milk, then roll dough into ball. Place balls on foil-lined cookie sheet. Press into thin round cookies about 1½- or 2-inches in diameter. Sprinkle with finely chopped pecans pressed lightly into cookies. Bake 10 minutes at 350°. Yield: 24 cookies.

Mamie Strieber Shepperd, BJ '38
Odessa

Apricot Sticks

½ cup sugar
½ cup (1 stick) butter
  or margarine
2 egg yolks
1 teaspoon grated
  lemon rind
1½ cups flour
¼ teaspoon baking soda
½ teaspoon salt
1 cup apricot jam
TOPPING:
2 egg whites
¼ cup sugar
½ cup finely ground
  pecans
  Powdered sugar

Cream sugar and butter. Add yolks, 1 at a time, and lemon rind. Add dry ingredients. Spread in greased 10½ x 15½-inch pan. Cover with apricot jam.

TOPPING: Beat egg whites until stiff peaks form. Combine with ¼ cup sugar and nuts. Spread over jam. Bake 45 minutes at 325°. Cool in pan. Cut into bars. Dust with powdered sugar. Yield: 40 bars.

Louise Farmer Boyer, BS '30
Austin

Chewy Brownies

½ cup (1 stick) butter or
  margarine
2 squares (1 oz. each)
  unsweetened
  chocolate
1 cup sugar
2 eggs, well beaten
¾ cup flour
¾ cup chopped nuts

Melt butter and chocolate in double boiler. Combine sugar and eggs and beat until creamy. Stir in flour and nuts. Bake in buttered 7 x 11-inch pan 25 minutes at 325°. Yield: 15 brownies.

T. Earnest Gammage, Jr., BA '39 LLB '39
Houston

College Chewy Brownies

1 cup (2 sticks) butter, melted
1 box (16 oz.) light brown sugar
2 large eggs
1 teaspoon vanilla
1½ cups chopped pecans
2 cups flour
¼ teaspoon salt
2 teaspoons baking powder

Cream butter and sugar. Add eggs, 1 at a time. Stir mixture thoroughly. Add vanilla. Use part of flour to dredge nuts to keep them evenly distributed in batter. Mix remaining flour with salt and baking powder. Add nuts, then flour mixture a little at a time, beating well after each addition. Spread mixture in greased 9 x 13-inch pan. Bake 15 minutes at 350° on lower oven rack; place pan on upper rack for 15 minutes more. (If slow to bake to light brown, put foil sheet across pan top during last 5 minutes.) Cool in pan, cloth covered, 10 minutes. While warm cut into squares or oblongs. Cool in pan keeping covered with cloth to retain original moisture. Store in covered container. These are best when eaten within 3 days. Yield: 20 to 24 pieces.

Emma Stullken Webb, '23
Elgin

Chinese Chews

CRUST:
1 cup (2 sticks) butter
1 cup light brown sugar
2 cups flour

FILLING:
4 eggs, lightly beaten
¼ cup flour
3 cups dark brown sugar
1 cup flaked coconut
2 cups coarsely chopped pecans or walnuts
1 teaspoon salt
½ teaspoon vanilla

TOPPING:
1 cup powdered sugar
1 tablespoon orange juice
½ teaspoon grated orange rind

Cream butter and brown sugar. Add flour. Spread evenly over a 8 x 12-inch pan. Bake 15 minutes at 350°. Remove from oven and cool. FILLING: Combine ingredients. Spread on crust layer. Bake 40 minutes at 325° or until cookie is firm. Remove from oven.

TOPPING: Combine ingredients and dribble over top while cookie is still warm. When thoroughly cooled, cut into fingers. Yield: 24 pieces.

Virginia Nalle Page, BJ '33 MJ '35
Austin

109

Carrot Yogurt Squares
A great snack for children

2 cups whole wheat
  flour
½ cup unbleached white
  flour
1 teaspoon baking soda
1 teaspoon baking
  powder
1 teaspoon salt
1 teaspoon grated lemon
  rind
8 ounces plain yogurt
1 cup finely grated
  carrots
½ cup molasses
1 egg, beaten
½ cup chopped nuts

Stir together the flours, baking soda, baking powder and salt. Set aside. Combine lemon rind, yogurt, carrots, molasses and egg. Stir well, add nuts. Add all dry ingredients and stir only until combined. Spread into buttered and floured 9-inch pan. Bake 25 to 30 minutes at 350°. Cool. Cut into squares, Yield: 16 squares.

Kathleen Kenny Reily, BS '77
Vaihingen, Germany

BUTTERSCOTCH BROWNIES. In a saucepan melt ¼ cup butter, add 1 cup brown sugar. Cool. Beat 1 egg into mixture, add 1 teaspoon vanilla. Sift together ½ cup flour, 1 teaspoon baking powder, ½ teaspoon salt; add to butter mixture. Stir in ½ cup chopped nuts. Spread in buttered 8-inch square pan. Bake 30 minutes at 350°. Cool, cut into 16 squares.

Priscilla Flawn, wife of UT President Peter Flawn
Austin

Cherry Coconut Squares

2 cups flour
1 cup shortening
6 tablespoons powdered
  sugar
4 eggs, slightly beaten
2 cups sugar
½ cup flour
1 teaspoon baking
  powder
½ teaspoon salt
2 teaspoons vanilla
1½ cups chopped pecans
1 cup coconut
1 cup maraschino
  cherries, quartered

Combine flour, shortening and powdered sugar. Mix well, pat firmly into bottom of ungreased 9 x 13-inch pan. Bake 20 to 25 minutes at 350°. Do not brown. Combine eggs and sugar. Add flour, baking powder, salt, vanilla, pecans, coconut and cherries. Spread mixture over top of baked pastry. Bake 25 minutes at 350°. Cut into squares to serve. Yield: 32 squares.

Carolyn Devault Crawford,
wife of John Crawford, Jr., BBA '61
Oakton, Virginia

Date Nut Squares

Easy to prepare; even better after they have been frozen

1½ cups sugar
1 cup flour
1 teaspoon baking powder
½ teaspoon salt
1 cup chopped dates
1 cup chopped nuts
3 eggs, beaten
2 teaspoons vanilla
½ cup (1 stick) butter, melted
Powdered sugar

Combine dry ingredients. Add dates, nuts, eggs, vanilla and butter. Bake in lightly greased 9 x 13-inch pan. Bake 30 minutes at 350°. Cool. Dust with powdered sugar, cut into squares. Yield: 30 to 36 bars.

Nancy Morris Wilson, MA '68
Dallas

QUICK FORTY-NINERS. *(Simple but delicious).* Beat 4 eggs, add 1 box (16 oz.) brown sugar, 2 cups biscuit mix, and 2 cups chopped pecans. Bake in greased 9 x 13-inch pan 35 minutes at 325°. Loosen from sides of pan while warm. Cool. Cut into 49 squares!

Don Chandler, BS '78
Houston

Dollie's Honey Nut Cookies

1 cup (2 sticks) butter or margarine
½ cup sugar
1 egg
¼ teaspoon salt
Grated rind of 1 lemon
3 cups flour

TOPPING:
1 cup (2 sticks) butter or margarine
½ cup honey
¼ cup sugar
1 cup brown sugar
¼ cup whipping cream
4 cups broken pecans

Cream butter and sugar. Add egg, salt and grated lemon rind. Mix well. Add flour. Line bottom and sides of greased 11 x 17-inch baking pan with dough. Prick with a fork. Bake 15 minutes at 375°.

TOPPING: Place butter, honey and sugars in deep saucepan, boil 3 minutes. Remove from heat, stir in whipping cream; boil up once and add pecans. Immediately spread hot mixture over dough. Bake 30 to 35 minutes at 350°. Cool, cut in squares: Yield: 48 Dollie's dainties.

Sara Armstrong Post, BS '67
Cuero

Lemon Bars
Delicious little lemon pies

1 cup (2 sticks) butter or
    margarine
2 cups flour
½ cup powdered sugar
    Dash salt
TOPPING:
4 eggs
2 cups sugar
6 tablespoons grated
    lemon rind
6 tablespoons fresh
    lemon juice
6 tablespoons flour

Combine ingredients for crust, pat into 10 x 15-inch jellyroll pan. Bake 15 minutes at 350°.

TOPPING: Beat eggs, add sugar, lemon rind (be sure to grate only the colored zest, none of the bitter white), lemon juice and flour. Pour over the baked crust. Bake 25 minutes at 350°. Yield: 35 bars.

Samuel L. Kone, CE '12
San Antonio

Chip Toffee Bars

1 cup (2 sticks) butter or
    margarine
1 cup brown sugar,
    firmly packed
2 teaspoons vanilla
2 cups flour
1 cup chocolate chips
1 cup chopped pecans

Cream butter and sugar; add vanilla. Combine with remaining ingredients. Spread mixture in buttered 9 x 13-inch pan. Bake 20 minutes at 350° or until browned. Cut into bars, cool in pan. Yield: 2½ dozen bars.

Suzanne Williams Nash, BA '67
Dallas

English Toffee Cookies

1 cup (2 sticks) butter
1 cup sugar
1 egg yolk
1 teaspoon vanilla
1 teaspoon cinnamon
2 cups flour
1 egg white, slightly
    beaten
1 cup chopped nuts

Cream butter and sugar. Beat in egg yolk. Add dry ingredients and mix well. Press dough evenly into greased 9½ x 14½ x 1-inch pan. Place shallow pan of water in the bottom of oven. Bake dough 15 minutes at 350°. Remove from oven. Brush slightly beaten egg white over top of dough. Sprinkle with nuts and press firmly into dough. Remove pan of water from oven. Return dough to oven, bake 15 to 20 minutes or until brown. Yield: 60 squares.

Sheila M. Gray, BBA '78
Houston

The Esther Hoblitzelle Parlor has as one of its dramatic focal points the Chandor portrait of Mrs. Hoblitzelle. Located on the fourth floor of the Academic Center, The University of Texas at Austin, the Hoblitzelle Room gives tasteful setting to the Chippendale furniture, enhanced by silk wallpaper, from the family home in Dallas. Items from the Yount silver collection give a regal patina to any table arrangement.

photo by Sherwood Inkley

Orange Gumdrop Cookies

An old-time memory from my childhood; was glad to see the recipe again.

2 cups brown sugar
½ cup shortening
3 eggs, beaten
2 cups flour
½ teaspoon baking
powder
½ teaspoon salt
1 teaspoon baking
soda
½ pound (1 cup) chipped
orange slices
1 cup chopped nuts
(optional)

Cream sugar and shortening. Add eggs. Add dry ingredients. Fold in chipped orange slices and nuts if using. Bake in greased 10 x 13-inch pan 30 minutes at 325°. Yield: 3 dozen.

Mary Hall Carter, BJ '77
Houston

CHUNKY CHINESE CRUNCHIES. Melt 1 package butterscotch morsels over low heat or in a double boiler. Add a small can salted peanuts and a can of Chinese noodles. Stir until noodles are coated. Drop from a spoon onto waxed paper. Refrigerate until set.

Judith Morrison Martin, BA '77 BJ '77
Houston

Marble Bars

Special make-ahead black and white brownies

1 cup (2 sticks) butter
4 squares (1 oz. each)
unsweetened
chocolate
2 cups sugar
3 eggs
1 cup flour
½ teaspoon salt
1 cup chopped nuts
1 teaspoon vanilla
TOPPING:
8 ounces cream cheese
½ cup sugar
1 egg
1 teaspoon vanilla

At low heat, melt butter and chocolate. Add sugar and eggs, beat well. Stir in flour, salt, nuts and vanilla. Spread evenly in heavily buttered 9 x 13-inch pan.

TOPPING: In mixer at low speed combine cream cheese, sugar, egg and vanilla. Increase speed to medium, beat 2 minutes. Drop mixture by large spoonfuls on top of batter. Use tip of knife to score top surface in a crisscross pattern. Bake 40 to 45 minutes at 350°. Cool in pan, cut into bars. Refrigerate 8 hours before serving. Will keep, refrigerated, 1 week. Yield: 3 dozen.

Sylvia Bone Waldrop, BS '56
Texarkana

Candies

Old-Fashioned Cream Caramels

2 cups sugar
¾ cup light corn syrup
⅓ cup butter
2 cups half and half cream, divided

In large saucepan, combine sugar, corn syrup, butter and 1 cup cream. Bring to boil, cook 5 minutes. Gradually stir in remaining cream. Cook to hard ball stage (250°), stirring constantly as mixture thickens. Pour into buttered 8-inch square pan. When thoroughly cooled, cut into 64 squares. Wrap in squares of waxed paper.

Sue Brooks Littlefield, BA '77 JD '80
Austin

Burnt Orange Caramels
For sweet Texans!

1 cup milk
½ cup half and half cream
1 can (14 oz.) sweetened condensed milk
2 cups sugar
½ cup (1 stick) butter
1 cup white corn syrup
2 teaspoons vanilla

Combine all ingredients except vanilla in a heavy saucepan. Cook slowly, stirring constantly, until candy reaches firm ball stage (242°). Remove from heat, stir in vanilla. Pour into buttered 7½ x 11½-inch pan. When cool, cut into bite-sized pieces and wrap in waxed paper. Cooking takes about 1 hour. Yield: 80 caramels.

Marie Blount Bassinger, BS '47
Fort Worth

Turtles
Do again—just like Lammes!

2 packages (6¼ oz. each) vanilla caramels
2 tablespoons evaporated milk
2 cups pecan halves
1 bar (7 oz.) milk chocolate, broken into squares
⅓ of a bar (4 oz. size) paraffin, broken into pieces

In double boiler, combine caramels and milk. Heat until caramels melt, stirring occasionally. Beat with wooden spoon until creamy. Stir in pecans. Drop from a teaspoon onto buttered waxed paper. Set aside 15 minutes. Combine chocolate and paraffin in double boiler. Heat until melted and smooth, stirring occasionally. Using toothpick, dip each turtle into chocolate mixture. Place on waxed paper to cool. Yield: 4 dozen chocolate turtles.

Carol A. Woodlock, BS '79
Dallas

114

Hand-Dipped Chocolates

½ cup (1 stick) butter,
  softened
1 can (14 oz.) sweetened
  condensed milk
1 teaspoon vanilla
2 pounds powdered
  sugar, sifted
2 cups chopped pecans
1 pound unsweetened
  chocolate
2 ounces paraffin

Combine softened butter with milk and vanilla, stir in powdered sugar. Mix with hands (heat from hands helps combine mixture), add nuts. Chill 3 or 4 hours. Shape into ¾ inch balls. Chill overnight. Melt chocolate and paraffin in double boiler (do not allow water to boil in lower pan or steam will cause chocolate to gray). Use cake tester or bamboo skewer to dip chocolate. Place on fine mesh rack to harden. Dippings may be remelted. Yield: 5 pounds authentic chocolates.

Carol A Woodlock, BS '79
Dallas

Cousin Tom's Brown Candy
6 pounds of candy for gifts and with excellent keeping quality

6 cups sugar, divided
2 cups milk
¼ teaspoon baking soda
½ cup (1 stick) butter
1 teaspoon vanilla
2 pounds pecan meats,
  broken

Melt 2 cups sugar in heavy skillet over low heat, stirring constantly with wooden spoon until sugar is a light brown color. At the same time, heat remaining 4 cups sugar and milk in large kettle over low heat. Simmer this mixture. As soon as melted sugar is browned, very slowly add to simmering milk, maintaining low heat and stirring constantly. Cook and stir until mixture reaches soft ball stage (238°) in cold water. Remove from heat and add baking soda, stirring until foam subsides. Add butter. Cool 20 minutes. Add vanilla and beat. Add broken pecan meats and mix. Pour into square pans, cool slightly, and cut into squares. Keep in a tin or wrapped in aluminum foil. Yield: 6 pounds.

"Cousin Tom told me if I didn't know why the nuts should be broken rather than chopped, I had no business trying to make this recipe."

Caroline Hunt Schoellkopf, BA '43
Dallas

John's Fudge

3 cups sugar
¼ teaspoon salt
1 cup evaporated milk
1 ounce unsweetened
    chocolate, melted
½ cup (1 stick) butter
    or margarine
3 tablespoons white
    corn syrup
½ teaspoon vanilla
1 cup chopped pecans

Place all ingredients, except vanilla and pecans, in large saucepan. Mix well. Bring to rolling boil, reduce heat to gentle boil. Stir frequently. Cook until soft ball stage (236°). Remove from heat, cool to 140°. Add vanilla and pecans. Beat with wooden spoon until candy thickens. Quickly pour into 9 x 13-inch buttered pan. Yield: 48 (2-inch) pieces.

John D. Ryder, BBA '65
Seguin

Olga's Fudge

1 cup (2 sticks) butter
4 cups sugar
1 can (13 oz.)
    evaporated milk
1 jar (7 oz.)
    marshmallow creme
2 packages (12 oz. each)
    chocolate chips
1 cup pecans
1 teaspoon vanilla
    Dash salt

Melt butter, add sugar and milk. Bring to boil. Stir constantly, boil 8 minutes, and remove from heat. Add marshmallow creme, chocolate chips, nuts, vanilla and salt. Mix thoroughly. Pour into buttered 9 x 13-inch pan. Yield: 48 (2-inch) squares.

Dick Rolle, '35
Houston

Microwave Fudge
Tastes just like fudge made the real way!

1 pound powdered
    sugar
½ cup cocoa
¼ cup milk
¼ cup butter or
    margarine
1 tablespoon vanilla
½ cup chopped nuts

Sift together powdered sugar and cocoa into glass baking dish. Add milk and butter. Cook in microwave 2 minutes at high. Remove bowl and stir. Add vanilla and nuts. Beat with a spoon until well mixed. Pour into buttered 5 x 7-inch pan. Set in freezer 20 minutes, or refrigerate 1 hour. Yield: 24 squares.

Glena Russell Pfennig, BJ '64
Baytown

Sour Cream Fudge

Double this recipe to avoid a fight for the last piece!

2 cups sugar
½ teaspoon salt
1 cup sour cream
2 tablespoons butter or margarine
½ cup chopped pecans or walnuts

Combine sugar, salt and sour cream. Cook, stirring occasionally, to soft ball stage (236°). Add butter. Cool at room temperature, without stirring, until lukewarm (110°). Beat until mixture loses gloss. Add nuts. Spread in buttered 8-inch square pan. When firm, cut into squares. Yield: 24 squares.

Bonnie Blades Allen, '51
Houston

Mashed Potato Candy

¼ cup hot mashed potatoes
1 teaspoon butter, melted
1¾ cups powdered sugar
½ teaspoon vanilla
¼ teaspoon salt
1½ cups shredded coconut

Combine potatoes and butter. Gradually add sugar, beat mixture until fluffy. Add vanilla, salt and coconut. Shape mixture into ½-inch balls. Roll in additional coconut. Yield: 36 balls.

Carol A. Woodlock, BS '79
Dallas

Add 1 teaspoon grated rind of lemon or orange, and yellow or orange food coloring accordingly. Also, dip balls in melted chocolate. Editor.

Peanut Brittle

2 cups sugar
1 cup water
1 cup white corn syrup
2 cups raw Spanish peanuts
1 teaspoon butter
1½ teaspoons baking soda

Combine sugar, water and syrup in large saucepan. Cook to soft crack stage (260°). Stir occasionally. Add peanuts. Cook to hard crack stage (290°). Stir constantly. Remove from heat, add butter and stir. Add baking soda, stir quickly, pour into ungreased 12 x 16-inch pan. Set aside until thoroughly cooled. Break into bite-sized pieces. Yield: many mouth-watering sweet bites.

John D. Ryder, BBA '65
Seguin

Buttermilk Pecan Pralines

3 cups sugar
1 teaspoon baking soda
   Pinch of salt
1 cup buttermilk
¾ cup white corn syrup
2 tablespoons butter
2 cups pecan halves

In large saucepan (5- or 6-quart size) combine sugar, baking soda, salt, buttermilk and corn syrup. Bring to boil, stirring constantly. Reduce heat to medium-low, continue cooking until mixture becomes caramel-colored and reaches soft ball stage (238°). Remove from heat, add butter and pecan halves. Beat until thick enough to drop from a spoon onto waxed paper. If mixture becomes too hard, return to heat and add small amount water. Stir until smooth. Yield: 44 to 48 pralines.

Sybil McKee Savage, BA '22
Sanderson

Variation: *Substitute 1 additional cup sugar for corn syrup, increase butter to ¾ cup, add 1 teaspoon vanilla.*

Billie Gault Vaughan, BS '71
Manor

Pecan Pralines

2 cups sugar
1 can (5.33 oz.)
   evaporated milk
¼ teaspoon baking soda
1½ cups pecans

Combine sugar, milk and baking soda in 2- or 3-quart size saucepan. Bring to boil, stirring constantly until light brown and until soft ball stage (238°), about 5 minutes. Remove from heat, add pecans. Stir until mixture begins to thicken. Drop onto waxed paper. Yield: 2 dozen.

Gladys Allen, wife of Tom Allen, BS '25 MS '27
San Antonio

Variation: *Substitute ⅔ cup milk for evaporated milk. Add baking soda when mixture comes to boil. Increase pecans to 2 cups.*

Janis Dechman Modrall, BA '53
Houston

Variation: *Substitute 1 pound box light brown sugar for white sugar. Omit baking soda. Increase pecans to 2 cups.*

Runelle Loyd Stembridge, BS '51
Gilmer

Easy Texas Butterscotch Pralines

1 package (3⅝ oz.)
    butterscotch
    pudding mix,
    non-instant
½ cup evaporated milk
1 cup sugar
½ cup brown sugar
1 tablespoon butter
1½ cups pecans, whole or
    large pieces

Combine pudding mix with evaporated milk and sugars. Cook slowly until mixture dissolves. Add pecans and boil slowly until candy reaches soft ball stage (238°). Stir gently, occasionally, during cooking and be careful not to stir candy onto sides of pan. To prevent crystalization, wash sides down with pastry brush dipped in water. Remove from heat. Beat until mixture thickens. Drop from spoon onto waxed paper. Yield: 30 pralines.

Theo Smith Eichler, BS '38
Austin

Mexican Pecan Candy

2 cups pecans
1½ cups sugar, divided
1 cup brown sugar
½ cup water
1 teaspoon vanilla
    (optional)
1 tablespoon butter
    (optional)

Combine pecans, 1 cup sugar, brown sugar and water in large saucepan. Bring to boil, cooking over low heat. At the same time, caramelize ½ cup sugar in cast iron skillet at low heat. Pour caramelized sugar into pecan mixture, cook until soft ball stage (238°). Add flavoring and butter if desired. Beat 2 or 3 minutes, then drop from a spoon onto waxed paper. Yield: 36 pecan candies.

Clydine Wagner Tweedy, BS '46
Minden, Louisiana

Buckeye Balls
Just like Reese's peanut butter cups—but in a ball

2 pounds peanut butter,
    creamy or crunchy
3 pounds powdered
    sugar
1 pound melted butter
    or margarine
1 bar (4 oz.) paraffin
24 ounces chocolate chips

Combine peanut butter, sugar and butter. Roll in hands to size of buckeye, about 1 inch. If necessary to make batter stick together, add a little milk, a few drops at a time. Chill balls. Melt paraffin and chocolate chips in double boiler. Using toothpick, dip balls in chocolate, leaving one small part uncovered to give buckeye effect. Yield: 7 pounds.

Susan J. Allen, BJ '78
Austin

Orange And White Apricot Balls

1 pound dried apricots
1 orange
2 cups sugar
1 package (8 oz.)
    coconut
Powdered sugar

Grind together apricots and orange in food chopper using fine grind blade. Cook apricot-orange mixture with sugar in top of double boiler until all sugar dissolves. Remove from heat, add coconut. Cool on rack. Shape into walnut-sized balls, roll in powdered sugar. Store several days in a closed container. Roll again in powdered sugar. Yield: 40 to 50 orange and white balls.

Runelle Loyd Stembridge, BS '51
Gilmer

Rum Or Bourbon Balls

2 cups crushed graham
    crackers or vanilla
    wafers
1 cup chopped pecans
2 tablespoons cocoa
1 cup powdered sugar
Pinch of salt
¼ cup rum or Bourbon
1½ tablespoons honey or
    light corn syrup

In food processor with steel blade, finely crush graham crackers and nuts. Add cocoa, sugar and salt. Add liquor and honey slowly to processor container until a ball forms. Chill. Form dough into balls. Roll in powdered sugar. Store in tightly covered tin box for at least 12 hours before serving. Yield: 60 intoxicating balls.

Elizabeth Lynn Rosen, BBA '80
New Orleans, Louisiana

Pecos Peanut Logs

1 loaf (1½ lbs.) white
    sandwich bread
¾ cup salad oil
¾ cup peanut butter

Trim crust from bread. Cut each slice into 5 finger-sized strips. Lightly toast crust and strips on cookie sheet for 1 hour at 200°. Pulverize crust in blender. (Corn flakes may be added for volume.) In blender combine salad oil and peanut butter. Dip strips in mixture and roll in crumbs. Place on cookie sheet. Bake 45 minutes at 200°. These freeze well. Yield: a baker's cord of logs.

Jerry Wilke English, '39
Leander

Spiced Pecans
Wonderful for gifts

½ pound (2 cups) pecans
1 cup sugar
1 teaspoon salt
1 teaspoon ginger
¼ teaspoon allspice
½ teaspoon cloves
½ teaspoon nutmeg
1 tablespoon water
1 egg white

Toast nuts 10 minutes at 250°. Sift together three times sugar, salt and spices. Add water to egg white and beat slightly. Add nuts into egg white, then drain. Put spice mixture in brown bag, add nuts, and shake well. Spread on greased cookie sheet. Bake 20 minutes at 250°. Serve warm. Yield: 3 cups spiced nuggets.

Ruth Ann Neves Powell, BS '72
Alvin

CAROLYN'S HOOK 'EM-IT'S-A-PARTY! Combine 1 jar salted peanuts with 1 box dark raisins. Excellent for snacking during the Longhorn games.

Carolyn Frost Keenan, BS '76 MA '78
Houston

TEXAS SALTED PECANS. Place 2 cups pecan halves in a jellyroll pan. Dot with 1½ tablespoons butter. Bake 20 to 25 minutes at 300°. Stir often so butter mixes and pecans toast evenly. Pour onto paper towel and salt the pecans immediately. Store in tightly closed pint jar. Yield: 1 pint.

Edwin Argyle Bailey, '64
Dallas

Hot Pepper Pecans
Highly seasoned

1 pound (4 cups) pecans
¼ cup (½ stick) butter
¼ cup Worcestershire
     sauce
1 teaspoon red pepper

Melt butter and add Worcestershire sauce and red pepper. Coat nuts, and spread on cookie sheet. Bake 25 minutes at 250°. Yield: 4 cups.

Caroline Hunt Schoellkopf, BA '43
Dallas

Variation: *Coat 1 pound pecans with ½ cup (1 stick) butter. Bake 20 minutes at 300°. Combine 2 teaspoons soy sauce, ½ teaspoon salt, and 2 or 3 dashes Tabasco. Pour over pecans, mix well. Drain on paper towels.*

Twyla Lynn Tranfaglia, BA '73 MLS '74
El Paso

Sugar Coated Nuts

½ cup liquid selected
    from flavor options
1½ cups sugar
 1 teaspoon white corn
    syrup
¼ teaspoon salt
2½ cups walnut or pecan
    halves

**FLAVOR
OPTIONS:**

Orange: ½ cup
   orange juice, 1½
   teaspoons finely
   grated orange rind
Sherry: ½ cup cream
   sherry, 1½
   teaspoons finely
   grated lemon rind
Spiced: ½ cup water,
   ½ teaspoon
   nutmeg, ½
   teaspoon cloves, 2
   teaspoons cinnamon
Mint: ½ cup milk,
   1 teaspoon pepper-
   mint extract, 2 to 4
   drops red or green
   food coloring

In 2-quart saucepan combine all ingredients except nuts. Cook to soft ball stage (238°). Add nuts and stir until creamy. Quickly drop candy mixture from a spoon onto waxed paper. Use forks to separate. Yield: MMMMMMmmmmmmm . . . many mouth-watering morsels . . . mmmmm . . . good!

Runelle Loyd Stembridge, BS '51
Gilmer

BRANDIED CRANBERRIES. Spread 1 package (16 oz.) fresh cranberries onto cookie sheet. Sprinkle with 2 cups sugar, cover tightly with foil. Bake 1 hour at 300°. Uncover, sprinkle with 4 tablespoons brandy and 1 cup sugar. Refrigerate. Delicious with turkey or with cream cheese on wheat crackers. Yield: 4 cups.

Oscar G. Zuniga, '54
Victoria

COUSIN ADA'S STUFFED DATES. Remove pits from large dates. Saute in butter, open side down. Simmer 5 minutes. Place whole almond in each date and roll in powdered sugar.

Sara May McCampbell Meriwether, BA '51
Austin

Super Caramel Corn

Best ever, have to beat the kids off with a stick.

5 quarts popped
    popcorn
1 cup (2 sticks) butter or
    margarine
2 cups brown sugar,
    packed
½ cup light corn syrup
1 teaspoon salt
½ teaspoon baking soda
1½ cups chopped mixed
    nuts

Spread freshly popped corn in large shallow pan. Keep warm in oven at 250°. Combine butter, brown sugar, syrup and salt in 2-quart saucepan. Cook until sugar dissolves. Continue to boil to firm ball stage (248°), about 5 minutes. Remove from heat. Stir in baking soda (mixture will foam). Take popped corn from oven, add nuts. Pour hot caramel mixture in a fine stream over the corn. Stir to mix well. Return to oven for 45 to 50 minutes, stirring every 15 minutes. Cool. Store in covered container. Yield: 5 quarts.

Lois Fenske Wolff, BA '47
Kenedy

Variation: *Omit nuts.*

Jamina Ford, wife of Tommy Ford, BS '65
Waco

Popcorn Cake

Sweet and salty treat for Longhorns, young or prime!

1 pound miniature
    marshmallows
½ cup (1 stick) butter or
    margarine
½ cup oil
2 quarts popped
    popcorn, lightly
    salted
2 cups peanuts, salted
    or plain
1 package (16 oz.) plain
    M&M's

Melt together marshmallows, butter and oil. Combine popcorn, peanuts and M&Ms. Pour butter mixture over popcorn combination, mix thoroughly, and pack firmly in a well-buttered 10-inch tube pan. Set aside 24 hours at room temperature. Remove from pan to serving plate. Serves 16 to 20.

Nancy Fiske Pellerin, BS '57
Austin
Patty Jay Fiske, BBA '27
Dallas

The 1910s

Pies, Pastries
Desserts

Beauty pages in the 1918 Cactus were censored by Helen Marr Kirby, dean of women, who insisted that the pages be removed before the yearbooks were distributed. This page was one that was removed.

$\mathcal{I}$n April 1914, University students indicated their willingness to enter military service in defense of the United States when more than 300 marched to the Governor's Mansion and urged the Governor to send them to guard the Mexican border. Students shouted, "On to Mexico!" as they marched four abreast from the Main Building down Congress Avenue.

James E. Ferguson was inaugurated as Governor of Texas on January 12, 1915, and during the same year launched his unexpected attack on the University. He began by trying to dictate to William J. Battle, president *ad interim*, how the University appropriations bill should be interpreted. When Robert E. Vinson was elected president in April 1916, several years of bitterness followed, because Ferguson thought he should have been consulted prior to the appointment. The Governor eventually called for the dismissal of Vinson and several other faculty members in May 1917 and said he would veto the appropriations bill if his demands were not carried out. One demand was abolition of all fraternities. At a meeting of approximately 100 faculty members, resolutions were adopted emphatically declaring that the Regents should be a free and autonomous board. Students met in protest of the Governor's actions on Monday morning, May 28. They were led by George Peddy, president-elect of the Students' Association, who had recently left the University to join the officers' training corps at Leon Springs. At the end of Peddy's speech, students marched to the Capitol and down Congress Avenue. Ferguson, outraged, vetoed the appropriations bill on June 2, 1917. The Attorney General declared that the Governor's failure to veto the totals on the bill left the bill intact. On August 24, the House of Representatives voted to impeach Ferguson on 21 articles, and on September 22, the Senate convicted him on 10 counts by a two-thirds majority vote. During the following fall, the Legislature conducted a thorough investigation of University affairs and praised its democratic administration.

Stephen Pinckney, a 1911 graduate, collected $1 each from 124 alumni and purchased a Longhorn steer to be the UT mascot. It arrived on a freight car in late November 1916 and at the Thanksgiving game was presented to "students of The University of Texas." His name was Bevo, which was also the name of a near-beer manufactured by the Budweiser Company that had a brewery in Austin. On February 12, 1917, Aggies branded Bevo with the numerals 13-0, the score by which A&M had beaten UT in their 1915 encounter. To save face, some students altered the brand to read "BEVO" by changing the "13" to a "B," the "-" to "E," and inserting a "V" before the "0." This first Bevo was barbecued in 1920 and served at a banquet for all who had lettered, including a group from College Station.

A few days before the US entered the World War on April 6, 1917, *The Texan* editor charged students to "keep cool." A committee of ten faculty members and ten students was authorized by the faculty to make recommendations in regard to "mobilization of forces of the University in behalf of the nation." One planned event was a Loyalty Day parade, "the biggest parade ever held in Austin."

The culture of the campus changed drastically during this decade. Texas women obtained the right to vote in primary elections in 1918, and more than 300 University women attended a mass meeting and heard a state leader for women's rights explain the new privilege and responsibility. Girls began to appear on campus with bobbed hair early in 1918. In May 1917, a group of men students peeled off their jackets and broke an ancient convention by entering the library coatless. Prohibition carried in Austin in a local option election in 1918, and students joined in the noisy celebration on Congress Avenue. Within a month, however, students had transformed Taylor (a small town in an adjoining wet county) into a pleasure resort!

Very few students had cars before the war. On Saturday and Sunday afternoons several couples might go for a walk in East Woods. Sometimes they would take along fruit to nibble or better still, a picnic lunch or a skillet in which to fry bacon and eggs. They might also walk to West Woods (present day Tarrytown) or take an extended jaunt to the Dam or to Mount Bonnell. A date to "walk" on a beautiful afternoon was far more fun than a streetcar ride downtown to a picture show. The hills in the spring were beautiful with mountain laurel, bluebonnets, paintbrush, and white lilies. Lacy mesquites and sprawling live oaks had a fragrance few could forget.

For walking, girls often dressed in Hoflin middy suits, ordered from Norfolk, Virginia. The pleated skirts came to the tops of their laced high-top shoes. The men wore their regular suits. Bathing suits, usually black, were actually short one-piece dresses with full skirts worn over black wool tights.

"Germans," held at the old Knights of Columbus hall downtown each month, were the big social events. Girls wore evening dresses and carried their slippers in an evening bag. Program dances were popular. Each couple had the first, fourth, eighth, twelfth, and first extra dances together. Dances were "tag" on the encores. The "John Paul Jones," when the stags joined the outer circle of boys, was great fun.

The ribbon clubs (interfraternity organizations) sponsored the most elaborate dances, but fraternities and sororities also had dances and numerous informal affairs, such as picnics, canoe trips, hikes, stunt parties, "baby" parties, smokers, and stag banquets. Twice a year, in the fall and spring, the YM and YWCA had a picnic in East Woods. Several hundred students met for the big event in front of the Woman's Building and walked across the campus and through the woods to the picnic site northeast of the campus. Group singing, hunting pecans along Waller Creek, and building a huge bonfire and roasting bacon over the coals were regular features of the affair.

During the week, library dates were popular. When the lights blinked at 8:45 p.m., students closed their books and, with their dates, walked the Perip, the twelve blocks around the original Forty Acres. The walk was paved in 1913, and new brilliant tungsten lamps illuminated the campus. Students might munch apples or popcorn as they walked, or if the boy was feeling affluent he would take his girl to Schutze's Cozy Corner at 24th and Guadalupe or to Charlie's Confectionery at 23rd for a thick chocolate malted milk. The Cozy Corner also made a delicious oyster loaf, which was a rare treat, and their chili and hot tamales were rated superb. A writer noted that "according to the most reasonable estimate, Varsity students drink annually sixty-five thousand or three hundred tons of soft drinks and use about a million straws . . . . Unsuspecting parents pay $50,000 to Austin fountains for 300 tons of Bryan's Delight and other beverages." Student enrollment at the time was 2,500.

The Car Shed, where students waited to board a street car on the west side of the campus, was a landmark. Students often met there to go on picnics or to make preparations for parades. Beck's Pond, a shallow puddle about three feet wide along the graveled walk at the northwest side of the old library (now Battle Hall) was created by the superintendent of grounds, for whom it was named. He piped in enough water to fall over some old stones left from construction of some of the buildings, planted willow trees, and placed a bench nearby. Crude as it was, Beck's Pond became a lover's rendezvous on the campus.

The dining room in B Hall was the only public dining facility on campus before 1912. Most students ate at boarding houses, fraternity and sorority houses, in B Hall or the Woman's Building. In the fall of 1912, the University opened a dining hall in a new frame building north of the Engineering Building (now Student Services Building). It was open to both men and women, but few women ate there at first. The B Hall dining room was closed and most residents ate at the "Caf," as students called the new facility.

The Freshman Reception, the Sophomore Reception, Junior Week, the Academic Reception, the Law Banquet, the Engineers' Open House and Banquet, and senior activities during Commencement Week were the annual class and department social affairs during the Teens. Class spirit remained high, except during wartime. Freshman elections continued to arouse interest of upperclassmen, and few classes failed to hear Clark Field (the athletic field) or some campus animal nominated for president.

Only two new permanent buildings were added during this decade, the Library (now Battle Hall) and Sutton Hall, both designed by famed architect Cass Gilbert. Numerous ugly wooden shacks covered the campus, and students continuously complained about their unattractiveness, the leaky roofs, the cold, the heat. By the end of 1919, the buildings on the campus, not counting temporary structures, numbered nine, two of which were dormitories. To satisfy pressing needs, the shacks provided quarters for a University Commons (the "Caf"), a men's gymnasium, a women's gymnasium, the Bureau of Extension, the University Interscholastic League, the Bureau of Government Research, the University Press, and several departments. Students complained that the campus was far from being first class, as the Constitution of 1876 mandated it to be.

Holiday Epicurean Treats

Open House

Christmas Morning Brunch

Wukasch's Meringue Delight
Wukasch sisters' favorite party item

6 egg whites
½ teaspoon cream of
    tartar
  Pinch of salt
1½ cups sugar, divided
  ICING:
  1 cup whipping cream
  1 pint fresh
  strawberries, sliced
  or 1 can (8 oz.)
    crushed pineapple,
    drained

Have egg whites at room temperature and beat until frothy. Add cream of tartar and salt, increase mixer speed and beat until stiff peaks form. Add ¾ cup sugar, 1 tablespoon at a time, beating constantly. Fold in remaining sugar. Grease 2 (9-inch) square pans. Line with brown paper on bottom and extend 2 or 3 inches above sides of pan (to make cake removal easier.). Grease paper, spread mixture evenly in pan, bake 35 minutes at 300°. Turn out onto cake rack, peel off paper. Cool. Ice like layer cake with cream mixture.

ICING: Whip cream, add fresh strawberries or crushed pineapple. Serves 16.

Lena Pettit Hickman, BA '15
Austin

Delicious Dessert
Great for children who are Oreo addicts

1 pound Oreo cookies
½ cup (1 stick) butter,
  melted
½ gallon vanilla ice
  cream, softened
1 carton (8 oz.) Cool
  Whip
1½ tablespoons chocolate
  syrup
½ cup chopped pecans

Finely crush cookies and combine with butter. (Cookies can be crushed easily in blender.) Reserve 1 cup cookie mixture. Spread remaining cookies in buttered 9 x 13-inch glass dish or pan. Cover cookies with ice cream, spread with Cool Whip. Dribble syrup over Cool Whip. Sprinkle with nuts and reserved cookie crumbs. Freeze until firm. Serves 20 Oreo addicts!

Rhonda Hodges, wife of Richard L. Hodges, BBA '74
Houston

Chocolate Marshmallow Roll

Could this be one of Charlie's Confectionery's specialties?

¾ cup sugar
4 eggs, separated
1 teaspoon vanilla
¾ cup cake flour
3 tablespoons cocoa
¾ teaspoon baking powder
¼ teaspoon salt
1 jar (7 oz.) marshmallow creme

FROSTING:

¼ cup (½ stick) butter
2 cups powdered sugar, sifted
2 tablespoons cocoa
2 tablespoons cream
1 teaspoon vanilla

Cream sugar and egg yolks until light and creamy. Add vanilla. Combine flour, cocoa, baking powder; add to creamed mixture, beating until thoroughly mixed. Whip egg whites with salt until stiff. Fold lightly into cake batter. Line bottom of 10 x 15-inch jellyroll pan with parchment paper or foil, grease and flour paper. Pour in batter, spread to cover all corners. Bake 13 minutes at 350°. Loosen edges and immediately turn out cake onto a towel that has been dusted with powdered sugar. Trim edges and roll cake immediately, using towel for support. Cool cake wrapped in towel. When cool, unroll carefully, spread with marshmallow creme (an updated '80's adaptation!). Roll again and frost.

FROSTING: Cream butter with powdered sugar and cocoa, add cream and vanilla. Spread onto cooled filled roll. Chill, slice to serve. Serves 15 to 18.

Doris Robinson Legg, BA '26
Slaton

CRUST:

½ cup (1 stick) butter or margarine
1 cup vanilla wafer crumbs

FILLING:

1 package (6 oz.) chocolate chips
1 cup chopped pecans
1 can (7 oz.) coconut
1 can (14 oz.) condensed milk

Hello Dollies

Combine butter and wafer crumbs. Press into 9 x 13-inch pan.

FILLING: Mix together chocolate chips, pecans, coconut and milk. Spread over crumb crust. Bake 30 minutes at 350°. Serves 20.

Barbara White Stuart, '55
Dallas

Chocolate Crumble Balls (CCBs)

This is the long-time favorite of SRD residents!

1½ quarts vanilla ice
    cream
1½ cups chocolate cookie
    crumbs (Hydrox or
    Oreo)

SAUCE:

½ cup (1 stick) butter
1 can (5.33 oz.)
    evaporated milk
2½ cups powdered sugar,
    unsifted
6 squares unsweetened
    chocolate
1 teaspoon vanilla
    extract

Crush cookies with filling to make 1½ cups crumbs. Using medium-size scoop, make balls of ice cream. Roll immediately in crumbs, place in serving dishes, top with sauce. After rolling in crumbs, ice cream balls may be frozen on a cookie sheet until ready to serve.

SAUCE: In double boiler melt butter; add milk, sugar and chocolate; cook 30 minutes or until chocolate melts. Remove from heat, add vanilla, stir vigorously. Sauce is best when served at room temperature. For a thinner sauce, add more milk or half and half cream. *Do not add water.* Sauce keeps indefinitely, refrigerated. Serves 8.

Natalie Townes, administrator
Scottish Rite Dormitory
UT campus

Variation: CCBs SAUCE, MICROWAVE METHOD. *Microwave butter and chocolate squares 2 or 3 minutes at high setting. Add milk and sugar, stir with whisk, cook 2 or 3 minutes more at high setting or until hot. Whisk until smooth. (If using round Corning Ware container, feel bottom of dish—when very warm to hot, then mixture inside container is thoroughly heated.)*

Anna M. Curry, BS '68 MD '72
Fresno, California

GINGERSNAP RUM BALLS. Cut 1 angel food cake into bite-sized pieces; dip pieces into a mixture of 2 sticks butter, 1 box (16 oz.) powdered sugar and 1 cup light rum. Roll dipped cubes in a combination of 1 pound finely chopped pecans and 1 large-sized box gingersnaps finely crushed into crumbs. Keep covered in air-tight container.

Sammie Farrier Marshall, '47
Temple

Gonga's Devil's Float
A sinful dessert . . . or a delight for all sinners

1 cup flour
¾ cup sugar
¼ teaspoon salt
2 teaspoons baking
    powder
1 square (1 oz.) Baker's
    chocolate
2 tablespoons butter or
    margarine
½ cup milk
½ cup chopped nuts
½ cup white sugar
½ cup brown sugar
4 tablespoons cocoa
1 cup cold water

Sift together flour, sugar, salt and baking powder. Melt chocolate and butter in milk in microwave or in double boiler. Cool. Combine with dry ingredients, add nuts and spread in buttered 8-inch square pan. Mix sugars with cocoa and sprinkle over chocolate mixture. Pour cold water on top, bake 45 minutes at 325°. Serve hot or chilled with whipping cream. Serves 10.

Mary Lou Hopson Nuhn, '44
Austin

Variation: *Omit pecans, add 1 teaspoon vanilla, and substitute 1 cup cold strong coffee for the cold water.*

Jeanne Schwarz Gilbert, '49
Houston

Mint Dazzler
Very rich . . . tastes like frozen fudge with marshmallow topping

CRUST:
¾ cup vanilla wafers
2 tablespoons powdered
    sugar
3 tablespoons butter

FILLING:
½ cup (1 stick) butter
1½ cups sifted powdered
    sugar
3 eggs, slightly beaten
3 squares (1 oz. each)
    unsweetened
    chocolate, melted

TOPPING:
1½ cups whipping cream
1 package (8 oz.)
    miniature
    marshmallows
½ cup (2 oz.) finely
    crushed peppermint
    stick candy

Prepare crust and press into 6 x 10-inch glass dish.

FILLING: Cream butter and sugar. Add eggs and melted chocolate, beat until light and fluffy. Spoon over crust. Set in freezer.

TOPPING: Whip cream. Gently fold marshmallows into whipped cream. Spread over chocolate layer. Sprinkle with crushed candy. Freeze until firm. To serve, cut into squares. Keeps well in the freezer. This recipe is great make-ahead dessert for a dinner party. Serves 12.

Mary Katherine Welhausen Borchers, BBA '45
Victoria

Chocolate Dream Dessert

FIRST LAYER:
½ cup (1 stick) butter
    or margarine
1 cup flour
1 cup chopped nuts

SECOND LAYER:
1 cup powdered sugar
8 ounces cream cheese,
    softened
1 teaspoon vanilla
1 cup Cool Whip

THIRD LAYER:
1 box (3¾ oz.) vanilla
    instant pudding
2 boxes (3¾ oz. each)
    chocolate instant
    pudding

FOURTH LAYER:
1 container (8 oz.) Cool
    Whip
  Sweet chocolate
    (optional)
  Chopped toasted
    pecans (optional)

Combine butter, flour and nuts. Spread mixture in bottom of 9 x 13-inch pan to form crust. Bake 15 minutes at 350°. Cool. Cream powdered sugar and cream cheese. Add vanilla. Fold in Cool Whip, spread over cooled crust. Combine puddings and mix with milk until thickened and smooth. Spread over second layer. (Puddings can be mixed individually to achieve more layers.) Spread with Cool Whip. Sprinkle with grated sweet chocolate or finely chopped toasted pecans. Chill overnight, or freeze. Butterscotch pudding may be substituted for chocolate puddings. Serves 20.

Dorothy M. Owens, friend of UT
Houston

John's Bananas Foster

4 tablespoons (½ stick)
    butter or margarine
½ cup brown sugar,
    firmly packed
4 bananas
1 tablespoon banana
    liqueur
1 tablespoon light rum
2 tablespoons brandy
  Vanilla ice cream

Dissolve brown sugar in butter in skillet over medium heat. Slice bananas lengthwise, then in half crosswise. Add bananas to butter mixture and cook bananas until tender but not mushy. Add liqueur and stir. Heat rum and brandy in small pan. Flame, then pour flaming mixture over bananas. Serve warm, not hot, over ice cream. Serves 6.

John W. Butler, Jr., BA '75
Arlington

Bill's Bananas Foster
A La Microwave

½ cup brown sugar
¼ cup dark rum
¼ cup (½ stick) butter
    or margarine
2 large bananas
6 to 8 butter cookies
    or vanilla wafers,
    crumbled

In a 1½-quart casserole stir together brown sugar and rum. Add butter. Cover. Microwave at high setting 4 or 5 minutes. Stir after 2 minutes until sugar is dissolved. Cut bananas lengthwise, then crosswise so there are 8 pieces. Add to syrup, stirring to cover each piece. Top banana mixture with crumbled cookies. Microwave at high setting 1 or 2 minutes until hot. Serve over ice cream. Serves 4.

William R. Birdwell, BA '69 DDS '73
Bryan

Use blender or food processor to make cookie crumbs easily. Editor.

Banana Split Dessert
Party treat for teenagers who will be future Longhorns

2 cups cracker crumbs
2 tablespoons sugar
½ cup (1 stick) butter or
    margarine
16 ounces cream cheese
1 box (16 oz.) powdered
    sugar
1 can (20 oz.) crushed
    pineapple, drained
5 bananas, sliced
1 cup whipping cream,
    whipped, or 1 carton
    (8 oz.) Cool Whip
½ cup chopped pecans
Chocolate syrup
Maraschino cherries

Combine crumbs, sugar and butter and press into 9 x 13-inch pan. Beat cream cheese until soft and fluffy, add powdered sugar. Spread over crust. Layer crushed pineapple and sliced bananas and top with whipped cream or Cool Whip. Sprinkle with chopped nuts. Refrigerate 24 hours. To serve, cut into squares, dribble chocolate syrup over each portion and top with cherry. Serves 10 to 12.

Louise Harrell Mulkey, BA '61
Panhandle

Italian Sweet Bowknots
Italian fried pastry to serve with coffee

6 eggs
3 tablespoons sugar
¼ teaspoon salt
½ teaspoon orange, almond or anise flavoring or 1 tablespoon anise seeds
3 cups flour
2 tablespoons butter
½ cup powdered sugar
Oil for deep-frying

Beat eggs lightly. Add sugar, salt and flavoring; beat thoroughly. Place flour in bowl, cut in butter. Add egg mixture. Knead until smooth ball is obtained. If dough is too soft, add a little more flour to make firm dough. Set aside 30 minutes. Divide dough into 4 sections. Roll paper thin. Cut into strips 6 x ¾ inches. Tie in individual bowknots. Fry bowknots in hot (375°) oil until lightly browned, turning once. Remove from oil with slotted spoon, drain on absorbent paper. Cool, sprinkle with powdered sugar. Yield: 6 or 7 dozen.

Anthony Petrick, Jr., BBA '65
Austin

Ragalach
Puffy crescents to serve with coffee or tea

1 cup (2 sticks) butter
8 ounces cream cheese
¼ teaspoon salt
2 cups flour
1 cup chopped walnuts
½ cup sugar
1 tablespoon cinnamon

Beat butter, cream cheese and salt until creamy. Mix in flour. Shape in 14 balls, chill overnight. On lightly floured, cloth-covered board, roll each ball into 6-inch circle. Cut each into quarters. Mix nuts, sugar and cinnamon and drop 1 teaspoon of this mixture atop each quarter. Pinch together edges of dough, then form into crescents. Place on ungreased cookie sheet. Bake 15 to 20 minutes at 350° or until lightly browned. These are best served fresh. Yield: 5 dozen.

Christine Sigmon Hines, BS '73
Waxahachie

Variation: STRAWBERRY FILLING. *Shape dough into 4 balls, roll each out to 9 x 12 inches. Cut dough into 3-inch squares. Fill each square with 1 teaspoon strawberry jam. Fold opposite points envelope fashion to form tiny tarts. Bake 10 to 12 minutes at 400°. Yield: 48 tarts.*

Nina Cook Segler, BBA '79
Dallas

Adelaide's Crullers

4 tablespoons butter
¾ cup sugar
2 eggs, beaten
4 cups flour
¼ teaspoon cinnamon
¼ teaspoon nutmeg
4 teaspoons baking
    powder
1 teaspoon salt
1 cup milk
    Oil for deep-frying

Cream butter and sugar. Add eggs. Sift together dry ingredients; add alternately with milk to creamed mixture. This makes a soft dough. Place dough in floured waxed paper. Refrigerate overnight. Roll out to medium thickness, cut as for doughnuts, and deep-fry in hot oil until golden. Drain on paper towels. Serve plain or sprinkled with powdered sugar. Yield: 36 doughnuts.

Mary Roberts Hardesty, MA '77
Austin

Gingerbread
And Lemon Sauce

A low calorie dessert with only 95 calories per serving!

1 cup flour
1 teaspoon baking soda
¼ teaspoon ground
    ginger
¼ teaspoon cinnamon
¼ teaspoon nutmeg
¼ cup packed brown
    sugar
¼ cup molasses
¼ cup water
2 tablespoons lemon
    juice

LEMON SAUCE:

¼ cup sugar
1 tablespoon cornstarch
½ teaspoon finely grated
    lemon peel
⅛ teaspoon nutmeg
¾ cup water
2 tablespoons lemon
    juice

Combine dry ingredients except for brown sugar. In small mixing bowl, combine brown sugar, molasses, water and lemon juice. Stir into flour mixture just until blended. Immediately pour into lightly buttered 8-inch square cake pan. Bake 20 minutes at 350°. SAUCE: Combine sugar, cornstarch, lemon peel and nutmeg. Add water. Cook, stirring constantly, until mixture is bubbly. Add lemon juice. Serve over warm gingerbread. Serves 12.

Joan Culver, wife of Joe Culver, BBA '53 MBA '58
Austin

Refrigerator Gingerbread
This batter keeps, refrigerated, 4 to 6 weeks

1¼ cups (2½ sticks)
    butter
1 cup sugar
4 eggs
1 cup molasses
2 teaspoons baking soda
1 cup buttermilk
4 cups flour
2 teaspoons cinnamon
1 teaspoon allspice
2 teaspoons ginger
½ cup pecans, chopped
½ cup raisins

Cream butter and sugar. Add eggs, 1 at a time, beating after each addition. Add molasses, beat well. Stir baking soda into buttermilk. When mixture foams, add to creamed ingredients. Sift together flour and spices. Add dry ingredients to creamed mixture. Add nuts and raisins. Cover and refrigerate until chilled. Keep refrigerated until ready to bake. Spread in greased loaf pan and bake 30 to 40 minutes at 350°, or bake in greased muffin tins 20 minutes at 400°. Serves 10 to 12.

Suzanne Williams Nash, BA '67
Dallas

Strawberry Pizza

1 cup flour
½ cup powdered sugar
½ cup (1 stick) butter
8 ounces cream cheese
½ teaspoon vanilla
½ cup sugar
¼ teaspoon lemon juice

TOPPING:

1 package (10 oz.)
    frozen strawberries
4 tablespoons sugar
1 tablespoon cornstarch
1 pint fresh
    strawberries, sliced

Combine flour and sugar, cut in butter. Pat this mixture into pizza pan. Bake 15 minutes at 325°. Cool. Beat together remaining ingredients until fluffy. Spread over cooled pastry.

TOPPING: Combine frozen strawberries, sugar and cornstarch. Cook over medium heat until thickened. Cool. Spread on top of cream cheese pastry. Arrange fresh strawberries as final topping. Cover with plastic wrap, refrigerate at least 2 hours. Cut into pizza-like wedges. Serves 8 to 10.

Catherine Baumstark Hurd, BS '69
Denver, Colorado

Variation: *Substitute 1 can (14 oz.) sweetened condensed milk for sugar in cream cheese layer, and increase lemon juice to ⅓ cup. For topping, use 2 packages (10 oz. each) frozen strawberries, 1 cup crushed pineapple (drained) and 5 tablespoons cornstarch. Omit fresh strawberries. Top with 1 cup walnut halves.*

Patsy Aliece Kirby, wife of Clarence Kirby, BS '58
Hays, Kansas

Stuffed Oranges Flambé

6 navel oranges
½ cup chopped dates
½ cup slivered almonds
½ cup shredded coconut
½ cup Grand Marnier
Brandy

Cut slice from top of each orange and scoop out contents. Save juice and as much pulp as possible. Discard membrane. Combine orange pulp, dates, almonds, coconut and Grand Marnier. Return to orange shells. Place in baking dish. Add reserved juice to contents of each orange, filling almost to the top. Bake, uncovered, 1 hour at 325°. Oranges may be flamed with 1 tablespoon brandy per orange. These keep well and may be made the day prior to serving. Serves 6.

Ann Barber Brinkerhoff, BA '49
Houston

Mommom's Peach Cobbler

PASTRY:
2½ cups flour
¾ teaspoon salt
¾ cup shortening,
   divided
7 or 8 tablespoons
   iced water

FILLING:
8 medium-sized peaches
2 tablespoons flour
1 cup sugar
1½ teaspoons cinnamon
   Butter

SYRUP:
1 cup sugar
¼ teaspoon cinnamon
4 teaspoons butter
2 cups water

PASTRY: Sift together flour and salt. Add half the shortening and cut in until like meal. Add remaining shortening and cut in until like large-sized peas. Sprinkle with iced water, pressing with a fork until dough can be made into a ball. Roll out dough into oval ⅛-inch thick. Place dough in buttered 8-inch square dish.

FILLING: Peel peaches, cut into slices. Sprinkle with flour, sugar and cinnamon, mixing well. Place filling in pastry-lined dish and dot with butter. Wrap pastry around filling and seal (to make stubborn edges stay sealed, moisten slightly with water and press together). Chill 1 hour.

SYRUP: Combine all ingredients in saucepan, boil 3 minutes. Pour boiling syrup over chilled cobbler. Bake immediately 5 minutes at 500° or until crust becomes golden colored. Reduce heat to 350°, bake 30 to 35 minutes more. Baste several times. Serve warm, chilled or reheated. Serves 6 to 8.

Mary Barnes James, BA '75 BJ '75
Houston

Strawberry Rhubarb Casserole

5 slices dry bread
½ cup (1 stick) butter
1 package (20 oz.)
    frozen cut rhubarb
1 package (10 oz.)
    frozen sliced straw-
    berries
Juice of 1 lemon
1½ cups sugar

Saute cubed bread in butter. Toss with thawed fruits, add lemon juice and sugar. Stir thoroughly. Bake in buttered 2-quart casserole 1 hour at 350° or until bubbly and crisp. Serves 6.

Patricia Doney Holt, '45
Fort Worth

CRANBERRY COBBLER. In bottom of 10-inch pie pan, spread 2 cups fresh cranberries, washed and drained. Sprinkle ½ cup sugar and ½ cup pecan pieces over the berries. Combine 2 eggs, 1 cup sugar, 1 cup flour and 1 stick (½ cup) butter. Beat well, pour batter over cranberries. Bake 45 minutes at 325°. Serve warm, topped with vanilla ice cream. Serves 8.

Samuel L. Kone, CE '12
San Antonio

Fruit Cobbler

Delicious. The batter starts at bottom and rises through fruit to top.

4 to 6 cups fresh
    fruit (peaches,
    blackberries, red
    plums, cherries, or
    whatever is most
    available)
1 cup sugar
¼ cup water
1 tablespoon lemon
    juice (optional)

BATTER:
1 cup flour
2 teaspoons baking
    powder
½ teaspoon salt
½ cup sugar
¾ cup milk
½ teaspoon almond
    extract (optional)
¼ cup (½ stick) butter,
    melted

Wash and peel fruit, if necessary; slice and combine with sugar, water and lemon juice (use especially with peaches to enhance flavor.) Heat almost to boiling.

BATTER: Combine ingredients using almond or other flavoring. Use melted butter to coat sides and bottom of 2½-quart deep-dish casserole. Pour in batter, pour hot fruit over batter. Bake, uncovered, 40 minutes at 375°. Serve at room temperature. Serves 6.

Patrice McCullen Schexnayder, BA '70
Friendswood

Peaches w/ nutmeg
Good & easy

Blueberry Mousse

1 can (14 oz.)
  blueberries
1 cup pineapple juice
2 packages (3 oz. each)
  lemon gelatin
1 banana, mashed
1 cup whipping cream,
  whipped, or 2 cups
  Cool Whip
1 cup broken nuts
  (optional)

Drain blueberries, reserve syrup. Heat reserved blueberry syrup with pineapple juice, pour over gelatin, and stir well to dissolve. Cool, refrigerate. When slightly congealed whip gelatin with electric mixer at high speed. Fold in banana, whipped cream and blueberries and nuts if using. Pour into buttered 9-inch square pan. Refrigerate until firm. Cut into 3-inch squares. Serves 9.

Samuel L. Kone, CE '12
San Antonio

Serve as dessert or as salad accompaniment to Longhorn Cheese Wafers. Editor.

Chocolate Mousse

½ cup (1 stick) butter
  or margarine
1 cup sifted powdered
  sugar
2 squares (1 oz. each)
  bitter chocolate,
  melted
2 eggs
1½ teaspoons vanilla
  Sweetened whipped
  cream
  Crushed pecans

Combine butter and sugar and beat until fluffy. Add chocolate, beating constantly. Add eggs, continue beating. Add vanilla. Pour into 4 dessert dishes, cover with waxed paper. Freeze. When ready to serve, top with whipped cream and crushed pecans. Since this mousse does not freeze hard, there is no need to thaw before serving. Serves 4.

Tom Landry, BBA '49
Dallas

Prune Whip

⅔ cup stewed prune
  puree
½ cup sugar
5 egg whites
1½ teaspoons lemon juice

Rub stewed prunes through strainer to remove skins and pits. Add sugar to puree, cook 5 minutes (mixture should be consistency of marmalade). Cool. Beat egg whites until stiff, fold in prune mixture and lemon juice. Pile lightly in buttered souffle dish or 6 individual baking dishes. Bake 30 to 40 minutes at 325°. Serve hot or cold with whipped cream. Serves 6.

Dan C. Williams, BS '35
Dallas

Syllabub
An old Colonial dessert and very rich!

1 cup whipping cream
3 teaspoons sugar
1 teaspoon grated
   lemon rind
1 teaspoon lemon juice
½ cup white wine

Whip cream, add sugar, beating well to dissolve sugar. Stir in lemon rind, juice and wine. Fold in beaten egg whites, combine thoroughly. Serve chilled—and soon! Serves 6.

Molly Moffet Gray, BFA '53
Alvin

Tipsy Pudding
A pudding with some zing

2 cups milk
4 egg yolks
½ cup sugar
2 packets (1 tablespoon
   each) unflavored
   gelatine
¼ cup water
4 egg whites
1 teaspoon vanilla
½ cup whiskey
1 cup chopped dates
1 cup white raisins
1 cup chopped nuts

Scald milk. Cool. Beat egg yolks with sugar. Add milk. Cook in double boiler until custard has thickened. Sprinkle gelatin in water, stir until dissolved and add to mixture in double boiler. Beat egg whites until stiff peaks form. Add vanilla and whiskey; fold gently into custard, adding dates, raisins and nuts. Put in mold. Chill until firm. Serve with whipped cream. Serves 10 to 12.

Marialice Shivers, wife of Allan Shivers, BA '31 LLB '33
Austin

Holee Pudding

1 package (4 oz.)
   German's sweet
   chocolate
4 eggs, separated
¾ cup sugar
1 tablespoon unflavored
   gelatin
1 tablespoon cold water
¼ cup boiling water
1 teaspoon vanilla

Melt chocolate in double boiler over hot water. Cool. Beat egg yolks with sugar until light and creamy. Add chocolate to egg mixture. Soften gelatin in cold water, then dissolve in boiling water. Add to chocolate mixture. Beat egg whites until stiff peaks form. Fold whites into chocolate mixture. Add vanilla. Pour into sherbet or champagne glasses. Refrigerate. Decorate with puffs of whipped cream before serving. Serves 6.

Jeanne Schwarz Gilbert, '49
Houston

Banana Pudding
Smooth, creamy, reminiscent flavor from childhood

4 cups milk
4 eggs
3 cups sugar
¾ cup flour
Pinch of salt
½ cup (1 stick) butter or
   margarine
2½ teaspoons vanilla
Vanilla wafers
5 bananas, sliced

Scald milk. Beat eggs, combine dry ingredients and add to eggs, beat until smooth. Pour slowly into scalded milk, cook at low heat stirring constantly until thickened. Remove from heat, add butter and vanilla. In large serving bowl, arrange layers of vanilla wafers, bananas, then pudding. Repeat layers, ending with pudding on top. Yield: many memorable mouthfuls.

Judy Perrone, wife of UT System Operations Officer
Charles H. Perrone
Manchaca

Christmas Plum Pudding

1 pound seeded raisins
½ pound seedless raisins
1 pound currants
½ pound white raisins
   (sultanas)
4 ounces citron peel
4 ounces orange peel
2 ounces lemon peel
¾ cup bread crumbs
1½ teaspoons nutmeg
1 cup chopped pecans
3½ tablespoons grated
   lemon rind
4 tablespoons lemon
   juice
10 ounces grated suet
3 cups sugar
3 eggs
1 cup brandy
½ teaspoon salt
Flour to make
   stiff mixture, about
   2 cups
Brandy (optional)

Mix together ingredients in order listed. Place mixture in greased and floured cooking basins (use suitable sizes for desired servings). Fill each basin ¾ to 1 inch from top to allow pudding to swell when baking. Cover each basin with waxed paper, then with foil and tie with string. Place basins in pressure cooker. Steam, with petcock open, 20 to 30 minutes. Close petcock, cook 1 hour at 15 pounds pressure. Release steam slowly, remove basins from cooker. Empty pudding(s) to be used into serving dishes and serve pudding warm. Sprinkle top of pudding with sugar, pour warm brandy over and ignite. Remaining pudding(s) should be stored, refrigerated, in the basin with waxed paper and foil covers. This pudding will keep 2 years and it is unnecessary to freeze. When desire to use, place basin in pressure cooker, close petcock and cook 1 hour at 15 pounds pressure. Release steam slowly, then remove basin from cooker. Empty pudding and flame with brandy. Yield: many happy returns!

Jeannette Monnier Selway, BS '55
Dallas

Cocada (Coconut Dessert)

2½ cups shredded
    coconut (fresh or
    dried)
¼ to ½ cup sugar,
    to taste
4 cups milk
5 egg yolks, beaten

Mix coconut, sugar and milk. Put over the fire to boil, moving continuously. When it thickens to a thin batter, retire it from the fire, let it cool slightly and add the beaten egg yolks. Mix everything thoroughly. Pour into greased 2-quart casserole. Bake 20 to 25 minutes at 350° or until it browns a little. If you like, you can put almonds or pignoli (pine nuts) on top as decoration. Serves 8.

Mauricio B. Madero, '33
Mexico City, Mexico

ZABAGLIONE. *Use 2 egg yolks for each serving. With each yolk use 1 teaspoon sugar and 2 tablespoons sherry or Marsala wine. Beat egg yolks; add sugar and beat until dissolved; add wine and beat well. Cook in double boiler, stirring constantly until thick and foamy. Serve very hot or very cold with fresh peaches.*

Mitzi Nuhn Dreher, BS '54 MS '56
Austin

Orange Custard
Texas-style Crème Anglaise

2 oranges
2 tablespoons sugar
1 can (13 oz.)
    evaporated milk
2½ cups milk, divided
3 tablespoons flour
1 cup sugar
3 egg yolks
1 teaspoon vanilla

MERINGUE:
3 egg whites
3 tablespoons sugar
½ teaspoon vanilla

Peel, section and dice oranges. Sprinkle oranges with sugar and set aside. Combine evaporated milk and 1½ cups milk and bring to simmer. Mix flour with sugar, add egg yolks, add remaining 1 cup milk and stir until smooth. Add slowly to simmering milk, stirring constantly. Cook at low heat until mixture coats back of wooden spoon. Do not boil. Stir in diced oranges and vanilla. Pour into 10-inch ovenproof bowl or 8 individual custard cups.

MERINGUE: Beat egg whites until soft peaks form, slowly add sugar and beat until stiff but not dry. Fold in vanilla. Spread over custard, sealing well to edges. Brown meringue at 450°. Serve hot or chilled. Serves 8.

Edith Royal, wife of former UT Football Coach
Darrell Royal
Austin

"Short" Pie Crust
Very rich!

3 cups flour
1½ cups Crisco
½ teaspoon salt
1 teaspoon vinegar
1 egg
5 tablespoons cold
  water

Combine flour, Crisco, and salt until mixture is in fine crumbs. With fork, mix together vinegar, egg and water. Pour over crumbs, combine quickly. Chill. Yield: 2 (9-inch) crusts.

Susan Dillon Tschudi, BA '71
Malibu, California

Green Grape Pie

1 unbaked 9-inch pie
  shell
1 cup sugar
2 tablespoons flour
1 cup milk
1 egg
1 can (16 oz.) green
  grapes, drained

Mix together sugar, flour, milk and egg. Add grapes, stir lightly. Pour into pie shell. Sprinkle cinnamon across top. Bake 1 hour at 350° or until custard is set. Serves 8.

Sara Armstrong Post, BS '67
Cuero

Fresh Peach Pie
Rated Four Star!

5 cups fresh peaches,
  peeled and sliced
¾ cup sugar
¼ cup brown sugar,
  firmly packed
2 tablespoons flour
¼ teaspoon nutmeg
¾ teaspoon cinnamon
1 tablespoon lemon
  juice
1 teaspoon grated lemon
  rind
2 tablespoons butter,
  melted
1 unbaked 9-inch double
  crust pie shell

Be sure peaches have good flavor. Peel and slice peaches. Mix sugars, flour and spices. Combine peaches with lemon juice and rind, then mix with sugar mixture. Pour into unbaked pie shell. Dribble melted butter across peaches. Place top crust, seal edges, bake 40 to 45 minutes at 400° or until brown. Serves 8.

Nita Hixson Galloway, BJ '51
Wilmington, Delaware

Prize Winner Apple Pie

CRUST:
- ⅔ cup shortening
- 2 cups flour
- 1 teaspoon salt
- 5 to 7 tablespoons water
- 1 teaspoon vanilla

FILLING:
- ¾ cup sugar
- ¼ cup brown sugar, firmly packed
- 3 tablespoons flour
- 1 teaspoon cinnamon
- ½ teaspoon nutmeg
- ½ teaspoon salt
- 5 cups sliced apples (tart, firm)
- 2 teaspoons lemon juice
- 2 tablespoons butter
- Milk

Prepare crust. Roll out ⅔ of dough to fit into 9-inch pie pan. Roll out remaining dough for top crust.

FILLING: Combine sugars, flour, spices and salt. Add apples. Stir in lemon juice. Pour filling into crust. Melt butter, dribble over filling. Cover filling with top crust. Pierce top with fork, brush with milk. Bake 45 minutes at 400° or until pastry is brown. Serves 8.

Nita Hixson Galloway, BJ '51
Wilmington, Delaware

Variation: *Use 1 cup sugar, omitting brown sugar. Decrease flour to 2 tablespoons. Bake in 6½ x 10½-inch deep-dish pie pan for 50 minutes.*

June Barrett, BS '54
Houston

Dewberry Cream Pie

- 4 cups dewberries
- 1 unbaked 10-inch pie shell
- 2 eggs, beaten
- 1½ cups sugar
- ½ cup flour
- ½ cup cream

TOPPING:
- 8 tablespoons flour
- 8 tablespoons sugar
- 4 tablespoons butter or margarine

Place berries in strainer, wash gently, being careful not to mash fruit. Fill pie shell with berries. Combine eggs, sugar, flour and cream. Pour over berries.

TOPPING: Combine ingredients, using pastry blender. Spread over pie. Bake 45 minutes to 1 hour at 325°. Serves 8.

Alice Gann Kaspar, BS '73
Ganado

Texas Pecan Pie
The ever-precious all-time Lone Star favorite

1 cup corn syrup
3 eggs, lightly beaten
Pinch of salt
1 teaspoon vanilla
1 cup sugar
2 tablespoons butter,
  melted
1 Texas-sized cup
  pecans, pieces or
  halves
1 unbaked 9-inch pie
  shell

Combine all ingredients. Pour into pie shell. Bake 15 minutes at 400°. Reduce heat to 350°, bake 30 minutes more. Yield: 8 darlin' little ole pieces.

Nancy Morris Wilson, MA '68
Dallas

Variation: *Add 1 egg more. Bake 1 hour at 350°.*

W.J. (Billie) Stark, LLB '49 BBA '50
Englewood, Colorado

Variation: *Substitute ½ cup brown sugar and use ½ cup white sugar. Add 1 tablespoon cream.*

Sybil McKee Savage, BA '22
Sanderson

Variation: *Add ½ cup water. Boil syrup, sugar, and water until syrup strings. Add to other ingredients, increasing pecans to 2 cups and adding 1½ teaspoons cinnamon.*

Nannette Avant Borden, BM '76
Corpus Christi

Variation: *Use only ½ cup sugar, 2 eggs, and divide syrup into ½ cup white corn and ½ cup maple. Add 2 tablespoons flour.*

Walter L. Geyer, BM '61
Dallas

Variation: *Use ½ cup white sugar and 1 cup dark corn syrup for sweetening.*

Amalee Turek Jones, BA '26
Grand Rapids, Michigan

Variation: SAUCY SOUTHERN PECAN PIE. *Substitute ¼ cup maple syrup for equal amount of corn syrup. Decrease sugar to ½ cup. Increase butter to ½ cup and pecans to 2 cups. Bake for 1 hour at 325°. Serve topped with whipping cream, if desired.*

John A. Bookout, MS '49 MA '50
Houston

Variation: *Add 1 egg more. Increase pecans to 1½ cups. Boil together sugar and 1¼ cups dark corn syrup 3 minutes before adding to other ingredients.*

Suzanne Williams Nash, BA '67
Dallas

Variation: *Decrease sugar to ½ cup. Increase butter to 4 tablespoons.*

Betty Dupree Carpenter, BA '48
Dallas

Variation: *Use ½ cup white sugar and ½ cup brown sugar. Add 2 tablespoons flour, increase pecans to 1¼ cups. Also, for CHOCOLATE PECAN PIE, add 2 ounces unsweetened chocolate, melted.*

Joe Kyle, Jr., BBA '73
Huntsville

Variation: *Reduce pecans to ½ cup and add ½ cup coconut. Bake 2 hours at 300° (secret seems to be in the baking!).*

Mary Fletcher White, BA '40
Oro Valley, Arizona

Variation: KENTUCKY DERBY PIE. *Increase butter to ½ cup, add 2 tablespoons Bourbon and ½ cup semisweet chocolate chips folded in with pecans.*

Roxie Potter, BS '75
New York, New York

Variation: GERMAN CHOCOLATE PIE. *Increase butter to ½ cup, add ½ bar German's sweet chocolate melted with the butter. Omit corn syrup, add 2 tablespoons flour. Use no crust, only buttered pie plate.*

Maxine Kubela Mebane, BS '35
San Angelo

Variation: *Use only ½ cup dark corn syrup and ½ cup light corn syrup for total amount of sweetening. Use 1½ cups pecans. Bake 15 minutes at 400°, reduce heat to 350° and bake 20 minutes more. Serve with scoop of vanilla ice cream on top of each serving.*

Wm. R. Archer, Jr., BBA '50 LLB '51
Houston

Buttermilk Pie

3 eggs
⅔ cup buttermilk
2 cups sugar
1 tablespoon flour
½ cup (1 stick) melted
 butter
1½ teaspoons vanilla
 Pinch of salt
1 unbaked 9-inch pie
 shell

Beat eggs, combine with buttermilk. Add other ingredients, mix thoroughly. Pour into unbaked pie shell; bake 10 minutes at 275°, then bake 50 minutes at 300°. Serves 8.

H. B. Amstead, BS '41 MS '49 PhD '55
Austin

Cottage Cheese Pie

1 carton (16 oz.) small
 curd cottage cheese
1½ cups sugar
3 eggs
1 teaspoon lemon
 extract
1 unbaked 10-inch pie
 shell

Beat eggs. Add sugar and cottage cheese and mix well. Add extract. Pour into unbaked 10-inch pie shell. Bake 15 minutes at 400°, then bake 15 minutes more at 350°. Do not overbake. Serves 8.

Denise Jaroszewski Chandler, BS '76
Houston

Cream Cheese Pie

16 ounces cream cheese
3 eggs, beaten
⅔ cup sugar
¼ teaspoon almond
 extract
TOPPING:
2 cups sour cream
3 tablespoons sugar
1 teaspoon vanilla

Beat cream cheese, add eggs, sugar and extract. Beat until creamy. Pour into buttered 10-inch pie pan. Bake 50 minutes at 325°. Cool 20 minutes. Combine topping ingredients and spread over pie. Return to oven, bake 15 minutes more. Cool, but do not chill. Serves 8.

Gail Hayes Cromeens, BS '70
Mineral Wells

Chocolate Meringue Pie

CRUST:

3 egg whites
Pinch of salt
Pinch of cream of
tartar
¾ cup sugar
½ cup nuts
½ teaspoon vanilla

FILLING:

1 package (4 oz.)
German's sweet
chocolate
3 tablespoons water
1 teaspoon vanilla
1 cup whipping cream
Chocolate shavings

CRUST: Combine egg whites, salt and cream of tartar and beat until foamy. Add sugar, 2 tablespoons at a time. Beat until very stiff. Fold in nuts and vanilla. Form into shell in buttered 9-inch pie pan. Bake 50 to 55 minutes at 300°.

FILLING: Combine chocolate and water in double boiler, stir and melt. Cool. Add vanilla, fold in stiffly whipped cream. Place in cooled, baked shell; sprinkle with chocolate shavings. Chill 2 hours before serving. Serves 8.

Betty Wenger Marburger, '55
Austin

Ye Olde College Inn's Chocolate Fudge Pie
Memories are made of this

½ cup (1 stick) butter or
margarine
3 squares (1 oz. each)
unsweetened
chocolate
4 eggs, slightly beaten
3 tablespoons white
corn syrup
1½ cups sugar
¼ teaspoon salt
1 teaspoon vanilla
1 unbaked 10-inch pie
shell

Melt butter and chocolate in double boiler. Beat eggs, add remaining ingredients. Add cooled chocolate mixture to eggs, mix well and pour into unbaked pie shell. Bake 30 minutes at 350° or until top begins to crack. Center will be moist and fudgy and forms its own crust on top. Garnish with ice cream. Serves 8 memory seekers.

Walter L. Geyer, BM '61
Dallas

Chocolate Candy Pie
Very, very rich . . . chocoholics downfall

½ cup milk
Chocolate bars with almonds (7½ ozs. total)
18 large-sized marshmallows
¼ teaspoon vanilla
1 cup whipping cream
1 chocolate or vanilla wafer 9-inch crust, baked and cooled

Combine milk, chocolate bars and marshmallows in double boiler. Cook at low heat, stirring occasionally, until melted. Cool. Add vanilla. Whip cream until stiff, fold into chocolate mixture. Pour filling into crust, chill overnight. Top with unsweetened whipped cream and chocolate curls shaved from another candy bar, if desired. Serves 6 to 8.

Louise Harrell Mulkey, BA '61
Panhandle

Peanut Butter Pie

1 unbaked 9-inch pie shell
⅓ cup peanut butter
¾ cup powdered sugar
FILLING:
4 tablespoons cornstarch
½ cup sugar
⅛ teaspoon salt
2 cups milk, scalded
3 egg yolks, slightly beaten
2 tablespoons butter
1 teaspoon vanilla
MERINGUE:
3 egg whites
½ teaspoon vanilla
¼ teaspoon cream of tartar
6 tablespoons sugar

Bake pie shell 10 to 12 minutes at 450°. Cool. Combine peanut butter and powdered sugar and spread across bottom of baked pie shell.

FILLING: In top of double boiler, combine cornstarch, sugar and salt. Stir in scalded milk. Combine small amount of this mixture with egg yolks. Add to milk mixture in double boiler and cook until mixture is thickened. Add butter and vanilla. Pour filling over peanut butter mixture.

MERINGUE: Beat egg whites with vanilla and cream of tartar until soft peaks form. Gradually add sugar, beating until stiff and until all sugar dissolves. Pile atop filling. Bake 12 to 15 minutes at 350°. Serves 8.

Adelle Neely Rannefeld, BA '42
Decatur, Alabama

Mommee's Syrup Pie

4 eggs
1 cup sugar
1 cup dark corn syrup
Pinch of salt
3 tablespoons butter
1 unbaked 9-inch pie
    shell

Beat eggs well. Add remaining ingredients, mix well. Pour into unbaked pie shell. Bake 5 minutes at 425°, reduce heat to 325° and bake until knife blade inserted in center comes out clean. Serves 8.

Ellen Brodnax, BA '41 MA '44
Fulton

Queenly Frozen Avocado Pie

1 cup pureed avocado
1 cup sour cream
1¼ cups sugar
½ cup fresh orange juice
½ cup pineapple juice
½ cup fresh lemon juice
¼ teaspoon almond
    extract
1 baked 9-inch pie shell
Whipped cream
Maraschino cherries

Combine avocado and sour cream. Add sugar gradually, alternating with juices. Add extract. Chill. Freeze crust. Pour filling into crust. Freeze overnight. Remove from freezer 10 minutes before serving. Top with whipped cream and maraschino cherry. Serves 8.

Bobbie Rainey Sublett, '31
Dallas

Sherbet Pie

A good make-ahead or emergency company dessert

1 package (2.5 oz.)
    Dream Whip
2 teaspoons sugar
½ teaspoon vanilla
2½ cups milk
10 coconut macaroon
    cookies, crushed
1 cup raspberry sherbet
1 cup orange sherbet
1 cup lime sherbet
½ cup chopped walnuts

Combine Dream Whip, sugar, vanilla and milk. Beat until soft peaks form, add crushed cookies. Line a 9-inch pie plate with half of this mixture. Mound sherbets by spoonfuls into the cookie crust. Cover with remaining whipped mixture. Sprinkle with walnuts. Freeze until firm. To serve, cut into wedges. Serves 8. This recipe can be doubled and served from 9 x 13-inch pan.

Louise Harrell Mulkey, BA '61
Panhandle

Orange Pie
Superb pie for Orangebloods everywhere!

PECAN CRUST:

2 cups flour
½ teaspoon salt
½ cup finely ground
  pecans
¼ cup milk
½ cup salad oil

FILLING:

1 cup sugar
3 tablespoons cornstarch
½ cup hot water
1 cup freshly squeezed
  orange juice
3 egg yolks, slightly
  beaten
3 tablespoons butter
1 tablespoon lemon
  juice
1 tablespoon grated
  orange rind
½ cup orange segments,
  cut into small
  pieces

TOPPING:

1 carton (8 oz.)
  whipping cream
½ cup sugar
1 teaspoon vanilla

CRUST: Sift together flour and salt, add pecan meal and mix well. Add milk to oil and add to flour mixture. Stir with fork until thoroughly combined. Roll out dough between 2 pieces of waxed paper. Put into 9-inch pie plate, flute edges. Bake 20 minutes at 375° or until golden. Cool.

FILLING: Mix sugar and cornstarch. Add water and orange juice, mix well. Cook in double boiler until mixture is thickened, stirring constantly. Beat small amount of hot mixture into beaten egg yolks. Add to hot mixture and cool until thick enough to set, about 10 minutes. Remove from heat. Add butter, lemon juice, orange rind and orange segments. Cool. Pour into cooled crust.

TOPPING: Whip cream with sugar and vanilla. Spread over pie. Refrigerate 4 hours before serving. Serves 8.

Judith Cody Colquitt, BS '60
Dallas

ORANGE APPLE PIE. Peel and thinly slice 3 large-sized or 4 small-sized tart apples. Put into unbaked 9-inch pie shell. Top apples with 1 cup sugar, 1 cup orange juice and sprinkle with cinnamon to taste. Cover apple mixture with additional pie dough, pierce dough for steam holes, and brush with egg glaze. Bake 40 to 50 minutes at 400° or until crust is brown.

Rhonda Hodges, wife of R. L. Hodges, BBA '74
Houston

Individual Cheesecakes

16 ounces cream cheese
¾ cup sugar
2 eggs
1 tablespoon lemon
    juice
1 teaspoon vanilla
    Vanilla wafers

TOPPING:

1 can (16 oz.) cherry,
    pineapple or
    blueberry pie filling

Combine all ingredients except vanilla wafers. Beat until smooth and fluffy. Line muffin tins with paper liners. Place a vanilla wafer in bottom of each paper liner. Fill each cup ⅔ full with batter. Bake 15 to 20 minutes at 350°. Cool. Top each cheesecake with 1 tablespoon favorite canned filling. Chill. Remove paper to serve. Serves 18.

Becky Barlow Rivers, BS '71 and Steve Rivers, '68
Bastrop

Louise Appleman, wife of Gordon Appleman, BA '59
Fort Worth

Golden Pecan Tassies

1 cup (2 sticks) butter,
    softened
9 ounces cream cheese,
    softened
2 cups sifted flour

FILLING:

2 eggs
1½ cups brown sugar
2 tablespoons butter,
    melted
    Dash salt
½ teaspoon vanilla
1 cup chopped pecans

Combine butter and cream cheese. Add flour gradually, mixing thoroughly. Using fingers, work into smooth dough. Shape into balls 1¼ inches diameter. Place each ball in small muffin cup; press dough to bottom and sides with thumb, making a shell.

FILLING: Beat eggs slightly. Gradually beat in brown sugar, butter, salt and vanilla. Sprinkle half the pecans over bottom of dough-lined cups. Spoon in brown sugar mixture, filling cups almost full. Sprinkle remaining nuts on top. Bake 15 minutes at 350°. Reduce heat to 250° and bake 10 minutes more. Yield: 6 to 7 dozen.

Beth Stephens Beck BA '79
Austin

155

The 1920s

Beverages
Appetizers, Dips

On Monday morning, May 28, 1923, Santa Rita #1 blew in. The oil strike on the University's extensive properties in West Texas precipitated a trend in oil mining that provided funds that would enable the University to move toward its constitutional mandate to be "first class." This is a picture of Santa Rita #1.

$\mathcal{T}$he moral revolt of the jazz age has been attributed to "the war, the motorcar, Freud, and bootleg gin," but probably the most important new feature of the postwar period was the change in the mores of women. Female University of Texas students reflected the changes taking place across the country; they bobbed their hair, shortened their dresses, smoked in public, and danced all the new steps to music provided by the jazz bands.

The postwar spirit of numerous campus organizations produced a social life at the University that received more attention in the state press than did academic accomplishments. Some one hundred and fifty clubs, societies, and groups existed on the campus in the mid-1920s, when enrollment was only 5,000, and complaints of over-organization, organizations without purpose, and over-emphasis on extracurricular activities came from both faculty and students. Fraternities and sororities were strong forces on the campus. Even though only a small percentage of the student body belonged to the Greek groups, their Rush Week, social life, and initiation activities heavily influenced the student culture.

Fraternities devised all types of activities for initiations. Parades up Guadalupe featuring costumed neophytes leading cows, goats, pigs, dogs, cats, ducks, or any other live animal or fowl afforded spectators entertainment. Pledges were sometimes tied together and sent up Congress Avenue picking up cigarette butts; some had to carry blocks of ice from the Colorado River bridge approximately 25 blocks to the campus; others had to walk from one side of town to the other looking for certain scraps of paper. One fraternity pledge was accidentally killed during mock initiation ceremonies in 1928.

Interest in athletics soared in the 1920s. Student interest was usually gauged by spirit shown at the big pre-game rallies. The official yell leader and his assistants were positions of prominence. Twice within five years students participated in strenuous money-making campaigns to have buildings for their athletic programs. They celebrated a successful financial drive with a giant mass meeting, a bonfire, and a shirt-tail parade down Congress Avenue.

An Aggie game in Austin on Thanksgiving Day in 1922 is an example of the elaborate spectacles afforded by athletic contests. More than

20,000 were present soon after the gates opened at one o'clock. Goal posts were decorated in orange and white and maroon and white. A&M's sweetheart was paraded up the sidelines. Cardboard megaphones were distributed to Texas "rooters" through the courtesy of the University Co-Op. At 1:47 the Texas rooting section gave 15 rahs for "Team," and then they gave a whistle yell. At 1:55, the A&M band marched on the field. They passed in front of the Texas section, playing "Good-bye to Texas University," followed by "Wildcat." Next, the Longhorn Band appeared and marched down the center of the field. Entering the southeast gate, 500 co-eds, dressed in white and wearing novel Texas armbands, marched up the goal line and around the field to the 50-yard line in front of the grandstand. Forming a huge "T," they marched to the center of the field, turned around, and sang, "Over Hill, Over Plain." Then they stooped down and spread orange confetti on the field in the shape of a huge "T," after which, led by their cheer leader, they ran to their special section in the bleachers and sang "Tex" and several other songs. Next, the Texas Cowboys, a new organization of 40 men, presented a 1922 version of "The Fall of Troy." Instead of a wooden horse, they had a huge steer from which they emerged dressed in full regalia of orange shirts, white kerchiefs, black sombreros, and leather chaps. They carried a sign which read, "Troy fell B.C. 1222; A&M fell A.D. 1922." A&M yell leaders rushed onto the field and were greeted by the Aggie band and rooters. Then the Texas yell leader led the A&M fans in 15 cheers for A&M, and the A&M yell leader led the Texas rooters in 15 rahs for Texas. The A&M team came on the field at 2:45. Ten minutes later, the Texas team appeared. At 2:57, the band played "The Eyes of Texas," and the game finally started at 3:03.

Old "flivvers," used cars that students bought for $35 to $100, were a fad during the middle and late 1920s. Regardless of their looks, they were correct for all occasions: gym hops, germans, and out-of-town football games.

The society pages of *The Daily Texan* told of dinner parties, buffet suppers, luncheons, smokers, banquets, and possum hunts. Dancing was the most popular activity for planned social affairs. An all-University dance, called the "german," usually was held in the Women's Gymnasium on Saturday nights in the 1920s. On dates, students went to a movie or a dance; or went automobile riding; or sat in a porch swing or in a dormitory lounge and talked, listened to a victrola or a radio, or played cards. In the spring, picnics and swimming parties, canoeing, broiling a steak at Bull Creek, or parking at Dillingham's Pasture took precedence.

Guadalupe Street between 21st and 24th Streets—called "The Drag" from time immemorial—was made up principally of drug stores, hamburger stands, cafes, and fruit shops. The drug stores served as gathering places for students who had an hour or so between classes in the afternoons. Students might drive up to the curb in a roadster with a rumble seat, honk the horn, and receive curb service, for their cherry cokes, limeades or chocolate sodas.

The changing Texas society, the changing purposes and standards of the University, and a new academic emphasis on specialization created a different spirit on the campus. A few selected words and phrases provide clues to the prevailing spirit: flappers, bobbed hair, short skirts, one-piece bathing suits, jelly beans, bell-bottom trousers, Oxford bags, Valentino pants,

160

Stacombed hair, drinking flivvers, Sunday movies, co-eds smoking, making whoopee, dances and dance bands, jazz, the Charleston, big rallies, building-fund drives, flash card stunts, stadium shows, crossword puzzles, barnyard golf, the comics, *College Humor*, aeroplane rides, chewing gum, and slang.

Scottish Rite Dormitory, housing 326 girls, was built in 1922 by the Scottish Rite Masons of Texas, and Kirby Hall, built for 112 by Methodist Women of five church conferences, opened in 1924. The University built Littlefield Dormitory in 1927 with funds left by Major George W. Littlefield.

The 1928 co-ed at Texas was considered as "collegiate" if she wore bright colors, had a raincoat with pin and ink sketches on it, rode in a model-T with signs painted all over it, and lived in a dormitory room surrounded with placards, tintypes, pennants, and caricatures. Girls living in S.R.D. were not permitted to smoke in the dormitory or on the grounds. For that prohibited cigarette, residents found it necessary to sit on the curb in front of the building. Junior girls dressed as men and escorted formally attired senior women to a Junior Prom. This tradition began near the turn of the century and continued through the 1930s. On the night of the Prom, junior men usually had a smoker.

Students started going to Dirty Martin's in 1926 and have continued to find it to be "a parlor of warmth, good-eatin' and human activity" ever since. It first opened at 2404 Guadalupe and later moved up to the 2800 block. A "Kum-bak" hamburger made from ground meat kept in ice water in a porcelain crock and known for its "everything-on-it" good taste was the favorite.

Student government concerned itself with such events as the chartering of Texas Student Publications, Inc.; raising money and making plans for Memorial Stadium, which was dedicated in 1924; celebrating the University's Fortieth Anniversary; designing and adopting the first official senior ring; abolishing the Honor System, which had never worked well anyway; and planning the big Student Union drive.

Ugly wooden shacks still covered the campus during the 1920s. The Regents decided in 1920 not to move the campus from its original location to the Brackenridge Tract on the Colorado River but to begin purchasing additional lands adjacent to the Forty Acres. Oil was discovered in 1923 on the vast expanse of University lands in West Texas when Santa Rita blew in. The discovery heralded a new era for the University. As money in the Available Fund (interest on the Permanent Fund) accumulated, the appearance of the campus would change, but the noticeable differences would not appear until the next decade. New permanent buildings constructed in the 1920s included Memorial Stadium, the Biological Laboratories, Garrison Hall, the Hal C. Weaver Power Plant, and T. U. Taylor Hall.

Presidents who served during the 1920s were Robert Ernest Vinson, William S. Sutton (*ad interim*), Walter Marshall William Splawn, and Harry Yandell Benedict.

Texas Political Fanfare

Mrs. Johnson's
White House Spiced Tea

6 teaspoons loose tea or
    8 tea bags
2 cups boiling water
1 can (6 oz.) frozen
    lemon juice
1 can (6 oz.) frozen
    orange juice
1½ cups sugar
2 quarts water
1 cinnamon stick

Pour water over tea, cool. Strain. Combine juices, sugar, water and cinnamon. Simmer mixture 20 minutes. If too strong, add more water. Add extra sugar to taste. Add tea to juice mixture. Yield: 16 to 20 cups.

"I like to serve this to guests on a cold winter's day here at the Ranch—just as I did at the White House."

Claudia Taylor (Lady Bird) Johnson, BA '33 BJ '34
Stonewall

QUICK HOT CHOCOLATE DRINK FOR LITTLE SIPS. Combine 1 (8-quart size) package nonfat dry milk, 1 (6 oz.) jar Coffee Mate, 1 (16 oz. size) Nestle's Quik, and half a box of powdered sugar. Store in covered container. Use ⅓ cup mix per 1 cup boiling water. Top each serving with a marshmallow. Makes about 60 cups.

Theresa Bus Block, BS '77
Del Rio

Mint Iced Tea

3 cups boiling water
12 large sprigs mint
6 tea bags
1 cup orange juice
¼ cup lemon juice
1 cup sugar
6 cups water

Pour boiling water over mint and tea bags, steep 3 to 5 minutes. Remove mint and tea bags. Cool. Combine juices with sugar and water. Stir to dissolve sugar. Combine mixtures. Chill before serving over ice. Garnish with sprig of mint. Serves 6.

Suzanne Williams Nash, BA '67
Dallas

Russian Tea

14 cups water
2½ cups sugar
½ cup fresh lemon juice
24 whole cloves
4 tablespoons loose tea
2 cups grape juice

Simmer together water, sugar, lemon juice and cloves. Add tea, steep 10 minutes. Strain, add grape juice. Serve hot. Yield: 16 to 20 servings.

Amy Lois Porter Oden, BA '21
Tyler

"Witches Brew" Spiced Punch

1 bag (12 oz.) whole
   cranberries
½ gallon apple cider
5 sticks cinnamon
8 whole cloves
5 oranges, unpeeled and
   sliced in rounds
4 lemons, unpeeled and
   sliced in rounds
6 tea bags
   Sugar or honey to
   taste

Combine cranberries, cider, spices and fruit in large-sized stainless or enamel saucepan. Simmer, covered, 3 hours at low heat. Strain in sieve or through several layers of cheesecloth. Add tea bags and steep 10 minutes. Remove bags and sweeten tea to taste. Yield: 16 servings, 5 ounces each.

Pat Howard, wife of Henry Howard, EE '59
Danbury

Hot Punch

2½ cups sugar
4 cups water
2 sticks cinnamon
8 whole allspice berries
10 whole cloves
1 whole fresh ginger
   root piece
4 cups orange juice
4 cups lemon juice
2 quarts apple cider

Combine sugar and water. Boil 5 minutes. Remove from heat and add spices. Cover and let brew 1 hour. Strain. Before serving, combine syrup, juices and cider. Bring quickly to boil and serve immediately. Yield: 4½ quarts.

Doris Weldon Stokes, '29
Duncan, Oklahoma

Pineapple Punch

¾ cup brown sugar
6 whole cloves
6 cardamom seeds
1 (3-inch length)
    cinnamon stick,
    broken into pieces
1 cup apricot nectar
1 cup orange juice
4 cups unsweetened
    pineapple juice
2 cups apple cider

Place sugar and spices in basket of 10-cup percolator, fill pot with juices. Perk through a cycle as for coffee. Serve hot. Yield: 16 servings, ½ cup each.

Louise Harrell Mulkey, BA '61
Panhandle

Mint Tea Punch

8 cups boiling water
2 large handfuls fresh
    mint
½ cup loose tea
2 cups sugar
1 cup lemon juice
1 can (46 oz.) pineapple
    juice

Pour boiling water over mint and tea. Steep 30 minutes. Strain. Add sugar, stir and cool. Add juices before serving. Serve over ice in glass garnished with sprig of fresh mint. Yield: 20 servings, 5 ounces each.

Sammie Farrier Marshall, '47
Temple

Frozen Punch

2 cups sugar
4 cups water
2 quarts pineapple juice
Juice of 8 oranges or
    1 can (12 oz.)
    orange juice, diluted
Juice of 8 lemons or 1
    can (12 oz.)
    lemonade, diluted
5 large-sized bananas,
    pureed
2 quarts gingerale

Combine sugar and water, bring to boil, stir until sugar dissolves. Cool. Combine with remaining ingredients except gingerale. Freeze. Before serving: remove from freezer, thaw slightly, add gingerale, stir and serve. Serves 50.

Grace Lewis Ley, BS '23
Cuero

Orange Cow
Just like the "real" Orange Julius!

⅓ cup (½ of 6 oz. can)
    frozen orange juice
    concentrate
½ cup milk
½ cup water
¼ cup sugar
½ teaspoon vanilla
5 or 6 ice cubes

Combine all ingredients in blender. Cover and blend until smooth, about 30 seconds. Serve immediately. Yield: 1 large Cow or 2 small servings.

Louise Harrell Mulkey, BA '61
Panhandle
Twyla Lynn Tranfaglia, BA '73 MLS '74
El Paso

Texas Punch
A political fundraiser's special

1 jug (3 liters) dry white
    wine
1 bottle (24.5 oz.)
    champagne
2 bottles (32 oz. each)
    gingerale
1 pint fresh strawberries
Ice ring or block

Chill all ingredients before combining. Mix as needed, pour over ice ring. Yield: 35 servings, 5 ounces each.

Jane Haun Macon, BA '67 JD '70
San Antonio

El Rancho's
Frozen Margaritas
A favorite of UT students and Exes

1 part white Sauza
    tequila
1 part deKuyper Triple
    Sec
1 part fresh lime juice
Crushed ice

Combine lots of first 3 ingredients. Fill blender container ¾ full with crushed ice. Pour in enough liquid mixture to cover ice plus 2 inches. Blend until smooth. Serve in 8-ounce brandy snifter which has been rubbed on the outer side of the rim with lime and rolled in salt.

El Rancho Restaurant
Austin

166

Sangria
Just like in Jerry Jeff's song "Viva Terlingua"

1 bottle (25.4 oz.)
    Burgundy wine
¼ cup sugar
¼ cup Cointreau
¼ cup brandy
1 orange, sliced or
    1 apple, sliced or
    ½ of each
12 ounces club soda
    Ice

Combine all ingredients except club soda and ice. Set aside 6 hours to ferment. Add club soda and ice to serve. Yield: 4 servings, 10 ounces each.

David R. Scheihagen, BS '77
Houston

Variation: *Add sliced lemon, lime and pineapple.*

Gay Freeze Maguire, '71
Austin

TODDY FOR TWO. Combine ¼ cup water, 1 tablespoon sugar, 1½ teaspoons lemon juice, and dash of ground cloves. Heat until very hot and until sugar dissolves. Remove from heat. Add ¼ cup Bourbon. Garnish each serving with a maraschino cherry. Serve immediately.

Ann Driscoll Hatchell, BS '65
Tyler

Granddad's Pink Drink
Festive and colorful holiday drink

FOR A CROWD:
1 can (6 oz.) frozen
    concentrate limeade
    or lemonade
3 cups water
1 gallon bottled
    cranberry juice
1 fifth (25.4 oz.) rum,
    vodka or Beretiaga

FOR 2:
6 ounces limeade or
    lemonade
12 ounces bottled
    cranberry juice
6 ounces rum or vodka
    or Beretiaga

FOR A CROWD: Mix limeade with water according to can directions. Add cranberry juice and liquor. Freeze in quart-sized containers. Serve in champagne glasses. Yield: 20 servings, 6 ounces each. FOR 2: Mix limeade with water according to can directions. Use *only* 6 ounces *mixed* limeade (give the remaining limeade to the kids) and combine with cranberry juice and liquor. Freeze and serve. Yield: 2 happy people.

Susan and Jim Kessler, Friends of UT,
Austin

Happiness Punch
A keep-in-the freezer treat for unexpected guests

1 can (12 oz.) frozen
  lemonade, undiluted
1 can (12 oz.) frozen
  orange juice,
  undiluted
5 cups water
3 cups (1 bottle, 25.4
  oz.) light rum

Combine ingredients until well mixed. Freeze in plastic container. Beverage will be slushy. Yield: 2½ quarts.

Theresa Bus Block, BS '77
Del Rio

Christmas Morning Milk Punch
A tantalizing treat for all Santas!

FOR A CROWD (25):
8 eggs
2 cups sugar
1 fifth (25.4 oz.) brandy
1 fifth (25.4 oz.) rum
2½ quarts milk

FOR 2:

1 egg
¼ cup sugar
2 ounces brandy
2 ounces rum
1 cup milk

Beat eggs in large mixing bowl. Add sugar gradually, beat thoroughly. Add brandy, rum and milk, beating until mixture is creamy. Refrigerate overnight. To serve, fill blender ⅔ full and add ½ cup ice. Blend. Serve from chilled container set in ice. Yield: 25 servings, 6 ounces each. FOR TWO: All ingredients may be put into blender and served immediately. Yields 2 servings, 6 ounces each.

Nell Allen Bell, '48
Tyler

Apricot Brandy
Tested with dried peaches also, very good.

2 pounds dried apricots
2 pounds rock candy
2 quarts vodka

Put all ingredients into a 1-gallon jar or crock. Cover and set in a cool closet for at least 6 weeks. Strain and bottle. Makes great gifts! Yield: special candlelight dinners and homemade brandy!

Patricia Doney Holt, '45
Fort Worth

Papa's Eggnog
A family recipe since before the Civil War

8 eggs, separated
5 tablespoons sugar,
    divided
½ cup Bourbon whiskey
1 cup (8 oz.) whipping
    cream
Freshly grated nutmeg

Beat egg yolks until creamy. While beating, add half the sugar and all the whiskey, a little at a time. The whiskey "cooks" the yolks. Beat egg whites until soft peaks form, gradually add remaining sugar. Fold yolk mixture into whites. Whip cream and fold into mixture. Serve in chilled cups. Sprinkle with freshly grated nutmeg. Pass the spoons. Serves 12.

Ellen Brodnax, BA '41 MA '44
Fulton

Kahlua
Inexpensive, plus the fun of home brewing

3 cups water
4 cups sugar
¾ cup instant coffee
1 fifth vodka, 100 proof
1½ vanilla beans
3 screw-top bottles

Bring water to full boil. Remove from heat. Add sugar and coffee. Stir until cool. When cool, add vodka. Put ½ vanilla bean in each bottle and divide coffee mixture equally among the bottles. Screw tops tightly and seal with masking tape. Store in dark place 3 weeks before serving.

Susan Chafin Jones, MA '76
Muskogee, Oklahoma

Scholz's Nachos
The all-time favorite from the famous beer garden

Pinto beans
Salt pork or bacon
Bacon grease
Kraft Smooth-melt
    American cheese
Tortilla chips
Jalapeño slices

Soak beans overnight in water to cover. Drain, rinse, cover with fresh water. Add salt pork, simmer until tender. Drain, prepare refried beans by cooking a small amount of cooked beans in hot bacon grease mashing into a paste as you stir. Top each tortilla chip generously with refried beans, cheese and jalapeño slices. Bake until cheese melts.

Scholz's Restaurant
Austin

Bolivian Tamales

6 ears fresh corn
6 ounces Cheddar
   cheese, grated
1½ teaspoons chili powder
½ teaspoon salt

Carefully shuck corn, peeling each shuck off without tearing. Wash and dry shucks. Cut corn off cob and grind with cheese. (This can be prepared in food processor.) Add chili powder and salt and mix well. Place spoonful of mixture on green shuck. Wrap tamale fashion. Lay tamales in single layer in lightly oiled pan or baking dish. Bake 15 minutes at 350°. When corn is in season, fresh green shucks can be frozen in plastic bags. Tamales can be made at any time using frozen corn. Serves: 8 to 10.

Harriet Kidder Matlock, '47
Long Beach, California

Texas Jalapeño Torte

Fantastic! I will use this recipe many, many times!

1 can (11 oz.) jalapeño
   peppers, seeded
   and sliced
10 ounces sharp
   Cheddar cheese,
   grated
4 eggs, beaten
   Dash Worcestershire

Line 10-inch glass pie plate with slices of jalapeño peppers. Cover with cheese. Add eggs. Bake 35 minutes at 350°. Serve hot. Amount of jalapeño peppers can vary according to taste. Serves 10.

Joe M. Kilgore, '39
Austin

Brenda Wilson Barber, BS '68
Palestine

Nannette Avant Borden, BM '76
Corpus Christi

Variation: *Use 2 cans (4 oz. each) chopped green chile peppers and 2 tablespoons cream with the Cheddar cheese and eggs.*

Kay Rose Sims, BS '72
Mountain Home, Arkansas

Hattie's Canape Tacos

1 onion, finely chopped
2 tablespoons butter
½ cup diced cooked
   shrimp
½ cup diced cooked
   lobster
½ cup diced cooked
   chicken breast
½ cup tomato juice
3 green chile peppers,
   peeled and minced
Pinch of thyme
Dash red pepper
1 tablespoon salt
18 corn tortillas
2 cups grated Longhorn
   cheese

LONGHORN SAUCE:

3 large-sized tomatoes,
   quartered
½ medium-sized onion,
   grated
6 tablespoons chili sauce
2 teaspoons dry mustard
1 tablespoon grated
   horseradish
½ teaspoon sugar
¼ teaspoon pepper
Dash red pepper
¾ teaspoon curry
   powder
6 tablespoons vinegar
1 clove garlic, sliced
1 tablespoon fresh
   parsley or fresh
   herbs, minced

Saute onions in butter until golden brown, add remaining ingredients except tortillas and cheese. Simmer 3 minutes, set aside. Fry tortillas in deep fat until soft. Remove, drain, cut into thirds. Place 1 teaspoon filling onto each piece. Fold in half, secure with a toothpick, place on cookie sheet. Bake at 450° until crisp. Sprinkle with grated cheese while very hot. Serve immediately with Longhorn Sauce. Yield: 54 munchies.

SAUCE: Combine all ingredients, simmer until fairly thick. Strain sauce, sprinkle with parsley or fresh herbs. NOTE: This sauce may also be used as a dip: add 3 tablespoons sauce to 1 cup sour cream or 1 cup mayonnaise. Combine thoroughly, serve with tortilla chips or fresh crisp vegetables.

Anthony E. F. Howard, BS '57
Tyler

Appetizing
Artichoke Squares

1 cup chopped onion
3 tablespoons butter or
   olive oil
4 eggs, well beaten
¼ cup fine dry bread
   crumbs
½ teaspoon salt
   Dash pepper
   Dash oregano
2 or 3 drops Tabasco
2 cups (8 oz.) shredded
   Cheddar cheese
2 jars (6 oz.) marinated
   artichoke hearts,
   drained and
   chopped
   Pimiento strips
   (optional)

Saute onion in butter until transparent. In mixing bowl, combine eggs, bread crumbs, salt, pepper, oregano and Tabasco. Stir in onion, cheese and artichokes. Spread in greased 7½ x 11-inch baking pan. Bake 18 to 20 minutes at 350°. Cut into 1-inch squares. Serve hot. Garnish with pimiento strips, if desired. Serves 25.

Penny Porter Helms, BFA '66
Austin

Zucchini Appetizers

3 cups grated zucchini
   (about 4 small-sized
   zucchini)
1 cup Bisquick
2 tablespoons minced
   parsley
½ cup finely chopped
   onion
½ teaspoon salt
½ cup grated Parmesan
   cheese
4 eggs, slightly beaten
½ teaspoon seasoned salt
½ teaspoon oregano
   leaves, crushed
   Dash pepper
1 clove garlic, minced

Combine all ingredients and mix well. Grease ovenproof 9 x 13 x 2-inch pan. Spread mixture in pan. Bake 25 minutes at 350°. Cool slightly. Cut into 2 x 1-inch bars. Serve warm, or reheat in microwave 2 minutes at medium setting. Yield: 48 bars.

Glynis Kirchhof Richter, BS '79
San Antonio

Variation: *Bake in tassie-sized muffin pans.*

Deanna Cook Murphy, BA '59
Houston

Cocktail Pizzas

72 slices party rye bread
 (2 loaves)
1 pound Cheddar
 cheese, grated
2 onions, finely chopped
1 can (4 oz.) chopped
 green chile peppers
1 can (14 oz.) pizza
 sauce
¼ cup salad oil
1 can (4 oz.) mushrooms,
 chopped
1 can (4½ oz.) chopped
 ripe olives
1 teaspoon Worcester-
 shire sauce
1 teaspoon vinegar

Toast bread lightly. Combine remaining ingredients. Spread on slices of bread. Broil 2 to 4 minutes or until bubbly. The mixture can be prepared and frozen for later use. Thaw, then spread on bread and bake 10 to 12 minutes at 350°. Yield: 72 pizzas.

Patricia Morgan Richardson, BS '69
Arlington

Pizza Things
Also makes a great snack for the kids!

2 pounds ground chuck
1 pound seasoned pork
 sausage (bulk)
1 box (16 oz.) processed
 cheese spread
1 can (14 oz.) pizza
 sauce
1 teaspoon Italian
 seasoning
1 teaspoon garlic
 powder
1 teaspoon onion
 powder
2 loaves party rye
 bread
 Parmesan cheese

Brown meats and drain. Dice cheese, combine with meat, add pizza sauce and seasonings. Cook at low heat until cheese melts. Spread on slices of party rye bread. Sprinkle with Parmesan cheese. Freeze. When ready to serve, arrange Pizza Things on cookie sheet, bake 10 minutes at 425°. Serve hot. Yield: 72 things.

Everett Tucker, BA '58
Poquoson, Virginia

Broiled Bread Puffs

1 can (4½ oz.) chopped
  black olives
½ cup thinly sliced green
  onions
1½ cups shredded sharp
  Cheddar cheese
½ cup mayonnaise
½ teaspoon salt
½ teaspoon curry
  powder
1 loaf sourdough French
  bread

Mix together all ingredients except bread.
Thinly slice bread and cut each slice in half.
Spread mixture on bread and broil 2 minutes
or until bubbly. Yield: 36 puffs. Serves
12 to 15.

Twyla Lynn Tranfaglia, BA '73 MLS '74
El Paso

LOUISE'S PITA PIE PIECES. Split pita bread in half. Cut each half into 4 pie
shaped pieces. Top each with thinly sliced sharp Cheddar cheese and 'spicy-
sweet' mustard. Bake at 400° until cheese melts. Serve very hot to 8 people.

Louise Freeman Eiseman, BFA '51
Dallas

Mushrooms Matamoros

1 pound large-sized
  fresh mushrooms
4 tablespoons (½ stick)
  butter, melted
3 teaspoons lemon juice
½ cup dry white wine
½ teaspoon salt
4 tablespoons (½ stick)
  butter, melted
  Lemon pepper to taste
  Worcestershire sauce
  Soy sauce
  Picante sauce
1 tin (3.66 oz.) smoked
  oysters

In saucepan, place cleaned mushrooms, stems
removed (reserve stems for soups or salads),
butter, lemon juice, wine and salt. Add
enough water to cover. Simmer 30 minutes. In
a second saucepan, combine second portion of
butter and season to taste with lemon pepper,
Worcestershire sauce and soy sauce. Place
drained mushroom caps (cup up) in shallow
pan. Put ¼ teaspoon picante sauce in each
cap. Drain canned smoked oysters and blot
dry. Place oyster in each cap. Spoon seasoned
butter over each cap. Bake 20 minutes at 250°.
Baste during baking. Serve hot. Serves 20 to 25.

Ken Nuhn, BArch '49
Austin

Cheese-Stuffed Mushrooms

3 ounces cream cheese,
    softened
4 green onions, finely
    chopped
4 tablespoons (½ stick)
    butter, melted
20 large-sized fresh
    mushrooms, stems
    removed
4 strips bacon, fried,
    drained and
    crumbled
Parmesan cheese

Combine cream cheese and onions. Brush butter onto mushrooms. Fill each mushroom with some of the cream cheese mixture. Top with crumbled bacon. Sprinkle with Parmesan cheese. Place on buttered cookie sheet. Broil 7 minutes, brushing with butter occasionally. Mushrooms also can be prepared in microwave. Cook 3 minutes at high. Serves 20.

Lynn Rosenfeld, BJ '72
Houston

Roquefort Pecan Balls

120 pecan halves
3 ounces Roquefort
    cheese
6 tablespoons (¾ stick)
    butter, softened

Toast pecans at 300° for 10 minutes or until lightly browned. Combine cheese and butter. Spread cheese mixture on pecan half, top with a second pecan half. Refrigerate until ready to serve. Yield: 60 pecan balls.

I. B. Hand, BBA '40 LLB '40
Weatherford

Spinach Balls

2 packages (10 oz. each)
    frozen chopped
    spinach
2 cups Pepperidge Farm
    Herb Seasoned
    Stuffing
1 cup finely chopped
    onion
6 eggs, beaten
¾ cup butter, melted
½ cup grated Parmesan
    cheese
1 tablespoon garlic salt
½ teaspoon thyme
1 tablespoon pepper

Cook spinach according to package directions, drain well. Add remaining ingredients, mix well. Form mixture into bite-sized balls and freeze. When ready to serve, thaw slightly and place on greased cookie sheet. Bake 15 minutes at 325°. Serve immediately. Yield: 65 to 70 balls.

Judith Lott Oliver, '30
Navasota

Variation: *Substitute 1 teaspoon minced garlic for garlic salt. Reduce pepper to ½ teaspoon, add ¼ teaspoon red pepper, 1 teaspoon monosodium glutamate, salt to taste. Use ice cream scoop to make mounds. Freeze. To serve, place frozen mounds on fresh tomato slice on foil-lined cookie sheet. Bake 20 minutes at 350°. Serve as a vegetable.*

Suzanne Adele Tausend, '79
Pasadena

Bite-Sized Turnovers

½ cup (1 stick) butter or
   margarine
3 ounces cream cheese
1 cup plus 2
   tablespoons flour
1 can (4½ oz.) deviled
   ham or 4 ounces
   prepared mincemeat
   or preserves

Cut butter and cream cheese into flour with pastry blender to the consistency of meal. Form into ball and roll out on floured board or pastry cloth. Roll to ⅛-inch thickness. Cut with round biscuit cutter. Thinly spread filling on rounds to within ⅛ inch of edges and fold over. Press edges with fork. Place on ungreased cookie sheet and bake 10 minutes at 400° or until golden brown. Turnovers may be frozen and then packaged for storage in freezer. If baked frozen, bake 15 minutes at 400°. Yield: 24 pastries.

Runelle Loyd Stembridge, BS '51
Gilmer

Variation: *Add 1 teaspoon dill weed and 3 ounces grated Cheddar cheese to pastry. Add 1 tablespoon chopped green pepper and 1 teaspoon chopped onion to filling.*

Sue Brooks Littlefield, BA '77 JD '80
Austin

Cream Cheese And Deviled Ham Appetizers

1 can (4½ oz.) deviled
   ham
8 ounces cream cheese,
   softened
½ teaspoon baking
   powder
30 small rounds of thinly
   sliced bread
1 egg yolk
1 teaspoon onion juice
1 teaspoon horseradish
¼ teaspoon hot sauce

Spread bread with deviled ham. Mix other ingredients and spread on ham. Bake 12 minutes at 375°. Serve warm. Appetizers may be frozen and baked as needed. Yield: 30 rounds.

Opal Thomson Rosson, BA '27 MA '39
Houston

Bookbinding as practiced by 20th century masters has produced some of the most exciting expressions of the book arts. The Humanities Research Center has a choice collection of contemporary bindings, and eight representative bindings are shown here:

(bottom row, left to right)
Philip Dusel (Berkeley, California), binding dated 1981 on *Candide* by Voltaire.
Michael Wilcox (Canadian), binding dated 1981 on *Moby Dick*.
Pierre-Lucien Martin (French), the greatest living binder. Binding dated 1974 on *Vents* by St. John Perse.

(center row, left to right)
Pierre Legrain (French, 1889-1929), the most influential designer of bindings of the twentieth century. Binding on *Pontoise ou La Folle Journee*, designed by Legrain, and executed by Rene Kieffer.
Georges Crette (French). Binding on *Adventures Prodigieuses de Tartarin de Tarascon*, designed by Raoul Dufy, and executed by Crette.
David Sellars and **Paul Collet** (British). Binding on *Epithalamion by Ida Graves, published 1980.*

(top row)
Arthur Johnson (British). Binding dated 1978 on *Extinct Birds* by Walter Rothschild.
Pierre-Lucien Martin (French). Binding dated 1960 on Virgil's *Bucoliques*.

photo by Sherwood Inkley

Ham Balls

1½ pounds ground
    smoked ham
1 pound ground lean
    pork
2 cups soda cracker
    crumbs
2 eggs
1 cup milk
SAUCE:
½ cup water
½ cup vinegar
1 teaspoon dry mustard
1½ cups brown sugar

Combine meats, crumbs, eggs and milk. Mix thoroughly. Form meat mixture into walnut-sized balls. Place in casserole.

SAUCE: Combine sugar, vinegar, water and mustard. Stir over low heat, until sugar dissolves. Pour sauce over meatballs and bake 1½ hours at 350°. Baste frequently. Serve warm from chafing dish as appetizers with toothpicks. Serves 20 to 25.

Ruth Butler Hunt, '27
Fairfield, Iowa

COCKTAIL HAM ROLL-UPS. Combine 3 ounces softened cream cheese with 1 teaspoon grated onion and enough salad dressing to make spreading consistency. Separate 1 package (3 oz.) Leo's sliced ham, spread mixture on slices and roll. Cut into 3 pieces each. Spear each piece with a toothpick for serving. Yield: 24 roll-ups.

Dora Eleanor Good Dean, BBA '58
Houston

Chipped Beef Spread

16 ounces cream cheese
4 tablespoons milk
5 ounces chipped beef,
    chopped
4 teaspoons finely
    chopped onion
3 teaspoons finely
    chopped green
    pepper
1 cup sour cream
½ teaspoon garlic
    powder
1 cup chopped pecans
4 tablespoons (½ stick)
    butter
¼ cup chopped pecans

Combine cream cheese and milk. Add chipped beef, onion, green pepper, sour cream and garlic powder. Mix well. Melt butter in ovenproof casserole. Add pecans, tossing to coat and bake 10 minutes at 350°; remove from casserole. Spread mixture into same buttered casserole, sprinkle with pecans. Bake 15 to 20 minutes at 350°. Keep hot on a serving tray. Serve with crackers. Serves 12 to 15.

Everett Tucker, BA '58
Poquoson, Virginia

Cocktail Meatballs

SAUCE:
¾ cup catsup
½ cup water
¼ cup cider vinegar
2 tablespoons brown sugar
1½ teaspoons salt
1 teaspoon pepper
1 tablespoon minced onion
2 teaspoons Worcester-shire sauce

MEATBALLS:
2 pounds ground beef
½ pound ground pork
⅓ cup catsup
1 tablespoon prepared horseradish
2 teaspoons Worcester-shire sauce
½ teaspoon salt
Pinch pepper
2 or 3 dashes Tabasco

Combine sauce ingredients, bring to a boil. Cook, refrigerate 24 hours prior to serving. MEATBALLS: Combine all ingredients and shape into small-sized balls, about 1-inch in diameter. Chill at least 1 hour before cooking. Saute a few meatballs at a time in large teflon skillet (use small amount of oil if necessary). Shake pan constantly to roll balls and maintain shape. Repeat until all meatballs are cooked. Drain. Warm sauce, add meatballs. Serve with toothpicks. Yield: 135 balls.

Carolyn Devault Crawford, wife of
John Crawford, Jr., BBA '61
Oakton, Virginia

Herb Pâté

½ pound chicken livers
4 tablespoons (½ stick) butter
⅓ cup sherry or sauterne
4 eggs
1 teaspoon finely chopped fresh tarragon
1 teaspoon salt

Place all ingredients into blender container. Blend at high speed until smooth. Line loaf pan with foil. Butter foil. Pour mixture into prepared pan, or into 6 individual buttered ramekins. Bake 40 minutes at 350° or until knife inserted in middle of pâté comes out clean. Cool. Serve as an appetizer with Melba toast, or for a brunch or luncheon. Cut into slices. Serves 6 to 8.

Deanna Cook Murphy, BA '59
Houston

MENU SUGGESTION: Serve accompanied by Marinated Green Beans, Sweet and Spicy "Orange" Marinated Carrots, hot French bread, a white wine, with Strawberry Pizza for dessert.

Oriental Chicken Wing'ums

4 pounds (22 to 24)
    chicken wings
⅓ cup soy sauce
2 tablespoons salad oil
2 tablespoons chili sauce
¼ cup honey
1 teaspoon salt
½ teaspoon ginger
¼ teaspoon garlic
    powder

Wash wings and pat dry, remove tips, (do not use tips, reserve for stockpot) and separate at joint. Combine remaining ingredients, pour over chicken. Cover, refrigerate 1 hour or longer, turning chicken occasionally. Remove chicken and reserve marinade. Place chicken on rack in foil-lined broiler pan, bake 30 minutes at 375°. Brush with reserved marinade. Turn chicken, bake 30 minutes longer or until tender, brushing occasionally with marinade. Yield: 44 to 48 wing'ums.

Susan and Jim Kessler, Friends of UT
Austin

Golden Crescent Shrimp And Dip
A fantastic hot finger-food treat

2 pounds giant Gulf
    shrimp
2 eggs
  Pinch of salt
1 cup flour
1 cup salad dressing
4 tablespoons
    Worcestershire
    sauce
  Oil for deep-frying

Peel and devein shrimp and butterfly*, leaving tail intact. Combine eggs and salt, beat well. Dip prepared shrimp in eggs, as you would for "chicken frys" and dust thoroughly with flour. Pop into very hot oil and deep-fry until golden brown. Mix salad dressing with Worcestershire sauce. Spoon into individual serving dishes as a dip for shrimp. Serves 6 to 8.

Liz Smith, BJ '50
New York, New York

BUTTERFLYING SHRIMP: Use medium to large-sized shrimp. Peel, devein, leaving tail intact. Hold shrimp so the underside is up, and using sharp knife, slice down length of shrimp almost to vein. Spread and flatten to form butterfly shape so that the vein trench operates as a hinge and allows shrimp to open flat.

179

Won Ton (Crab Puffs)

**WON TON
PASTE:**

2 cups flour
1 teaspoon salt
2 eggs, slightly beaten
3 to 5 tablespoons
    water

FILLING:

8 ounces cream cheese,
    softened
12 ounces fresh or
    canned crabmeat
3 green onions, minced
    Oil for frying

Sift flour and salt. Add eggs and enough water to bind mixture. Turn onto floured board, knead until smooth. Cover and set aside 15 minutes. Roll out paste very thin on floured board and cut into 3-inch squares.

FILLING: Combine cream cheese, crabmeat and onion. Place teaspoonful of filling in center of square. Position won ton square in palm of hand with one corner pointed toward you. Moisten edges with water and fold corner nearest you over to opposite corner. Press firmly to seal. Fold third corner across its opposite side about ¾ inch below top point. Moisten and seal. Fold fourth corner across in same way. Deep-fry in hot oil until golden brown. Serve with Sweet Hot Mustard Sauce. Yield: 8 or 9 dozen puffs.

Irene Reeb Meitzen, BA '65
San Angelo

East Bay Shrimp Spread
One bite and you'll want another!

12 ounces cream cheese,
    softened
2 teaspoons Worcester-
    shire sauce
2 tablespoons
    mayonnaise
    Garlic powder or
    onion powder
    Dash Tabasco
    Dash paprika

TOPPING:

8 ounces chili sauce
2 to 3 pounds fresh
    shrimp, cooked and
    chopped
    Chopped parsley

Combine cream cheese with all ingredients, except topping, and beat until light and creamy. Adjust seasonings to taste. Pack firmly into 9-inch cake pan lined with plastic wrap. Chill. Turn onto serving platter, remove plastic wrap. Spread mold with chili sauce. Top with chopped shrimp and sprinkle with chopped parsley. Cover, chill overnight. Serve with assorted crackers. Serves 20 to 25.

Everett Tucker, BA '58
Poquoson, Virginia

Deviled Oysters

3 dozen or 3 jars (10 oz. each) oysters
2½ cups soda cracker crumbs, divided
1 cup finely chopped celery
1 cup finely chopped onion
1 cup finely chopped green pepper
1 clove garlic, minced
½ cup finely chopped parsley
1 tablespoon butter or oil
2 eggs, well beaten
1 teaspoon salt
2 tablespoons catsup
½ teaspoon red pepper
2 tablespoons Worcestershire sauce
2 tablespoons lemon juice
Rock salt

Drain oysters reserving liquor and finely chop in food processor or food grinder. Combine 2 cups cracker crumbs with enough oyster liquor to moisten. Saute celery, onion, green pepper, garlic and parsley in butter or oil until barely tender. Add oysters and eggs to vegetables, mix well. Add moistened crumbs, cook over low heat 20 minutes, stirring often. Add salt, catsup, red pepper, Worcestershire sauce and lemon juice. Pile into oyster shells, dust with remaining cracker crumbs, dot with butter. Place shells on rock salt in shallow pans. Bake 15 to 20 minutes at 400° or until hot. Yield: 48 filled shells.

Jeanne Ferguson, wife of Paul L. Ferguson, BS '57
Tyler

Smokey Salmon Appetizer Ball Or Spread
very good
Habit-forming, very delicious

1 can (16 oz.) red sockeye salmon
8 ounces cream cheese
1 medium-sized onion, grated
1 teaspoon pickle relish, drained
1 teaspoon liquid smoke
½ teaspoon lemon juice
½ cup chopped walnuts

Drain salmon well, remove skin and bones. Combine salmon with remaining ingredients, except nuts, in large mixing bowl. Place mixture on plastic wrap and form into ball. Cover and chill overnight. Several hours before serving, roll in chopped nuts. When used as a spread, mix nuts into mixture. Chill until ready to serve on crackers or dark bread. NOTE: You may use 2 small cans Smoked Alaskan Salmon. Substitute salt for the liquid smoke. Serves 6 to 8.

Louise Stromberg Bates, BS '34
Alice

Oysters Rockefeller

A very special dish to be served to someone special!

12 oysters
3 tablespoons butter
1 tablespoon chopped shallots
¼ cup white wine

SPINACH BASE:

1 package (10 oz.) frozen chopped spinach or 1 pound fresh spinach
1 tablespoon chopped shallots
2 tablespoons butter
1 teaspoon Worcestershire sauce
¼ teaspoon anisette liqueur or Pernod
12 oyster shells
Rock salt

MORNAY SAUCE:

1 cup milk
½ bay leaf
1 small-sized onion
3 whole cloves
2 tablespoons butter
2 tablespoons flour
1 egg yolk
2 tablespoons cream
2 tablespoons grated Parmesan cheese
2 tablespoons grated Gruyère cheese
Salt, pepper and red pepper to taste

Open fresh oysters. Remove oysters, keep a half shell. Saute oysters and shallots in butter. Add wine. Do not cook oysters at too high heat or too long.

SPINACH BASE: Prepare spinach according to package directions, drain and finely chop. Saute shallots in butter, season with Worcestershire, Pernod, salt and pepper to taste. Add to spinach.

SAUCE: Scald milk with bay leaf and onion studded with cloves. Strain. Cool. Melt butter, add flour and cook over low heat 3 to 5 minutes. Remove from heat, slowly stir in milk in 3 portions, whisking after each addition. Return mixture to heat, cook stirring with whisk until sauce is thickened. Mix yolk with cream, beating well. Add 2 tablespoons sauce, combine and return mixture to saucepan. Stir; add cheeses, constantly stirring until cheeses melt. Add seasonings.

TO ASSEMBLE: Fill shallow pan ½-inch deep with rock salt. Place oyster shells on salt. Press to make each shell level. Place a spoonful of spinach inside each shell. Add prepared oysters. Cover with Mornay Sauce. Broil 4 to 5 minutes until golden brown. Serve as first course with crisp French bread and white wine. Serves 2.

Harding Lawrence, BBA '42
Dallas

Herring Copenhagen

1 dozen herring fillets
   in brine
1 whole herring in brine
1 cup white vinegar
½ cup sugar
¼ teaspoon allspice
½ teaspon white pepper
4 bay leaves
½ cup chopped white
   onion

Place fillets and whole herring in large enamel or earthenware bowl. Add cold water to cover. Soak herring overnight to remove excess salt, changing water several times. Drain herring. Cut each fillet crosswise into 1-inch pieces. Place pieces in enamel or earthenware bowl. Prepare whole herring in similar manner; cut crosswise into 1-inch pieces and place in second bowl. Place remaining ingredients in saucepan. Bring to boil. Simmer 1 minute. Remove from heat. Cool to room temperature. Pour most of marinade over fillets. Pour remainder over whole herring pieces. Cover bowls. Marinate herring, refrigerated, 6 hours or longer. Drain, reserve marinade. Serve herring plain, using pieces cut from whole herring for garnish or use in many ways for main dish or salad offerings. Serves 25.

Walter Cronkite, '33
New York, New York

Crabmeat Mold

1 can (6½ oz.) crabmeat
1 tablespoon unflavored
   gelatin
3 tablespoons crab juice
   and water
1 can (10¾ oz.) cream
   of mushroom soup
6 ounces cream cheese
3 green onions, finely
   chopped
1 cup finely chopped
   celery

Drain crabmeat and reserve juice. Check crabmeat for shells. Soften gelatin in juice (add water to juice to make 3 tablespoons). Heat soup, add gelatin and cream cheese. (Hand mixer may be needed to mix cream cheese thoroughly.) Fold in remaining ingredients. Pour into greased 1½-quart mold. Chill at least 24 hours. Keeps refrigerated several days. Serve with party rye, pumpernickel, or brown bread. Serves 10 to 12.

Becky Burns Hoffman, BS '68
Seabrook

Panama Ceviche

4 pounds firm, fresh
    white fish (red
    snapper, pompano,
    corvina)
Juice of 12 limes,
    or enough to cover
    fish
Pinch of salt
Freshly ground pepper
1 tablespoon white
    vinegar
3 large-sized white
    onions
3 chili picante peppers
    or 1 large-sized
    chile pepper

Cut skinned, boned fish into ½-inch cubes. Place in ceramic or glass bowl. *Do not use metal or plastic.* Cover with freshly squeezed lime juice. Add salt, pepper and vinegar. The lime juice "cooks" the raw fish to a firm consistency. Dice onions and peppers. Add to fish, do not stir. Refrigerate 4 hours. Before serving, mix well and adjust seasonings. Serve as an appetizer with crackers. Serves 50.

Robert L. Herndon, BS '66
Woodbridge, Virginia

Variation: *To make CEVICHE À LA AGGIE, add 4 finely chopped tomatoes, 1 cup finely chopped celery, 1 cup coarsely chopped stuffed green olives and jalapeño peppers to taste. Reduce onion to 2 large-sized.*

Joe McMordie, Aggie husband of
Virginia Calhoun McMordie BS '46
Elgin

Stuffed Jalapeños

1 can (11 oz.) mild
    jalapeños, seeded
3 ounces cream cheese
1 tablespoon
    mayonnaise
1 can (7 oz.) tuna
2 tablespoons lemon
    juice
Vegetable oil
Paprika

Drain jalapeños and soak in iced water. If whole jalapeños are used, slice in half lengthwise and remove seeds. Change water every few hours. Combine tuna, cream cheese, mayonnaise and lemon juice. Drain jalapeños. Shine each jalapeño with vegetable oil. Fill each with tuna mixture and dust with paprika. Serves lots of people.

NOTE: May omit tuna, use more cream cheese and add ⅓ cup finely chopped walnuts or pecans. Yield: 18 hot halves.

Louise Sromberg Bates, BS '34
Alice

Jalapeño Log

Very enticing, slices form a pinwhell effect

1 pound Velveeta
cheese, softened
8 ounces cream cheese,
softened
1 envelope dry onion
soup mix
2 to 4 tablespoons
jalapeño pepper
sauce
½ cup finely chopped
pecans

Between 2 large pieces of waxed paper roll the softened Velveeta to ⅛-inch thickness. With a spatula spread cream cheese across top of Velveeta. Mix onion soup, jalapeño sauce and pecans. Spread this mixture over cream cheese. Roll the cheese into a log. Refrigerate until firm. Serve with round crackers. Serves 6 to 8 people.

Irene Reeb Meitzen, BA '65
San Angelo

SUBSTITUTE JALAPEÑO SAUCE. *If jalapeño sauce is unavailable, use 3 medium-sized canned jalapeños (stemmed and seeded) and 1 tablespoon jalapeño juice from the can. Use food processor to chop nuts, then add jalapeños, juice, and onion soup mix to make a smooth-spreading consistency. Editor.*

Artichoke And Mushroom Herb Vinaigrette

2 boxes (9 oz. each)
frozen artichoke
hearts, quartered
2 pounds fresh
mushrooms, sliced
1 cup vinegar
½ cup peanut oil
1½ teaspoons salt
½ teaspoon pepper
½ teaspoon thyme
½ teaspoon oregano
1 bay leaf
1 clove garlic

Cook artichokes according to package directions, decreasing cooking time to half the time indicated. Drain, combine with remaining ingredients. Refrigerate 12 hours. Serve chilled with toothpicks. Serves 25.

Roxie Potter, BS '75
New York, New York

Curried Olives

1 tablespoon minced
   onion
1 tablespoon curry
   powder
2 tablespoons lemon
   juice
½ cup salad oil
1½ cups stuffed olives,
   drained

Combine all ingredients in glass jar. Refrigerate
at least 3 days. Shake occasionally. When all
olives are served and the jar is empty, add
more olives and set aside, refrigerated, 3 days
before serving. Yield: munchies for many.

H.C. Pfannkuche, '22
Austin

Stuffed Celery Sticks

1 can (3 oz.) smoked
   oysters
1 cup farmer's cheese*
2 tablespoons cream
1 teaspoon soy sauce
   Celery
   Paprika

Chop oysters. Combine oysters with farmer's
cheese, cream and soy sauce. Mix well. Fill
crisp celery sticks with cheese mixture, sprinkle
with paprika. Refrigerate until ready to serve.
Serves 8 to 12.

Kathleen Kenny Reily, BS '77
Vaihingen, Germany

*Farmer's cheese is a very dry cottage cheese
purchased in bags, not cartons. Regular cottage cheese is too soupy for this recipe. A
substitute: 8 ounces cream cheese. Editor.*

Eggplant Nibbles

1 medium-sized eggplant
2 hard-cooked eggs,
   finely chopped
1 kosher dill pickle,
   finely chopped
¼ cup mayonnaise
½ teaspoon salt
¼ cup finely chopped
   onion
¼ teaspoon garlic
   powder
1 carton fresh green
   sprouts
   Cherry tomatoes

Wash eggplant and pierce skin with fork. Bake
in shallow pan 1 hour at 400°. Peel, drain and
chop fine in food processor or food grinder.
Add remaining ingredients, mix well and
refrigerate until well chilled. To serve, spread
mixture on Triscuit crackers, sprinkle with
fresh sprouts or chopped fresh parsley, top
each nibble with a slice of cherry tomato.
Yield: 30 nifty nibbles.

Jamie Carter Snell, BJ '73
Beaumont

186

Avocado Cherry Tomatoes

30 large-sized cherry
 tomatoes
Salt
Sugar
2 medium-sized
 avocados, pureed
2 tablespoons sour
 cream
2 tablespoons minced
 parsley
3 teaspoons fresh lime
 juice
3 teaspoons fresh lemon
 juice
2 teaspoons salt
¼ teaspoon Tabasco
¼ teaspoon sugar

Cut thin slice from top of cherry tomatoes. With a small-sized melon ball cutter, scoop out and discard seeds and pulp. Sprinkle inside of tomato shells lightly with salt and sugar. Invert shells on paper towels to drain 30 minutes. Combine pureed avocados with remaining ingredients. Mix well. Fill tomato shells with avocado mixture using a small knife or piping bag. Arrange tomatoes on serving dish. Serve chilled. Serves 6.

Barbara White Stuart, '55
Dallas

PORT WINE CHEDDAR DIP. In blender, combine ½ pound sharp Cheddar cheese (shredded), 8 ounces softened cream cheese and ⅓ cup port wine. Blend until smooth. Whip ⅔ cup heavy cream. Fold in blended ingredients. Keep refrigerated, but serve at room temperature.

Ruth Ann Neves Powell, BS '72
Alvin

Liptauer Cheese

8 ounces cream cheese,
 softened
½ cup butter, softened
1 tablespoon anchovy
 paste
1 tablespoon paprika
1 tablespoon chopped
 chives (frozen if
 fresh unavailable)
¼ teaspoon prepared
 mustard
½ teaspoon caraway
 seeds
Dash salt
Radish slices

In blender, combine all ingredients. Mold into a tower shape and chill. Surround base with sliced radishes. Serve with radishes, green onions and toast rounds. Serves 6.

Priscilla Flawn, wife of UT President Peter Flawn
Austin

Cheese Ball

1 can (8 oz.) crushed
    pineapple
8 ounces cream cheese,
    softened
1 tablespoon seasoned
    salt
5 tablespoons chopped
    green pepper
½ medium-sized onion,
    finely chopped
2 cups chopped pecans
    (reserve portion of
    pecans in which to
    roll mixture)

Drain pineapple 3 or 4 hours before adding all other ingredients. Mix well. Form into ball. Roll in reserved pecans. Serves 24.

Kimberly Fojtik, BBA '79
Greenwood, South Carolina

Gouda Wellington

Good and unusual, a special for cheese lovers!

1 round (8 oz.) Gouda
    cheese, wax
    covering removed
½ can (8 oz. size)
    crescent rolls
½ cup jalapeño jelly

Using a method of preparing rolls described in Chicken Cordon Bleu*, use 4 rolls to wrap Gouda with dough. Bake on cookie sheet at 450° until browned, about 15 minutes. Turn off oven. Spoon slightly warmed jelly over top of Wellington. Set in oven 5 to 15 minutes. Serve warm. Serves 10 to 12.

Shirlee McCulley Page, BBA ' 65
Houston

*See Index, Chicken Cordon Bleu.

Cheese Pastries

2½ cups flour
1 cup butter or
    margarine
1 cup sour cream
3 cups grated Cheddar
    cheese
Seasoned salt
Pepper
Paprika

Mix flour, butter and sour cream to form dough. Chill overnight. Divide dough into 4 balls. On a floured surface roll each ball into 6 x 12-inch rectangle. Sprinkle with seasoned salt, pepper, and ¾ cup cheese. Roll like a jelly roll, sealing edges with water. Dough can be frozen. To bake, sprinkle with paprika, slice roll into ¾-inch portions. Bake 30 minutes at 350°. Serve warm. Serves 60.

Nancy Bell Cooper, BA '67
Tyler

Longhorn Cheese Wafers

1 cup (2 sticks) butter
1 package (10 oz.) sharp
    Cheddar cheese,
    grated
2 cups flour
3 dashes Worcestershire
    sauce
¼ teaspoon Tabasco
2 cups Special K cereal
    or puffed rice cereal

Bring butter and cheese to room temperature, then cream together. Add flour, mix well. You may need to work flour in with hands. Add Worcestershire sauce, Tabasco and cereal. Drop mixture from a teaspoon onto a greased cookie sheet. Bake 20 minutes at 325°. Very spicy and crispy. Yield: 4 dozen.

Debbie Deering Owen, BS '79
Dallas

Variation: *Omit Worcestershire sauce and Tabasco. Use Rice Krispies for cereal. Add ½ teaspoon red pepper.*

Kathleen Tempel Elkins, '41
Shreveport, Louisiana

Variation: *Omit Worcestershire sauce and Tabasco. Add 1 teaspoon red pepper, 2 teaspoons salt. Substitute 2 cups chopped nuts for cereal. Roll into cylinder. Chill, slice, bake.*

Dora Eleanor Good Dean, BBA '58
Houston

Variation: *Follow Variation #1, adding ½ teaspoon salt. Roll into long cylinder 1½-inches in diameter. Chill. Slice into thin slices. Bake 10 minutes.*

Nina Cook Segler, BBA '79
Dallas

Cheese Fondue With Beer

16 ounces Cheddar
    cheese, shredded
½ cup beer
2 teaspoons Worcester-
    shire sauce
½ teaspoon dry mustard
    Dash garlic powder
    Dash Tabasco
1 tablespoon cornstarch
2 tablespoons cold
    water

Have cheese at room temperature. With mixer at low speed, beat cheese until creamy. Gradually add beer and beat at medium speed until fluffy. Add Worcestershire sauce, mustard, garlic, Tabasco and beat well. Melt cheese in fondue pot set on top of range. Combine cornstarch and water and mix into cheese. Cook and stir until thick and bubbly. Transfer to fondue burner. Serve with crusty French bread cubes. Serves 6 to 8.

Sue Brooks Littlefield, BA '77 JD '80
Austin

189

Chicken Cheese Fondue
Serve for a cozy dinner for 4 or party fare for a dozen

3 to 4 pounds chicken
    breast
8 ounces cream cheese,
    softened
¾ cup milk
2 tablespoons sherry
¼ teaspoon salt
    Dash garlic powder
½ cup Parmesan cheese
    Bread cubes*

Debone and cut chicken into bite-sized pieces. Bake, covered, 20 minutes at 350°. Bake, uncovered, 10 minutes to brown. Combine softened cream cheese with milk and sherry; mix in blender or electric mixer until smooth. Cook at low heat until bubbly. Add salt and garlic powder, stir in Parmesan cheese. Transfer to fondue pot. Dip baked chicken or bread cubes in cheese.

David R. Scheihagen, BS '77
Houston

NOTE: Cut Beer Bread into cubes and toast until brown.

MENU SUGGESTION: Serve with Artichokes and Mushroom Herb Vinaigrette, chilled white wine (Soave would be tasty), and Chocolate Mousse.

"BUM STEER'S" RED-EYE CHEESE. "Combine 1 package each (6-oz. size) softened Cheddar cheese spread, Cheddar with jalapeno spread, and Cheddar with bacon spread. Shape into 2-inch round log. Chill 4 hours. Roll in chili powder. Serve with crackers to Longhorn friends with lots of Texas beer."

Carolyn Frost Keenan, BS '76 MA '78
Houston

Crabmeat Zatarain
Family recipe of the Zatarain mustard clan

½ cup (1 stick) butter
1 clove garlic, minced
8 ounces cream cheese
    Dash red pepper
1 teaspoon Worcester-
    shire sauce
    Salt to taste
1 pound fresh lump
    crabmeat

In top of double boiler, melt butter. Add minced garlic and cream cheese. Season with dash of pepper and Worcestershire sauce. Cook until cheese melts and all ingredients combine in a smooth texture. Fold in fresh crabmeat. Serve warm in chafing dish with your favorite crackers. Serves 8.

Dick Rolle, '35
Houston

Hot Crab Dip

2 tablespoons minced
  onion
1 can (6½ oz.) crabmeat
8 ounces cream cheese,
  softened
1 tablespoon milk
2 teaspoons Worcester-
  shire sauce
  Salt and pepper to
  taste
  Tabasco to taste
  Slivered almonds
  (optional)

Combine all ingredients and mix well. Pour
into greased 8-inch pie pan. Bake 15 minutes
at 350°. Slivered almonds may be sprinkled
on top before baking. Serves 8 to 10.

Ruth Butler Hunt, '27
Fairfield, Iowa

Variation: *Omit milk and onion. Add ½ cup
mayonnaise, 1 can (10¾ oz.) condensed
tomato soup, and 1 clove garlic, minced. Serve
warm.*

Roxie Potter, BS '75
New York, New York

FOOTBALL TUNA DIP. Combine 16 ounces cream cheese (softened), ½ cup
mayonnaise, 1 teaspoon Worcestershire sauce, 1 tablespoon chopped onion and
2 cans (7 oz. each) albacore tuna in a 1-quart casserole. Garnish top with
slivered almonds. Bake 30 minutes at 325°. Serve hot or warm. Yield: 5 cups.

Penny Porter Helms, BFA '66
Austin

Super Sausage Cheese Dip

1 pound hot sausage
1 pound ground beef
1 large-sized onion,
  chopped
1 small-sized green
  pepper, chopped
2 pounds Velveeta
  cheese
1 can (10¾ oz.)
  mushroom soup
1 can (10 oz.) tomatoes
  with green chile
  peppers
1 tablespoon chili
  powder

Brown ground beef and sausage. Drain. Saute
onion and green pepper. Add remaining
ingredients and simmer until cheese melts.
Serve hot with corn chips. Serves 20 to 25.

Michael G. Shirley, BA '70 JD '72
Texas City

Longhorn Picadillo Dip

1 pound ground beef
    or venison
½ green pepper, chopped
4 medium-sized
    tomatoes, peeled
    and chopped
6 tablespoons tomato
    paste
½ cup tomato sauce
1 tablespoon instant
    minced onion
⅔ cup water
¼ teaspoon oregano
½ cup dark raisins,
    rinsed and drained
½ cup white raisins,
    rinsed and drained
    Salt to taste
    Pepper to taste
    Slivered almonds

Saute meat, drain. Add remaining ingredients except almonds. Simmer slowly about 30 minutes. If meat mixture is too thick to use as a dip, add more water. Serve in a chafing dish with almonds sprinkled on top. Use tostados for dipping. Serves 20.

Lisa Evans Strickhausen, BS '77
Corpus Christi

Hot Cheesy Beef Dip
Great served cold as a spread

⅓ cup chopped pecans
1½ tablespoons butter,
    melted
1 jar (2½ oz.) dried beef
8 ounces cream cheese,
    softened
2 tablespoons milk
¼ cup finely chopped
    green pepper
¼ cup finely chopped
    green onion
1 clove garlic, minced
½ teaspoon white pepper
½ cup sour cream

Saute pecans in butter 3 to 5 minutes, drain on paper towels and set aside. Place dried beef in container of blender or food processor; chop finely and set aside. Combine cream cheese and milk in a medium-sized mixing bowl, beat at medium speed with electric mixer until smooth. Stir in beef, green pepper, onion, garlic and white pepper, mixing well. Stir in sour cream. Spoon into greased 1-quart casserole. Sprinkle pecans on top. Bake 25 minutes at 350°. Serve dip hot with assorted crackers. Yield: 2 cups.

Ruth Butler Hunt, '27
Fairfield, Iowa

Green Chile Pepper Dip

1 pound ground beef
¼ cup chopped green
   onions
1 can (8 oz.) tomato
   sauce
1 can (4 oz.) green chile
   peppers, chopped
1 teaspoon Worcester-
   shire sauce
1 pound American
   cheese, diced
   Dash garlic powder

In large skillet, brown meat. Add green onions, cook over low heat until soft but not browned. Add remaining ingredients. Cook, stirring occasionally, until cheese melts. Add garlic powder. Serve in crockpot or chafing dish. If recipe is doubled use only half the cheese, then taste and add more cheese accordingly. Too much cheese could give too strong a cheese taste. Yield: 1 quart.

Ane Watson Casady, BA '70
Richardson

BURR'S BEAN DIP. Combine 1 can (10½ oz.) bean dip with 2 tablespoons juice from can of jalapenos. Add 2 tablespoons mayonnaise. Serve with Doritos.

Dorothy Hudson Burr, BBA '26
Corpus Christi

Chile Con Queso
Spicy and just hot enough

1 tablespoon bacon
   grease
2 tablespoons grated
   onion
1 can (4 oz.) green chile
   peppers, chopped
1 large-sized clove
   garlic, minced
½ pound Velveeta cheese
2 cups grated Cheddar
   cheese
⅓ cup or more canned
   milk

Saute onion in bacon grease. Add chiles, garlic and Velveeta. When Velveeta begins to melt, add Cheddar. Transfer to double boiler or crockpot. Add milk to desired texture. Stir until well blended. *Do not boil.* This recipe doubles easily. Serves 12.

Walter L. Geyer, BM '61
Dallas

Variation: *Substitute 2 cups cottage cheese (pureed to liquid in blender) for Cheddar cheese and canned milk.*

Twyla Lynn Tranfaglia, BA '73 MLS '74
El Paso

Hot Artichoke Dip

Easy and great . . . make this a dip in the microwave . . . 5 minutes at medium setting

1 can (14 oz.) artichoke
   hearts
1 cup Hellman's
   mayonnaise
1 cup grated Parmesan
   cheese

Drain artichoke hearts and chop. Combine ingredients, mix well. Place in greased 8-inch round baking dish. Bake 10 to 15 minutes at 350°. Serve with crackers or corn chips. Serves 6 to 8.

Nancy Mitchell Meyers, BS '75
Midland

Variation: *Use ½ cup Parmesan cheese.*

Patricia Martin Younts, BS '53
Louy Younts, '51
Del Rio

Variation: *Substitute 1 cup grated Cheddar cheese for the Parmesan and add dash Tabasco. Bake until bubbly. Sprinkle top with Parmesan and paprika.*

Louise Stromberg Bates, BS '34
Alice

Variation: *Use 2 cans of artichokes, add 2 tablespoons minced onions.*

Jinny Chappell Smith, BA '66
Dallas

Spicy Cheese 'N' Black-Eyed Pea Dip

4 cans (15 oz. each)
   black-eyed peas,
   drained
3 canned jalapeños,
   seeded and chopped
2 tablespoons jalapeño
   liquid from can
1 small-sized onion,
   chopped
2 cloves garlic, minced
1 can (4 oz.) green chile
   peppers, chopped
½ pound Old English
   cheese, grated
1 cup (2 sticks) butter

Combine first 6 ingredients in blender or food processor. Melt butter and cheese in microwave. Then stir in black-eyed pea mixture. Serve hot or chilled with corn chips. Serves 20 to 25.

Mary Lou Hopson Nuhn, '44
Austin

Dips

International Bean Dip
Best bean dip ever tasted

1 can (15 oz.) refried
    beans
4 ounces cream cheese,
    softened
12 ounces sour cream
1 bunch green onions,
    finely chopped
½ can (12 oz.) Ortega
    salsa
1 packet (1¼ oz.) taco
    seasoning
½ can (4 oz.) diced
    green chile peppers
Dash oregano
Salt and pepper to
    taste
1 cup grated Monterrey
    Jack, Longhorn or
    Cheddar cheese

Combine all ingredients except grated cheese in ovenproof dish. Sprinkle top with grated cheese. Bake 1 hour at 300°. Serves 15.

Roxie Potter, BS '75
New York, New York

Hot Broccoli Dip

1 package (10 oz.)
    frozen chopped
    broccoli
½ cup chopped onion
½ cup chopped celery
½ cup chopped
    mushrooms
3 tablespoons butter
1 can (10¾ oz.) cream
    of mushroom soup
1 roll (6 oz.) garlic
    cheese
Generous squeeze of
    fresh lemon juice

Cook broccoli, drain. Saute onion, celery and mushrooms in butter until soft. Add to broccoli. Combine mushroom soup and cheese. Cook in double boiler over low heat until cheese melts. Add broccoli mixture and lemon juice. Serve hot in chafing dish with corn chips or Melba toast rounds. Serves 25.

Peter S. Solito, '42
Houston

Variation: *Substitute 1 roll (6 oz.) jalapeño cheese for garlic cheese.*

Maria Luisa Flores, BA '77 JD '80
Austin

195

Okie Dip

2 cups sour cream
2 packages (.6 oz.)
    Good Seasons
    Italian Mix
Juice of 1 lemon
2 tablespoons
    mayonnaise
1 avocado, finely diced
1 tomato, peeled and
    chopped
Dash Tabasco

Combine all ingredients and set aside, refrigerated, 4 hours. Serve with corn chips to 6 loyal T-sips living in Oklahoma.

Bobbie Sloan Peltier, wife of Al E. Peltier, BS '51
Tulsa, Oklahoma

Caroline's Appetizer With Crudités

4 tablespoons jalapeño
    jelly
4 ounces picante sauce
8 ounces cream cheese,
    softened
CRUDITÉS:
    Thinly sliced jícama,
    turnip and squash
    Carrot and celery
    sticks
    Cauliflower and
    broccoli flowerets

Microwave jelly at high setting 30 seconds. Add picante sauce and cream cheese. Mix well. Refrigerate. Serve as dip with crudités. Yield: 1¾ cups.

Caroline Hunt Schoellkopf, BA '43
Dallas

Fresh Vegetable Dip

1 small-sized onion
8 ounces cream cheese
½ teaspoon salt
1 pint Hellman's
    mayonnaise
3 ounces Roquefort
    cheese
Garlic powder to taste

In food processor, using steel blade, chop onion until fine. Change to plastic blade and add softened cream cheese, salt and mayonnaise. Blend quickly and add cheese and garlic powder. Chill. Serve with celery sticks, cauliflower and broccoli flowerets, and carrot slices cut diagonally. Yield: 3½ cups.

Charlotte Plemmons Warren, BJ '76
Austin

CRUDITÉS. *The assortment of raw vegetables used for crudites are endless. Remember: the fresher the vegetable, the more crisp and better its service. Slice with a sharp knife or use a slicer (food processor produces uneven slices; do not use). Arrange sliced vegetables on ruffled lettuce leaves, alternating the colors, shapes, and flavors; place a bowl of dip in center of tray. Be sure all pieces are cut only into 1 bite-size tidbit, or the pieces will be re-dipped after the first bite. Prepare vegetables ahead of serving time, seal tightly in plastic bags. If vegetables are not crisp enough, soak in iced water; drain, blot each piece dry or dip will not adhere.*

To serve:

Jerusalem artichokes — scrub, do not peel, slice. This vegetable must be sliced at last minute or will discolor.

Asparagus — cut diagonally to insure more dipping area.

Broccoli — select heads that are all green, remove flowerets intact with 2-inch stem. Peel lower stem, slice diagonally.

Carrots — peel, slice diagonally.

Cauliflower — Separate into flowerets allowing a 2-inch stem, slice lengthwise into small bite-size pieces.

Celery — remove strings (most important), cut diagonally into ½-inch pieces.

Cucumber — scrub skin, score lengthwise with fork, slice ¼-inch thick.

Jícama — a Mexican tuber, peel and thinly slice.

Mushrooms — firm, large-sized, closed around stem on underside. Trim end of stem, slice cap and stem in one piece.

Red or green pepper — Cut into ½-inch strips. Great color variety for trays.

Squash — zucchini, crookneck, patty pan. Select very young squash, use all unpeeled and cut into slices or wedges (patty pan).

Turnip — purple top, young. Peel, thinly slice but not much ahead of serving time in order to avoid discoloring. Editor.

Dill Dip

1 cup sour cream
1 cup mayonnaise
1 tablespoon instant
   minced onion
1 tablespoon dried
   parsley flakes
1 teaspoon dill weed
1 teaspoon Beau Monde
   seasoning

Stir together all ingredients until smooth. Refrigerate at least 4 hours before serving so that flavor can blend and mellow. Serve with assorted fresh vegetables. Serves 8 to 10.

Becky Burns Hoffman, BS '68
Seabrook

Spinach Surprise Dip

1 package (10 oz.)
   frozen spinach
½ cup fresh parsley,
   chopped
2 teaspoons grated
   onion
½ cup mayonnaise
½ teaspoon salt
1 tablespoon fresh
   lemon juice

Thaw spinach, drain very well. In blender, combine all ingredients and blend until smooth. Chill until ready to serve. Serve with assorted fresh vegetables. Serves 8 to 10.

Everett Tucker, BA '58
Poquoson, Virginia

Variation: *Use ½ cup chopped onion, 1 cup Hellman's mayonnaise, 1 teaspoon salt, 1 teaspoon pepper. Omit lemon juice.*

Frances Combest Rountree, BBA '38
Waco

Variation: *Use ½ cup chopped green onion, 2 cups Hellman's mayonnaise, 1 teaspoon salt, ½ teaspoon pepper. Omit lemon juice.*

Dora Eleanor Good Dean, BBA '58
Houston

LUCILLE PEREZ'S NEW ORLEANS DIP. Drain 1 can (14 oz.) artichoke hearts and finely chop. Combine with 1 cup mayonnaise, 1 package Good Seasons Italian Dressing mix and juice of ½ lemon. Chill. Serve with rounds of wheat crackers or garlic-flavored Melba rounds.

Dick Rolle '35
Houston

El Rancho's Guacamole

6 avocados
2 tomatoes, finely
   chopped
1 teaspoon salt
½ teaspoon pepper
   Juice of 1 lemon
2 small-sized cloves
   garlic, minced
2 tablespoons salad oil
2 tablespoons chopped
   onion or chopped
   green onion
   (optional)
2 tablespoons chopped
   fresh jalapeño
   (optional)

Peel and mash avocados, add remaining ingredients using optional items as desired. Cover tightly, chill. Serve on shredded lettuce as salad or as dip with tortilla chips. Serves 8 as salad, 12 to 16 as dip.

El Rancho Restaurant
Austin

Montegia Polre

A south-of-the-border treat for a herd of Longhorns

1 dozen avocados
1 dozen tomatoes
2 large-sized purple
   onions
1 large-sized white
   onion
3 bunches green onions,
   tops included
1 can (14 oz.) pitted
   black olives,
   drained
1 bottle (10 oz.) salad
   olives, drained

DRESSING:

1 cup lime juice
½ cup salad oil
1 clove garlic, minced
2 tablespoons
   monosodium
   glutamate
   Salt and pepper to
   taste

Finely chop all ingredients. Texture should be crunchy, not pureed. Add dressing and season to taste. Marinate, refrigerated, at least 4 hours before serving. Serve with tortilla chips. Serves 25.

Marjorie Price, wife of Meredith Wayne Price, BBA '70
Eden

Mucho Picante Cheese Dip

Only for those with insulated mouths: warn your guests about this hot dip!

3 jars (5 oz. each) Old
   English cheese
3 ounces cream cheese
7 large-sized canned
   jalapeños
1 tablespoon juice from
   can of jalapeño

Cream Old English cheese and cream cheese until fluffy. Remove seeds and stems from jalapeños and mince finely. Combine cheeses. Add juice to yield a dip consistency. Refrigerate. Bring to room temperature 20 minutes before serving. Serve with chips and warning. Serves 6 insulated-mouthed friends or 36 timid tongues or a gross of unsuspecting Aggies!

Marietta Watson "Bitsy" Wynne, BS '54
Tyler

Mexican Dip Or UT Caviar
Also good as relish on hot dogs

2 large tomatoes, finely
    chopped
3 green onions, chopped
1 can (4½ oz.) chopped
    black olives,
    undrained
1 can (4 oz.) chopped
    green chile peppers
3 tablespoons olive oil
1 teaspoon garlic salt
1½ teaspoons vinegar
2 canned jalapeños,
    chopped
1 tablespoon jalapeño
    liquid (taken from
    canned jalapeños)
  Salt and pepper to
    taste

Combine all ingredients and mix well.
Refrigerate 5 or 6 hours. Serve with tortilla
chips. Yield: 3 cups.

Jan Bixler Bennett, BS '72
Houston

Theresa Valenta Pesek, '49
Harlingen

Shrimp Dip
A cocktail treat for 6 Longhorns

8 ounces cream cheese,
    softened
¾ cup mayonnaise
3 tablespoons catsup
  Juice of 1 lemon
1 pound cooked shrimp,
    peeled, deveined
    and chopped
1 rib celery, chopped
1 medium-sized onion,
    chopped
  Salt and white pepper
    to taste

Combine cream cheese, mayonnaise, catsup
and lemon juice until smooth and creamy.
Fold in remaining ingredients. Season to taste.
Cover and refrigerate overnight. Serve with
crackers or corn chips. Serves 6.

Elizabeth Ann Kibbe, BBA '78
Austin

Variation: *Substitute 1 carton (8 oz.) sour
cream for mayonnaise. Omit catsup. Substitute
2 cans (4½ oz. each) shrimp, drained, for
cooked shrimp, add dash red pepper.*

Barbara White Stuart, '55
Dallas

Variation: *Reduce mayonnaise to 2
tablespoons. Add 1 teaspoon Worcestershire
sauce, dash vinegar, dash Russian dressing.
Substitute 2 cans (4½ oz. each) shrimp,
drained, for cooked shrimp.*

Judith Morrison Martin BA '77 BJ '77
Houston

Dilled Crab Dip

8 ounces cream cheese, softened
1 cup mayonnaise
¼ cup sour cream
1 tablespoon dill weed
3 green onions, minced
1 or 2 teaspoons instant beef bouillon (1 crushed beef cube)
1 teaspoon Louisiana red pepper sauce
2 cups fresh crabmeat or 2 cans (6½ oz. each) crabmeat

Beat cream cheese until light and creamy. Add mayonnaise and sour cream, mixing well. Stir in remaining ingredients. Serve with fresh vegetables or chips. Yield: 4½ cups.

Erika Reeb, Friend of UT
Corpus Christi

Cold Artichoke Dip

1 can (14 oz.) artichoke hearts, drained
⅓ cup mayonnaise
1 tablespoon grated onion
Juice of ½ lemon
4 strips bacon, cooked crisp and finely chopped
Salt and pepper
Dash Tabasco

Mince artichoke hearts. Add other ingredients. Mix well. Add salt, pepper and Tabasco to taste. Chill. Serve with crackers, corn chips, or crudités for dipping. Yield: 1 cup.

Marialice Shivers, wife of Allan Shivers, BA '31 LLB '33
Austin

Oyster Dip

8 ounces cream cheese, softened
1 teaspoon grated onion
1 tablespoon chopped parsley
2 tablespoons dry sherry
1 can (3.6 oz.) smoked oysters, drained and chopped
2 tablespoons cream
¼ teaspoon salt
Freshly ground pepper to taste

Combine cream cheese, onion, parsley and sherry. Stir in remaining ingredients. Chill before serving. Yield: 1⅔ cups.

Theresa Bus Block, BS '77
Del Rio

Panamanian Shrimp Dip

2 pounds cooked
   shrimp, finely
   chopped
1 cup finely chopped
   celery
1½ cups finely chopped
   green onions
½ cup salad dressing
16 ounces cream cheese,
   softened
1 packet unflavored
   gelatin
   Juice of 1 large-sized
   lemon (about 3
   tablespoons)
1 can (10¾ oz.) tomato
   soup

Combine shrimp, celery, onions, salad dressing and cream cheese. Dissolve gelatin in lemon juice, set aside. Heat undiluted soup to boiling. Add gelatin mixture. Stir into shrimp combination, stir well. Chill 6 hours. Serve with corn chips as a dip, or serve nestled in a bed of lettuce as a salad. Freezes well. Yield: 6 cups.

Jan Bixler Bennett, BS '72
Houston

Big Red Onion-Cheese Sandwiches
These will be wiped out at half-time as the Horns wipe out OU!

1 large-sized red onion
½ cup red wine vinegar
   Garlic salt
   Lemon pepper
6 ice cubes
1 box (4 oz.)
   Liederkrantz or
   Limburger cheese
12 slices pumpernickel
   bread or 1 loaf
   Homemade Dark
   Pumpernickel Bread
   Instant Remoulade
   Sauce (See Index)

Thinly slice onion, place in deep bowl, cover with boiling water. Set aside 10 minutes. Drain, marinate in vinegar, salt and lemon pepper: add ice cubes. Refrigerate several hours before serving. Spread 1 slice of bread with one-sixth of softened cheese, top with onion slices, spread second slice of bread with Instant Remoulade Sauce. Enjoy! If you weren't offensive during first half, you will be now! Yield: 6 smelly sandwiches!

Bobbie Sloan Peltier, wife of Al E. Peltier, BS '51
Tulsa, Oklahoma

Toasted Cheese Sandwiches
Tasty treat for half-time

1½ cups (3 sticks) butter
    or margarine,
    softened
1 teaspoon onion
    powder
1½ teaspoons Worcester-
    shire sauce
    Dash cayenne
1 pound sharp Cheddar
    cheese, grated
1¼ teaspoons dill weed
¾ teaspoon Tabasco
1 teaspoon garlic salt
2 loaves (1½ lbs. each)
    thin sliced bread

Combine all ingredients except bread. For each sandwich, place 3 slices bread together, trim crusts. Spread cheese mixture between and on top of 2 bottom slices. Top with third slice. Cut into 3 finger-sized sandwiches. Spread cheese mixture on top and all sides of each sandwich (should look like miniature frosted cakes). Place sandwiches on cookie sheet, not touching each other. Freeze, then wrap in foil. When ready to serve, remove foil, place frozen sandwiches on cookie sheet, bake 20 minutes at 350°. Yield: 42 tasty treats.

Opal Thomson Rosson, BA '27 MA '39
Houston

CHEWY CRACKERS. Combine ½ box (18 oz. size) Quick Oats, 1 envelope (5½ oz.) buttermilk biscuit mix and 1 can (10¾ oz.) cream of mushroom soup. Season to taste. Take handfuls of the stiff dough and roll flat in additional biscuit mix. Saute slowly in vegetable oil. Yield: 24 dodgers.

M. Julie Cooper, '12
Corpus Christi

That Favorite Sandwich

1 package Stouffer's
    frozen Welsh
    Rarebit
    Tabasco (optional)
4 slices baked chicken
    or turkey breast
4 slices toast
    Sliced tomato
    (optional)
8 strips bacon, fried
    crisp
4 tablespoons grated
    Parmesan cheese

Heat rarebit and add Tabasco if using. Place chicken slices on toast, top with tomato if using and 2 strips bacon. Cover with rarebit, sprinkle with 1 tablespoon Parmesan per sandwich. Broil until cheese melts. Serves 4.

"My version of the sandwich served at the Baker Hotel Coffee Shop in Dallas. The hotel is gone but the memories linger on."

Rosemary Fanning Pinson,
wife of Robert M. Pinson, BA '41
Dallas

The 1930s

Soups, Chowders Stews, Chilies

Despite protests from loyal alumni, Old Main was taken down during the 1934-1935 school year to make room for the present Main Building with its tower, which was completed in 1937. In this picture, some students in the early 1930s were walking from Old main to the Old Law Building.

$\mathcal{T}$he economic depression, increased interest in world affairs, and a change in the social pace marked the campus in the early 1930s. Signs of the nation-wide depression appeared, but enrollment figures did not decline. Most flashy roadsters were replaced with cooperatively owned flivvers; low-priced rooms were in demand; more students chose the 25¢ lunch; local bookstores found an increasing demand for second-hand books; and hitchhiking became a national pastime. One student wrote that his regular menu consisted of pinto beans and cornbread. Girls chose cotton dresses for formals and asked their dates not to buy corsages.

A straw poll in the early 1930s regarding drinking in Texas colleges showed that college students were wet by a slight majority, even though prohibition laws were still in effect until 1935. Comic strips were popular but University students thought Harold Teen, published in *The Texan*, was too high-schoolish. Campus drugstore cowboys and cowgirls bought an average of 5,245 gallons of ice cream each month in 1930 when enrollment was 6,000, and spent an estimated $37.50 per day for chewing gum. Jig-saw puzzles hit the campus, and professors, co-eds, and strong athletes succumbed to the fascination of fitting minute pasteboard blocks together.

Although the elaborate entertainments and social affairs that formerly marked Rush Week and the beginning of school had been abandoned, certain activities still dominated the social calendar. Dances every Saturday night in Gregory Gymnasium (and later in the Texas Union) replaced those formerly sponsored by interfraternity organizations (ribbon clubs) and various town groups. The Thanksgiving Ball continued to be a big social event in the years when the A&M football game was played in Austin. The Inaugural Ball every other year and the annual Round-Up Ball were special affairs. Approximately 20,000 attended the Inaugural Ball of Governor Ross Sterling in 1931 in Gregory Gymnasium. Governor W. Lee O'Daniel was inaugurated in Memorial Stadium in 1939, and one of his several balls was held in Gregory Gym. During the depression years, March 2 and April 1 celebrations were less rowdy; student interests again were changing.

Movies continued to increase in popularity and "road houses" appeared on the outskirts of town. "Navajo parties" were listed as "probably the most famous and most popular of Texas traditions." "Take a Navajo [a blanket], an alarm clock, and your best girl, rent a Ford and start out," a student wrote. Dillingham's pasture, eight miles out on the Georgetown turnpike, was the best known place to park.

Radios blared the swing music of Paul Whiteman from open windows in unairconditioned dormitories. Students attended tea dances in the Texas Union and danced to the music of Guy Lombardo and Benny Goodman. They also attended "germans" on Saturday nights. A large number of stags (men without dates) at the dances provided students the opportunity to make new friends. Being "stuck" with one dancer was an embarassment to both partners.

A study in the fall of 1931 showed that the total average monthly expenditure for women was $68.68; for men, it was $58.68. Among the women, 9.3% held part-time jobs; 24% of the men worked. Of the women, 6.6% had cars and reported that they spent an estimated $10.87 per month for gas and oil; 13.6% of the men owned cars or motorcycles and spent an estimated $7.64 per month for gas and oil. Rented cars were used by 50% of the women, but 19.2% used them less than four times a month; 49.5% of the men used rented cars, with 39.1% using them less than four times per month. The women paid an average of $12.41 for room and $26.09 for board per month; the men averaged $10.39 for room and $23.84 for board. Ninety-nine percent of both groups attended the movies, but 13.8% saw fewer than three per month. Among the women, 32.4% spent an average of $3.15 per month on cigarettes and 69.8% spent an average of $2.41 at a beauty shop. Among the men, 53.3% reported they smoked and spent an estimated $4.12 per month for cigarettes.

A student waiter in one of The Drag restaurants described the eating habits of students in 1931. The most popular order throughout the day was for a hot roll and a cup of coffee. Before eight o'clock classes, students rushed in from rooming houses and fraternity and sorority houses for a quick breakfast. Around ten o'clock many would come back for a more leisurely meal of orange juice, grapefruit, cereal, scrambled eggs, and waffles. Most students had noon and evening meals at boarding houses or dormitories, but during the afternoon they drank coffee, cokes, milk, and fruit drinks. Between 9:30 and 10:00 at night, another rush occurred; students leaving the library and others on dates drank coffee, milk, or fountain drinks and perhaps ate pie, toast, a hot roll, or occasionally a sandwich or "a half order of scrambled eggs." From eleven until twelve o'clock, business was better. Boys came by after taking their dates home and had scrambled eggs, waffles, and three-decker sandwiches. An after-dance rush was common. The boys did not care particularly what they ate, yet they enjoyed the noisy fellowship. During final examination week, students ate more and drank more coffee than at any other time.

Hilsberg's at 101 East 21st Street was a good place to get a steak, and Wukasch's at 2002 Guadalupe was a favorite place for Sunday dinner, which usually consisted of turkey and dressing, peas, Waldorf salad, angel food roll, and ice tea. Sunday dinners cost 50¢, while week-day dinners were only 35¢. Two other favorite haunts in the 1930s were Miss Norwood's Tearoom, on Rio Grande, and the nearby College Inn, famous for its frozen fruit salad. Miss

Anna Janzen presided at the University Commons, in a shack before moving to the new Texas Union. Her fried chicken was 25¢, and a big slice of her delectable devil's food cake was only 10¢.

In February 1930, an editor of *The Daily Texan* expressed pessimism concerning the future of student government at the University. Most of the powers of self-government once given to the students had been gradually withdrawn by University administrators as the student body grew larger, so that student interest lagged. The principal powers of the Students' Assembly during the 1930s were to elect a representative to the Athletic Council, elect two members of the Publications Board, appropriate all monies of the Students' Association, apportion the Blanket Tax proceeds among the organizations that received a share of them, control arrangements for student celebrations, enact regulations for the welfare of the student body, and prepare amendments to the constitution of the Students' Association.

Students pointed out as "important accomplishments" of the Students' Assembly the formation of the Cultural Entertainment Committee, which used an appropriation from the Blanket Tax to bring plays, entertainers, and speakers to the campus; and the assumption of control of the all-University dances and the Thanksgiving Ball. They helped the Ex-Students' Association with the first Round-Up in 1930 and the first Round-Up parade in 1934. In the spring of 1933, the Students' Assembly helped organize the Texas Union.

The dedication of nine new buildings at Round-Up time in 1933 (UT's fiftieth anniversary) marked the beginning of another change in the physical appearance of the campus. The de-shacking of the campus had begun! Two additional buildings, including the new Main Building with its Tower and carillon were completed before 1940.

President H. Y. Benedict served until 1937 when, near the end of the spring semester, he died suddenly of a heart attack. John W. Calhoun was *ad interim* president until Homer Price Rainey took office in 1939.

Lone Star Centennial Celebrations

Texas Chile - p. 231
Crispy Onion Rings - p. 257
Cheesy Jalapeño Cornbread - p. 22
Red River Mud Cake - p. 79

Texas Orange Stew - p. 230
Toasted Cheese Sandwiches - p. 203
Easy Texas Butterscotch Pralines - p. 119

Cold Tomato Soup - p. 211
Lone Star Red Beans And Rice - p. 361
Crackling Bread - p. 24
Texas Jam Cake - p. 72

Gulf Coast Seafood Gumbo - p. 223
Lady Bird's Popovers - p. 29
Texas Pecan Pie - p. 148

Cold Avocado Soup

3 avocados
2 tablespoons lemon
    juice, divided
1 can (10¾ oz.) chicken
    broth
2 dashes pepper
2 dashes red pepper
1 cup plain yogurt
GARNISH:
    Green onions, thinly
        sliced
    Parsley, minced
    Cilantro, minced
    Paprika

Peel avocados. Puree 2 avocados; finely dice the third avocado. Toss diced avocado with 1 tablespoon lemon juice and set aside. Combine pureed avocado with remaining ingredients. Season to taste. Cover and chill. Before serving, fold in diced avocado. Portion into 4 chilled bowls. Garnish as desired. Serves 4.

Harvey "Chick" Wallender, Jr., BS '36
Tyler

Cold Tomato Soup

3 cups tomato juice
2 tablespoons catsup
4 green onions, minced
    Salt to taste
    Dash thyme
½ teaspoon curry
    powder
    Freshly ground black
        pepper
    Grated rind of ½
        lemon
2 tablespoons lemon
    juice
1 tablespoon sugar
1 cup sour cream
    Chopped parsley

Combine all ingredients except sour cream and parsley. Chill. Before serving stir in sour cream. Serve in chilled bowls. Garnish with chopped parsley. Serves 4 to 6.

Sylvia Cook, BA '65
Austin

Persian Cucumber Soup

½ cup currants
1 cup cold water
3 cups plain yogurt
1½ cups half and half
  cream
1 hard-cooked egg
6 ice cubes
¼ cup chopped green
  onions
2 teaspoons salt
½ teaspoon pepper
1 English cucumber,
  unpeeled, or
  2 American
  cucumbers, peeled
1½ cups finely chopped
  pecans
12 ice cubes
1 tablespoon chopped
  parsley or 1
  tablespoon chopped
  fresh dill

Soak currants in the cold water 5 minutes. Combine undrained currants with yogurt and cream. Finely chop egg, add to yogurt mixture. Add 6 ice cubes, green onions, salt and pepper. Slice cucumber paper thin in food processor or with potato peeler. Add cucumber to yogurt mixture. Refrigerate 3 hours or overnight. Toast pecans 5 minutes at 350°. Cool. Divide pecans equally into 12 soup cups. Ladle chilled soup over pecans, garnish each cup with 1 ice cube and chopped parsley or dill. Serves 12.

Dolores Simmons Snyder, BS '54
Irving

Chicken Curry Soup
A gourmet soup . . . rated as one of the top five in the world by my neighbor

2 tablespoons butter
1 small-sized onion,
  sliced
3 small-sized apples,
  peeled, quartered,
  cored and sliced
  (3 cups)
2 tablespoons flour
2 or 3 teaspoons curry
  powder
½ teaspoon salt
4 cups hot chicken
  broth
2 cups half and half
  cream
1 cup dry white wine
½ to 1 cup finely
  chopped cooked
  chicken (optional)

Saute onion and apples in butter until soft but not brown. Combine flour, curry and salt; add to apple mixture. Gradually add hot broth, stirring constantly over medium heat. Simmer, stirring often, 10 minutes or until mixture is thickened. Cool. Puree mixture. Return to skillet. Stir in cream and wine. Add chicken. Serve hot or chilled. Serves 6 to 8.

Madeline Bynum Closmann, BJ '49
Houston

Chilled Strawberry Soup
Great for breakfast, or a first course for a light summer meal

1 quart fresh
    strawberries,
    washed and hulled
1 cup orange juice
1¼ teaspoons instant
    tapioca
⅛ teaspoon allspice
⅛ teaspoon cinnamon
½ cup sugar
1 teaspoon lemon peel
1 tablespoon lemon
    juice
1 cup buttermilk

Puree strawberries in food processor or blender, strain into 4-quart saucepan. Add orange juice. Mix tapioca with 4 tablespoons pureed strawberry mixture. Add to saucepan with allspice, cinnamon and sugar. Cook 1 minute or until thickened. Remove from heat. Pour soup into a large-sized bowl, add remaining ingredients, mix well. Cover, chill at least 8 hours before serving. Serves 8.

Connie Carpenter, BBA '80
Houston

Cheese Soup
From the Driskill Heritage Society
1886 Luncheon and Socializing Parlor

¼ cup butter
½ cup finely diced onion
½ cup finely diced carrot
½ cup finely diced
    celery
¼ cup flour
1½ tablespoons cornstarch
4 cups chicken broth at
    room temperature
4 cups milk at room
    temperature
Pinch of baking soda
1 pound processed
    cheese, Old English,
    cut into pieces
1 teaspoon salt
White pepper to taste
1 tablespoon dried
    parsley flakes
Dash red pepper
    (optional)
Paprika

Melt butter in heavy saucepan. Saute vegetables until tender. Stir in flour and cornstarch. Cook until bubbly. Add stock and milk *gradually*, blending into a smooth sauce. Add baking soda and cheese pieces. Stir until thickened. Season with salt and pepper. Add parsley. Before serving, heat thoroughly in a double boiler. Do not boil. Garnish with paprika. Serves 6 to 8.

Beth Stephens Beck, BA '79
Austin

Beer Cheese Soup
Yummy! And you can drink the rest of the beer!

¼ cup butter
2 tablespoons grated onion
¼ cup flour
2 cups beer
2 cups grated Swiss cheese
4 cups milk
Parsley

In large saucepan, saute onion in butter but do not brown. Add flour and cook until mixture bubbles, stirring constantly. Remove from heat, gradually add beer, whisking until smooth. Return to low heat, stirring constantly until mixture is thickened. Add cheese and stir until melted. Gradually add milk, heat thoroughly, but do not boil. Garnish with snipped parsley. Serves 6.

Verna Sykes Farris, BS '74
Hurst

MENU SUGGESTION: Serve with Alabama Hush Puppies, Vegetable Salad, and Tom Landry's Fresh Peach Pie.

ZUCCHINI SOUP FOR A WEIGHT WATCHER. Combine 1 cup cooked zucchini with 1 tablespoon onion flakes, 1 cup buttermilk and 1 cup chicken bouillon. Serve hot or chilled. Garnish with chopped chives. Yield: 3 cups.

Lena Pettit Hickman, BA '15
Austin

Kota Supa Avagolemono
Superb Hellenic classic lemon-chicken soup

1 hen (5 or 6 pounds)
3 quarts water
½ cup uncooked rice
1 tablespoon butter (optional)
SAUCE:
4 eggs
Juice of 2 lemons
3 tablespoons water
Salt and pepper

Clean and thoroughly wash hen, place in large stockpot, add water. Bring to boil, reduce heat to medium flame, cook 1 hour or until tender. Remove hen from broth, degrease. Add rice to broth, and if broth is thin, add butter. Cook 20 minutes. Remove from heat, add 1 cup chopped chicken and sauce. Serve immediately.

SAUCE: Beat eggs until light and frothy, add lemon juice and water, beating constantly. Add some hot broth to egg mixture, then stir sauce into soup. Serves 8 to 10.

Sylvia Bone Waldrop, BS '56
Texarkana

Chinese Corn Soup

Subtle in flavor, having a texture between a clear broth and cream soup

1 chicken breast, cooked and minced
3 egg whites
6 cups chicken stock
1 can (12 oz.) white shoepeg corn
4 tablespoons cornstarch
4 tablespoons water
Salt to taste
1 slice Chinese ham, chopped
Fresh parsley, chopped

Toss chicken in egg whites. Set aside. Bring stock to boil. Add corn, return to boil. Mix cornstarch with water into paste, add to soup and cook until mixture thickens. Lower heat and quickly mix in chicken. Stir thoroughly. Salt to taste. Remove from heat, serve in hot soup bowls and garnish with ham and parsley. Serves 6. NOTE: Chinese ham is very salty—may substitute Virginia ham, or other cooked ham. Again, salt to taste.

Maria Luisa Flores, BA '77 JD '80
Austin

Russian Cabbage Borscht

Basic peasant soup of Russia

1 lamb shank
2 beef short ribs
1 soup bone
2 quarts water
2 onions, chopped
2 ribs celery, sliced
1 green pepper, chopped
3 whole carrots
1 tablespoon salt
½ head small-sized cabbage, shredded
Garlic salt
1 can (16 oz.) stewed tomatoes
2 cans (8 oz. each) tomato sauce with mushrooms
1 tablespoon soy sauce
¼ teaspoon Tabasco
1 tablespoon catsup
Juice of ½ lemon
1 tablespoon sugar
Sour cream

In 5-quart stockpot place meats, water, onion, celery, green pepper, carrots and salt. Simmer 1 to 1½ hours. Remove meat pieces and carrots. Puree remaining vegetables. Set aside carrots. Return meat to pureed mixture. Sprinkle cabbage with garlic salt, stir thoroughly and add to soup. Add tomatoes and tomato sauce, soy sauce, Tabasco, catsup, juice of ½ lemon and sugar. Cook until cabbage is soft. Chop carrots and add to soup. Chill soup. Skim excess fat. Remove meat from bones and chop. Return meat to soup. Reheat and serve hot borscht, topped with dollop of sour cream, with dark Pumpernickel Bread. Serves 6.

Ronya Kozmetsky, wife of UT Dean George Kozmetsky
Austin

Mushroom Onion Soup

1 pound fresh
  mushrooms, sliced
2 large-sized onions,
  thinly sliced
1 clove garlic, minced
¼ cup (½ stick) melted
  butter
6 cups chicken broth
2 tomatoes, peeled and
  chopped
1 cup dry white wine
1 teaspoon salt
½ teaspoon pepper
1 cup croutons
½ cup Parmesan cheese

Saute mushrooms, onions and garlic in melted butter in heavy 4-quart pan. Add broth, stir in tomatoes, wine, salt and pepper. Simmer 1 hour. Serve with croutons sprinkled with Parmesan cheese. Serves 10.

Sue Brooks Littlefield, BA '77 JD '80
Austin

Ann Brinkerhoff's Famous Onion Soup

4 large-sized red onions
½ cup (1 stick) butter
4 cans (10¾ oz. each)
  consommé,
  undiluted

Slice onions as thinly as possible. Saute very slowly in butter, but do not brown, in a black iron pot. This can take 2 hours. Add consommé, bring to a "barely simmer." The longer you cook the soup, the better the flavor. Keeps well in refrigerator, and is almost better when reheated. Serves 8 to 10.

Ann Barber Brinkerhoff, BA '49
Houston

Tortilla Soup

3 corn tortillas, cut
  into thin strips
Salad oil
4 cups chicken broth
1 medium-sized tomato,
  peeled and chopped
4 green onions, chopped
  with part of tops
Grated Parmesan
  cheese

Saute tortilla strips until crisp in a frying pan containing about ⅛ inch hot salad oil. Drain strips on paper towels. Bring to a boil the chicken broth with chopped tomato, onion and tortilla strips. Simmer slowly 20 minutes. Top each serving with grated Parmesan cheese. Serves 4.

Elizabeth "Bitsy" Graham Hill, BA '44
Austin

Tomato Cream Soup

A stand-up soup drink for brunch or before the game

1 can (48 oz.) tomato
    juice
1½ teaspoons baking soda
    Salt and pepper to
    taste
½ cup (1 stick) butter
1 medium-sized onion,
    finely chopped
1 medium-sized green
    pepper, finely
    chopped
3 ribs celery, finely
    diced
6 cups milk
6 cups water
4 cups chicken broth
    Butter and chopped
    parsley (optional)

Bring to boil tomato juice, baking soda, salt and pepper. Saute vegetables in butter. Boil milk and water, combine with tomato juice. Add chicken broth. Adjust seasonings. Serve in mugs. If desired, float squares of butter on top of soup, or garnish with fresh chopped parsley. Serves 20.

Trudy Iverson Kokernot, BS '71
Boerne

Winning Game Soup

2 cans (10¾ oz.)
    chicken broth
1 can (6½ oz.) minced
    clams
1 bottle (6 oz.) clam
    juice
    Pinch Beau Monde

Combine ingredients and heat thoroughly. Puree in blender. Put into Thermos bottles and head for the game. Or serve at home, after the game, in demi-tasse cups. Top with a spoon of whipped cream. Serves 2 at the game, 6 at home.

"Nothing tastes better, including Bourbon and branch, at a chilly day football game than a thermos of hot soup. I like Clam Broth Bellevue which I call Winning Game Soup. The recipe came from the longtime bachelor and maitre'd of the Hotel Regis who, upon retirement, fled to Vatican City to join a monastery."

Liz Carpenter, BJ '42
Austin

217

Curried Zucchini Soup
A cold soup for sophisticated palates

3 tablespoons butter
2 or 3 medium-sized
  onions, thinly sliced
1 large-sized clove
  garlic, thinly sliced
1 tablespoon good-
  quality imported
  curry powder
8 medium-sized or 6
  large-sized unpeeled
  zucchini, scrubbed
  and sliced ¼-inch
  thick
  Salt
  Freshly ground pepper
3 cups chicken stock
  Lemon juice
  Red pepper
1½ cups heavy cream
1½ tablespoons dark rum

Melt butter in large heavy saucepan and add onions and garlic. Cook at low heat until soft but not browned. Stir in curry powder and cook very slowly 2 minutes, then add zucchini. Cover, cook over low heat 6 minutes until zucchini is just beginning to become tender. Season with 2 or 3 teaspoons salt and pepper to taste, then add chicken stock. Cover, raise heat slightly, and simmer 8 minutes until zucchini is tender but still retains some crisp texture. Puree in blender, using an on-off technique, constantly checking to avoid too smooth a puree. The crisp bits add a pleasant texture. Season to taste with salt, pepper, a few drops of lemon juice and a dash of red pepper. Chill. Just before serving, stir in cream and rum. Correct seasoning, if necessary. Serves 8.

Denton A. Cooley, BA '41
Houston

Easy Vegetable Soup

1½ pounds beef for stew
2 quarts water
2 cans (14 oz. each)
  stewed tomatoes
½ cup chopped onion
1 can (12 oz.) whole
  kernel corn
1 can (16 oz.) cut green
  beans
2 cups chopped celery
1 can (10½ oz.)
  jalapeño bean dip
1 tablespoon salt
½ teaspoon ground
  pepper
2 bay leaves
½ teaspoon seasoned salt
1 large-sized potato

Cut meat into bite-sized pieces; place in 2-gallon Dutch oven; add water, tomatoes, and onion. Heat until steaming, do not boil. Add corn, green beans and celery. Plop the whole can of jalapeño dip into the soup, this will eventually dissolve; however, you may want to stir it around to break it up. Add salt, pepper, bay leaves; sprinkle in salt. Cook at low heat, being careful not to let it boil over, 1 hour 45 minutes. Peel potato, cut into large bite-sized chunks and add to soup mixture. Cook soup until potatoes are tender. Serves 12.

Mary Ann Flowers, BA '78
Dallas

Spanish Bean Soup

1 ham hock
1 quart water
1 medium-sized onion,
    chopped
1 clove garlic, minced
3 potatoes, diced into
    1-inch cubes
1 teaspoon paprika
1 can (15 oz.) garbanzo
    beans, undrained
2 sausage links, sliced
    Yellow food coloring

Boil ham hock 1 hour in 1 quart water. Add onion, garlic, potatoes and paprika. Cook at low heat 1 hour more. Add beans and sausage. Simmer 2 hours. Debone ham, remove skin and fat. Cut remaining meat into small pieces. Return to soup. Puree ½ cup mixture to thicken soup. Add food coloring to give authentic Spanish coloring. Serves 6 to 8.

Roxie Potter, BS '75
New York, New York

Pasta E Fagioli
Bean soup with pasta

1 cup dried white beans
2 quarts water
2 tablespoons olive oil
½ pound cooked smoked
    ham, cubed
½ cup finely chopped
    onion
¼ cup finely chopped
    celery
½ teaspoon finely
    chopped garlic
1½ teaspoons salt
    Freshly ground black
    pepper
½ cup 1-inch pieces
    spaghetti
    Grated Parmesan
    cheese

In 4-quart saucepot bring beans and water to boil and boil 2 minutes. Remove from heat, set aside 1 hour. Drain beans, reserve liquid. Add enough water to bring liquid to 2 quarts. Heat oil in large saucepan; stir in ham, onion, celery and garlic stirring frequently for 10 minutes or until mixture is lightly colored. Add beans and water; season with salt and pepper. Bring to boil, then simmer partially covered until beans are tender, at least 1 hour. Skim fat. With slotted spoon, remove half the beans from the soup and purée in a blender. Return purée to soup. Simmer, stirring constantly, 2 minutes. Add spaghetti, simmer 15 minutes more. Adjust seasoning to taste, ladle into hot soup bowls, sprinkle each serving with grated cheese. Serves 4 to 6.

Kathleen Kenny Reily, BS '77
Vaihingen, Germany

219

Bean Soup À La Gooch

3 strips bacon,
    finely crumbled
1 large-sized onion,
    finely diced
2 ribs celery,
    finely diced
2 large-sized fresh
    jalapeños,
    pulverized
2 cans (10¾ oz.) bean
    and bacon soup
1 can (16 oz.) navy
    beans
¼ cup diced green
    pepper
1 cup shredded Cheddar
    cheese
1 can (10 oz.) tomatoes,
    drained and
    pulverized
½ teaspoon garlic
    powder
1 teaspoon pepper
1 can (10 oz.)
    Snap-E-Tom
    Cocktail Tomato
    Juice

If microwave available, put bacon, onion, celery and jalapeño in plastic or china bowl. Cover with paper towel and cook 4 minutes. If microwave unavailable, put bacon, onion, celery and jalapeño in saucepan, add 3 cups water and cook at low heat 1 hour until bacon is very tender. Stir occasionally. Add water as needed to prevent sticking. Add bacon and bean soup and navy beans; use masher to crush substantially but not entirely the whole beans. Add remaining ingredients. Add water as needed, but not too much as this should be a thick soup. Simmer at low heat until mixture comes to boil. Serve in Thermos cups, if available, or warmed soup bowls. Serves 10 to 12.

J.A. Gooch, '29
Fort Worth

Split Pea Soup

1 pound dried green
    split peas
2 quarts water
1 meaty ham bone
1 cup chopped onion
¼ teaspoon garlic salt
¼ teaspoon marjoram,
    crushed
    Pepper to taste
1 cup chopped celery
1 cup chopped carrots
1 teaspoon salt

In large saucepan, cover peas with water. add ham bone, onion, garlic salt, marjoram and pepper. Bring to boil, cover, and simmer 2 hours, stirring occasionally. Remove ham bone and cut meat from bone. Dice meat, add to soup with celery and carrots. Simmer 45 minutes. Add salt and pepper to taste. Serves 8 to 10.

MENU SUGGESTION: Serve hot with Tolbert's Cornbread, Spinach Salad, and Orange Apple Pie.

Glynda Harrell Eschle, BS '63
Groom

Sausage Bean Chowder

1 pound pork sausage,
  bulk
2 cans (16 oz. each)
  kidney beans
1 can (29 oz.) tomatoes,
  chopped
1 quart water
1 large-sized onion,
  chopped
1 bay leaf
1½ teaspoons seasoned
  salt
½ teaspoon garlic salt
½ teaspoon thyme
⅛ teaspoon pepper
1 cup diced potatoes
½ green pepper, chopped

Brown sausage. Drain. In large Dutch oven combine beans, tomatoes, water, onion, bay leaf, salts, thyme and pepper. Add sausage. Cover and simmer 1 hour. Add potatoes and green pepper. Cover and simmer 15 to 20 minutes until potatoes are soft, but not mushy. Remove bay leaf before serving. Serves 8.

Bonnie Blades Allen, '51
Houston

Manhattan Clam Chowder

4 strips bacon,
  finely diced
1 cup chopped onion
2 cans (16 oz. each)
  clams, undrained
2 cans (16 oz. each)
  whole peeled
  tomatoes, coarsely
  chopped
3 medium-sized
  potatoes, diced
1 cup diced carrots
1 cup diced celery
1 teaspoon chopped
  parsley
1 bay leaf
1 teaspoon thyme
  Salt and pepper to
  taste
  Finely shredded
  cabbage (optional)
  Diced green pepper
  (optional)

Saute bacon pieces, add onion, and cook 5 minutes. Add undrained clams, tomatoes, potatoes, carrots, celery, parsley and seasonings. Cover and simmer until potatoes are soft but still firm. Remove bay leaf. (If desired, add cabbage and green pepper and simmer with vegetable ingredients.) Serve in hot tureen with oyster crackers. Serves 4 to 6.

Harding Lawrence, BBA '42
Dallas

Shrimp Chowder
A thick, hearty Louisiana potage

6 strips bacon
1½ cups chopped onion
1½ cups chopped celery
½ medium-sized chopped
    green pepper
3 cloves garlic, chopped
1 pound raw shrimp,
    peeled and deveined
2 teaspoons salt
Pepper to taste
Red pepper to taste
3 cups milk
1 cup half and half
    cream
1 cup water
4 tablespoons butter
3 tablespoons fresh
    parsley or 2
    teaspoons dried
    parsley flakes
1½ cups instant potato
    flakes
¼ cup minced green
    onions

Fry bacon crisp and set aside. Saute onion, celery, green pepper and garlic in bacon grease. Add shrimp and seasonings, simmer until shrimp turn pink, about 5 minutes. In deep saucepan, heat to a boil the milk, cream, water, butter and parsley. Add instant potato flakes, stir well. Add shrimp mixture, cook at very low heat about 10 minutes. Garnish each serving with crumbled bacon and green onions. This chowder may be made ahead and reheated. Keep refrigerated. Serves 6.

Lee Elledge, '43
Oakdale, Louisiana

Corn and Tuna Bisque

2 tablespoons butter
2 tablespoons flour
1 teaspoon curry
    powder
2 cups milk
1 chicken bouillon cube
1 can (17 oz.) cream-
    style corn
1 can (7 oz.) tuna
Salt and ground
    pepper to taste

Melt butter in top of double boiler. Add flour and curry and cook briefly, stirring constantly. Add milk and chicken bouillon cube. Simmer, stirring occasionally, until sauce has thickened. Stir in corn including liquid and bring to boil. Add flaked tuna. Correct seasoning and serve immediately. Serves 6 to 8.

Carolyn Williams Marks, BS '60
Dallas

Shrimp Gumbo

½ cup chopped onion
¼ cup chopped green
    pepper
1 clove garlic, minced
¼ cup (½ stick) butter
    or margarine
1 can (10¾ oz.)
    condensed chicken
    gumbo soup,
    undiluted
1 can (16 oz.) tomatoes
1 can (16 oz.) cut okra
1 can (12 oz.) vegetable
juice cocktail
1 teaspoon salt
1 teaspoon sugar
¼ teaspoon Tabasco
½ cup cold water
1 tablespoon cornstarch
2 pounds shrimp,
    peeled and deveined

Saute onion, green pepper and garlic in butter until onion is golden. Stir in soup, tomatoes, okra, vegetable juice, salt, sugar and Tabasco. Bring to boil. Simmer, covered, 10 minutes. Blend cornstarch into cold water. Stir into soup, bring to boil, stirring constantly until soup thickens. Add shrimp, cook 3 minutes more. Serve over rice. Serves 6 to 8.

Carol A. Woodlock, BS '79
Dallas

Gulf Coast Seafood Gumbo
You need a bib and pliers to eat this!

2 onions, chopped
1 clove garlic, minced
½ cup (1 stick) butter
1 can (20 oz.) whole
    peeled tomatoes
  Salt and pepper
    to taste
2 bay leaves
1 dozen Gulf Coast
    crabs
2 tablespoons bacon
    grease
1 large slice of ham,
    diced
1 pound shrimp, peeled
    and deveined
1 quart oysters,
    undrained
  Cooked rice

Saute onions and garlic in butter, add tomatoes and seasonings, simmer 30 minutes. Clean crabs well, peel out bodies, leave claws whole, saute in bacon grease. Add crabs with ham and remaining seafood to tomato mixture. Simmer 30 minutes more. Serve over rice. Serves 6 to 8.

Kittie Fae Robinson Jinkins, BS '19
Galveston

223

Microwave Crab Soup

1st place winner in Joske's Great American Recipe Contest

2 cups crabmeat or
  1 can (12½ oz.)
  tuna
2 cans (10¾ oz.) cream
  of mushroom or
  cream of celery
  soup
1½ cups milk
1½ cups half and
  half cream
2 tablespoons butter
3 hard-cooked eggs,
  chopped
1 teaspoon Old Bay
  Seasoning or
  seafood seasoning
1 teaspoon Worcester-
  shire sauce
  Pinch garlic salt
¼ teaspoon pepper
¾ cup dry sherry
  Fresh parsley (optional)

MICROWAVE: Place all ingredients except crab or tuna in 3-quart casserole. Cover and microwave at high setting 4 minutes. Stir, cover and microwave 5 minutes more. Stir in crabmeat or tuna, cover and microwave 6 to 8 minutes or until thoroughly heated. Garnish each serving with parsley if desired.

RANGE: In heavy saucepan, add milk, half and half cream and seasonings. Bring to simmer. Add remaining ingredients, cook at low heat 10 to 15 minutes. Do not boil. Serves 8.

Erika Reeb, Friend of UT
Corpus Christi

Veal Stew
With Ravioli Dumplings

1 pound veal or
  Texas baby beef
3 tablespoons flour
1 teaspoon salt
½ teaspoon pepper
4 teaspoons salad oil
½ cup chopped onion
1 clove garlic, minced
1½ cups water
1 can (15 oz.) beef
  ravioli in sauce
2 tablespoons minced
  parsley
¼ teaspoon oregano
1 package (10 oz.)
  frozen green peas
  (optional)

Cut meat into 1-inch cubes. Combine flour, salt, and pepper; dredge meat. Brown in oil. Add onion and garlic, cook 5 minutes. Add water, cover, simmer 30 minutes or until meat is tender. Stir in remaining ingredients. Cover, simmer 15 minutes more. Serves 4.

Madeline Bynum Closmann, BJ '49
Houston

Meadowbrook—The dining room at Meadowbrook, the President's house at The University of Texas at Austin, displays generations of gifts to the University. The furniture was given to Home Economics by Mary E. Gearing, first Department Chairman of Home Economics. The wallpaper was a gift from James L. Britton, III and the silver service was given by A. Baker Duncan in memory of his mother. The table appointments have come from an on-going Development Board program through which friends of the University donate linen, china, crystal and silver.

photo by Sherwood Inkley

Wedding Stew

*From northern Mexico, a delight for a big
crowd of hungry Texans*

1½ pounds ground lean
    beef
1 pound ground pork
2 or 3 cans (29 oz. each)
    tomatoes
2 green peppers,
    chopped
1 clove garlic, minced
2 medium-sized onions,
    chopped
½ teaspoon ground
    cinnamon
1 teaspoon oregano
1 teaspoon cumin
1 tablespoon chili
    powder or to taste
1 cup raisins or currants
1 teaspoon dried
    coriander leaves or
    fresh cilantro to
    taste
2 slices bread, crumbled
    or ¼ cup masa
    harina
Salt to taste
PILÓN (A little
   something extra):
½ cup chopped nuts
1 can (11 oz.) mandarin
    oranges, chopped
1 cup crushed
    pineapple, drained,
    or 1 cup chopped
    apple or 1 cup
    chopped pear or
    other firm fruit

In Dutch oven at medium heat, brown meat.
For a lean stew, most of the fat may be
removed with this technique: place cooked
meat in colander over a bowl, and pour 2
cups boiling water over cooked meat.
Refrigerate the drippings until fat rises and has
solidified. If time is short, stir several ice cubes
into drippings to solidify fat. Discard fat.
Return drained meat and defatted liquid to
Dutch oven. Add remaining ingredients, except
the pilón, and simmer 30 to 45 minutes.
During last minutes of simmering, add any or
all of the "little something extra" ingredients.
Serves 10 to 12.

*Joe Belden, BJ '39
Eugenia Nash Belden, MA '36
Dallas*

Caldillo
Stew . . . not too soupy

1½ pounds cubed beef
¾ cup diced onion
   Bacon grease
1½ cups fresh tomatoes,
   peeled and diced
¾ cup canned green chile
   pepper strips
½ cup beef stock
½ cup chicken stock
½ tablespoon salt
½ tablespoon pepper
¼ teaspoon cumin
⅛ teaspoon garlic
   powder
1 pound cubed potatoes

Saute beef and onion in bacon grease. Add tomatoes, chile strips, stocks and seasonings. Cook, uncovered, over low heat until beef is tender, about 30 minutes. Add cubed potatoes. Simmer, covered, 30 minutes more. Serves 8.

C.T. Wells, BS '37 MS '37, PhD '39
Houston

Mary's Slow-Cooking Stew

1½ pounds stew meat,
   cubed
1 can (16 oz.) whole
   new potatoes,
   drained
2 cups carrots, cut in
   ½-inch slices
8 ounces fresh
   mushrooms, sliced
1 envelope dry onion
   soup mix, no liquid
   added
1 can (10¾ oz.) Golden
   Mushroom soup,
   undiluted
1 bay leaf
1 cup red wine

Combine all ingredients in crockpot. Cook all day at low temperature setting! This makes lots of gravy, and the wine adds a wonderful flavor! Serves 6.

Mary Lins Shetler, BA '79
Houston

Elephant Stew

1 elephant
 Salt and pepper
2 jack rabbits (optional)

Cut elephant into small bite-sized pieces. This should take about 2 months. Brown in large skillet, making enough gravy from the drippings to cover. Cook over mesquite campfire about 4 weeks at 465° or until tender. Serves 3,836 people. If more folks are expected, the 2 jack rabbits may be added, but do this only if necessary as most people do not like to find hare in their stew.

"This recipe was very popular back in my grandfather's day. In fact, it was so popular that most hunters are hard-pressed to find any elephants in Texas now. However, adding the hares was so unpopular that most cooks would just as soon serve small portions than add the rabbits . . . so that's why there's still so many jack rabbits around today."

Mary Barnes James, BA '75 BJ '75
Houston

Five Hour Stew
Perfect for the busy bachelor or housewife

2 pounds lean beef
 stew meat
1 cup coarsely diced
 celery
1 cup diced onion
1 cup sliced carrots
1 cup diced new
 potatoes
2 cans (10 oz. each)
 Snap-E-Tom
 Tomato Cocktail
 Juice
2 tablespoons instant
 tapioca
 Salt and pepper to
 taste

Combine all ingredients in stewpot with tightly fitting lid. Season to taste. Cover and cook 5 hours at 250°. Do not uncover anytime during cooking. Serve with cornbread and green salad or fruit salad. Serves 6 to 8.

Ruth Brooks Teague, '39
Austin

Oven Stew

A company dish that requires no more attention than an occasional stir

3 pounds lean stew
    meat, cubed
3 large-sized carrots,
    sliced
2 ribs celery, sliced
1 can (6 oz.) mush-
    rooms, undrained
1 can (16 oz.) stewed
    tomatoes
1 jar (16 oz.) whole
    boiled onions*
    (drained) or 8 or 9
    small-sized onions
1 package (10 oz.)
    frozen peas or
    green beans
1 teaspoon salt
1 teaspoon sugar
1 teaspoon pepper
½ cup tapioca
½ cup sherry or dry red
    wine
2 bay leaves
½ cup beef consomme
    or 1 beef
    consomme cube
    dissolved in ½ cup
    hot water
3 or 4 potatoes, cubed

Place all ingredients into heavy Dutch oven or casserole with tightly fitting lid. Cover and bake 6 hours at 300°. Your favorite vegetables can be substituted, but do not use the juices from canned vegetables. The meat does not have to be browned because the browning takes place during cooking. The tapioca thickens the stew. Serve with green salad and hot corn bread. Serves 6 to 8.

Fletcher Metcalfe Croom, '36
Houston

Gail Hayes Cromeens, BS '70
Mineral Wells

*COOKING ONIONS. *To keep whole onions from telescoping in the cooking process of a stew or a roast, peel the onion and in the root end cut an X to a depth of ¼ to ½ inch (depending on size of onion). Editor.*

Carter's Beef Stew

I grew up hating stew . . . until I tried this one!

2 pounds beef chuck,
   cut into 1½-inch
   cubes
2 tablespoons butter
2 cups boiling water
1 teaspoon Worcester-
   shire sauce
1 clove garlic, minced
1 medium-sized onion,
   sliced
1 bay leaf
1 tablespoon salt
1 teaspoon sugar
½ teaspoon pepper
½ teaspoon paprika
   Dash allspice or cloves
6 carrots, scraped
1 pound (18 to 24
   count) small white
   onions
4 medium-sized
   potatoes, peeled

In Dutch oven, brown cubed chuck in butter. Add boiling water, Worcestershire sauce, garlic, onion, bay leaf and seasonings. Cover and simmer 1 hour, stirring occasionally. Remove bay leaf and garlic. Cut carrots into 1½-inch chunks, leave onions whole, and cut potatoes into large-sized chunks. Add carrots, onions and potatoes to stew. Cover, simmer 30 minutes more. Serves 6 to 8.

Spear whole clove of garlic with toothpick for easy removal. Editor.

Mary Hall Carter, BJ '77
Houston

Football Season Stew

2 pounds stew meat,
   cubed
1 can (16 oz.) peas or
   whole kernel corn
1 cup carrots, sliced
2 onions, quartered
1 teaspoon salt
¼ teaspoon pepper
1 can (10¾ oz.) tomato
   soup
1 soup can water
3 medium-sized
   potatoes, cubed

Combine all ingredients in large, tightly covered casserole. Bake 5 hours at 275°. Serves 6 to 8.

Louise Buckner Milburn, BBA '48
Odessa

"Texas Orange" Stew

2 cups dried lima beans
Vegetable oil
1½ pounds beef stew meat
5 cups water
2 cans (16 oz. each)
    whole tomatoes,
    pureed
2 cups uncooked
    cabbage, grated
2 cups canned whole
    new potatoes,
    quartered
Salt and pepper to
    taste

Cover lima beans with water and set aside overnight. In Dutch oven brown meat in small amount of oil. Add water and lima beans (drained). Cover and simmer 2 hours. Add tomatoes, cabbage and potatoes. Season to taste. Bring to boil, simmer 30 minutes. Other ingredients, such as "orange-colored carrots" may be added. Serves 6.

Judith Morrison Martin, BA '77 BJ '77
Houston

Chili De Sangre Anaranjada

2 pounds coarse ground
    beef
3 pounds pork
    tenderloin, diced
¼ cup comino (cumin
    seeds)
2 tablespoons cilantro
    seeds (whole
    coriander)
6 cloves garlic, minced
1 tablespoon oregano
½ cup Ron Oso Negro
    Superior (dark rum)
36 pods El Paso Valley
    chile peppers (dried
    red peppers)
¼ cup masa harina

Combine beef and pork and brown in iron skillet. Grind cumin in spice grinder at least 2 times. Repeat for coriander. Add garlic, oregano and all spices to the meat mixture. Add Oso Negro and mix well. Marinate overnight. Remove all seeds from red chile peppers. Cover pods with water, boil 20 minutes. Pour hot chile water into blender and puree. Strain skin from puree; discard skin. (If no blender available, do as the Mexicans do: scrape the red chile pulp off the pods with a knife.) Mix seasoned meat with red sauce. Add salt to taste. Simmer until thickened. Serves 20.

SPECIAL INSTRUCTIONS: No beans! No onions! Add masa harina only if you're not person enough for the straight stuff! (Or if you want it thicker.) CAUTION: Red chile can blister tender hands. So, rubber gloves are advisable, or wash hands well before touching eyes or skin.

"This recipe has never been written down. In fact, family tradition says this chili can't be made from a written recipe. So, if it doesn't work, have an Aggie over."

Humboldt C. Mandell, Jr., BS '57
Seabrook

Texas Prison System Chili

May you never have to eat any of this behind bars.

25 pounds coarse ground
    beef
½ pound cumin
¼ pound chili powder
⅛ pound paprika
2 handsful crushed dry
    red pepper
    (optional)
¼ to ½ pound finely
    chopped garlic

Combine all ingredients in hot cooking container and close tight. Allow to cook 15 minutes at medium high heat before stirring once. When meat has heated enough to change color, stir and simmer 30 to 40 minutes. Do not add water or any other ingredients. Correct seasoning to desired strength. If you desire to thicken the chili, add necessary amount of cracker meal.

George J. Beto, MA '44 PhD '55
Huntsville

Texas Chili

The smell of this chili cooking brought my family running.

3 pounds lean beef
¼ cup salad oil
6 cups water
2 bay leaves
6 tablespoons chili
    powder
1 tablespoon salt
10 cloves garlic, minced
1 teaspoon comino seeds
1 teaspoon oregano
    leaves, crushed
½ teaspoon red pepper
¼ teaspoon pepper
1 tablespoon sugar
3 tablespoons sweet
    Hungarian paprika
1 tablespoon dried
    onion flakes
3 tablespoons flour
6 tablespoons cornmeal

In a 6-quart saucepan, sear beef (cubed or coarsely ground) in salad oil until beef color is gray, not brown. Add water, bay leaves, chili powder, salt, garlic, comino seeds, oregano, red pepper, pepper, sugar, paprika and onion flakes. Simmer, covered, 2 hours. Cool. Refrigerate overnight so flavors will mellow. Remove top layer of solidified fat. Reheat. With a little cold water make a paste of flour and cornmeal. Add paste to chili. To obtain a smooth texture, cook and stir 5 to 7 minutes after thickening has been added. Remove bay leaves before serving. Serves 6.

Shirley Coin Kleiman, BBA '47
Victoria

Home Drug Chili
Cafe fare around the campus in the 30's.

¼ cup olive oil
3 pounds chili meat
3 or 4 cups hot water
6 tablespoons chili
    powder
3 teaspoons salt
10 cloves garlic, chopped
1 tablespoon ground
    comino seeds
1 tablespoon oregano or
    marjoram
1 teaspoon red pepper
1 tablespoon sugar
3 tablespoons paprika

THICKENING:

3 tablespoons flour
6 tablespoons cornmeal
    or masa harina
1 cup water V-8 juice

At high heat in a 6-quart iron skillet heat oil until it smokes. Add chili meat and sear well. Add hot water, simmer 1½ hours. Add seasonings, simmer 30 minutes more.

THICKENING: Combine flour, cornmeal or masa harina and water into smooth paste. Stir into chili. Stir and simmer until thickened, about 10 minutes. This chili goes well over 2 or 3 tamales per serving, topped with chopped onions.

William K. Miller, BA '34 LLB '34
Austin

Five Alarm Chili
Serve with the remaining 6-pack, a green salad, and hot cornbread.

3 pounds beef stew
    meat, trimmed lean
    and cubed
1 pound lean beef,
    ground round
3 fresh jalapeños,
    chopped
1 clove garlic, minced
2 tablespoons cumin
2 tablespoons chili
    powder
1 tablespoon salt
1 teaspoon pepper
1 can (15 oz.) tomato
    sauce
1 can (12 oz.) beer
1 onion, chopped
V-8 juice

Brown the cubed stew meat and ground round. Add jalapeños, garlic, cumin, chili peppers, salt and pepper. Mix well; add tomato sauce, beer and onion. Bring to boil, reduce heat, and simmer chili, covered, 4 hours. Chili may be frozen in airtight containers and reheated with ¼ cup water over low heat. Serves 6 to 8.

David M. Gould, BA '76
Houston

Quick Chili

Quick, easy, and looks like a regular bowl of "Texas Red"

1 pound ground beef
1 onion, chopped
1 clove garlic, minced
2 tablespoons butter
  Salt and pepper to
    taste
1 tablespoon chili
    powder
½ can (6 oz. size) tomato
    paste or 1½ cups
    tomato juice or
    1 can (10¾ oz.)
    tomato soup
2 cups water
1 can (16 oz.) pinto or
    kidney beans

Brown meat, onions and garlic in butter. Season with salt and pepper. Add chili powder, tomato paste, water and beans. Simmer 10 minutes. If using tomato juice or tomato soup, decrease water accordingly so chili will not be soupy. Serves 6 to 8.

Amalee Turek Jones, BA '26
Grand Rapids, Michigan

Variation: *Omit tomato paste and water. Substitute 1 can (14 oz.) tomatoes and 1 can (10 oz.) tomatoes and green chile peppers. Cook 1 hour or in slow cooker for 8 hours.*

Judy Walker Mayo, BS '71
Dallas

Venison Chili

Are you game for this?

2 pounds lean venison
4 tablespoons oil
1 medium-sized onion,
    finely chopped
4 cloves garlic, minced
2 cups tomato juice or
    2 cups canned
    tomatoes
4 tablespoons chili
    powder
½ teaspoon salt
½ teaspoon ground
    cumin
½ teaspoon oregano
1 can (10¾ oz.)
    consomme

Trim 2 pounds lean venison from shoulder or tag ends of the ribeye. Cut into 1-inch cubes. Heat oil in heavy Dutch oven, add meat and brown slightly. Reduce heat; add onion, garlic, tomato juice, chili powder, salt, cumin, oregano and consomme. Simmer 1 hour. Add boiling water if the liquid reduces too much. Serves 4.

Maurine Redfearn Bartos, BS '57
Waco

The 1940s

Vegetables

After Pearl Harbor, December 7, 1941, campus activities assumed a new look. Shown here is part of the first graduating class at the Naval Flight Preparatory School, established in January 1943.

$\mathcal{T}$he 1940s were marked by the Second World War, the firing of UT President Homer Price Rainey, and the return of large numbers of veterans to the campus after the War. The War claimed the lives of many students, including that of J. Ward Fouts, the 1940-1941 president of the student body.

Homer Price Rainey became president of the University in the fall of 1939 after an eighteen-month search by the Board of Regents. The general consensus was that he would lead the University to the heights of greatness mandated in the 1876 Constitution of Texas. On November 1, 1944, he was fired by the Regents in a dispute about academic freedom, and students and faculty members demonstrated in protest. The reverberations of the controversy troubled the University for many years. Theophilus S. Painter was appointed acting president and became president in 1946.

The building program, slowed in the 1940s because of the War, picked up speed. The Music Building on the South Mall, the Petroleum Engineering Building, the E. P. Schoch Laboratories, and the Student Health Center were added. The University, under a $1-a-year lease agreement with the War Assets Administration in 1946, acquired the multi-million dollar magnesium plant, eight miles northwest of Austin, which subsequently became the Balcones Research Center. Use of the plant for research released valuable space on campus for teaching.

Life magazine featured the entire University football team on its cover on November 17, 1941. On the following Saturday, a Baylor team tied Texas 7 - 7 in Waco, and TCU later beat the Longhorns 14 - 7. Gloom filled the campus.

In many ways, the University felt the cultural impact of the Second World War. Female enrollment was greater than that of male. The total number of students was not quite 7,000 in 1945, 3,800 of which were women and 3,174 were men. A woman was elected *Texan* editor in 1944, and another became president of the student body in 1945 when the male president resigned. Dim-out regulations darkened the Tower for two years, and the Tower chimes were silent for a while when the University had no carillonneur. Gasoline and sugar rationing changed the life styles of students and faculty alike. Victory gardens were popular; planting a garden was patriotic, and canning and preserving the vegetables were common undertakings. Student government conducted bond-selling campaigns. Many students married before the young men went off to the service. Heretofore, few married students were enrolled at the University, but being married was no longer unusual or frowned upon.

The manpower shortage upset one of the strongest University traditions in 1944 when women students were admitted to the Longhorn band. But even in wartime the break in tradition was only partial: women did not wear uniforms or march in the band at athletic events. They played only at band concerts. Erosion of the all-male tradition would be gradual.

A Navy V-12 Unit was established on the campus in 1943, and a V-5 program was in existence for a while. In 1945, a Reserve Officers Training Corps (ROTC) was established with the same status as other departments in the University. All three units of the armed forces—Army, Navy, and Air Force— were represented. Young men had the option to graduate out of a Reserve Corps and leave the University in a normal four-year period with both a degree and a commission. Military uniforms were common on the campus as students drilled and attended classes.

Students and University supporters were aroused in 1945 when a legislator proposed a constitutional amendment that would divide income from the University Permanent Fund among all state-supported institutions of higher learning. The proposal was defeated, though it would be heard again.

In 1946-47 the famous Heman Sweatt case, which opened the University to its first Black, began litigation. Denied entry in 1946, Sweatt began pursuing his rights through the courts.

Counseling and advising facilities, particularly for freshmen, were improved. In 1946 student government made a thorough investigation of the Student Health Service, comparing it with other university health services and ultimately submitting the report to University officials. The study resulted in expanded health services, including a new building.

The University Tea House, operated by the Home Economics Department, opened on the campus in 1939 and became one of the favorite eating places in Austin. It was one of only ten places in Texas listed in Duncan Hines' *Adventures in Good Eating*. Everything in the Tea House was designed to encourage pleasurable, relaxed dining: the view of Waller Creek, the flagstone floor, the twin rock fireplaces flanked by massive Welsh cupboards, the generous use of copper accessories, and an old grandfather clock. Service was swift and was performed by white-jacketed student waiters. Food was well-prepared and reflected under-six-flags Texas tastes. French gumboes and creoles, Spanish-influenced Mexican foods, and Dixie dishes with plenty of hot breads were favorites. The Tea House was used as a Navy mess hall during the War, and later it became a convenience cafeteria until it was removed in 1969.

Another special place was opened in Austin in 1945 by Chester and Mary Koock when they converted the Henry Faulk family home, Green Pastures, into what was to become one of Austin's finest restaurants. Austinites

238

and visitors to the capital city have always boasted the finest Mexican restaurants in Texas, and these, too, began to proliferate. One of the most popular was El Matamoros, established in 1947 at 504 East Avenue by Monroe Lopez.

As the War ended, hundreds of veterans returned to the campus under the new GI Bill of Rights. Consequently enrollment escalated to an all-time high of more than 17,000 by 1947. University officials obtained army barracks and moved them to the Brackenridge Tract near the Miller Dam as "temporary" housing for married students. The University entered Shack Era II when 14 new temporary buildings were moved to the campus in 1947 from Camp Wallace, near Galveston, as part of a Federal Works Administration project. The buildings housed 36 classrooms, four chemistry laboratories, a Health Service annex, a cafeteria, an engineering workshop, faculty offices, and (with singular appropriateness) the Veterans' Administration.

A $40,000 lighting system was installed in 1947 on the intramural playing fields (where Jester Center now stands). The Interfraternity Council contributed $11,000 to the project, and the Athletic Council gave the balance, approximately $29,000. Students celebrated at a special dedication program.

In these pre-television days, Alpha Phi Omega and the Texas Union co-sponsored Grid-Graph parties, play-by-play accounts of out-of-town football games. The Grid-Graph was a large board marked to resemble a football field, and the position of the ball at a given time was shown by a small spotlight shining through the translucent screen on which the field was marked. Large groups of students gathered at the Union or Gregory Gymnasium or in front of the University Co-Op to "watch" an out-of-town game.

The Round-Up parade of 1947 was spectacular; it featured 54 floats in four divisions: most beautiful, most educational, most unique, and most comical. Led by the Longhorn Band, the parade wound down Guadalupe, past the Capitol, down Congress, to the Colorado River bridge. Following the band were State and University officials and visiting and local sweethearts riding in convertibles. Cowboys, celebrating their twenty-fifth anniversary, had a prominent place in the parade. That night a capacity crowd of 6,500 packed Gregory Gymnasium for the climax of the celebration, announcement of the new University sweetheart. At 10 p.m. guests began dancing to big band music.

Student government was active and important on the campus in the late 1940s. Student elections were marked by a revival of the old-time pre-war spirit and noisy gaiety. They became more elaborate when the Student Assembly voted to increase the campaign spending limit from $10 to $15 per candidate. Preceding elections, Drag and campus alike were scenes of chorus girls, wheelbarrows, battered cars, baby carriages, monkeys, and noisy loud speakers. The American Veteran's Committee sponsored Stump Speaking, while Orange Jackets, APO's, and Mortar Board members officiated at the polls.

As the decade ended, many young men were involved in yet another war, this time in Korea.

Stars and Stripes Jubilee

Texas Brisket - p. 285
Cuban Black Beans - p. 242
Sauerkraut Salad - p. 382
Pull-Apart Vegetable Bread - p. 21
Spirited Marble Cake - p. 73

Korean Chicken - p. 306
Swedish Potato Pancakes - p. 258
Mexican Green Beans - p. 244
Irish Soda Bread - p. 20
Dutch Baby - p. 28

Italian Shrimp - p. 315
Squash And Things - p. 250
Asparagus Vinaigrette - p. 241
Red Hot Salad - p. 395
Blueberry Kuchen - p. 40

Asparagus Vinaigrette

1½ pounds green or white
    asparagus
Salt

VINAIGRETTE
DRESSING:

2 tablespoons white
    wine vinegar
Salt
Pepper
1 tablespoon Dijon
    mustard
6 tablespoons salad oil
2 hard-cooked eggs,
    chopped
2 medium-sized shallots,
    finely chopped
1 tablespoon chopped
    fresh parsley

Snap asparagus stems to remove tough ends. Submerge in water, set aside. In bottom of double boiler, bring 3 inches water to a boil, tie the asparagus in bundles and stand them in the water, tips up. Cover by inverting inner double boiler pan over standing bundled asparagus. Boil 8 minutes for green asparagus, 10 minutes for white asparagus. Drain thoroughly.

DRESSING: Add salt, pepper and mustard to vinegar. Slowly add oil, whisking until thick. Fold in eggs, shallots and parsley. Arrange the asparagus on serving platter. Spoon dressing over center of asparagus, leaving tips and ends uncoated. Serve warm or at room temperature. Serves 4.

Connie Carpenter, BBA '80
Houston

Sylva Maley's Baked Beans

2 cans (31 oz. each)
    pork and beans,
    undrained*
1 large-sized onion,
    chopped
½ cup brown sugar
1 tablespoon chili
    powder
1 tablespoon Worcester-
    shire sauce
6 strips bacon

Combine all ingredients except bacon. Place 3 strips bacon in 3-quart casserole. Pour in bean mixture. Place remaining bacon strips on top of beans. Bake 4 to 6 hours at 250°. Serves 8 to 10. *If drier beans are preferred, drain the beans before using.

Mary Ann Maley, BA '54
Smithville

Cuban Black Beans

1 pound black beans
5 cups water
½ jalapeño pepper
1 bay leaf
  Olive or corn oil
1 green pepper, diced
1 medium-sized onion,
  chopped
1 to 4 (as desired) cloves
  garlic, minced
1 can (6 oz.) tomato
  paste
1 teaspoon cumin
  (comino)
20 chopped green olives
1 can (2 oz.) chopped
  pimientos
  Salt to taste
1 tablespoon sugar

Wash black beans and place in pan with water to cover; soak overnight. Drain, place in pressure cooker and cover with 5 cups water. Add the pepper half and bay leaf. Cook 45 minutes at 15 pounds pressure. Cool. Cover bottom of frying pan with olive or corn oil. Saute pepper, onion and garlic. Stir in tomato paste, cook 1 minute. Add cumin, cook 3 minutes more. Stir in olives and pimientos. Add contents of frying pan to beans, salt to taste and simmer 1½ hours or until tender. Add sugar to neutralize acidity of peppers and stir. Serves 6 to 8.

John K. Dannelley, '73
Amarillo

Variation: *Omit tomato paste, olives and pimientos. Add 1 cup diced ham and ½ cup dark rum before final simmering. To serve, puree in blender 3 cups bean mixture. Return and combine with remaining mixture. Serve in hot soup bowls, garnish with sieved hard-cooked eggs, a dollop of sour cream, and Lake Caddo Relish (See Index).*

Gladys Bravenec Howard, BS '55
Tyler

Variation: *Substitute green pepper for jalapeño and omit tomato paste. Add ½ teaspoon oregano and 1 teaspoon vinegar. Serve with steamed rice.*

Jack Wrather, BA '39
Los Angeles, California

MEXICAN BEANS. Wash and sort 2 cups dried pinto beans, add water to cover, soak overnight. To cook, drain, then cover with fresh water. Cook 6 hours. Saute 1 small-sized onion (chopped) in oil until soft, mash 1 cup cooked beans and add to onion with 1½ tablespoons chili powder mixed with ½ cup water and 1 clove minced garlic. Add 1 teaspoon whole comino seed. Add salt and pepper to taste and ½ cup canned tomatoes. Add this mixture to beans and simmer an additional hour.
Serve with Corn Pone and longneck bottles of beer. Editor.

Mary Hall Carter, BJ '77
Houston

Penelope's Bean Bake
Very tasty, good even cold!

2 cans (16 oz. each)
    pork and beans
1 large-sized apple,
    chopped
¼ cup raisins
½ cup chopped onion
½ cup brown sugar
¼ cup sweet relish
1 tablespoon prepared
    mustard
½ cup catsup
4 strips bacon, fried
    and crumbled

Combine all ingredients in a 2-quart casserole.
Bake uncovered 1½ hours at 250°. Serves 6.

Penny Porter Helms, BFA '66
Austin

WEANIE LOTTA. Combine 1 can (16 oz.) pork and beans with ¼ teaspoon dry mustard, 2 tablespoons brown sugar, ¼ cup combined catsup and barbecue sauce. Add 1 package (12 oz.) beef franks (cut into bite-sized pieces) and 1 chopped onion. Place in a 9-inch pan and cover with 1 cup grated cheese. Bake 30 minutes at 350°. Serves 4.

Dana Humble Dodson, BS '77
and Dwain Dodson, BS '76 MS '77
Lake Jackson

Green Bean Casserole

1¼ cup mayonnaise
1 medium-sized onion,
    grated
1 teaspoon dry mustard
1 teaspoon Worcester-
    shire sauce
1 teaspoon salt
1 can (8 oz.) water
    chestnuts, drained
    and sliced
2 cans (16 oz. each)
    Blue Lake green
    beans, whole
1 cup grated Cheddar
    cheese

Combine all ingredients except beans and cheese. In buttered 2-quart casserole layer beans, then mayonnaise mixture, then cheese. Repeat layers ending with cheese. Bake at 325° until hot and bubbly, about 30 minutes. Serves 6 to 8.

Eleanor Ann Van Zandt Gerrard, BA '42
Victoria

Mexican Green Beans
Excellent with turkey and dressing

4 cans (16 oz. each)
   green beans,
   drained
1 can (8 oz.) sliced
   water chestnuts,
   drained
1 can (10¾ oz.) cream
   of mushroom soup
1 jar (8 oz.) jalapeño
   Cheese Whiz

Combine beans and water chestnuts in buttered 3-quart casserole. Heat together soup and Cheese Whiz in saucepan until cheese melts. Pour cheese mixture over beans and water chestnuts. Mix well. Bake 30 minutes at 350°. Serves 12 to 15.

Kathy Fife, BS '80
Austin

TAKE A WOK, CHINESE STYLE. Thinly slice and cut diagonally 1 pound fresh green beans and 2 cups celery. In wok, heat 2 tablespoons salad oil. Add beans, saute 1 minute at high heat, stirring constantly. Add celery, saute 1 minute more. Add ½ cup chicken broth. Cover and cook 2 minutes. Add 1 teaspoon cornstarch mixed with 2 tablespoons cold water. Toss vegetables thoroughly. Season with salt and pepper. Sometimes, substitute fresh mushrooms for the celery and fresh asparagus for the green beans. Serves 6.

Shirley Coin Kleiman, BBA '48
Victoria

Beans In Sour Sauce

1 can (16 oz.) French-
   cut green beans
1 small-sized onion,
   chopped
1 tablespoon bacon
   grease
1 tablespoon flour
1 tablespoon sugar
¼ cup vinegar
½ cup liquid from
   beans
½ teaspoon salt
   Pepper to taste

Drain beans, reserve liquid. Saute onion in grease. Stir in flour and sugar. When smooth, gradually add vinegar and liquid. Add beans, salt and pepper. Heat thoroughly before serving. Serves 4.

Edith Mae Sanders Livingston, BBA '41
Austin

244

Zesty Green Bean Casserole

2 tablespoons butter or
   margarine, melted
1½ tablespoons flour
½ cup milk
1 can (10 oz.) tomatoes
   and green chile
   peppers drained
   (reserve liquid)
½ pound American cheese,
   cubed
2 cans (16 oz. each)
   French-style green
   beans, drained

Combine butter and flour, cook over low heat until bubbly. Gradually add milk, cook until smooth and thickened, stirring constantly. Add liquid from tomatoes and chiles. Add cheese, stirring until melted. Combine sauce, beans, tomatoes and chiles. Pour into lightly buttered 1½-quart casserole. Bake 20 minutes at 450° or until bubbly. Serves 6.

John T. Ryder, BA '68
San Antonio

Broccoli Mold

3 packages (10 oz. each)
   chopped, frozen
   broccoli
1 can (10¾ oz.)
   consommé
2 packets unflavored
   gelatin
4 hard-cooked eggs,
   chopped
¾ cup mayonnaise
1½ teaspoon salt
4 teaspoons Worcester-
   shire sauce
4 teaspoons lemon juice
   Dash Tabasco

Cook broccoli according to package directions. Drain. Soften gelatin in small amount of consommé. Heat remaining consommé, add softened gelatin and stir well. Combine all ingredients and pour into mold, or pour into bread pan and slice to serve. Serves 10 to 12.

NOTE: Lightly brush mold with mayonnaise before pouring in mixture.

Trudy Iverson Kokernot, BS '71
Boerne

245

Broccoli Souffle

1 tablespoon chopped
   onion
2 tablespoons butter
1 package (10 oz.)
   frozen chopped
   broccoli, thawed
   and drained
3 eggs, beaten
½ cup milk
½ cup cream
1 teaspoon salt
   Dash pepper
   Dash nutmeg
   Paprika

Saute onion in butter. Mix all ingredients, except paprika and pour into buttered 1½-quart casserole. Sprinkle with paprika. Bake in hot water bath 45 minutes at 350°. Serves 6.

Lena Pettit Hickman, BA '15
Austin

Almond Broccoli Casserole With Cheese Sauce

1½ pounds fresh broccoli
   or 2 packages
   (10 oz. each) frozen
   broccoli spears
2 tablespoons butter
2 tablespoons flour
1½ cups milk
¾ cup grated cheese
½ teaspoon salt
¼ teaspoon pepper
¼ cup toasted chopped
   almonds
4 strips crisp bacon,
   crumbled
½ cup buttered bread
   crumbs

Cook broccoli until slightly tender. Drain, place in greased 1½-quart casserole. Prepare a sauce of butter, flour, milk, cheese, salt and pepper. Sprinkle broccoli with almonds, top with cheese sauce. Sprinkle casserole with bacon and crumbs. Bake 20 minutes at 350° or until bubbling. Serves 6.

Charlotte Curtis Henderson, BA '37
Baytown

Aunt Margaret's Broccoli Rice Casserole

2 packages (10 oz. each)
    frozen chopped
    broccoli
½ cup chopped onion
½ cup chopped celery
½ cup (1 stick) butter or
    margarine
1 cup cooked rice
1 can (10¾ oz.) cream
    of mushroom soup
1 can (10¾ oz.) cream
    of chicken soup
1 jar (8 oz.) Cheese
    Whiz

Cook broccoli according to package directions. Drain. Saute onion and celery in butter, combine with broccoli. Add rice, soups and Cheese Whiz. Place in buttered 3-quart casserole. Bake 30 minutes at 300°. Serves 8 to 10.

Barbara Koy, wife of Ernie Koy, BA '66
Bellville

Variation: *Use 1 cup each of celery and onion. Substitute cream of celery soup for both soups.*

Kittie Fae Robinson Jinkins, BS '19
Galveston

Variation: *Use only 1 package broccoli. Omit cream of chicken soup.*

Jan Bixler Bennett, BS '72
Houston

Variation: *Use only 1 package chopped broccoli, uncooked.*

Amy Purcell Powell, BS '55
Navasota

Variation: *Omit celery, increase onion to 2 large-sized and chopped, omit Cheese Whiz, top with 1 cup grated sharp Cheddar cheese and 1 cup bread crumbs.*

Peter S. Solito, '42
Houston

Marinated Broccoli

1 bunch fresh broccoli
1 cup salad oil
1 cup cider vinegar
1 tablespoon
    monosodium
    glutamate
1 tablespoon dill weed
1 teaspoon garlic salt
1 teaspoon salt

Remove stems from broccoli, peel and cut into strips. Separate tops into flowerets. Marinate broccoli in combined remaining ingredients 24 to 48 hours. Store in covered plastic or crockery dish and shake or stir occasionally. Drain 2 hours before serving. Serves 6.

Harriet Schmitt Livingston, BS '69
Fort Worth

Vegetables

German Red Cabbage
Very colorful and perfect with pork or venison roast

½ cup salad oil
1 onion, chopped
1 apple, chopped
2 to 3 pounds red
   cabbage, sliced
½ cup sugar
3 bay leaves
1 tablespoon salt
1 teaspoon pepper
Dash cinnamon
Dash cloves
½ cup white vinegar
2 cups beef bouillon

Heat oil, combine and add remaining ingredients. Cook at low heat 30 to 40 minutes, turning occasionally. Remove bay leaves before serving. Serves 10.

Mamie Strieber Shepperd, BJ '38
Odessa

Cheese Scalloped Carrots

12 carrots, scraped and
   sliced
¼ cup (½ stick) butter
1 onion, minced
3 tablespoons flour
1 teaspoon salt
¼ teaspoon dry mustard
2 cups milk
Pinch of pepper
¼ teaspoon celery salt
½ pound Cheddar cheese
   slices
1½ to 2 cups buttered
   fresh bread crumbs*

Cook carrots until tender in small amount of boiling water. Drain. Saute onion in butter 2 to 3 minutes; stir in flour, salt, mustard and milk. Cook, stirring until smooth. Add pepper and celery salt. In buttered 2-quart casserole, arrange layer of carrots, then layer of cheese slices. Repeat until both are used, ending with carrots. Cover with sauce. Sprinkle with bread crumbs. Bake, uncovered, 25 minutes at 350° or until golden. This recipe may be prepared early in day and refrigerated until baking time. If refrigerated, increase baking time to 35 to 45 minutes. Serves 8.

John T. Ryder, BA '68
San Antonio

See Index, Fresh Bread Crumbs.

248

Parsleyed Carrot Vichy

2 cups thinly sliced
    peeled carrots
½ cup boiling water
2 tablespoons butter
¼ teaspoon salt
1 teaspoon lemon juice
    Chopped parsley

Combine all ingredients except parsley in heavy saucepan, cover and simmer carrots until water is absorbed. Serve sprinkled with chopped parsley. Serves 4.

Audrey Fritz Cooper, wife of Richard Cooper, BBA '56
San Antonio

Shoestring Carrots

12 medium to large-sized
    carrots
    Salt
¼ cup dark brown
    sugar, firmly
    packed
¼ cup butter
    Dash ground nutmeg
    Salt to taste

Peel carrots and cut into julienne slices using a sharp knife or using the French-fry disc of food processor. (The julienne disc cuts too fine.) The strips should be matchstick size. Briefly steam, or boil covered in a small amount of salted water. Drain, toss with remaining ingredients. Serves 4 to 6.

Merle Tooke Lewis, BA '53 MLS '70
Waterville, Maine

FOOD PROCESSOR CARROT-CELERY MIX: Cut 6 peeled carrots and 8 ribs celery into feeder-tube lengths. Boil in chicken broth to cover until softened but still crisp. Drain, cool, slice with French-fry blade. Add 4 to 6 chopped green onions. Marinate overnight in a vinaigrette dressing. Serve as appetizers or on lettuce leaves as a salad, or as a cold vegetable.

Sandra Lauer, wife of John Lauer, LLB '59
Kentfield, California

Carrot and Squash Casserole

6 carrots
6 yellow squash
3 tablespoons chopped
   onion
¼ cup (½ stick) butter
2 tablespoons flour

Scrub carrots and unpeeled squash and cut into large-sized pieces. Cook in water to cover. Drain and puree. Saute onion in butter until limp, add flour, stir. Add vegetables and beat mixture until well mixed. Pour into 2-quart casserole, bake 1 hour at 350°. Serves 6 to 8.

Carolyn Kongabel Vance, BS '55
Houston

SQUASH AND THINGS. Cook 6 to 8 peeled and sliced tender yellow squash and 1 tablespoon instant minced onion in salted water. Drain well. Add 4 tablespoons (½ stick) butter or margarine, 1 can (10 oz.) tomatoes and green chile peppers, 1 cup grated Cheddar cheese, 1 teaspoon salt and ½ teaspoon pepper. Stir, pour into buttered 2-quart casserole. Top squash with crushed saltine crackers and 2 tablespoons melted butter. Bake 30 minutes at 350°. Serves 6.

Shirley Coin Kleiman, BBA '48
Victoria

Aunt Jane's
Cauliflower Mountain
A hasty, tasty microwave classic

1 medium-sized
   cauliflower
½ cup mayonnaise
¼ cup prepared mustard
1 teaspoon horseradish
   (optional)
1 cup grated sharp
   Cheddar cheese

Wash cauliflower, place in glass dish with stem side up. Microwave at high setting 5 or 6 minutes until center of stem is soft, not mushy. Remove and turn right side up. Combine mayonnaise, mustard and horseradish. Spread over top of cauliflower (as if frosting a cake). Cover with cheese and microwave at high setting 2 or 3 minutes until cheese is completely melted and bubbly. Serve immediately. Serves 4 to 6.

Carolyn Frost Keenan, BS '76 MA '78
Houston

Colorful Corn Casserole

¼ cup butter
¼ cup flour
2 teaspoons salt
1 tablespoon sugar
1¾ cup milk
1 onion, chopped
½ cup chopped green
   onions
3 cups fresh corn
   kernels or 1½
   packages (10 oz.
   each) frozen corn
   kernels
3 eggs, beaten
Dash garlic powder
1 can (2 oz.) chopped
   pimientos
Jalapeño juice

Melt butter; add flour, salt and sugar; cook until bubbly. Add milk gradually and cook until mixture has thickened. Stir in onions and corn. Remove from heat; add eggs, garlic powder, pimientos and 1 tablespoon juice from jar of jalapeños. Pour into well-buttered 9-inch square casserole. Bake 45 minutes at 325° or until slightly browned. Serves 8.

Penny Porter Helms, BFA '66
Austin

NEVER FAIL SOUTHERN CORN PUDDING. Beat 2 eggs slightly. Add 1 can (17 oz.) cream-style corn, ¾ cup milk, 2 tablespoons flour, and 2 tablespoons sugar. Stir thoroughly. Season with salt and pepper to taste. Pour into greased 2-quart casserole and bake 1 hour at 350° or until pudding is set. Serves 6 to 8.

Eleanor Ann Van Zandt Gerrard, BA '42
Victoria

Corn Casserole
Great for company

4 eggs, beaten
¾ cup milk
4 tablespoons sugar
4 tablespoons flour
2 cans (12 oz. each)
   yellow whole
   kernel corn, drained
2 tablespoons butter

Combine all ingredients except butter. Pour into buttered 1½-quart casserole. Dot with butter. Bake 45 minutes at 375°. Serves 8.

Margaret Blair, BS '74
Phoenix, Arizona

Variation: *Substitute 2 cans cream-style corn for whole kernel corn and add 1 egg. Use 1 stick butter and 1 can (13 oz.) evaporated milk. Bake in a water bath.*

Linda Hughes Sharkey, BS '71 MED '73
St. Croix, Virgin Islands

Vegetables

Family Dinner Special Corn Casserole

4 tablespoons (½ stick) butter
1 large-sized onion, chopped
2 cans (12 oz. each) whole kernel corn, drained
2 tomatoes, peeled and chopped
Salt and pepper to taste
3 tablespoons milk or cream
1 cup grated sharp Cheddar cheese

Saute onion in butter until limp. Add corn. Simmer 3 to 5 minutes more. Add tomatoes. Season to taste. Cook 10 minutes to reduce liquid. Glaze baking dish with milk or cream, add sauteed ingredients and top with cheese. Bake 30 minutes at 350°. Serves 6 to 8.

Susan Weber Munson, BFA '67
William B. Munson, IV, LLB '67
Denison

MARY'S EGGPLANT SOUFFLE. Cook 1 eggplant, drain, peel and mash. Add 2 tablespoons flour, 2 tablespoons butter, salt, pepper and garlic salt to taste. Combine 2 egg yolks, beaten, with 2 tablespoons catsup and 1 cup milk. Stir into eggplant mixture. Add 1 cup grated Longhorn cheese. Fold in 2 egg whites, whipped to stiff peaks. Bake in buttered 2-quart souffle dish 45 minutes at 350°. Serves 4.

Edith Royal, wife of former UT Football Coach Darrell Royal
Austin

Squash Corn Casserole
Wonderful side dish, especially with Mexican food

3 pounds squash
1 can (16 oz.) cream-style corn
4 eggs, slightly beaten
1 onion, chopped
1 small-sized green pepper, chopped
2 tablespoons butter, melted
1¼ teaspoons salt
¼ teaspoon pepper
1 cup grated Cheddar cheese
Dash paprika

Steam unpeeled squash until tender. Cut into chunks. Combine squash, corn and eggs. Saute onion and pepper in butter until golden brown. Add onion and pepper mixture to squash. Add salt and pepper. Pour into buttered 2-quart casserole, sprinkle with cheese and paprika. Bake, uncovered, 40 minutes at 350° or until light and bubbly. Cool 15 minutes before serving. Serves 8.

Roxie Potter, BS '75
New York, New York

252

SCALLOPED EGGPLANT. Peel 1 medium-sized eggplant. Slice and cook in salted water until tender. Drain well and mash. Add 2 tablespoons butter, 1 tablespoon onion, 2 eggs (beaten), 1 cup milk and salt and pepper to taste. Place in buttered 8-inch baking dish, top with buttered cracker crumbs and bake 30 minutes at 350°. Serves 4.

Nell Jones Herndon, BA '30
Bastrop

Half Century Eggplant
This recipe dates from late '20s

2 small-sized eggplants
  (about 2 cups)
1 small-sized onion,
  minced
2 tablespoons bacon
  grease
1 cup soft bread
  crumbs*
1 egg, slightly beaten
  Dash sage
  Dash red pepper
  Salt and pepper to
  taste

Drop whole eggplants into boiling water and cook until tender. Cool. Peel and finely chop. Saute onion in bacon grease, add eggplant and remaining ingredients. Combine thoroughly. Pour into buttered 1-quart casserole. Bake, uncovered, 1 hour at 350°. Serves 6.

Bessie Kilgore Merner, BA '30 MA '32
Faribault, Minnesota

Variation: *Make topping of ½ cup buttered bread crumbs, ½ cup Parmesan cheese, 1 teaspoon dried parsley flakes and dash paprika. Bake, uncovered, 30 minutes at 375°.*

Amy Lois Porter Oden, BA '21
Tyler

*FRESH BREAD CRUMBS. To prepare fresh bread crumbs use 2- to 4-day-old bread, crusts trimmed. Pull apart with fork into small pieces or chop coarsely in food processor. To make ½ cup buttered bread crumbs, use 2 bread slices (crusts trimmed) and place ¼-inch pat of butter in center of each slice. Fold corners of bread to center to make small square. Drop into food processor, use quick on-off procedure. Add dried parsley flakes, paprika, and Parmesan cheese to make seasoned crumbs. Editor.

Fried Eggplant

1 medium-sized
  eggplant, unpeeled
1 egg
1 cup heavy cream
2 cups soya flour*
  Salt and pepper to
  taste
5 cups peanut oil

Slice eggplant into ½-inch French-fry fingers. Beat egg until frothy, add cream and mix thoroughly. Combine soya flour, salt and pepper. Heat peanut oil to 365°. Dip eggplant in cream mixture, then in soya mixture. Drop fingers, 1 at a time, into oil until surface is full. Do not fry too many fingers at one time as the fingers should bubble to the top. Eggplant should be a golden brown after 3 or 4 minute's frying. Drain on paper towel, sprinkle salt over fingers while still hot. Serves 3 or 4.

*NOTE: Soya flour has three times the protein of regular flour and truly compliments the eggplant flavor. Soya flour is available at health food stores.

Gem Meacham, BA '72
Odessa

Mushroom Casserole

1 pound large-sized
  mushrooms,
  thickly sliced
2 tablespoons butter or
  margarine
1 cup sour cream
2 tablespoons flour
  Garlic salt
  Salt and pepper
1 tablespoon dried
  onion flakes
1 tablespoon chopped
  chives
½ cup grated Cheddar
  cheese
½ cup grated Monterrey
  Jack cheese
  Red pepper

Saute mushrooms in butter until slightly tender. Place in well-buttered baking dish. Combine sour cream, flour, garlic salt, salt and pepper to taste, dried onions and chives. Simmer until heated but do not boil. Pour over mushrooms. Top with cheeses and red pepper (sprinkled ever so lightly!) Bake 15 minutes at 350°. Serves 8.

Twyla Lynn Tranfaglia, BA '73 MLS '74
El Paso

Sauteed Mushrooms

2 pounds fresh
   mushrooms
¼ cup chopped onion
4 tablespoons (½ stick)
   butter or margarine
⅓ cup sherry
2 tablespoons pineapple
   juice
1 tablespoon soy sauce
¼ teaspoon garlic salt

Clean mushrooms. If very large-sized
mushrooms, slice in half. Saute onion in
butter until transparent. Add remaining
ingredients and mushrooms. Cook, covered, 5
minutes. Then cook, uncovered, 10 minutes.
Serves 6 to 8.

Emrys Ann Ryder Wuest, '60
Seguin

Hominy
With Green Chile Peppers
Great with steak

2 cans (20 oz. each)
   white hominy
2 cans (4 oz. each)
   chopped green chile
   peppers
Sour cream
Butter
Salt
Pepper
1 cup grated
   Monterrey Jack
   cheese
1 carton (8 oz.)
   whipping cream

Drain and rinse hominy. Butter a 3-quart
casserole. Divide hominy into 3 portions.
Layer 1 portion in bottom of casserole. Dot
with sour cream and butter and season with
salt and pepper. Add a layer of green chile
peppers. Repeat layers, ending with hominy on
top. Pour whipping cream over layers. Cover
with shredded cheese. Bake 25 to 30 minutes at
350° or until lightly browned. Serves 6 to 8.

Virginia Stanberry Williams, '35
Austin

Variation: *Omit 1 can green chile peppers, add
2 teaspoons chili powder. Add ½ chopped
onion sauteed in 2 tablespoons butter. Use 8
ounces sour cream, omit whipping cream.
Substitute sharp Cheddar cheese for Monterrey
Jack.*

Priscilla Flawn, wife of UT President Peter Flawn
Austin

Sula's Stir-Fry Okra
Tender, crisp, delicious—the only way to cook okra

2 cups thinly sliced
   fresh okra
1 tomato, peeled
¼ cup sliced green
   onion
1 teaspoon fresh lemon
   juice
¼ teaspoon thyme
   leaves, crushed
1 teaspoon salt
   Dash pepper
1 tablespoon salad oil
2 tablespoons butter

Trim stem ends of okra and slice as thinly as possible. Quarter tomato, then slice quarters lengthwise into thin wedges. Thinly slice onion, using both white and green parts. Squeeze lemon juice to measure. Combine seasonings and add to lemon juice. NOTE: All ingredients must be prepared before beginning to cook. In wok or large skillet, heat oil and butter. Add all ingredients, tossing and stirring constantly over high heat. Cook 3 to 5 minutes if using wok, or cook 5 to 8 minutes in skillet. Serve immediately. Serves 4.

Jane Cornick Jamison, BS '66
Austin

Cheese-In-Okra

1 tablespoon butter
2 cups halved cherry
   tomatoes
1 package (10 oz.)
   frozen sliced okra
1 cup chopped green
   pepper
1 can (16 oz.) cream-
   style corn
4 green onions,
   green tops chopped
   and white bulb
   minced
   Seasoned salt and
   pepper to taste
½ teaspoon thyme
   leaves, crushed
1 cup diced Cheddar
   cheese
1 cup diced Monterrey
   Jack cheese

Using butter, generously coat 2-quart casserole. Cover bottom with ⅓ of tomatoes, okra, green pepper and corn. Sprinkle ⅓ of chopped green onion tops, salt, pepper and thyme as second layer. Add layer of ⅓ of cheeses. Repeat each layer two more times. Sprinkle minced white onion over top layer of cheese. Bake, uncovered, 40 minutes at 350°. Serves 6.

Dale Merlo, BS '75
Austin

Crispy Onion Rings

2 large-sized onions
1 can (12 oz.) Seven-Up
BATTER:
1 cup flour
1 or 2 teaspoons
    cornstarch
¼ cup milk
1 egg, slightly beaten
    Dash salt
1 cup water
    Oil for deep-frying

Slice onions into thick rings. Place onions in mixing bowl and cover with Seven-Up. Set aside overnight as this makes the onions very crisp and provides a wonderful flavor.

BATTER: Combine flour, cornstarch, milk, egg, salt and water. Drain onion rings and pat dry. Heat oil to 350°. Dip onion rings into batter and fry in hot oil 3 to 5 minutes. Serves 8 to 10.

Carol Hebdon, wife of Jack C. Hebdon, Jr., BBA '77
San Antonio

Onion Casserole
A replacement for potatoes with beef or venison steak

2½ cups soda cracker
    crumbs
½ cup (1 stick) butter or
    margarine, melted
4 cups thinly sliced
    onion
SAUCE:
1 cup milk
2 eggs
1 teaspoon salt
¼ teaspoon pepper
1½ cups grated Cheddar
    cheese

Combine cracker crumbs and ⅓ cup butter. Pat into bottom of 9 x 13-inch baking dish. Saute onion in remaining butter and spread over crust.

SAUCE: Combine milk, eggs, salt and pepper over low heat. Add cheese and heat, whisking constantly until cheese melts. Pour sauce over onion. Bake 40 to 45 minutes at 300°, or until knife inserted in center of mixture comes out clean. Serves 6 or 7.

Jo Ann Nelson Law, '43
Fort Worth

My Mama's Purple-Hull Peas
Ann Campbell's East Texas Speciality

2 ham hocks or bacon
    end pieces (about
    1 lb.)
12 cups water
10 cups fresh shelled
    purple hull peas
1 onion, sliced
¼ cup sugar
2 tablespoons salt

Add ham hocks or bacon pieces to water, bring to boil. Add peas, onion, sugar and salt. Cover, boil 2½ hours. Serves 1 running back and 3 rookies.

Earl Christian Campbell, BS '79
Houston

Swedish Potato Pancakes With Chives
Old recipe made easy in food processor

4 potatoes
2 tablespoons chives
2 teaspoons salt
    Freshly ground
    pepper
3 tablespoons butter
3 tablespoons salad oil

Peel potatoes and grate. Quickly add chives, salt and a few grindings of pepper. Heat butter and oil in skillet over medium high heat. Fry pancakes 2 minutes each side, flattening with spatula. Serves 6 to 8.

Nancy Morris Wilson, MA '68
Dallas

COUNTRY POTATOES. Cook 6 peeled and sliced potatoes in salted water. Drain and mash until lumpy. Add ½ cup butter, 1 cup sour cream, ½ cup chopped green onion, salt and pepper to taste. Place in buttered 1-quart casserole and top with 1½ cups grated sharp Cheddar cheese. Bake 20 minutes at 325° or until heated through and cheese is melted. Serves 6 to 8.

Patti W. Livingston, BA '75
Houston

Refrigerator Mashed Potatoes

Keeps 2 weeks—great for busy homemakers!

5 pounds potatoes
6 ounces cream cheese
1 cup sour cream
2 teaspoons onion salt
1 teaspoon salt
¼ teaspoon pepper
2 tablespoons butter

Cook peeled potatoes in boiling salted water until tender. Drain. Cream until smooth. Add remaining ingredients, beating until light and fluffy. Cool. Store in tightly covered container in refrigerator. Keeps 2 weeks. To use, place desired amount in buttered casserole, dot with butter. Bake 30 minutes at 350°. The taste is of baked potato with sour cream and chives. This recipe is good to make ahead and serve at large dinner parties. Yield: 8 cups or 12 servings.

Carolyn Devault Crawford, wife of
John Crawford, Jr., BBA '61
Oakton, Virginia

CROCCHE DI PATATE (ITALIAN STYLE MASHED POTATO CROQUETTES). Combine 3½ cups mashed potatoes with 2 eggs (beaten), ½ cup grated Parmesan cheese, and 1 tablespoon finely chopped parsley. Roll into fat sausage shapes, each about 2-inches long. Coat with bread crumbs and refrigerate 1 hour. Heat enough olive oil for deep frying, add croquettes a few at a time and fry until golden brown. Serves 4 to 6.

Kathleen Kenny Reily, BS '77
Vaihingen, Germany

Cheesy Potatoes Supreme

1 cup (2 sticks) butter or margarine, divided
1 package (32 oz.) frozen hash brown potatoes
½ cup chopped green onion
2 cups grated sharp Cheddar cheese
1 cup sour cream
1 can (10¾ oz.) cream of chicken soup
2 cups crushed cornflakes

Melt ½ cup margarine in 3-quart casserole in slow oven. Combine potatoes, onion, cheese, sour cream and soup. Place in casserole. Bake, covered, 30 minutes at 350°. Saute cornflakes in remaining butter. Spread on top of mixture. Bake, uncovered, 15 minutes more. Serves 8 to 10.

Marsha Herndon Wheless, BBA '76
Corpus Christi

Variation: *Reduce butter to ¼ cup to combine with cornflakes which are added at beginning of baking. Bake, covered, 40 minutes.*

Gay Freeze Maguire, '71
Austin

259

Nut-Covered
Sweet Potato Balls
A different look for Thanksgiving company!

2 cups cooked, mashed
    sweet potatoes
4 tablespoons (½ stick)
    butter
Cinnamon and
    nutmeg to taste
½ cup finely crushed
    cornflakes
½ cup sugar
⅔ cup chopped pecans
8 slices canned
    pineapple
2 tablespoons butter
2 tablespoons honey
1 teaspoon water

Season hot sweet potatoes with butter, cinnamon and nutmeg. Add cornflakes and sugar. Shape into 8 balls. Roll balls in pecans. Chill at least 30 minutes, or overnight. Arrange atop pineapple slices in buttered baking dish. Bake 15 minutes at 375°. Combine butter, honey and water in small saucepan. Bring to boil, stirring frequently, over low heat. Boil 1 minute. Spoon sauce over potato balls. Bake 5 minutes more. Serves 8.

*Carolyn Devault Crawford, wife of
John Crawford, Jr., BBA '61
Oakton, Virginia*

ORANGE AND SWEET POTATO BAKE. Alternate slices of canned sweet potatoes with slices of unpeeled orange in buttered casserole. Top with a combination of ⅓ cup melted butter, ½ cup brown sugar and 1 can (8 oz.) crushed, drained pineapple. Bake 30 minutes at 350°. Sprinkle with miniature marshmallows and bake 10 minutes more.

*Shirley Coin Kleiman, BBA '48
Victoria*

Sweet Potato Pone
Super easy for food processor owners

2 cups grated raw
    sweet potato
1 cup milk
1 cup sugar
2 eggs, slightly beaten
1 cup pecans, coarsely
    chopped
3 tablespoons butter,
    melted
1 cup miniature
    marshmallows

Grate sweet potatoes in food processor. Add remaining ingredients except marshmallows. Bake in buttered 8-inch square casserole 1 hour at 375°. Remove from oven, place marshmallows on top of casserole and return to oven until marshmallows are lightly browned. Serves 6.

*Dan C. Williams, BS '35
Dallas*

Pecan Sweet Potatoes

4 large-sized sweet
    potatoes, peeled
    and halved
¾ cup brown sugar,
    packed
1 teaspoon cinnamon
    Water
6 tablespoons (¾ stick)
    butter
½ cup chopped pecans

In saucepan, cover sweet potatoes with water and cook until tender. Drain. Arrange in buttered 1-quart baking pan. Mix brown sugar, cinnamon, butter and a few tablespoons water. Cook 3 minutes. Pour over potatoes, sprinkle with pecans. Bake 30 minutes at 350°. Serves 6 to 8.

Rhonda Hodges, wife of Richard L. Hodges, BBA '74
Houston

Hot Spinach

2 packages (10 oz. each)
    frozen chopped
    spinach
4 tablespoons butter
3 tablespoons chopped
    onion
2 tablespoons flour
½ cup evaporated milk
½ cup spinach liquid
½ teaspoon pepper
¾ teaspoon celery salt
1 small clove garlic,
    minced
1 teaspoon Worcester-
    shire sauce
    Dash red pepper
1 roll (6 oz.) jalapeño
    cheese
2 cups fresh buttered
    bread crumbs*

Cook spinach according to package directions, omitting salt. Drain, reserving ½ cup spinach liquid. Melt butter, saute onions until tender. Add flour, mix well. Add evaporated milk and reserved spinach liquid. Add pepper, celery salt, garlic, Worcestershire sauce and red pepper. Add jalapeño cheese (cut into small pieces) and melt in the sauce. Add spinach. Put in 1-quart buttered casserole and top with bread crumbs. Bake at 350° until bubbly. Serves 6 to 8.

Lynda Johnson Robb, BA '66
McLean, Virginia

*See Index, Fresh Bread Crumbs.

Herbed Spinach Bake
With options this can be a luncheon entree.

1 package (10 oz.)
 frozen chopped
 spinach, thawed
1 cup cooked rice
2 eggs, slightly beaten
⅓ cup milk
1 teaspoon salt
 Pepper to taste
4 tablespoons chopped
 onion
1 cup grated Cheddar
 cheese
½ teaspoon rosemary or
 thyme, crushed
OPTIONS:
 Cooked eggplant
 (peeled and chopped)
 and 1 jar oysters
 sauteed with onion
 Crabmeat
 Shrimp
 Mushrooms

Combine all ingredients, add an option if you choose. Pour into buttered baking dish. Bake 20 to 25 minutes at 350°. Serves 8.

Erika Reeb, Friend of UT
Corpus Christi

Spinach Supreme Casserole

3 packages (10 oz.
 each) frozen
 spinach
¼ cup (½ stick) butter
 or margarine
4 tablespoons dried
 onion flakes
1 can (10¾ oz.) cream
 of mushroom soup
1½ rolls (6 oz.) garlic
 cheese, diced
¼ cup slivered almonds
3 tablespoons toasted
 sesame seeds

Cook spinach according to package directions, drain thoroughly. Melt butter, add spinach, onion, soup and garlic cheese. Mix well at medium heat until all ingredients are combined and cheese is melted. Stir in almonds. Pour into buttered 3-quart casserole. Bake, covered, 20 minutes at 350° or until bubbly. Just before serving, garnish with sesame seeds. Serves 10 to 12. If prepared ahead of time and refrigerated, increase baking time to 40 minutes.

Susan Scott Birdwell, BS '69
Bryan

Texas Spinach Souffle

2½ pounds fresh spinach
    or 2 packages (10
    oz. each) frozen
    chopped spinach
2 tablespoons butter
  Juice of 1 lemon
1 onion, finely chopped
2 eggs
¼ cup milk
  Salt and pepper to
    taste
  Worcestershire
    sauce to taste

Cook spinach, drain, chop. Melt butter until brown. Add lemon juice, onion and spinach. Beat eggs, add milk. Combine egg and spinach mixtures. Pour into well-buttered 1-quart mold. Set mold in pan of water, bake 25 minutes at 350° or until set. Serves 4 to 6.

Conrad Bering, '17
Houston

SPINACH STUFFED ZUCCHINI. Parboil whole zucchini 3 to 5 minutes, split in half lengthwise, remove seeds. Drain well (turn halves upside down), pile thawed Texas Spinach Souffle onto cored, drained halves. Place in buttered pan. Sprinkle with Parmesan cheese, bake 30 minutes at 350°.

Louise Appleman, wife of Gordon Appleman, BA '50
Fort Worth

Rolled Spinach Pudding

2 pounds fresh spinach
4 eggs, beaten
1 clove garlic, minced
1 small-sized onion,
    finely grated
¼ teaspoon nutmeg
½ cup (1 stick) butter,
    melted
  Salt and pepper to
    taste
  Soda cracker meal

Cook spinach until wilted. Drain, press to extract all liquid. Puree spinach using food grinder or food processor. Add eggs, garlic, onion, nutmeg, melted butter, salt and pepper. Add enough soda cracker meal to yield consistency of meat loaf so that roll will hold shape. (Too much cracker meal will make a dry pudding.) Mix well. Form into long roll and wrap tightly in foil. Bake 1 hour at 250°. Serve hot. Serves 4 to 6.

Myrtle Ligon, wife of Jack A. Ligon, BA '50
San Antonio

Tomato Cheese Biscuit Bake

4 cups peeled,
    quartered, and
    sliced ripe tomatoes
1 large-sized green
    pepper, quartered
    and sliced
Pinch of salt

BISCUIT TOPPING:
¼ tablespoon shortening
1½ cups flour
1 teaspoon salt
1 teaspoon baking
    powder
¼ teaspoon baking soda
1 cup grated Colby
    cheese
Buttermilk to moisten
    dry ingredients

Cook tomatoes and green pepper with salt until pepper is almost tender. Place mixture in 8-inch casserole. Combine dry ingredients. Cut in shortening, stir in cheese and enough buttermilk to drop-dough consistency. Drop from a tablespoon onto top of tomato mixture until entire surface is covered. Bake 20 minutes at 375° or until biscuits are golden brown. Serves 6.

Judy Walker Mayo, BS '71
Dallas

Grilled Tomato Cups
Quick and easy in microwave

4 medium-sized
    tomatoes
Salt and pepper to
    taste
½ cup soft bread
    crumbs*
¼ cup shredded sharp
    Cheddar cheese
2 tablespoons butter or
    margarine, melted
2 tablespoons dried
    parsley flakes

Halve tomatoes, sprinkle with salt and pepper. Combine bread crumbs, cheese and butter. Portion the mixture on tomato halves. Sprinkle with parsley. In microwave, heat prepared tomatoes, uncovered, in glass dish at reheat (medium) setting until cheese is melted; or broil in oven until cheese melts. Serves 8.

Judith Morrison Martin, BA '77 BJ '77
Houston

Variation: *For 5 or 6 tomatoes (halved), use ½ cup sour cream, ½ cup mayonnaise, ¼ cup grated Parmesan cheese, 1 teaspoon garlic salt, 3 green onions (chopped), juice of 1 lemon and 1 teaspoon parsley. Cook as above. Serves 10.*

Susan and Jim Kessler, Friends of UT
Austin

*See Index, Fresh Bread Crumbs.

Sweet Squash Pie
Include in buffet after Horns sweetly squash the Houston Cougars!

2 pounds medium-sized
  yellow squash,
  peeled
¼ cup chopped onion
3 eggs, beaten
1 teaspoon salt
¾ cup sugar
½ teaspoon white
  pepper
¼ cup (½ stick) butter,
  melted
30 soda crackers

Cook squash and onion in water to cover. When tender, press through coarse sieve. Add remaining ingredients except crackers. Pour into 9-inch casserole. Finely crush saltine crackers. Sprinkle over top of squash until entire surface is covered. Bake 45 minutes at 350°. Serves 6 to 8.

*Idanell Brill Connally, '40
Houston*

BUTTERNUT SQUASH. Peel and dice into 1-inch squares 3 butternut or acorn squash weighing 1 pound each. Layer squash in 9-inch square casserole. Dot with butter and salt. Sprinkle with 1 cup light brown sugar and a few drops lemon juice. Bake 45 minutes to 1 hour at 350°. Serves 6 to 8.

*Conrad Bering, '17
Houston*

Yellow and White Squash Casserole

1 pound yellow summer
  squash, peeled and
  sliced
1 pound white summer
  squash, peeled and
  sliced
½ cup onion, chopped
3 tablespoons butter
2 eggs, beaten
1 cup grated sharp
  Cheddar cheese,
  divided
½ teaspoon salt
  Pepper to taste
  Cornflake crumbs

Steam squash about 15 minutes. Drain. Saute onion in butter, add squash, eggs, ½ cup cheese, salt and pepper. Lightly butter a 2½-quart casserole, sprinkle with remaining cheese. Pour in mixture. Sprinkle with cornflake crumbs. Bake 30 minutes at 350°. Serves 6 to 8.

*Denton A. Cooley, BA '41
Houston*

Creole Squash

4 cups cooked squash,
  drained (yellow
  or zucchini)
½ teaspoon salt
½ teaspoon dark brown
  sugar
2 eggs, beaten
¼ teaspoon paprika
2 tablespoons cream
3 tablespoons catsup
4 tablespoons grated
  Cheddar cheese

Mix together all ingredients except catsup and cheese. Beat 1 minute. Spread in buttered 2-quart baking dish. Mix catsup and cheese and top squash mixture. Bake 15 minutes at 350°. Serves 6 to 8.

Zula Thompson Vizard, BA '33 MA '35
San Antonio

BAKED ACORN SQUASH AND HOMEMADE PORK SAUSAGE. Gather 2 medium-sized acorn squash from the garden, wash, divide in half, and remove seeds from cavity. Place in pan, add a pat of homemade butter and a tablespoon of honey to each cavity. Be sure the honey was manufactured from orange blossoms from the Rio Grande. In another pan, place 4 homemade pork sausage patties. Bake squash and sausage at 375° until done. Remove from oven. Pour out the butter and honey from the squash cavity and place a sausage patty in each. Serves 4.

Whynell Aston, BBA '46
Mehlville, Missouri

Spaghetti Squash
For those on wheat-free diets

1½ pounds spaghetti
  squash
2 tablespoons butter,
  melted
Dash nutmeg
Pinch of sugar

Cut squash in half, scoop out seed and fiber. Brush interior with melted butter. Cover tightly with plastic wrap. Place in microwave, bake at high setting 6 or 7 minutes. Remove from microwave, cool 4 minutes. Remove spaghetti string from shell, toss with more butter, a dash of nutmeg, pinch of sugar or serve as pasta with your favorite Italian concoction. Serves 4 to 6.

Evelyn Cheatham Bochow, MBA '53
Tyler

Zucchini Cheese Bake

3 medium-sized zucchini
1 large-sized onion
1 large-sized green
    pepper
2 medium-sized
    tomatoes
½ pound Cheddar
    cheese, grated
2 tablespoons butter
Salt and pepper

Slice all vegetables into ¼-inch slices, slicing the zucchini lengthwise. Layer in 10-inch square baking dish in the following order: zucchini, onion, pepper, cheese and tomatoes. Repeat layers two more times, sprinkling with salt and pepper between layers. Dot top of mixture with butter. Cover and bake 40 minutes at 400° or until tender yet still somewhat crisp. Serves 8.

Jennifer McNeil Jackson, BS '70 MEd '75
Austin

GREAT ZUCCHINI PATTIES. Shred zucchini, add enough egg to bind, salt and white pepper to taste. Make into patties and roll lightly in flour, saute in butter.

Nancy Brown Negley, '58
San Antonio

Zucchini Boats

6 small-sized or 1
    large zucchini
½ pound ground chuck
½ cup chopped onion
1 clove garlic, minced
½ cup minced green
    pepper
1 teaspoon oregano
2 tablespoons olive oil
1 can (8 oz.) tomato
    sauce, divided
¾ cup grated Parmesan
    cheese, divided
½ cup crushed herbed
    stuffing mix

Halve squash lengthwise, scoop out seeds and pulp leaving a ¼-inch shell. Chop seeds and pulp and set aside. Saute meat, onion, garlic, green pepper and oregano in olive oil until onion is tender. Add chopped pulp and seeds, ¼ cup tomato sauce, ½ cup cheese and stuffing mix; combine thoroughly. Spoon mixture into zucchini shells. Arrange stuffed zucchini in 9 x 13-inch pan. Pour remaining sauce over and around zucchini. Sprinkle with remaining cheese. Cover and bake 45 minutes at 375° or until zucchini is tender. Uncover and bake 5 minutes more. Serves 6.

Jerry Wilke English, '39
Leander

Calabaza
(Mexican-Style Squash)
Even my 2-year-old ate this vegetable!

2 strips bacon, chopped
½ onion, chopped
1 tomato, peeled and
   chopped
1 teaspoon garlic salt
   Salt and pepper to
   taste
2 zucchini (1 lb.),
   sliced

Saute bacon in skillet. Add all ingredients except the zucchini. Cover pan, cook for 1 minute. Add zucchini to pan and cook, covered, over medium heat 20 minutes. Stir as needed. Serves 4.

Susan Fortson Magee, BA '76 MLS '78
Brownsville

Variation: *Omit bacon. Add 1 green pepper (chopped). Use oil to saute onion, pepper, tomato and 2 tablespoons minced chives. Omit garlic salt. Add Parmesan cheese just before serving.*

Irene Reeb Meitzen, BA '65
San Angelo

Variation: *Use yellow squash for zucchini, add ½ green pepper and ¼ teaspoon comino seed. Omit garlic salt.*

Vera Lee Giles, wife of Rogan Giles, BBA '51 LLB '53
Austin

Variation: *Omit bacon, use combination of zucchini and yellow squash, add 1 canned jalapeño (minced) and ½ teaspoon coriander. Cook only 10 minutes and cover with strips of Monterrey Jack cheese. Broil 2 minutes.*

Twyla Lynn Tranfaglia, BA '73 MLS '74
El Paso

ITALIAN SQUASH. Cook 8 unpeeled, sliced zucchini and 1 small-sized onion, diced, in salted water. Drain well and mash into small pieces. Add ½ can Mountain Pass tomatoes and green chile peppers, 1 cup (5 slices) diced Old English sharp cheese, 1 egg, beaten, and ¾ cup fine bread crumbs. Mix well and place in buttered 2-quart casserole or in individual baking cups. Cover with bread crumbs browned in butter. Bake 30 minutes at 350°. Serves 6.

Walter L. Geyer, BM '61
Dallas

Jo's Zucchini-Rice-Salami Casserole

Serve with salad for complete luncheon or as side dish for brisket or turkey

4 medium-sized
   zucchini, sliced
1 medium-sized onion,
   sliced
4 to 6 jalapeño peppers
1 pound Monterrey Jack
   cheese
2 cups sour cream
4 green onions, chopped
1 teaspoon sugar
½ teaspoon onion salt
½ teaspoon celery salt
   Dash Worcestershire
    sauce
   Salt and pepper to
    taste
1 cup cooked rice
1 large-sized tomato,
   sliced
8 to 10 slices Thuringer
   or hard salami

Parboil zucchini and onion 10 minutes, drain. Split jalapeños, remove seeds and slice into strips. Cut ½ pound cheese into narrow strips, place on jalapeño strips. Grate remaining cheese. Mix sour cream with chopped green onion and seasonings. Taste and adjust accordingly. In buttered 9 x 13-inch casserole, place rice, then a layer of cheese-filled chiles, then zucchini-onion mixture and tomato slices; top with salami slices. Pour sour cream mixture over layers, sprinkle with grated cheese. Bake 30 minutes at 350°. This casserole can be prepared a day ahead and refrigerated until ready to bake. Serves 12.

Jo Shropshire Hannon, BBA '47
Austin

Zucchini Casserole

3 medium-sized
   zucchini, grated
3 strips bacon, fried
   and crumbled
½ cup chopped
   mushrooms
¼ cup chopped onion
   Dash garlic salt
½ cup butter, melted
1¼ cup soda cracker
   crumbs
1 egg, beaten
¼ teaspoon pepper
½ teaspoon salt
½ cup grated Swiss
   cheese

In a buttered casserole, combine all the ingredients except cheese. Top mixture with the cheese. Bake 40 minutes at 350°. Serves 8 to 10.

Marilyn Reneau, BS '70
Dallas

Martha's Vegetable Delight

1 package (10 oz.) baby
   lima beans
1 package (10 oz.) tiny
   green peas
1 package (10 oz.)
   French-cut green
   beans
1 green pepper, sliced
1 cup sour cream
¾ cup mayonnaise
1 can (3 oz. grated)
   Parmesan cheese

Cook each vegetable according to package directions. Drain. Combine with green pepper. Place mixture in greased 9-inch square casserole. Combine sour cream, mayonnaise and cheese. Spread over vegetables. Bake 20 minutes at 350°. Serves 6.

Suzanne Williams Nash, BA '67
Dallas

Variation: *Omit green pepper, add ½ cup slivered almonds. Substitute 1 cup whipping cream, whipped, for sour cream. Fold vegetables into cream mixture. Bake 30 minutes at 350°.*

Gail Hayes Cromeens, BS '70
Mineral Wells

Vegetable Trio With Zippy Sauce

1 cup mayonnaise
2 hard-cooked eggs,
   chopped
3 tablespoons lemon
   juice
2 tablespoons minced
   onion
1 teaspoon Worcester-
   shire sauce
1 teaspoon prepared
   mustard
¼ teaspoon garlic salt
   Dash Louisiana hot
   pepper sauce
1 package (10 oz.)
   frozen French-style
   green beans
1 package (10 oz.)
   frozen green peas
1 package (10 oz.)
   frozen baby lima
   beans

Combine all ingredients except frozen vegetables. Heat and stir mixture at low heat until thoroughly warmed. Cook vegetables according to package directions; drain. Combine vegetables and pour warmed sauce over mixture. Serves 8 to 10.

Helen Johnson Jones, BA '39 MLS '51
Austin

Five Vegetable Casserole
Less than 950 calories for the whole casserole

6 medium-sized
   zucchini, unpeeled
   and sliced
¼ cup (½ stick) butter
   or margarine
1 green pepper, chopped
1 onion, chopped
10 large-sized fresh
   mushrooms, sliced
¼ cup flour
   Salt to taste
1 tablespoon paprika
3 large-sized tomatoes,
   peeled and chopped
2 tablespoons brown
   sugar
1 cup shredded
   Gruyère cheese

Place zucchini in bottom of buttered 8-inch square casserole. Melt butter and saute pepper, onion and mushrooms. Stir in flour, salt and paprika. Add tomatoes and brown sugar. Pour mixture over zucchini, cover with cheese. Bake 1 hour at 350°. Serves 6 to 8.

Robert Ellen Colbert, wife of
Lester L. Colbert, BBA '25
Naples, Florida

Blender Hollandaise

3 egg yolks
¼ teaspoon salt
3 tablespoons lemon
   juice
½ cup (1 stick) butter,
   melted
   Dash red pepper

Beat egg yolks and salt in blender at high speed. Add lemon juice. Add melted butter in a slow stream. When all butter is added, turn off blender. Add red pepper. Serve immediately, or hold for short period of time in water bath. Yield: ¾ cup.

Minifred Boyles Trigg, '56
Bastrop

Amy Purcell Powell, BS '55
Navasota

271

The 1950s

Barbecue, Beef
Poultry, Seafood

In 1958, the University celebrated its 75th anniversary. The Round-Up parade that year featured floats built around that theme.

*J*ohn Clellan Holmes described young people of the 1950s as the "beat generation." Others called them the "silent generation" and accused them of being apathetic. They enjoyed James Dean and Marlon Brando, rocked to Elvis Presley, and read Dylan Thomas poetry.

The University of Texas had its first chancellor, James P. Hart, who served from 1950 to 1953. Logan Wilson came to the University to become president and later chancellor. Harry Ransom, who had been on the faculty since 1935, had moved into the administration, successively as dean, provost, president, and chancellor.

Bigness was cheered during the 1950s: big University (with 14,000 students in 1950 and more than 18,000 in 1959), big band, big dances, big Round-Up parade and revue, big varsity carnival, big fraternities and sororities, big ROTC, big black-faced Cowboy minstrels. The 1950s was truly a period when *extra*curricular activities blossomed.

The 1950s also produced UT students Wales Madden, Kathy Crosby, Willie Morris, Loyd Hand, Bill Moyers, Celia Buchan, Ronnie Dugger, and Betsy Rawls.

This decade was a time of quiet rebuilding after the tumultuous years following the firing of President Homer P. Rainey in 1944. President Logan Wilson laid to rest much of the bitterness that had developed and avoided confrontation with any of the warring factions that still debated the issues of the early 1940s. Faculty salaries rose and academic standards improved. Dr. Wilson broke the custom of using monies from the Available Fund for building construction only. He pleaded for "more brains, less bricks."

A building program in the 1950s produced the Experimental Science Building, Journalism (now Geography) Building, Pharmacy Building, Townes Hall, ROTC Building, Engineering Laboratories, and Batts, Benedict, and Mezes Halls on the South Mall. Old B Hall finally was taken down in 1952.

The Heman Sweatt case, after four years of litigation, ended in 1950 when the University was ordered to accept blacks for graduate study where substantially equal facilities were not offered in Negro state schools. The Board of Regents in July 1955, decreed complete racial desegregation, beginning in 1956-1957, and the immediate desegregation of the main University graduate school. Few blacks enrolled, however, because housing was still segregated, as were most facilities in the University area. Students conducted "Steer Here" campaigns to try to desegregate Drag business establishments. In the spring of 1957, Barbara Smith, a young black woman, was cast in the lead of a University production of *Dido and Aeneas*. Publicity, pressure and controversy followed, and Barbara was removed from the part. Her removal caused further criticism of the University, but Barbara was applauded two decades later for her performance as Marian Anderson in ABC's mini-series "Franklin and Eleanor."

Some students in mechanical engineering built "Smokey," the spirit cannon, in 1953. Harley Clark, head yell leader and later student body president, introduced the "Hook 'em Horns" signal at a Friday night pep rally in Gregory Gymnasium before the Texas Christian University football game in 1955. He and his friend, Henry Pitts, decided that the sign, made by extending the index and little fingers and tucking the middle and ring fingers beneath the thumb, would be appropriate for UT students because it resembled the head of a Longhorn. Colonel (now Brigadier General) D. Harold Byrd presented "Big Bertha," reportedly the world's largest drum, to the Longhorn Band in 1955. He obtained it from the University of Chicago, which no longer had a football team.

In 1958, the University celebrated its seventy-fifth anniversary. Beginning with a convocation in January, a Committee of 75 and a Conference on Expectations worked for a year to form a blueprint for the next twenty-five years of University development. Faculty and staff, alumni, students, and distinguished educators from other universities attended the convocation.

Girls in their penny loafers and white socks and with full skirts supported by crinoline petticoats and boys with duck-tail and flat-top hair cuts were later described as "conformists" by critics of the campus culture. Jitterbugging was the popular style of dancing. Sock hops, western hops, and big formals filled the campus social calendar. Drinking was forbidden but tolerated at the dances. Rules were difficult to enforce, and chaperones began to go out of style. Students gathered in groups to watch television, including the McCarthy hearings in 1954. Torchlight parades down The Drag before each pep rally, a once-a-week affair during the fall, were led by the Longhorn Band, Bevo, the Silver Spurs, and the Cowboys, followed by large numbers of students. In May 1952, the University community experienced its first panty raid, a fad that had had a big build-up in national magazines and full coverage in newspapers across the nation. Throughout the 1950s and into the early 1960s, these raids occurred periodically when students were inspired by spring weather and sought relief from the pain of studying.

The quiescence of the 1950s at the University reflected a general torpidity of national life and a Texas culture still emerging from an unsophisticated attitude toward higher education. Varsity football stirred more enthusiasm than did any other activity. Following a football game, the entire campus community became a beehive of activity that included dances, beer-busts, barbecues, backyard parties for old grads, and church socials. Banning freshman from having cars on campus caused bigger protest from students than did any national or state incident.

The cost of an education at the University during the 1950s did not increase rapidly. The *General Information Bulletin* reported that estimated expenses, not including incidentals, for the 1950-1951 long term would average between $442 and $724.50. Board ranged from $250 to $470; room, from $90 to $150. Books cost between $20 and $40, while fees and deposits were between $62 and $84.50. Laundry cost from $20 to $40.

Before the 1950s ended, the Russians had sent Sputnik into space, and its impact would again bring significant cultural change to the campus.

Menus

Longhorn Round-Up Barbecues

UT Caviar - p. 200
Steak and Ribs With Texas Barbecue Sauce - p. 279
Deviled Eggs - p. 343
Papa's Potato Salad - p. 381
Penelope's Bean Bake - p. 243
Champion Egg Bread - p. 20
Quick Texas Pecan Sheath Cookies - p. 101
Whoopie Pies - p. 102

Scholz's Nachos - p. 169
#1 Broiled Chicken - p. 302
Texas Rice Patties - p. 355
Spinach Supreme Casserole - p. 262
Texas Union Fruit Salad - p. 396
Dilly Casserole Bread - p. 19
Kinsolving Peanut Butter Cheesecake - p. 69

278

Texas Barbecue Sauce
Older than UT; use for all meats

2 cups (4 sticks) butter
1 cup salad oil
½ cup vinegar
   Juice of 2 large-sized
     lemons
3 tablespoons catsup
   Worcestershire sauce
     to taste
½ cup dried parsley
     flakes*
1 or 2 tablespoons chili
     powder (optional)
   Salt and pepper

Melt butter; add oil, vinegar, lemon juice and catsup. (Desired amount of sweetness may be determined by varying amount of catsup.) Mix well and heat. Add Worcestershire sauce and parsley flakes. Add chili powder for a spicy taste. Salt and pepper meat before beginning to cook and before adding the sauce. Keep sauce hot, stir and sop throughout the cooking process. Best way to cook meat is over hickory. If this is unavailable or inconvenient, then hickory flakes should be added to the charcoal or use hickory-flavored salt on the meat. Yield: 4 cups.

*The parsley flakes keep the sauce on the meat during grilling; it is important to get as much of the sauce as possible on the meat during the cooking. *Contributor's addition.*

"This recipe came from Bastrop, Texas, and was in use there definitely as early as the Civil War, probably before. In 1957 a 90-year-old man who had cooked at local barbecues all of his life shared this recipe. The recipe had been handed down from his father who had been a slave and who is known from newspaper accounts to have cooked at a barbecue at the Bastrop Military Institute in 1860 during a visit by Governor Sam Houston whose son attended the institute."

Maureen Mooney Jenkins, '59
John H. Jenkins, '63
Austin

Barbecue Sop and Sauce
Enough for moppin' and dippin' 50 pounds of meat

SOP: Combine all ingredients, cook until boiling. Keep hot and brush onto meat while cooking slowly.

SAUCE: Combine all ingredients, cook slowly until thickened. Pour over cooked meat before serving, pass remaining sauce in bowl for more "dippin.'" Yield: hefty "helpin's" for a herd of hungry 'Horns.

Amy Purcell Powell, BS '55
Navasota

SOP:
- 1 quart 45% vinegar
- ½ gallon water
- Salt
- Pepper
- 1 cup (2 sticks) butter
- 2 onions, sliced
- ½ tablespoon prepared mustard
- Tabasco

SAUCE:
- ½ gallon catsup
- ½ pound onions, minced
- 1 green pepper, minced
- 2 cups vinegar
- ½ cup (1 stick) butter
- 6 ounces Worcestershire sauce
- ¼ pound sugar
- Juice of 2 lemons

Beer Barbecue Sauce
Enhances rather than covers flavor of meat

Saute onion in oil. If you scorch the onion, discard and begin again. Add all other ingredients using only 6 ounces beer in sauce (you know what to do with the rest of the beer!). Simmer, stirring, until sauce comes to slow boil. Yield: 2 quarts.

Gillett Sheppard, LLB '56
Longview

- ¼ cup salad oil
- 3 tablespoons minced onion
- 1 large bottle (44)oz.) catsup
- 5 ounces Worcestershire sauce
- 5 ounces soy sauce
- Juice of 1 lemon (drop rind into saucepan)
- ¼ cup brown sugar
- 1 six-pack beer
- 1 teaspoon Tabasco
- ½ teaspoon garlic salt
- Salt to taste
- Red pepper to taste
- Cracked pepper to taste

South Of The Border Barbecue Sauce
An unusual herbed variation

1 cup (2 sticks) butter
½ cup peanut oil
1 lemon, thinly sliced
4 tablespoons lemon juice
2 onions, finely chopped
3 cloves garlic, minced
1 teaspoon pepper
1 teaspoon salt
½ teaspoon ground cumin
1 bottle (5 oz.) Worcestershire sauce
2 cans (8 oz. each) tomato sauce
1 bottle (32 oz.) catsup
2 tablespoons red wine vinegar
1½ tablespoons fresh cilantro leaves
2 cups water

Heat butter and oil until bubbling; add sliced lemon, lemon juice, onions and garlic. Cook 20 minutes or until soft. Add spices, stir well. Add liquids, cook 1 hour. Add finely chopped cilantro leaves and water, cook at a slow boil 1 hour. Spices can be varied to taste. For more "picante" flavor, add more cumin or even pepper sauce. Use as is or strain, mashing solids in strainer. Yield: ¾ quart.

James. T. Holman, BJ '59
Palestine

Number 1 Barbecue Sauce
Dark, thick sauce especially good for brisket

1 onion, minced
3 tablespoons butter
1¼ cups strong, black coffee
1 bottle (14 oz.) catsup
1 bottle (10 oz.) Worcestershire sauce
¼ cup cider vinegar
½ teaspoon pepper
1 tablespoon salt
¼ cup sugar

Saute onion in butter. Mix with remaining ingredients. Stir constantly until mixture begins to boil, then lower heat and simmer 30 minutes. The longer this sauce is stored in refrigerator, the better the flavor. Yield: 1 quart.

Judy Walker Mayo, BS '71
Dallas

Chunky Barbecue Sauce
A thin sauce for chicken and for 'pouring over'

¼ cup (½ stick) butter
2 cans (8 oz. each)
   tomato sauce
½ of a packet dry onion
   soup mix
5 ounces Worcestershire
   sauce
½ jalapeño, stemmed
   and seeded
½ cup olives
1 can (4 oz.)
   mushrooms,
   undrained
2 cloves
½ teaspoon ground
   cumin
¼ cup capers
½ teaspoon monosodium
   glutamate
1 teaspoon sugar
½ teaspoon garlic salt
   Freshly ground pepper
   to taste
1½ cups dry red wine

Melt butter; add tomato sauce, dry soup mix, Worcestershire sauce; boil 15 minutes. Chop jalapeño, olives and mushrooms; add to mixture; add mushroom liquid, spices and seasonings; simmer 30 minutes. Add wine, simmer 10 minutes more. Sauce is to be used for basting chicken; use remaining sauce to pour over chicken when serving and to pour over potato salad and red beans. Yield: 1½ quarts.

Jose Correa, BS '47
Houston

Diedra Ann Barbecue Sauce
Make ahead; keeps well when refrigerated.

¼ cup chopped onion
1 clove garlic, minced
2 tablespoons oil
1 tablespoon flour
½ cup orange juice
   Juice of 1 lemon
½ cup catsup
1 cup brown sugar
2 tablespoons prepared
   mustard
2 tablespoons
   Worcestershire
   sauce
½ teaspoon ground
   cloves

Saute onion and garlic in oil, sprinkle in flour, cook and stir until light brown. Add orange juice, lemon juice, catsup, brown sugar, prepared mustard, Worcestershire sauce and cloves. Simmer 15 minutes. Use for sop for all meats. Keep refrigerated. Yield: 2½ cups.

John P. Reeves, BA '51
Texas City

Auntie Lillian's Barbecue Sauce
An ideal recipe for wild game cookery

½ cup (1 stick) butter, melted
¼ cup sugar
¼ teaspoon red pepper
½ teaspoon prepared mustard
1 bottle (14 oz.) catsup
½ bottle (5 oz. size) Worcestershire sauce
2 cloves garlic, minced
1 large-sized onion, grated
Juice of 1 lemon
Tabasco to taste
1 cup cooking oil (optional)

Combine and heat ingredients. Eliminate oil if using sauce for oven cooking. Oil keeps the meat moist while cooking on the grill. Yield: 1 quart.

Julie Dryden Crow, BS '75
Austin

EASY BARBECUE SAUCE: In saucepan, combine 1 can (8 oz.) tomato sauce, rinse can with water and add to tomato sauce with 1 teaspoon Tabasco, 1½ tablespoons Worcestershire sauce, 1 teaspoon liquid smoke, 1 tablespoon chili powder and salt to taste. Heat, sop over meat while cooking. Enough for 1 frying chicken.

Carol A. Woodlock, BS '79
Dallas

Sweet Hot Mustard Sauce

½ cup Coleman's mustard
1 cup white wine vinegar
2 eggs
1 cup brown sugar
½ teaspoon salt

Sift mustard and combine with vinegar in top of double boiler. Set aside 2 to 4 hours, or overnight. Taste after 2 hours because the longer the mustard is combined with the vinegar, the hotter the effect. Beat in eggs, sugar and salt. Place over hot water and cook 10 minutes after water begins to boil. Stir constantly. Pour into jars and cool. Keep refrigerated. Yield: 1 pint.

Deanna Cook Murphy, BA '59
Houston

Murray Burgers
A juicier, tastier cheeseburger

FOR EACH SERVING:
½ pound ground beef
2 tablespoons diced
   onion
1 jalapeño, diced
   Salt and freshly
    ground pepper to
    taste
2 slices American or
   Cheddar cheese
   Hamburger bun
   Mayonnaise or
    mustard
   Lettuce
   Tomato

Divide beef for each serving into 2 equal portions. Flatten each portion between sheets of waxed paper into a thin, round patty, about 6 inches in diameter. Place onion and jalapeño, salt and pepper to taste on 1 patty. Top with cheese slices. Place second patty atop the cheese. Pinch edges of two patties tightly together. Grill on barbecue pit 2 minutes per side, turning carefully. When done, place on heated bun, one side spread with mayonnaise, the other side spread with mustard. Top with lettuce and tomato. Feeds one hefty Horn!

Patricia Reichenbach Murray, BA '72
Cambridge, Massachusetts

DIRTY MARTIN'S KUM-BAK HAMBURGERS. Men who have worked for 32 years at Dirty's roll fresh ground meat into balls by hand. They make 6 or 7 balls per pound, a little more than 2 ounces each. These are kept refrigerated in a crockery pot on ice at constant temperature to prevent any dryness. When a hamburger is ordered, a ball of meat is taken from the refrigerator and placed on the grill where it is flattened with a spatula. It should be turned frequently. As the patty fries and the grease begins to collect on top, the bun is opened and each side is dabbed on the frying meat in order to absorb a little grease. Then the bun is toasted on another grill while the meat finishes cooking. Each hamburger is completed with the fixin's ordered.

Lone Star Brisket
Dutch oven or crockpot slow cooking makes this a tasty treat.

6 pounds beef brisket,
   well-trimmed
2 onions, sliced
1 clove garlic, minced
¾ cup brown sugar
½ cup vinegar
1 cup catsup
1 cup water
1 tablespoon salt
   Freshly ground pepper

Place brisket in Dutch oven and brown on all sides. Add onions and garlic, saute until browned. Add remaining ingredients. Cook, covered, until meat is tender, 2½ to 3 hours. Serves 8 to 10.

Phyllis Horn Rozen, BS '68
Corpus Christi

Good Golly Miss Molly Spareribs

5 or 6 pounds
    spareribs
2 lemons, thinly sliced
    Salt and pepper
1 large-sized onion,
    chopped
2 cups catsup
3 tablespoons chili
    powder
2 teaspoons celery seed
½ cup Worcestershire
    sauce
½ cup vinegar
½ cup brown sugar
1¾ cups water
    Tabasco to taste

Place spareribs in large shallow pan, meaty side up. Place lemon slices on top of ribs. Sprinkle with salt and pepper. Roast 30 to 40 minutes at 450°. Combine remaining ingredients, boil 5 minutes and pour over ribs. Cool and refrigerate, if desired, until time to charcoal. Spread charcoal on bottom of grill. Light charcoal, burn down 1½ hours. Place ribs on grill, close cover, leaving vent open enough to keep charcoal burning. Smoke and grill 2 hours, basting frequently and turning occasionally. Serves 6. Serve with bowls of leftover sauce for dipping ribs.

Murph Holley, BBA '50
Fort Worth

TWENTY-FOUR HOUR BRISKET. Use any size brisket, season to taste, wrap in foil, bake 12 hours at 200°. Turn over brisket, bake 12 hours more. Open the foil the last 2 hours for browning and add any seasoning desired. Nothing to it.

R.J. Smith, '50
Gonzales

Texas Brisket

Best brisket I've ever eaten. I didn't use a knife, it was so tender.

1 brisket, 4 or 5 pounds
2 teaspoons meat
    tenderizer
1 bottle (4 oz.) liquid
    smoke
1 teaspoon celery salt
1 teaspoon paprika
¼ teaspoon nutmeg
¼ teaspoon garlic
    powder
1 teaspoon onion salt
1 tablespoon brown
    sugar

Sprinkle brisket with meat tenderizer, cover with liquid smoke. Refrigerate overnight, covered with foil. Next day, sprinkle brisket with mixture of remaining ingredients. Cover tightly with foil, bake 2 hours at 300°. Loosen foil, bake 5 hours more at 200°. Remove meat from pan, set aside 1 hour before slicing. Strain any grease from pan juices (or chill in deep freezer for easy removal). Slice brisket very thin across grain, serve with hot de-greased liquid or barbecue sauce of your choice. Serves 5 or 6.

Jim Young, BA '48
Corpus Christi

London Broil
Great for charcoal grilling

1½ pounds flank steak
1 clove garlic, sliced
½ cup corn oil
¼ cup vinegar
½ teaspoon salt
Dash pepper
1 teaspoon dry mustard
1 teaspoon Worcester-
   shire sauce
Dash red pepper
Dash Tabasco

Score surface of meat on both sides, and place steak in large shallow pan. Combine all ingredients, mix well and pour over steak. Marinate at least 7 hours. Remove meat from marinade. Broil steak 2 to 3 inches from heat, allowing 3 to 4 minutes each side. Carve across grain into thin slices. Serves 5 or 6.

Sara Dobarganes, BS '79
Houston

BRISKET COOKED IN BEER. "Sprinkle garlic powder, salt and pepper on 3- to 4-pound beef brisket. Mix ¼ cup chili sauce, 2 tablespoons brown sugar and 1 can (12 oz.) beer in pan. Place the meat in the sauce, cover with 1 sliced onion. Cover tightly with foil. Bake 3 hours at 350°. Uncover and bake 30 minutes more to brown the meat. Serve with the remainder of the 6-pack. Serves 5 or 6.

Charles M. Wilson III, BBA '70 JD '74
Rockwall

Beef Tenderloin
À La James Mason

1 beef tenderloin, 4 or 5
   pounds
Freshly cracked
   pepper
1 can (12 oz.) pineapple
   juice
1 bottle (5 oz.)
   Worcestershire
   sauce
2 tablespoons Kikkoman
   soy sauce
½ cup (1 stick) butter,
   melted

Trim tenderloin, rub with pepper. Combine juice, Worcestershire sauce and soy sauce. Marinate the beef, refrigerated, at least 3 hours. Turn the meat at least twice in the marinade. Before cooking remove beef from marinade and add butter to marinade. Cook at low heat over charcoal or gas broiler 45 minutes to 1 hour. Baste frequently with butter mixture. Serves 10 to 12.

Joe C. Thompson, Jr., BBA '62
Dallas

Tournedos La Rue

6 tournedos of beef
   (2-inch thick slices
   of beef tenderloin,
   trimmed of fat)
¾ cup butter, divided
2 shallots, finely
   chopped
½ cup brandy
2 tablespoons fresh
   chopped tarragon
1 cup imported Madeira
   wine
1 cup beef stock or beef
   bouillon
1 teaspoon arrowroot
3 large-sized white
   mushrooms, thinly
   sliced (truffles may
   be substituted)
Salt to taste
Freshly ground black
   pepper to taste

Saute meat in ½ cup butter as desired—rare, medium or well done. Add shallots and brown lightly. Heat and ignite brandy. While flaming, pour over meat. Remove meat to platter and keep warm. To sauce remaining in skillet, add tarragon and ½ cup wine and cook until sauce is reduced to one-third of its original quantity. Add beef stock and boil 5 minutes. Mix arrowroot with remaining Madeira, add to sauce in pan. Season with salt and pepper. Remove from heat, add remaining ¼ cup butter. Place sliced mushrooms on tournedos and pour sauce over them. Serves 6.

Texas Union Dining Services
Austin

Steak Shish Kebabs

MARINADE:
½ cup olive oil
¼ cup fresh lime juice
½ cup fresh lemon juice
1 clove garlic, minced
1 teaspoon lemon
   pepper
1 teaspoon seasoned
   salt
3 pounds steak
1 onion
2 green peppers
8 cherry tomatoes
8 metal or bamboo
   skewers
Cooked rice

Combine ingredients for marinade. Cut steaks, onion and peppers into 1 x 1½-inch chunks, (do not cut tomatoes). Marinate steak and vegetables 2 to 3 hours. Alternate meat, onion and peppers on skewers. Cook over charcoal or under double broiler 4 minutes. Add tomatoes to ends of skewers. Turn, cook other side 2 minutes. Serve over rice. Serves 8.

Jo Laynne Hill Boies, MM '72
Austin

Texas-Style Chicken Fried Steak

8 veal cutlets or
    tenderized round
    steaks, cut ½-inch
    thick
3 eggs
3 tablespoons milk
  Flour
  Garlic salt
  Pepper
  Salad oil

GRAVY (OPTIONAL):
  Remaining seasoned
    flour
2 cups warm milk
  White pepper
  Salt

If using round steak, cut into serving pieces about 5-inches in diameter. Combine eggs with milk, beat with fork until ribbon forms. Combine flour with garlic salt and pepper. In well-seasoned cast iron skillet, pour oil to ½-inch depth, heat at moderate to hot flame (setting at 6 or 7 on control heat burner). Dip cutlets into egg mixture, then into seasoned flour; shake off excess; dip again into egg mixture, again into flour. Place immediately into hot fat (cutlets must NOT be allowed to sit with coating before frying). Cook until crisp on first side, do not move or coating will be disturbed. Turn carefully, cook other side. Drain on paper towels. Drain oil from skillet, leaving about 3 tablespoons and browned bits. Add 3 tablespoons of the left-over seasoned flour and cook, stirring to incorporate all bits until flour smells "nutty," do not brown. Add warm milk and cook, stirring until thickened. Taste for seasonings, add white pepper and salt. Serve on mounds of fluffy creamed potatoes. Serves 8.

Judy Newton,
wife of UT Regent Jon Newton, BA '63 LLB '65
Austin

MENU SUGGESTION: Serve with Sula's Stir-Fry Okra and John's Bananas Foster.

MIDNIGHT SPECIAL. Saute 1 pound bulk hot sausage and ½ pound ground beef seasoned with garlic salt and pepper. Stir together in skillet, mixing well. Drain on paper towels. Put into 3-quart casserole. Beat 15 eggs with salt and pepper and soft scramble. Place on top of meat. Mix 1 can (10¾ oz.) cream of chicken soup and ½ cup sour cream. Spread over top of eggs. Top with grated Longhorn cheese and paprika. Bake 15 to 20 minutes at 350°. If made earlier, refrigerate, bake 30 minutes at 350°. Serves 12 midnight raiders.

Twyla Lynn Tranfaglia, BA '73 MLS '74
El Paso

The Beginnings of Perry Mason — the study of Erle Stanley Gardner on the fourth floor of the Academic Center, The University of Texas at Austin. While the room itself is an authentic recreation of the original, all items in the room are Gardner's personal effects profiling the ambience in which he worked. While his first short story was published in 1923, it wasn't until 1932 that Gardner dictated his first Perry Mason novel in three and a half days — *The Case of the Velvet Claws,* published by Morrow in 1933. Eighty-two other Perry Mason titles followed.

photo by Sherwood Inkley

Beef Burgundy

3 pounds round steak
    or beef tenderloin
Salt and pepper
¼ cup cooking oil
3 tablespoons brandy
1 clove garlic, crushed
2 cans (10¾ oz. each)
    beef bouillon
3 beef bouillon cubes
1 cup Burgundy wine
3 tablespoons chopped
    onion
½ cup sliced mushrooms
    (optional)
2 teaspoons Worcester-
    shire sauce
¼ teaspoon ground
    thyme
2 bay leaves
1 can (12 oz.)
    tomato paste

Cut meat into 1½-inch cubes. Salt and pepper, brown on both sides in oil. Add brandy and garlic. Warm bouillon and dissolve cubes. Add with wine to meat mixture. Add onion, mushrooms and remaining ingredients except tomato paste. Cover skillet tightly and simmer 45 minutes to 2 hours, depending on quality of meat used. Add tomato paste, heat and serve immediately. Serves 4 to 6.

Susan Fortson Magee, BA '76 MLS '78
Brownsville

Brandywine Beef

3 pounds boneless
    chuck
Salt
Freshly ground pepper
Dash cinnamon
2 tablespoons cooking
    oil
1 small-sized onion,
    sliced
1 clove garlic (optional)
3 tablespoons brandy
    or Bourbon
1 bay leaf
½ cup dry white wine

Sprinkle meat with salt, pepper and cinnamon. (Be stingy with cinnamon!) In large pot, heat oil until hot but not smoking. Add meat and brown well on all sides. Add onion slices and brown them. Add garlic and reduce heat. Then heat brandy, ignite and spoon burning brandy over meat until the flame dies. Add bay leaf and wine. Cover tightly and simmer 1½ hours or until meat is fork tender but not too soft. The meat should retain some firmness. After first hour of cooking, turn the meat over and taste gravy to adjust seasonings. When meat is done, remove to warm serving platter. Remove bay leaf, increase heat under liquid and boil rapidly until reduced by one-third. To serve, cut meat into ½-inch slices and serve with gravy spooned over the slices. Serves 4 to 6.

Betty Wright, wife of Jim Wright, '41
Washington, DC

Gourmet Beef Stroganoff

3 pounds top round
   steak
1½ teaspoons salt
½ teaspoon pepper
½ teaspoon onion
   powder
½ pound (2 sticks) butter
2 cups sliced onion
4 drops Tabasco
1 tablespoon Worcester-
   shire sauce
¼ cup dry white wine
3 cups water
2 packets MBT Beef
   Broth or 2 beef
   bouillon cubes
Dash nutmeg
1 pound fresh
   mushrooms, sliced
½ cup (1 stick) butter
1 cup water
½ cup cornstarch
1 cup sour cream
4 tablespoons cream
   sherry
Rice or noodles,
   cooked
Fresh chives, chopped
Chutney and pickle
   relish

Slice beef ¼-inch thick and cut into strips ¾ x 2 inches. Season with salt, pepper and onion powder, set aside 2 hours. Saute beef in butter. Add onion, Tabasco, Worcestershire sauce, wine, water, broth, nutmeg; bring to a boil. Reduce heat, simmer 30 minutes. Saute mushrooms in butter. Add to beef mixture. Mix together water and cornstarch. Add to beef and simmer until mixture has thickened. Just before serving, add sour cream and sherry. Serve over rice or noodles. Garnish with fresh chives. Use chutney and pickle relish as accompaniments. Serves 12.

Frances Combest Rountree, BBA '38
Waco.

ARLINE'S CASSEROLE. Brown 1 pound ground beef with 1 onion, chopped; add 1 can tomatoes with green chile peppers, 1 can ranch-style beans, 1 can cream of mushroom soup, 1 small-sized can chopped green chile peppers. Line 2-quart casserole with Doritos, add beef mixture, top with shredded cheese. Bake 20 minutes at 375°. Serves 8.

Rosemary Fanning Pinson, wife of
Robert M. Pinson, BA '41
Dallas

Quick And Easy Beef Stroganoff
Very easy, the best stroganoff I've ever eaten!

1 cup chopped onion
¾ cup cooking oil
2 pounds round steak
  Flour for dredging
1 teaspoon salt
½ teaspoon pepper
1 teaspoon garlic
    powder
  Water
¼ cup soy sauce
1 tablespoon Worcester-
    shire sauce
1 can (10¾ oz.) cream
    of mushroom soup
1 carton (8 oz.) sour
    cream
  Cooked rice or
    noodles

Saute onion in oil, remove onion from skillet. Cut steak into bite-sized strips. Dredge in flour, salt, pepper and garlic powder. Saute steak in oil remaining in skillet. Drain oil, return onion to skillet. Cover with water. Stir in soy and Worcestershire sauces. Simmer 1 hour. Add more water if needed. Just before serving, stir in soup and sour cream. Heat thoroughly, do not boil. Serve over rice or noodles. Serves 6 to 8.

Runelle Loyd Stembridge, BS '51
Gilmer

Round Steak Diablo
A special by the author of "Cooking Without Looking"

1 round steak (1½ to 2
    lbs.), cut 1-inch
    thick
¼ cup flour
3 tablespoons shortening
1 teaspoon salt
¼ teaspoon coarsely
    ground pepper
1 cup sliced onion
3 tablespoons minced
    fresh jalapeños
1 can (12 oz.) vegetable
    juice cocktail

Score fat edges of steak. Dredge steak with flour. Heat shortening in deep skillet at medium low heat. Add steak, brown each side 10 minutes. Sprinkle with salt and pepper. Cover with onion and fresh jalapeños. Heat juice and pour slowly into side of skillet. Cover and simmer 1 hour. Serves 4.

Esther Knudson Tipps, MS '56
Austin

Pepper Steak Caballero

1½ pounds sirloin
    steak, cut into
    ¼-inch strips
1 tablespoon paprika
2 cloves garlic, minced
2 tablespoons butter
1 cup sliced green
    onion with tops
2 green peppers, sliced
2 large-sized fresh
    tomatoes, peeled
    and diced
1 cup beef broth
¼ cup water
2 tablespoons cornstarch
2 tablespoons soy sauce
3 cups hot cooked rice

Sprinkle steak with paprika and set aside while preparing other ingredients. Saute steak and garlic in butter until steak is browned. Add onion and green pepper. Cook until vegetables are wilted. Add tomatoes and broth. Cover and simmer 15 minutes. Mix water with cornstarch, add soy sauce. Stir into steak and cook until mixture has thickened. Serve over fluffy rice. Serves 6 people.

Verna Sykes Farris, BS '74
Hurst

Round Steak Oriental

2 pounds round steak
  Salt and pepper to
    taste
  Garlic salt to taste
2 tablespoons butter
1 medium-sized onion,
    sliced
1 green pepper, cut into
    strips
1 can (16 oz.) tomatoes,
    undrained
1 cup beef broth,
    divided
2 tablespoons cornstarch
2 tablespoons soy sauce
  Hot cooked rice

Cut steak across grain into thin strips. Sprinkle with salt, pepper and garlic salt. Brown meat in butter in Dutch oven or electric skillet. Add onion and green pepper, stir in tomatoes and ¾ cup broth. Cover, simmer 30 minutes. Combine remaining broth with cornstarch and soy sauce, stir into steak and boil rapidly until mixture thickens. Serve over hot rice. Serves 6 to 8.

Becky Barlow Rivers, BS '71
and Steve Rivers, '68
Bastrop

Beef Chow Mein
A quick microwave meal for heart patients

1 pound sirloin steak or
   1 pound ground
   sirloin
1 medium-sized onion,
   sliced
1 green pepper, cut into
   thin strips
1 cup fresh bean sprouts
   or 1 cup canned
   bean sprouts,
   drained and rinsed
½ cup brown sugar,
   firmly packed
2 tablespoons cornstarch
¼ cup red wine vinegar
3 tablespoons soy sauce
1 can (15¼ oz.)
   pineapple chunks,
   drained, reserving
   ¾ cup liquid
1 can (8 oz.) bamboo
   shoots, thinly sliced
Hot cooked rice

Slice steak on diagonal into ½ x 4-inch strips. Place in buttered 3-quart baking dish. Cook in microwave at high setting 7 or 8 minutes if strips, 4 or 5 minutes if ground. Stir in onions, pepper, and sprouts, if using fresh; (if using canned, add later with pineapple). Microwave, covered, 2 minutes at high. Combine sugar and cornstarch; add vinegar, soy sauce and ¾ cup reserved pineapple liquid. Stir into meat mixture. Microwave at high, uncovered, 4 or 5 minutes, stirring once or twice. Add pineapple, canned sprouts and bamboo shoots. Microwave 2 or 2½ minutes or until thoroughly heated. Serve on bed of hot rice. Serves 4.

Dorothy Shepperd Shelby, BA '32
Tyler

Real Good Beef Short Ribs

⅓ cup oil
3 pounds beef short ribs
1 clove garlic, minced
½ cup soy sauce
¼ cup white wine
1 medium-sized onion,
   chopped
⅓ cup chopped celery
¼ teaspoon chili powder
¼ teaspoon pepper
1 can (8 oz.) tomato
   sauce
6 to 8 carrots, peeled
4 potatoes, peeled and
   quartered

Pour oil into large casserole with tightly fitting lid. Brown ribs. Add remaining ingredients. Cover and bake 2 hours at 325°. Serves 4 people.

Patricia Doney Holt, '45
Fort Worth

Tangy Rump Roast

5 to 6 pound boned
   rump roast
⅓ cup flour
2 tablespoons salad
   oil
2 teaspoons salt
   Pinch of pepper
   Monosodium gluta-
      mate to taste
   Beau Monde to taste
   Mei Yen to taste
¼ cup prepared
   horseradish
¾ cup Burgundy wine
½ package dry onion
   soup mix
2 bay leaves
6 whole allspice
   Pinch of celery seeds
   Pinch of leaf oregano,
      crushed
3 tablespoons wine
   vinegar
1 medium-sized onion,
   sliced
2 cups small-sized white
   onion*
8 small-sized carrots,
   scraped
3 potatoes, peeled and
   quartered
3 tablespoons flour
½ cup water

Dredge meat in flour. In Dutch oven or electric skillet, brown meat on all sides in hot oil, turn and sprinkle with salt, pepper, monosodium glutamate, Beau Monde and Mei Yen. Spread all sides with horseradish. Heat Burgundy, add dry onion soup mix, pour slowly over roast. Add bay leaves, allspice, celery seeds, oregano, vinegar and sliced onion. Cover and simmer, turning occasionally, 3½ hours. Add 2 cups small onions, carrots and potatoes. Cover, simmer 1 hour or until beef and vegetables are fork-tender. Skim grease from broth. Add enough water to make 2½ cups. Combine 3 tablespoons flour and ½ cup water, stir into liquid. Cook until gravy thickens. Serves 10 to 12.

Susan and Jim Kessler, Friends of UT
Austin

See Index, Cooking Onions.

EASY HAMBURGER SUPPER. Brown 1 pound ground beef and combine with 1 can chili beef soup, 1 can tomato soup, 1 cup cooked macaroni and 1 cup shredded cheese. Bake 20-25 minutes at 350°. Serves 4.

Madeline Bynum Closmann, BJ '49
Houston

very good

French Provincial Roast

Very tender, best pot roast I've ever eaten

3 to 5 pounds beef arm
    roast or chuck roast
1 tablespoon shortening
1 clove garlic, minced
2 tablespoons red wine
    vinegar
⅓ cup water
1 can (8 oz.) tomato
    sauce
1 bay leaf
1 teaspoon bouquet
    garni or Italian
    seasoning
¼ teaspoon rosemary
1 teaspoon salt
12 whole cloves
1 medium-sized onion,
    halved crosswise

In Dutch oven, brown roast in shortening. Add garlic during last seconds of browning. Add vinegar, water and tomato sauce. Add seasonings except for cloves. Insert cloves into onion halves. Place onion on the roast. Cover, cook at low heat 3 to 4 hours, or in oven at 300°. Turn roast once and re-cover with onion pieces. Serves 6 to 8.

Sandra Daniel Billingsley, '60
Greenville

Pot Roast Indienne

4 pounds lean beef
    (chuck or round)
1 teaspoon salt
2 tablespoons lemon
    juice
3 strips bacon
1 clove garlic, minced
⅔ cup chopped onion
¼ cup chopped parsley
4 whole cloves
½ teaspoon cinnamon
½ bay leaf
1 cup canned whole
    tomatoes
1 teaspoon sugar
1 cup orange juice
1 pound small-sized
    fresh mushrooms
    (optional)

Season meat with salt and lemon juice. Fry bacon until crisp, remove from pan. Add meat to bacon grease. Brown on all sides. Combine garlic, onion, parsley, cloves, cinnamon, bay leaf, tomatoes and sugar. Add to beef. Crumble bacon over meat. Bring to boil, reduce heat, cover and simmer 10 minutes. Add orange juice, cover and simmer 3 hours or until meat is tender. Add whole mushrooms, if using, during last 10 minutes of cooking. If needed, add water to keep mixture moist. Serves 6 to 8.

Twyla Lynn Tranfaglia, BA '73 MLS '74
El Paso

Southwestern Spiced Roast
Yummy sandwich fixin's with barbecue sauce

8-pound sirloin tip
  roast
1 teaspoon comino seed
2 teaspoons chopped
  parsley
½ teaspoon red pepper
½ teaspoon garlic salt
½ teaspoon marjoram
1 teaspoon poppyseed
1 teaspoon seasoned salt
2 teaspoons pepper
2 teaspoons onion
  powder
1 teaspoon celery seed
¼ teaspoon oregano
¼ teaspoon thyme
2 bay leaves

Brown meat on all sides and place in baking dish. Combine all seasonings and rub on meat. Top with bay leaves. Cover, bake 10 hours at 250° or until meat falls apart. *Do not add water.* Remove bay leaves. Stir meat and juices together, shredding meat. Spoon mixture onto hamburger buns or flour tortillas. Serve with barbecue sauce. Yield: enough for 20 buns or 30 tortillas.

Penny Porter Helms, BFA '66
Austin

An excellent spread is Sweet Hot Mustard Sauce. Editor.

Beef And Biscuit Casserole

1 pound ground beef
1 teaspoon salt
1 can (16 oz.) pork
  and beans
½ cup barbecue sauce
1 tablespoon brown
  sugar
1 tablespoon dried
  onion or ⅓ cup
  chopped yellow
  onion
1 can refrigerator
  biscuits
1 cup shredded
  Cheddar cheese

Saute beef. If using yellow onion, saute with beef. Drain. Stir in remaining ingredients except biscuits and cheese. Heat until bubbly. Pour into 2-quart casserole. Cut biscuits in half to form 20 half circles. Place cut-side-down around edge of casserole. Sprinkle with cheese. Bake 25 to 30 minutes at 375°, or until biscuits are golden brown. Serves 4 to 6.

Madeline Bynum Closmann, BJ '49
Houston

Sweet and Sour Meatballs

Very colorful, a different combination of textures

5 slices bread
½ cup milk
1 egg, beaten
2 pounds ground beef
  Dash salt
  Dash pepper
  Dash garlic salt
¼ cup flour
¾ cup water
½ cup salad oil
3 cans (8 oz. each) tomato sauce
¾ cup vinegar
¾ cup sugar
½ cup sweet gherkin pickles, cut into ½-inch slices
2 small-sized green peppers, cubed
2 carrots, sliced diagonally
1 tablespoon salad oil
1 can pineapple chunks, drained

Trim crust from bread, cut into ½-inch cubes, combine with milk and egg. Set aside 5 minutes, then press together. Add meat, salt, pepper and garlic salt. Shape into 1-inch meatballs, roll in flour. Heat oil, brown meatballs, drain. In heavy saucepan, combine water, tomato sauce, vinegar, sugar, salt, pickles and meatballs. Simmer, uncovered, 10 to 15 minutes. Saute pepper and carrots in hot oil until tender crisp. Add to meatballs, add pineapple, simmer until hot. Serve over hot rice or fine egg noodles. Serves 6.

Dorothy Ann Cooley, BS '80
Houston

Cherry Tomato Meatballs

1 egg, beaten
¾ cup soft bread crumbs (2 slices bread, crust removed)
½ cup milk
¼ cup finely chopped onion
¾ teaspoon salt
½ teaspoon oregano
  Dash pepper
1 pound lean ground beef
12 cherry tomatoes

Combine egg, bread crumbs, milk, onion, salt, oregano and pepper. Add ground beef. Mix well. Shape about ¼ cup meat mixture evenly around each cherry tomato to form round meatballs. Place in 9 x 13 x 2-inch baking pan. Bake 25 to 30 minutes at 375°. Serves 4.

Dale Merlo, BS '75
Austin

Marsha's Meatballs

2 tablespoons salad oil
½ medium-sized onion, chopped
1 cup catsup
1 teaspoon lemon juice or vinegar
¼ cup sugar
1 pound ground beef
  Salt and pepper to taste

Heat oil in saucepan. Add onion and saute until translucent. Stir in catsup, add lemon juice or vinegar and sugar. Taste. If sauce is too sweet, adjust with additional lemon juice. If too sour, adjust with sugar. Bring sauce to boil. When boil begins add walnut-sized balls of ground beef. When all meatballs are added, cover pan, reduce to low heat. Cook 15 minutes. When meatballs on top appear brown and firm, gently stir mixture to allow meatballs to settle into sauce. Simmer 25 to 30 minutes more. Remove from heat, set aside to cool until fat rises to surface. Skim fat. Reheat. Serve meatballs over bed of white rice. Serves 4 to 6.

Marsha Newman Greiner, '64
Oklahoma City, Oklahoma

Mushroom Meatloaf

1 pound ground beef (round or chuck)
2 tablespoons chopped green pepper
1 small-sized onion, chopped
½ cup chopped fresh mushrooms
1 tablespoon barbecue sauce
1 tablespoon catsup
¼ teaspoon salt
  Dash pepper
1 egg, beaten
¼ cup milk
¼ cup crushed seasoned croutons
  Dash Worcestershire sauce

Combine thoroughly all ingredients. Pour into buttered bread pan. Bake 1 hour at 400°. Serves 4.

Dale Sandgarten Udashen, BA '75
Dallas

Meat Loaf

1 can (4 oz.) mushroom
  pieces
1 medium-sized onion,
  minced
1 medium-sized green
  pepper, minced
½ teaspoon monosodium
  glutamate
½ teaspoon celery flakes
½ teaspoon sage
½ teaspoon salt
½ teaspoon dry mustard
1 carrot, minced
1 rib celery, chopped
¼ teaspoon garlic
  powder
¼ teaspoon pepper
1 tablespoon Worcester-
  shire sauce
1 tablespoon soy sauce
1 cup milk
2 eggs
1 cup bread crumbs
1 pound lean ground
  beef
½ pound ground pork

Combine all ingredients except beef and pork.
Mix well. Set aside 1 hour. Add beef and
pork. Mix thoroughly. Spoon into greased
5 x 8 x 3-inch loaf pan. Bake 1 hour 15
minutes at 350°. If you like, pour 1 can (8 oz.)
tomato sauce across top during last 15
minutes, or serve hot sauce separately. The
meat loaf can be spooned into smaller pans
and frozen for later baking. Serves 8.

Fred Ramsey, '57
Palestine

Texas Meat Pie
The best meat pie I ever ate.

1 unbaked 10-inch pie
  shell
½ pound ground beef
½ cup mayonnaise
½ cup milk
2 eggs, beaten
1 tablespoon cornstarch
¾ cup grated Cheddar
  cheese
¾ cup grated Swiss
  cheese
⅓ cup chopped onion
  Salt and pepper to
  taste

Brown beef. Drain and set aside. Mix
mayonnaise, milk, eggs and cornstarch until
smooth. Add beef, cheeses, onion, salt and
pepper. Pour into pie shell. Bake 35 to 40
minutes at 350°. After 25 or 30 minutes,
garnish top of pie with strips of bacon or, using
cookie cutter and remaining pie dough, cut a
shape of state of Texas for top of pie.
Serves 6 to 8.

Susan Weber Munson, BFA '67
Denison

Beef

Sicilian Meatroll

2 eggs, beaten
⅔ cup (1 slice) soft bread
    crumbs
½ cup tomato juice
2 tablespoons chopped
    parsley
½ teaspoon dried
    oregano, crushed
    Salt to taste
½ teaspoon pepper
1 clove garlic, minced
2 pounds lean ground
    beef
8 thin slices boiled ham
6 ounces (1½ cups)
    shredded Mozzarella
    cheese
3 slices Mozzarella
    cheese, each slice
    halved diagonally
    Tomato wedges
    (optional)

Combine eggs, bread crumbs, tomato juice,
parsley, oregano, salt, pepper and garlic. Mix
in ground beef. On foil or waxed paper, pat
meat mixture into a 10 x 12-inch rectangle.
Arrange ham slices on top, leaving small
margin around edges. Sprinkle shredded cheese
over ham. Starting from one short end,
carefully roll up meat, using foil or waxed
paper to lift. Seal edges and ends. Place roll,
seam side down, in 9 x 13-inch pan. Bake 1
hour 15 minutes at 350°. Bake until done,
although center of meat will be pink because
of ham. Place cheese wedges on top of
roll.Return to oven 5 minutes. Garnish with
tomato wedges. Serves 8.

Susan and Jim Kessler, Friends of UT
Austin

Dilly Meat Stuffed Zucchini

4 large-sized zucchini
1 pound ground beef
1 small-sized onion,
    finely chopped
2 tablespoons
    Worcestershire
    sauce
1 teaspoon dill weed
½ teaspoon salt
½ cup water
8 slices Swiss cheese,
    halved

Slice zucchini in half lengthwise. With a
spoon, scoop out seeds to make boats. Set
aside. Combine meat, onion, Worcestershire
sauce, dill weed and salt. Mix well. Fill
zucchini boats with meat mixture and place in
9 x 13-inch casserole. Add water to bottom of
dish, cover, bake 45 minutes at 375°. Remove
from oven, arrange 2 halved cheese slices on
top of each zucchini. Return to oven 5 minutes
more. Serve immediately. Serves 8.

Margaret Otto Bryan, BS '76
Dallas

300

Sauerkraut Agnes
A quick and easy supper dish . . . served with cornbread and a salad

5 strips bacon
1 large-sized onion, chopped
1 can (16 oz.) whole tomatoes
1 can (20 oz.) sauerkraut
Salt to taste
1 package (16 oz.) frankfurters

In large skillet, fry bacon until crisp. Remove bacon, saute onion in bacon grease. Reduce heat, add tomatoes. Wash sauerkraut in a colander until brine is diminished. Mix the kraut with tomatoes and onions. Salt lightly, add crumbled bacon and whole frankfurters. Cover and simmer 30 minutes until franks have plumped from steaming. Serves 4.

"Reminds me how much we loved Agnes Brown, who worked for my family nearly 40 years—she knew how to get the most out of a little!"

George Christian, BJ '71
Austin

Smoked Turkey
Serve after Horns smoke out the Aggies!

20-pound turkey
Salad oil
1 small stalk celery
2 medium-sized onions
1 head iceburg lettuce
1 medium-sized apple
1 tablespoon salt
1 tablespoon oil
1 teaspoon sage or poultry seasoning
1 medium-sized orange

Brush turkey inside and outside with salad oil. Chop celery (use ribs and leaves), onion, apple and lettuce. Combine with salt, oil and sage. Stuff vegetable and apple mixture in cavity. Score the orange and insert in cavity. (Stuffing keeps turkey moist during baking and is discarded after cooking.) Using a *covered* barbecue grill, build fire of charcoal and add oak bark, hickory chips, or anything to make lots of smoke. Cook turkey over slow fire (about 140° to 150°) 8 hours or more. Do not allow the fire to become too hot; long, slow cooking is the secret so that the smoke penetrates the meat. The skin will turn a dark mahogany color. Cool at least 30 minutes before slicing and serving. This is a sumptuous feast for cocktail parties or buffet after-game party. Serves 20.

J. S. Bleymaier, BBA '50
Columbia, Maryland

Number 1 Broiled Chickens

Any number of small (no larger than 2 lbs. each) frying chickens, halved
Plenty of butter
Stack of lemons
Salt and pepper
Paprika
Sugar
2 ounces of Bourbon (Wild Turkey preferably)

Wash and dry chicken halves. Marinate in lemon juice (just rub lemon juice inside and out) and leave an hour or so. Melt butter. Salt and pepper chickens inside and out, then rub melted butter all over them with your hands. While butter is still soft and warm, sprinkle sugar all over chickens. Finally sprinkle paprika all over the sugared chickens. Place on grill about 10 inches over hot coal fire (inside of chicken half down first) and close the top. Turn in 20 minutes and continue turning as needed. May be basted with the pan drippings of butter, salt and pepper, paprika, etc., used in preparing. Allow 1 to 1½ hours to cook (test for doneness with fork). During this period, sip the Wild Turkey.

"Mary John and I have served this to our friends for years—and have NEVER responded to their request for the recipe—and do not intend to! But nothing is too good for the Horns so . . ."

Ralph Spence, BBA '42
Tyler

MRS. DENTON'S CHICKEN WITH BACON RICE. Place 4 to 6 strips bacon in bottom of 7 x 10-inch casserole. Add 1 cup uncooked long-grain rice. Wash and salt chicken pieces (4 to 6 boneless breasts), place on rice. Sprinkle with: dash garlic powder, 1 tablespoon paprika, dash nutmeg, 1 tablespoon dried parsley flakes, 1 teaspoon oregano. Add 1 can (10¾ oz.) cream of chicken soup. Add ⅔ cup water. Cover tightly, cook 1½ to 2 hours at 350°. Serves 4 to 6.

Carol Pirrung Mann, MA '75 MLS '77
Mesquite

Variation: *Add 1 chopped onion, 1 tablespoon chopped green pepper. Substitute ½ cup white wine and ½ cup milk for water.*

Michael G. Shirley, BA '70 JD '72
Texas City

Stagecoach Inn's Barbecued Chicken
Recollection of a special dinner at Salado

3-pound frying chicken
3 medium-sized onions,
   thinly sliced
SAUCE:
1½ cups tomato juice
¼ teaspoon red pepper
2 teaspoons salt
¼ teaspoon pepper
¼ teaspoon dry mustard
4½ tablespoons
   Worcestershire
   sauce
1 bay leaf
1 teaspoon sugar
½ cup cider vinegar
3 cloves garlic, minced
3 tablespoons butter

Cut lengthwise or into quarters. Arrange in single layers, skin side up, in roasting pan. Sprinkle with salt and pepper. Pour in enough hot water to cover bottom of pan. Arrange onion slices over chicken and tuck some slices under wings and legs. Bake, uncovered, 30 minutes at 350°. Turn chicken and bake 30 minutes more. Remove from oven, drain grease keeping ¾ liquid in bottom of pan.

SAUCE: Combine all ingredients and heat. Turn chicken skin side up and pour sauce over chicken. Bake 1 hour at 350° or until fork shows chicken is done. Baste frequently with sauce from pan juices. Serves 4.

Barbecued Chicken By J.P. And Me

SOP:
1 can (10¾ oz.) chicken
   and rice soup
   Water
1 lemon, juice and rind
½ cup vinegar
1 tablespoon Worcester-
   shire sauce
½ medium-sized onion,
   chopped
2 tablespoons salt
½ can (12 oz.) beer
SAUCE:
1½ cups sop
½ bottle (14 oz. size)
   catsup
   Lemon juice

Strain soup, discard rice and pieces in strainer. Add 2 soup cans water to strained broth. Juice the lemon and slice rind, add to broth with vinegar, Worcestershire sauce and onion. Bring to boil, simmer briefly. Remove from heat and reserve about 1½ cups of this liquid to be used for barbecue sauce. Add beer to the "sop." To the reserved liquid, add catsup and lemon juice to taste. Heat just before serving with barbecued chickens.

"Sop is used to baste chickens while barbecuing. Make a small mop or use a pastry brush to brush chickens with sop while cooking. This recipe may also be used for barbecued ribs, steaks or chops."

William Bryan Finklea, LLB '50
Dallas

Chicken Marinate
A chicken cook-out for a crowd

4 or 5 frying chickens,
 halved
 Paprika
2 cups corn oil
1 cup fresh lemon juice
1 cup red wine vinegar
2 tablespoons salt
2 tablespoons cracked
 pepper or seasoned
 pepper
4 or 5 bay leaves
1 tablespoon tarragon
1 tablespoon oregano,
 crushed
 Soy sauce

Wash chickens, sprinkle liberally with paprika. Place halves breast down in pan. Combine together remaining ingredients, stirring well to dissolve salt. Taste, add soy sauce to cut tart lemon taste. (If not tart enough, add more lemon juice.) Pour over chicken halves and marinate, refrigerated, at least 3 hours. Remove from marinade, grill on low fire, basting frequently with marinade. Serve to a herd of Longhorns, about 20 of 'em.

Susan Weber Munson, BFA '67
Denison

MENU SUGGESTION: Serve with Mamie Shepperd's Potato Salad, Tomato Vinaigrette and Picosa Fresh Peach Ice Cream.

Pork and Chicken Adobo

1 chicken, cut into
 serving pieces
1 kilo (2.2 lbs.) pork
 with little fat,
 cut into 2-inch
 cubes
3 to 5 cloves garlic,
 crushed
10 to 15 peppercorns
¼ cup vinegar (the
 vinegar of sweet
 mixed pickles is
 excellent)
⅓ cup soy sauce
 Hot cooked rice

Marinate chicken and pork in vinegar, salt, garlic and peppercorns for at least 4 hours, preferably refrigerated overnight. Add 1½ cups water to marinade and boil until meat is tender. Strain stock, set aside. In its own fat, saute meat until golden brown; add 1 teaspoon salad oil if needed. Add soy sauce and brown thoroughly. Add stock, simmer until a thick sauce is produced. Serve with hot rice. Serves 8 to 10.

Carmen G. Kanapi, PhD '67
Manila, Phillipines

Sweet And Sour Pineapple And Chicken

A complete meal that serves 4 at 445 calories per serving

2 whole chicken breasts, boneless (1 to 1½ pounds)
2 tablespoons soy sauce
1 teaspoon cornstarch
½ teaspoon salt
2 cups plus 2 tablespoons salad or peanut oil, divided
3 medium-sized onions, cut into eighths
3 medium-sized carrots, sliced diagonally
1 large-sized green pepper, cut into 1-inch chunks
2 cloves garlic, chopped
1 small-sized pineapple, peeled, cored, and cut into 1-inch chunks (about 2 cups), reserve juice for sauce

BATTER:
¾ cup flour
2 tablespoons cornstarch
¼ teaspoon baking soda
¼ teaspoon salt
¼ teaspoon sugar
Pinch of baking powder
¾ cup cold water

SAUCE:
½ cup reserved pineapple juice
½ cup chicken broth
½ cup dark brown sugar
¼ cup water
2 tablespoons cornstarch
3 tablespoons catsup
3 tablespoons cider vinegar
2 tablespoons soy sauce

Skin and debone chicken, cut into ½-inch chunks. Combine soy sauce, cornstarch and salt. Mix well, add chicken and toss until well coated, set aside. In large skillet or wok, heat 2 tablespoons oil. Add onions, carrots, pepper and garlic. Cook, stirring quickly (stir-fry) at medium heat 3 minutes. Remove vegetables, add pineapple and stir-fry 2 minutes. Add pineapple to vegetables, wipe skillet clean and set aside.

BATTER: Combine ingredients and beat with fork until smooth. In wok or skillet, heat remaining 2 cups oil to 365°. Add chicken to batter, toss until well mixed. Using slotted spoon drop chicken pieces into hot oil, a few at a time. Cook 4 or 5 minutes until crisp and browned. Remove chicken to serving platter, keep warm in oven. Cook remaining chicken.

SAUCE: Combine ingredients and add to skillet or wok in which vegetables were cooked. Heat sauce to boil, stirring constantly. Cook until sauce has thickened and sugar has dissolved. Add vegetables and pineapple to sauce, cook 1 or 2 minutes. Pour sauce and vegetables over chicken. Serve immediately with a side dish of steamed rice. Serves 4 to 6.

Marta Gray, BS '79
Houston

Variation: QUICK SWEET AND SOUR CHICKEN. *Omit Batter and Sauce. Add chicken with vegetables and stir-fry until mixture is cooked.*

Jennifer McNeil Jackson, BS '70 MEd '75
Austin

Korean Chicken

1 chicken
½ cup soy sauce
½ cup sesame oil or
   salad oil
¼ cup sugar
¼ teaspoon salt
¼ teaspoon pepper
2 cloves garlic, minced
3 green onions, chopped
1 teaspoon monosodium
   glutamate
2 tablespoons sesame
   seeds, browned and
   crushed

2 tbs ginger

Cut chicken into serving pieces. Combine remaining ingredients and pour over chicken. Marinate at least 1 hour or more. Drain, broil chicken until done, basting with marinade once on each side. This marinade is also delicious for barbecued steak. Serves 4.

Irene Reeb Meitzen, BA '65
San Angelo

CURRIED CHICKEN CASSEROLE. Simmer 4 whole chicken breasts in seasoned water 30 minutes. Drain. Debone, cut into bite-sized pieces. Spread 2 cans (16 oz. each) whole green beans (drained) into 9 x 13-inch casserole. Top with chicken, salt and pepper to taste. Combine 2 cans (10¾ oz. each) cream of chicken soup, ½ teaspoon curry powder, 2 teaspoons dry onion soup mix, ⅓ cup mayonnaise, 4 drops Tabasco, and 1 can (8 oz.) chopped water chestnuts. Pour mixture over chicken. Sprinkle top with 1 can (3 oz.) onion rings. Bake, uncovered, 30 minutes at 350°. Serves 4 to 6.

Adele Houssels Black, BS '29
Austin

Chicken Paprika

1 frying chicken (2½ to
   3 lb.)
   Juice of 1 lemon
1½ teaspoons salt
2 tablespoons butter
2 onions, sliced
2 tablespoons paprika
1 cup sour cream
   Cooked egg noodles

Cut chicken into pieces and rub pieces with lemon and salt. Melt butter in large deep skillet, add sliced onions and paprika. Toss ingredients to combine flavors. Add chicken, cover, simmer about 45 minutes or until chicken is tender. Turn the chicken several times while simmering. Add sour cream before serving over noodles. Serves 4 to 6.
NOTE: This recipe cooks 6 hours in crockpot at low heat.

Sara Dobarganes, BS '79
Houston

Chinese Chicken With Zucchini

1 cup diced chicken
  breast, uncooked
1 clove garlic, crushed
1 tablespoon oil
2 tablespoons soy sauce
1½ cups diced zucchini
¼ cup mushroom slices
½ cup bamboo shoots,
  sliced matchstick
  size
1 tablespoon cornstarch
¼ cup water
1 cup toasted slivered
  almonds
  Steamed rice

In wok or heavy skillet, stir-fry chicken and garlic in oil at high heat. When chicken is "white," add soy sauce and continue stirring 3 minutes. Add zucchini, mushrooms and bamboo shoots. Cover, cook 3 to 5 minutes. Combine cornstarch with water, add and stir 1 minute. Serve with steamed rice, garnish with almonds. Serves 4.

Jamie Carter Snell, BJ '73
Beaumont

Incredible Chicken À La Blair

Best flavored baked chicken ever eaten

1 baking hen, 4 or 5
  pounds
1 lemon
  Seasoned salt
  Pepper
1 tablespoon dried
  tarragon leaves
4 or 6 strips bacon

PECAN RICE
DRESSING:

1 chicken bouillon cube
1 cup uncooked rice
½ cup chopped pecans
½ teaspoon Fines Herbs
  Seasonings

Wash and dry hen, rub with cut lemon, salt and pepper. Crush tarragon and pat inside and outside hen. Arrange bacon strips over chicken. Bake, breast up, 30 minutes at 400°. Remove bacon and place in cavity. Bake 30 minutes more at 400° on one side, turn to other side and bake 30 minutes more.

DRESSING: Remove chicken from oven, pour drippings and fat from pan. Add enough water, and the bouillon cube, to equal 2½ cups total liquid. Add to pan and stir to loosen particles. Empty contents into saucepan; add rice, pecans and seasonings. Cook rice until tender. Return chicken to roasting pan. Bake, breast up, 10 to 30 minutes more as needed until skin is brown and crisp and thigh moves easily. Serve with the dressing as a side dish. Serves 8.

Margaret Blair, BS '74
Phoenix, Arizona

Bess Powell Ezelle, '26
Sanderson

307

Cotolette Di Pollo
Alla Valdostana
Succulent Italian stuffed chicken fillets

4 split chicken breasts,
  skinned and
  deboned
4 thin slices Fontina or
  Swiss cheese
4 thin slices Prosciutto
  or smoked ham
2 tablespoons oil
1½ cups dry bread
  crumbs
4 tablespoons (½ stick)
  butter or margarine
2 eggs

Split chicken breast horizontally into 2 thin slices. To do so, lay boned breasts on cutting board, grasp thick end of meat and cut into it slowly, sliding knife handle along board for guidance. Pound meat lightly with palm of hand. Insert a slice of cheese and a slice of ham between 2 chicken fillets. Seal by pounding gently around edge of chicken. Whip eggs, dip fillets into egg batter, then quickly into bread crumbs. Pat lightly with hand, making sure sandwiches are thoroughly coated with crumbs. In heavy skillet, brown butter at medium heat. Add oil, fry chicken sandwiches 2 or 3 minutes on each side until golden brown on both sides. Serve immediately. Serves 4.

Kathleen Kenny Reily, BS '77
Vaihingen, Germany

Variation: CHICKEN CORDON BLEU. *After filling chicken fillets with cheese and ham, rub 1 tablespoon soft butter over each fillet coating both sides well. Use 2 cans (8 oz. each) crescent rolls to enclose fillets in following manner. Take 2 rolls, section, brush with butter, fold and roll to 5-inch square. Place prepared chicken cutlet on top of dough, cover with 2 rolls prepared in same manner. Seal edges with fork dipped in flour. Prepare remaining breasts in same manner. Brush with egg glaze made with egg yolk and 1 teaspoon water. Bake 50 minutes at 325°. Reglaze after 30 minutes. Serve with cheese sauce. Serves 4.*

David R. Scheihagen, BS '77
Houston

MENU SUGGESTION: Excellent with Marinated Broccoli and chilled white wine, perhaps a Soave.

Poulet Montfort
Grand Prize Original Recipe Winner

2 broiler halves
1 pair sweetbreads
1 tablespoon lemon
    juice
Butter
1 cup white wine
¼ cup sliced ripe olives
½ cup sliced artichoke
    hearts
1 cup sliced mushrooms
½ cup cognac
Rice for two, cooked
    with chicken stock
Chopped fresh parsley
Salt and pepper to
    taste

Cover sweetbreads with salted water to which 1 tablespoon lemon juice has been added. Simmer until done, 2 to 5 minutes. Cool. Separate and remove membrane. Refrigerate. Salt and pepper broiler halves, saute in small amount of butter until golden. Save buttered sauteing skillet for later use. Place chicken in covered roasting pan, add white wine. Bake 45 minutes at 350°. Slice sweetbreads; combine with ripe olives, artichoke hearts and mushrooms in the buttered sauteing skillet. Cook over medium heat, stirring frequently until hot; add juice from roasting pan as needed to keep mixture moist. Taste for flavor and add warm cognac. Set aflame and loosen drippings in skillet. Place broiler halves on bed of cooked rice and surround with mushrooms-sweetbread mixture. Ladle remaining juices over chicken and sprinkle with fresh parsley. Serve with asparagus, the ideal vegetable, very dente! Serves 2.

Steve Castlebury, BA '43
Dallas

Jefferson Chicken Pudding
Had a big picnic? Fried chicken left over? Try this!

2½ to 3 pounds fried
    chicken pieces
1½ cups flour
1½ teaspoons baking
    powder
1 teaspoon salt
2 eggs, beaten
1½ cups milk
3 tablespoons oil
Pepper

Combine dry ingredients and sift. Add eggs to milk and oil. Combine wet and dry ingredients, beat until batter is smooth. Pour into buttered 2-quart baking dish. Place fried chicken pieces in batter, sprinkle with pepper. Bake 45 minutes at 350°. Serves 6.

"I received this recipe from a friend in Charlottesville, Virginia."

Walther John Ives, MA '51
San Antonio

309

Viva La Chicken

4 whole chicken breasts
    or 8 split breasts
1 can (10¾ oz.) cream
    of mushroom soup
1 can (10¾ oz.) cream
    of chicken soup
1 cup milk
1 onion, grated or
    finely chopped
1 can (4 oz.) green
    chile salsa
12 corn tortillas
1 pound Cheddar
    cheese, grated

Wrap chicken breasts in foil. Bake 1 hour at 400°. Reserve liquid from baked chicken. Debone and cut chicken into large-sized pieces. Mix soups, milk, onion and chile salsa. Cut tortillas into 1-inch squares or strips. Butter large shallow baking dish. Put 2 tablespoons reserved liquid in bottom of dish. Place a layer of tortillas, then chicken, then soup mixture; top with cheese. Repeat layers, ending with soup mixture and cheese on top. Refrigerate 24 hours so seasonings can blend. Bake 1 to 1½ hours at 300°. Serves 8 to 10.

Tex Schramm, BJ '47
Dallas

Chicken Tetrazzini

1 hen, 5 or 6
    pounds
1 clove garlic
2 ribs celery with tops
2 bay leaves
½ teaspoon dried thyme
½ teaspoon dried
    rosemary
1 package (8 oz.) small-
    sized noodles
½ cup (1 stick) butter
¾ cup flour
4 cups milk
½ pound Old English
    cheese
1 medium-sized onion,
    finely chopped
1 large-sized green
    pepper, chopped
1 can (8 oz.) sliced
    mushrooms
1 can (8 oz.) Parmesan
    cheese

Cook hen in plenty of water seasoned with garlic, celery and herbs. Cool in broth overnight. Next day, remove hen, strain broth and bring broth to boil. Add noodles and cook according to package directions. Drain. Make a white sauce using butter, flour and milk. Add cheese to sauce and mix well. Skin, debone and dice hen. Add to sauce with onion, pepper, mushrooms and noodles. Combine ingredients at least 4 hours before serving. Bake 45 to 60 minutes at 350°. Sprinkle with Parmesan cheese before serving. Serves 8 to 10.

Joe J. Fisher, BBA '63
Beaumont

Baked Chicken Supreme

2 frying chickens or
    8 large chicken
    breasts
2 cups sour cream
¼ cup lemon juice
4 teaspoons Worcester-
    shire sauce
4 teaspoons celery salt
2 teaspoons paprika
4 cloves garlic, chopped
½ teaspoon pepper
1¾ cups packaged dry
    bread crumbs
½ cup butter
¼ cup shortening

Cut chicken into serving pieces, dry with paper towels. Combine sour cream, lemon juice, Worcestershire sauce, celery salt, paprika, garlic and pepper. Thoroughly coat each piece of chicken with this mixture. Cover and refrigerate overnight. Next day roll chicken pieces in crumbs, coating evenly. Arrange in single layer in large shallow pan. Melt butter and shortening and spoon over chicken. Bake, uncovered, 1 hour at 350°. Remove to warm serving dish. Serves 8.

Ray Roberts, '33
Washington, D C

WINE CHICKEN. Brown 4 chicken breasts in ½ cup (1 stick) butter. Remove to 1½-quart casserole. Brown 1 onion (minced) in butter, add 2 teaspoons paprika and 3 tablespoons flour; brown. Add ½ cup chicken bouillon, ¾ cup white wine, pour over chicken. Cover, bake 1 hour at 350°. Serves 4.

Suzanne Adele Tausend, '79
Pasadena

Chicken À L' Orange

1 frying chicken
¼ cup butter, melted
    Salt, pepper, paprika
    to taste
¼ cup flour
1 large-sized onion,
    thinly sliced
½ cup sliced mushrooms
½ green pepper, thinly
    sliced
1 cup orange juice
1 tablespoon brown
    sugar
½ teaspoon salt
1 teaspoon grated
    orange rind
1½ tablespoons water
1 tablespoon cornstarch

Wash and dry chicken, cut into serving pieces. Dip pieces in melted butter. Combine flour, salt, pepper and paprika. Roll pieces in flour mixture. Pour remaining butter into 2-quart casserole. Arrange chicken in casserole and sprinkle with onion, mushrooms and green pepper. In saucepan, mix orange juice, brown sugar, salt and orange rind. Combine water and cornstarch and stir into orange juice mixture. Cook over low heat until mixture thickens. Pour over chicken. Bake, covered, 1 hour at 375°. Uncover during last 15 minutes of baking. This recipe may be doubled, and the second recipe frozen uncooked. Serves 4.

Jeanette Anne Fleming, BS '76
Pearland

Chicken Divan

2 boneless chicken
  breasts
2 tablespoons butter,
  melted
1 package (10 oz.)
  frozen broccoli
  spears
1 can (10¾ oz.) cream
  of mushroom soup,
  undiluted
½ cup milk
½ cup shredded Cheddar
  cheese
¼ cup bread crumbs
  Paprika

Place chicken breasts in 9-inch square pan, drizzle with butter. Bake 40 minutes at 375°. Cook broccoli according to package directions, drain. Arrange broccoli around chicken. Combine soup, milk and cheese, pour over chicken and broccoli. Sprinkle with bread crumbs and paprika. Bake 20 minutes more. Serves 2.

Nita Hixson Galloway, BJ '51
Wilmington, Delaware

CHICKEN AND RICE WITH HOLLANDAISE. Bake 4 deboned chicken breasts in oven 1 hour at 400°. Season with salt and pepper. Cook ¾ cup rice and saute ⅓ cup chopped onion and 3 tablespoons chopped parsley in 2 tablespoons butter. Add a little chicken drippings to rice when it's done. Arrange rice on plate. Put chicken on rice and cover with Blender Hollandaise. Serves 4.

Minifred Boyles Trigg, '56
Bastrop

Chicken Broccoli Cheese Casserole

1 package (10 oz.)
  chopped broccoli
1 jar (8 oz.) Cheese
  Whiz
⅓ cup milk
½ cup chopped onion
½ cup chopped celery
½ cup chopped
  mushrooms
3 tablespoons butter
1½ cups cooked rice
1 chicken (about 3 lbs.),
  cooked, deboned
  and diced

Cook broccoli according to package instructions, drain. Add Cheese Whiz and milk, stir until melted. Saute onion, celery and mushrooms in butter. Add to broccoli. Stir in rice and diced chicken. Place in buttered 9 x 14-inch casserole. Bake, uncovered, 30 minutes at 350°. Serves 6 to 8.

Bess Harris Jones, BJ '34
Austin

Variation: *Increase broccoli to 3 packages, omit milk, celery and mushrooms. Add 1 can (10¾ oz.) cream of chicken soup and ½ soup can water. Serves 12.*

Sally Baumgardner Hoffman, BS '75
Austin

Chicken Diable

1 frying chicken (about
   3 pounds)
4 tablespoons butter
½ cup honey
¼ cup Dijon mustard
1 teaspoon salt
OPTIONS:
1 teaspoon curry
   powder
1 tablespoon lemon
   juice
½ teaspoon garlic
   powder

Wash and dry chicken. Cut into serving pieces. Melt butter in shallow baking pan and slightly brown chicken pieces. Mix remaining ingredients, using at least one of the options, and pour over chicken pieces. Coat well. Bake 45 minutes at 375°, turning once. Serves 4.

Patricia Doney Holt, '45
Fort Worth

Chicken Breasts Eden Isle

6 chicken breasts,
   boned, skinned,
   and halved
2 cans (10¾ oz.) cream
   of chicken soup
3 ounces cream cheese
1 carton (8 oz.) sour
   cream
   Toasted sliced
   almonds
   Steamed rice

Place uncooked chicken breasts in buttered 9 x 12-inch baking dish. In blender, combine soup and cream cheese until smooth. Stir in sour cream. Pour over chicken. Cover tightly with foil. Bake 2 hours at 325°. When baked, remove foil, brown lightly under broiler, cover with toasted sliced almonds. Serve with rice. Serves 4 to 6.

Billie Krausse, wife of Dan Krausse, BS '47
Fort Worth

Variation: *Substitute 1 can (10¾ oz.) cream of mushroom soup for 2 cans cream of chicken soup. Omit cream cheese, add 1 teaspoon Worcestershire sauce and 1 tablespoon flour (addition of flour reduces tendency of sour cream to curdle during baking). Bake only 1 hour. Sauteed fresh mushrooms may be added before serving.*

Katherine Young, MS '44
San Jose, California

Variation: *Top casserole with 20 Ritz crackers (crushed), 1 teaspoon poppyseed and ¾ cup (1½ sticks) melted butter.*

Sharen Ann Kirksey, BS '76
Beaumont

313

Judy's Chicken Supreme

4 to 6 chicken breasts,
  split
½ cup (1 stick) butter
2 cups canned whole
  new potatoes,
  quartered
1 onion, sliced
2 carrots, peeled and
  sliced
½ cup lemon juice
½ teaspoon lemon
  pepper
¼ teaspoon salt
  Dash paprika
  Dash garlic salt
  Dash celery salt

In a frying pan saute chicken breasts in butter.
Remove chicken to 2-quart casserole. In remaining butter, saute potatoes, onions and
carrots. Remove and set aside. Add lemon
juice and spices to the frying pan. Stir to
loosen the drippings. Pour over the chicken.
Add vegetables and cover tightly. Bake 1 hour
at 350° or until chicken is tender. Serves 4.

Judith Morrison Martin, BA '77 BJ '77
Houston

Burgundy Chicken

1 frying chicken (about
  3 pounds)
  Salt
  Paprika
  Seasoned pepper
  Garlic powder
1 medium-sized onion,
  chopped
½ green pepper, diced
½ cup diced celery
1 can (4 oz.) sliced
  mushrooms, drained
  and liquid reserved
1 teaspoon curry
  powder
¾ cup Burgundy wine
1 chicken bouillon cube
  Steamed rice

Cut chicken into serving pieces, remove skin.
Sprinkle with salt, paprika, pepper and garlic
powder. Layer in Dutch oven with onion,
green pepper, celery and mushrooms. Stir
curry powder with Burgundy, mix bouillon
cube with heated liquid from mushrooms,
combine mixtures and pour over chicken.
Bake, uncovered, 15 minutes at 350°. Cover
and cook until very tender, about 1 hour.
Serve over steamed rice. Serves 4 to 6.

Charlotte Curtis Henderson, BS '37
Baytown

Barbecued Shrimp
À La Manale's

New Orleans specialty, served with French bread to soak up juices!

2 pounds fresh unpeeled
    shrimp
¼ pound unsalted butter
½ cup best imported
    olive oil
4 cloves garlic,
    finely chopped
1 tablespoon fresh
    rosemary leaves or
    1 teaspoon dried
    rosemary
1 tablespoon fresh
    oregano leaves or
    1 teaspoon dried
    oregano leaves,
    crushed
1 teaspoon salt
1 tablespoon dried
    Creole seasoning
    mix
1 tablespoon freshly
    cracked pepper
½ teaspoon red pepper

Use shrimp with heads if possible (25 to 30 count) or 1 pound headless. Melt butter, cool; add oil, garlic, herbs and seasonings. Place shrimp in metal baking pan, pour over the butter mixture, marinate 30 minutes at room temperature. Start a charcoal fire in large barbeque barrel, let burn 30 minutes, place shrimp in pan and place on gray coals. Close barrel, cook 10 minutes; stir, cook 10 minutes more. Serves 2, leaves them finger-licking happy!

Dolores Simmons Snyder, BS '54
Irving

Variation: *Use 1 cup (2 sticks) butter, no olive oil, garlic, herbs or seasonings. Add 4 tablespoons Worcestershire sauce, freshly ground pepper and lemon juice. Spoon over shrimp. Bake 20 minutes at 400°, then broil 3 minutes more.*

Barbara White Stuart, '55
Dallas

Italian Shrimp

2 pounds raw shrimp
6 cloves garlic
6 tablespoons olive oil
1 tablespoon oregano
3 cups chicken stock
    Juice of 2 lemons
    Salt and pepper

SAUCE:
½ cup (1 stick) butter
4 tablespoons arrowroot

Peel and devein shrimp. Cook garlic in oil. Discard garlic. Add remaining ingredients. Simmer until shrimp is pink. SAUCE: Melt butter in saucepan. Add arrowroot to make a roux. Add to shrimp mixture. Boil until slightly thickened. Serve with tiny loaves of French bread. Serves 8.

Carol Pirrung Mann, MA '75 MLS '77
Mesquite

Shrimp Casserole
The kids even liked this!

½ cup (1 stick) butter or
    margarine
1½ cups chopped onion
2 ribs celery, chopped
1 green pepper, chopped
2 cloves garlic, minced
1½ cups chopped raw
    shrimp
¼ cup chopped pimiento
¼ cup chopped parsley
1 can (10¾ oz.) cream
    of mushroom soup,
    undiluted
4 slices bread, crusts
    trimmed
2 cups cooked rice

Saute onion, celery, green pepper and garlic in butter 15 minutes at medium heat. Add shrimp, pimiento, parsley and soup. Cook 5 minutes. Soak bread in water, press moisture out, add with rice to shrimp mixture. Toss gently to combine. Place in buttered 2-quart casserole. Bake 25 minutes at 350°. Serves 4 to 6.

Elizabeth Ann Kibbe, BBA '78
Austin

Shrimp Pie

1 pound shrimp,
    cooked, peeled and
    cleaned
2 tablespoons butter,
    melted
1 cup sliced celery
1 cup thinly sliced onion
1 can (10¾ oz.) cream
    of celery soup
1 can (4 oz.)
    mushrooms, stems
    and pieces, drained
1 teaspoon Worcester-
    shire sauce
  Dash freshly ground
    pepper
1 tablespoon finely
    chopped parsley
2 cups cooked, creamed
    and well-seasoned
    Irish potatoes

Saute onions and celery in butter until tender. Combine remaining ingredients except potatoes and parsley. Pour shrimp mixture into greased 2-quart ovenproof casserole. Combine potatoes and parsley. Spoon around top edge of casserole as garnish. Sprinkle with paprika. Bake 15 to 20 minutes or until lightly browned at 450°. Serve with green salad, toasted English muffins, sherbet and macaroons. Serves 5 or 6.

Bobbie Rainey Sublett, '31
Dallas

Baked Stuffed Shrimp

24 jumbo shrimp
1 medium-sized onion,
  minced
1 green pepper, chopped
6 tablespoons butter,
  divided
1 cup fresh crabmeat or
  1 can (6½ oz.)
  crabmeat
1 teaspoon dry mustard
1 teaspoon Worcester-
  shire sauce
½ teaspoon salt
2 tablespoons
  mayonnaise
  Butter
2 tablespoons flour
1 cup milk
2 tablespoons sherry
  Parmesan cheese,
  grated
  Paprika

Clean and remove heads and shells from shrimp, leaving tails. Butterfly* shrimp and open flat. Saute onion and green pepper in 4 tablespoons butter until soft but not brown. Add crabmeat, dry mustard, Worcestershire sauce, salt and mayonnaise. Set aside. Make white sauce using remaining 2 tablespoons butter, flour and milk. Add to crab mixture with sherry, mixing thoroughly. Stuff butterflied shrimp with crabmeat mixture. Dot with butter. Sprinkle with Parmesan cheese and paprika. Arrange in shallow baking dish. Bake 35 minutes at 350°. Serves 4 to 6.

Barbara White Stuart, '55
Dallas

See Index, Butterflying Shrimp.

Shrimp Santorini
Brings back memories of Greece

1 clove garlic, minced
1 or 2 tablespoons sliced
  green onion
  (optional)
¼ cup butter
1 tablespoon dried
  parsley
¼ teaspoon paprika
  Dash red pepper
¾ cup dry white wine
1 tablespoon lemon
  juice
½ pound shrimp, peeled
  and deveined
½ cup fresh mushrooms,
  halved
  Hot cooked rice

Saute garlic and green onion (if using) in butter until lightly browned. Add parsley, paprika and red pepper. Stirring constantly, add wine and lemon juice. Simmer 10 minutes. Just before serving, add shrimp and mushrooms. Cover and cook 5 minutes. Serve over hot rice. Serves 2.

Joe Frantz, BJ '38 MA '40 PhD '48
Austin

Stir-Fry Scampi

16 jumbo-sized fresh
   shrimp, peeled and
   deveined
4 tablespoons butter
   Salt to taste
   White pepper to taste
1 clove garlic, minced
4 tablespoons minced
   parsley
1 cup white wine
   Cooked rice

Peel, devein and butterfly* shrimp. In wok, combine butter, salt, pepper, garlic, parsley and wine. Simmer 3 minutes. Add shrimp. Simmer 5 minutes more. Serve with rice. Serves 4.

Helen Dixon Brown, MA '34
San Antonio

*See Index, Butterflying Shrimp.

INSTANT REMOULADE SAUCE. Mix in equal parts Hellman's mayonnaise and Zatarain's Creole Mustard.

Dick Rolle, '35
Houston

Texas-Louisiana Shrimp Creole
An after-game special for a crowd of hungry spectators

6 strips bacon, fried and
   crumbled
¾ cup butter or
   margarine, melted
1¼ cups flour
2 cups chopped celery
2 cups chopped onion
2 cups chopped green
   pepper (use both
   red and green
   pepper for colorful
   effect)
1 can (16 oz.) tomatoes
1 can (8 oz.) tomato
   sauce
6 cups water
   Salt and pepper to
   taste
5 pounds shrimp, peeled
   and deveined
   Cooked rice

Fry bacon in a 12-quart saucepan. Set bacon aside and make a roux with bacon grease, butter and flour. Add celery, onion and green pepper; saute until limp. Add tomatoes, tomato sauce, water, salt and pepper to taste. Simmer the mixture, covered, 30 minutes. More water may be added if mixture becomes too thick. Add shrimp, simmer 5 minutes. Serve over cooked rice. Serves 20.

Tom Harlow, BBA '58
Austin

Shrimp And Wild Rice Casserole

1 box (6 oz.) long-
    grain and wild
    rice
2 cups cooked shrimp
1 can (10¾ oz.)cream of
    shrimp soup
1 cup chopped onion
1 tablespoon butter
½ teaspoon curry
    powder
1 carton (8 oz.) sour
    cream

Cook rice according to package directions. Saute onion in butter. Combine all ingredients with rice mixture. Place in buttered 8-inch square casserole dish. Bake 25 minutes at 300°. This recipe can be prepared ahead and refrigerated until ready to bake. Serves 4 to 6.

Madeline Bynum Closmann, BJ '49
Houston

TEXAS STYLE SHRIMP BOIL. Simmer 15 minutes: 8 cups water, ¼ cup sliced onion, 1 clove garlic, 1 bay leaf, 2 ribs celery with leaves, 1½ tablespoons salt and red pepper to taste. Add ½ lemon (sliced), 2 pounds raw shrimp; and boil, uncovered, 5 minutes. Drain. Cool. Peel and devein shrimp. Serve with cocktail sauce.

Carol A. Woodlock, BS '79
Dallas

Easy Shrimp Creole
Quick and spicy

¾ cup (1½ sticks)butter
2 onions, finely chopped
2 ribs celery, finely
    chopped
1 large-sized tomato,
    seeded and chopped
¼ cup chopped green
    pepper (optional)
1 can (7 oz.) Herdez
    home-style Mexican
    sauce
12 ounces cooked, frozen
    shrimp (thawed)

Saute onions and celery in butter until tender. Add tomato and green pepper (if using); cook 5 minutes. Add sauce; cook 5 minutes more. Add shrimp; cook just enough to warm them. Salt and pepper to taste. Serve over rice, Chinese vegetables or chow mein noodles. Serves 4.

Lucy Green, BA '72
San Antonio

Hampton Crab Imperial

1 pound backfin
    crabmeat
1½ teaspoons chopped
    pimiento
1½ teaspoons chopped
    green pepper
3 tablespoons butter,
    divided
2 tablespoons flour
1 cup milk
1 egg yolk, beaten
¼ teaspoon dry mustard
1 teaspoon capers,
    drained
1½ teaspoons Worcester-
    shire sauce
1 cup mayonnaise
    Salt and pepper to
    taste

Examine the crabmeat carefully for any bits of shell or cartilage. Refrigerate. Saute pimiento and green pepper in 1 tablespoon butter. Melt remaining butter in a heavy skillet, stir, adding flour. Cook 3 minutes, stirring constantly. Remove from heat, add milk, whisk and return to heat. Cook until smooth. Add 1 tablespoon hot mixture to egg yolk, whisk and return mixture to cream sauce. Mix well, add sauteed vegetables. Remove from heat and add ¾ cup mayonnaise. Fold in crabmeat carefully so lumps will remain intact. Spoon into shells or shallow baking dishes. Spread remaining mayonnaise atop each crab filling. Bake 30 to 35 minutes at 350°. Sprinkle with paprika and serve immediately. Serves 6.

Randolph H. Lewis, '40
Houston

Variation: *Omit capers and Worcestershire sauce. Increase green pepper to 1 green pepper, chopped, and pimiento to 1½ teaspoons.*

David L. Parsley, BBA '66
Sue Armintor Parsley, Friend of UT
Nederland

Mother's Deviled Crab

2⅔ cups king crabmeat
4 tablespoons butter,
    divided
2 tablespoons flour
1 cup warm milk
1 tablespoon minced
    fresh parsley
2 teaspoons lemon juice
1 teaspoon dry mustard
½ teaspoon horseradish
1 teaspoon salt
2 hard-cooked eggs
½ cup bread crumbs

Drain and sort through crabmeat for shell and cartilage. Melt 2 tablespoons butter over low heat, add flour and stir well to make roux. Gradually add milk, whisking until thick. Add seasonings. Mix well. Fold in crabmeat and eggs. Portion into 6 buttered crab shells or ramekins. Top with bread crumbs combined with remaining 2 tablespoons butter. Bake 10 minutes at 400°. Serves 6.

Vera Lee Giles, wife of Rogan Giles, BBA '51 LLB '53
Austin

Hot Crab Salad

1 cup cooked rice
1 can (6½ oz.) crabmeat
5 hard-cooked eggs, chopped
⅔ cup evaporated milk
¼ teaspoon red pepper
1½ cups mayonnaise
¼ teaspoon salt
¼ teaspoon tarragon leaves, crushed
2 tablespoons chopped onion
1 tablespoon minced parsley
½ cup grated Cheddar cheese

Combine rice, crabmeat and eggs. Add remaining ingredients except cheese. Mix and place in buttered 8-inch square casserole. Sprinkle top with cheese. Bake 30 minutes at 350°. Serves 4.

Diane Akers, wife of UT Football Coach Fred Akers
Austin

Delicious Stuffed Crab

½ cup butter
½ cup diced green pepper
2 cups diced celery
1 cup minced onion
1 tablespoon Worcestershire sauce
1 cup heavy cream
1 pound crabmeat
3 cups Pepperidge Farm Herb Seasoned Stuffing
Dash Tabasco
Paprika
Salt and pepper

Saute green pepper, celery and onion in butter. Combine Worcestershire sauce and cream. Fold together crabmeat, sauteed mixture, stuffing and seasonings. Bake in crab shells 30 to 40 minutes at 350°, or bake in casserole 40 minutes at 350°. Serves 6.

Erika Reeb, Friend of UT
Corpus Christi

Crabmeat Casserole

1 pound crabmeat
1 cup milk
⅔ cup mayonnaise
1 can (10¾ oz.) cream
    of shrimp soup
2 cups cooked egg
    noodles
1 cup grated Cheddar
    cheese
1 can (3 oz.) French-
    fried onion rings

In a buttered 2-quart casserole, combine crabmeat, milk, mayonnaise, soup and noodles. Sprinkle top with cheese . Cover, bake 30 to 35 minutes at 350°. Remove cover, sprinkle with onion rings. Bake, uncovered, 8 to 10 minutes more. Serves 8.

Dorothea Gannaway Casberg, BFA '45
Hale Center

Seafood Trio

¾ cup chopped onion
¾ cup chopped green
    pepper
4 tablespoons (½ stick)
    butter or margarine
1 can (6 oz.) sliced
    mushrooms, with
    juice
⅔ cup flour
2 teaspoons salt
¼ teaspoon pepper
4 cups milk
1½ cups grated American
    cheese
1 teaspoon lemon juice
1 teaspoon dry mustard
½ teaspoon Worcester-
    shire sauce
1 package (12 oz.)
    crabmeat
1 package (12 oz.)
    cooked lobster
    meat
1 package (8 oz.)
    cooked shrimp
1 teaspoon chopped
    parsley
½ cup sherry

Saute onion and green pepper in butter. Add mushrooms and juice, flour, salt and pepper. Stir in milk, whisk until mixture thickens. Stir in cheese, lemon juice, dry mustard and Worcestershire sauce. Whisk until cheese melts. Shred lobster and crabmeat into large pieces, add with shrimp to cheese mixture. Heat to boiling but do not boil. Add sherry. Serve over pastry shells or Chinese noodles. Less lobster and more shrimp may be used. Serves 8 to 10.

Loraine McNeil Jackson, '46
Marble Falls

Lobster Maciel — Exc.

3 cups diced lobster*
½ cup (1 stick) butter
2 cups half and half
    cream
2 tablespoons cornstarch
1 teaspoon curry
    powder
½ cup sherry
    Salt to taste
2 cups cooked rice
½ pound (2 cups) grated
    Swiss cheese

+ Seafood seasoning to taste

Cook lobster in shell, if raw; cool, peel and dice. Bring butter and cream to boil, add cornstarch and curry powder mixed in sherry until smooth. Cook until sauce has thickened. Add lobster and salt to taste. Cover bottom of buttered 2-quart casserole with rice. Top with lobster mixture. Sprinkle with grated cheese. Bake 15 minutes at 325° or until cheese slightly browns. Serves 6 to 8.

*Shrimp, crab, crawfish, or chicken may be substituted for lobster.

Eleanor Ann Van Zandt Gerrard, BA '42
Victoria

TCU Frog Legs
A larrupin' treat to celebrate a victory over the Horned Toads!

8 large-sized frog legs
    Salt and pepper to
    taste
½ cup flour
2 tablespoons butter
2 tablespoons oil
2 cloves garlic, crushed
1 small-sized onion,
    finely chopped
¾ cup stock, beef or
    chicken
1 tablespoon lemon
    juice
    Hot steamed rice
    Parsley

Gig 4 large-sized frogs, cut off hind legs close to body, cut off and discard feet. Separate legs and, beginning at top, strip off skin. Soak in iced water (this helps diminish the twitching). Drain, combine salt and pepper with flour. Heat oil and butter in large skillet, add garlic and onion. Dredge frog legs in seasoned flour. Brown in hot oil. Reduce heat, add stock and lemon juice. Cover, braise 10 minutes or until frog legs are tender. Remove legs. Serve on hot rice with pan sauce poured over legs. Sprinkle with parsley. Serves 4.

Dixi Rhodes Clay, wife of Jerry H. Clay, BS '59
Tyler

Tuna Devils

1 cup mayonnaise
¾ cup canned milk or
    cream
6 hard-cooked eggs,
    chopped
⅓ cup minced onion
¾ teaspoon salt
    Pepper to taste
1½ cups fresh bread
    crumbs*, divided
2 cans (7 oz. each) tuna
    packed in water,
    drained
¼ cup sliced stuffed
    green olives
    Paprika

Combine mayonnaise, milk, eggs, onion and salt. Gently fold in 1 cup bread crumbs and crabmeat. Spread into buttered individual scallop shells. Top with remaining bread crumbs, olives and paprika. Bake 20 minutes at 350°. Serves 6 to 8.

Peggy Gross Lerner, BA '49
Dallas

Variation: *Substitute 1 cup crabmeat for tuna, add 2 teaspoons minced parsley, reduce onion to 3 teaspoons. Omit olives and paprika. Bake in 2-quart casserole.*

Suzanne Adele Tausend, '79
Pasadena

*See Index, Fresh Bread Crumbs.

Tuna Au Gratin

2 cans (7 oz. each) tuna
1 can (16 oz.) peas,
    drained
1 can (10¾ oz.) cream
    of mushroom soup
1 soup can milk
1 can (4 oz.) mushroom
    stems and pieces
    (optional)
1 package (5 oz.)
    noodles, finely
    crushed
1 jar (2 oz.) pimientos
2 tablespoons chopped
    green peppers
2 tablespoons finely
    chopped onion
12 ounces Longhorn
    cheese, sliced

Combine all ingredients except cheese slices. Layer in buttered 3-quart casserole using half the mixture, cover with half the cheese slices. Spread remaining mixture over cheese. Cover, bake 45 minutes at 350° or until noodles are tender. Top with remaining cheese slices, bake until cheese melts. Serves 6.

Millie Haehnel, wife of Bill Haehnel, '39
Austin

Tuna Vegetable Medley

1 pound fresh green
   beans
¼ cup oil
8 ounces fresh
   mushrooms, sliced
1 cup celery, sliced
   diagonally
1 green pepper, diced
1 red pepper, diced
4 green onions, sliced
3 cans (7 oz. each) tuna,
   drained, and liquid
   reserved
Salt to taste
1 tablespoon cornstarch
1 tablespoon sugar
1 teaspoon
   monosodium
   glutamate
2 tablespoons soy sauce
1 cup white wine
Cooked rice

Parboil green beans 3 minutes, drain. In hot oil in wok or skillet (use oil reserved from tuna if packed in oil), saute mushrooms, celery, peppers and green onions. Add green beans and tuna. Mix together cornstarch, sugar, monosodium glutamate, salt, soy sauce, and wine (use water reserved from tuna, if packed in water; mix with wine). Pour over tuna mixture. Cover and simmer 5 minutes. Serve with rice. Serves 6.

Helen Dixon Brown, MA '34
San Antonio

TIMELESS THRIFTY TUNA. Combine 1 can (7 oz.) tuna, 1 can cream of chicken soup, 1½ cups cooked rice, 1 tablespoon minced onion, and ¼ cup milk. Bake in buttered 2-quart casserole, topped with buttered bread crumbs. Bake 30 minutes at 375°. Serves 4.

Susan Elkins Allen, BBA '75
Richardson

Chow Mein Cashew Casserole
Quick and easy—right out of the pantry

1 can (7 oz.) tuna
½ cup chopped celery
¼ cup chopped onion
1 can (10¾ oz.)
   mushroom soup
1 can (3 oz.) chow mein
   noodles
½ cup chopped cashew
   nuts
¼ cup water

Combine all ingredients reserving a half can of noodles for topping. Bake in greased 1-quart casserole 30 to 40 minutes at 350°. Serves 4.

Carolyn Devault Crawford, wife of
John Crawford, Jr., BBA '61
Oakton, Virginia

Red Snapper Fillets
À La Creole

3 tablespoons butter or
  margarine
1 small-sized onion,
  chopped
1 green pepper, chopped
1 clove garlic, minced
1 tomato, chopped
½ cup sliced
  mushrooms
2 tablespoons lemon
  juice
½ teaspoon thyme
½ teaspoon pepper
½ teaspoon salt
3 tablespoons chili sauce
6 drops Tabasco
1 tablespoon chopped
  parsley
2 tablespoons capers
  (optional)
½ cup cooked small
  shrimp
¼ cup white wine
6 red snapper fillets

Saute onion, green pepper, garlic, tomato and mushrooms in butter. Add lemon juice, thyme, pepper, salt, chili sauce and Tabasco. Simmer 5 minutes. Add parsley, capers, shrimp and white wine. Place fillets in buttered casserole, spoon sauce over fillets. Bake 15 minutes at 400°. Serves 6.

Madeline Bynum Closmann, BJ '49
Houston

JVW's Champagne-Poached
Fish

4 strips bacon
1 can (4 oz.)
  mushrooms, drained
4 green onions, sliced
3 tablespoons lemon
  juice
¼ teaspoon garlic salt
1 cup champagne or
  white wine
1 teaspoon tarragon
1 tablespoon butter
2 pounds white fish
  fillets (trout)
Lemon slices

Cut bacon into 1-inch pieces. Saute until cooked, but not crisp. Add drained mushrooms and onions, cook briefly. Add lemon juice and salt, then fillets. Cover with champagne or wine, dot with butter, sprinkle with tarragon. Arrange lemon slices on top of fillets. Cover and poach 8 to 10 minutes at low heat. Serves 8.

Cindy Wilson Walker, BS '79
Houston

Red Snapper With Green Beans Amandine
A quick, Southern-style dish from New Orleans

4 red snapper fillets,
  cut ¾-inch thick
2 cups water
2 tablespoons lemon
  juice
1 teaspoon salt
1 package (10 oz.)
  French-cut green
  beans
1 cup skim milk
½ cup Swiss cheese,
  cubed
2 tablespoons flour
1 tablespoon butter
¼ teaspoon salt
1½ cups cooked shrimp,
  chopped or whole,
  small-sized shrimp
1 tablespoon dry sherry
2 tablespoons slivered

Place fish in large skillet. Add water, lemon juice and salt; bring to boil. Reduce heat, cover and simmer 10 minutes or until fish flakes easily when pierced with a fork. Prepare green beans according to package directions. Drain. In blender, combine milk, cheese, flour, butter and salt. Blend until smooth. Put cheese mixture into a saucepan. Cook and stir until bubbly and thickened. Add shrimp. Cook and stir to mix, add sherry and green beans. Drain fish, and remove to warm serving platter. Spoon sauce over fish and sprinkle with almonds. Serves 4.

Sara Avant, BS '78
New Orleans, Louisiana

Fillets Of Bass Au Gratin

1 onion, chopped
1 cup fresh mushrooms,
  chopped
1 clove garlic, minced
2 tablespoons butter
2 pounds bass fillets
  Salt and pepper to
  taste
½ cup white wine
1 cup fresh buttered
  bread crumbs*
  Fresh chopped parsley
1 lemon

Saute onion, mushroom and garlic in melted butter. Cook, without browning, until limp. Spread vegetables in buttered 3-quart baking dish. Top with fish fillets. Season to taste and pour in white wine. Cover with foil, bake 15 minutes at 350°. Remove from oven, uncover and sprinkle with bread crumbs. Return to oven, uncovered, bake 6 to 8 minutes more. To serve, sprinkle with fresh chopped parsley and lemon wedges. Serves 8.

Maurine Redfearn Bartos, BS '57
Waco

*See Index, Fresh Bread Crumbs.

Rolled Stuffed Flounder Fillets With Bechamel Sauce

¼ cup chopped onion
¼ cup chopped green pepper
4 tablespoons (½ stick) butter
1 can (3 oz.) broiled chopped mushrooms, drained with liquid reserved
1 can (6½ oz.) crabmeat, drained
½ cup soda crackers, coarsely crumbled
2 tablespoons parsley, minced
1 teaspoon lemon juice
½ teaspoon salt
Pepper to taste
Dash Louisiana hot sauce
8 flounder fillets, (about 2 pounds)

SAUCE:
3 tablespoons butter
3 tablespoons flour
¼ teaspoon salt
Milk
⅓ cup dry white wine
4 ounces (1 cup) shredded Swiss cheese
½ teaspoon paprika

Saute onion and green pepper in butter until soft but not browned. Add mushrooms, flaked crabmeat, crackers, parsley, lemon juice, salt, pepper and hot sauce. Spread mixture over flounder fillets. Roll fillets and place seam side down in buttered 7 x 12 x 2-inch baking dish. SAUCE: In saucepan, melt butter, add flour and salt and cook 4 minutes. Do not allow mixture to brown. Remove from heat. Add enough milk to reserved mushroom liquid to make 1½ cups. Slowly add to flour mixture, whisking until smooth. Add wine and return to heat. Cook and stir until mixture has thickened. Pour over fillets. Bake 25 minutes at 400°. Sprinkle with cheese and paprika. Bake 10 minutes more or until fish flakes easily with fork. Serves 8.

Susan and Jim Kessler, Friends of UT Austin

Sole Meunière

2 pounds sole fillets or
    flounder fillets
Salt
Flour
¼ cup (½ stick) butter
1 lemon
Chopped parsley

Be sure fillets have all bones removed. Sprinkle fillets lightly with salt and dust each fillet with flour. Melt butter in skillet. Saute fillets in a single layer until golden brown on each side. Repeat until all fillets are sauteed, adding butter if needed. Remove fillets to dish and keep warm in oven (200°). Squeeze juice of lemon into remaining liquid in skillet, stir, and pour over fish. Sprinkle with parsley. Serve immediately. Serves 6.

John D. Ryder, BBA '65
Seguin

Turbot Provençale
Microwave special for heart patients

2 pounds frozen or
    fresh turbot fillets
4 green onions, sliced
1 cup sliced fresh
    mushrooms
2 tomatoes, peeled and
    cut into wedges
1 clove garlic, minced
⅓ cup dry white wine
1 tablespoon lemon
    juice
¼ teaspoon thyme
¼ cup water
2 tablespoons cornstarch

Place fillets (thawed, if using frozen) in greased 3-quart glass casserole. Layer onions, mushrooms and tomatoes atop fillets. Combine garlic, wine, lemon juice and thyme; pour over fillets. Cover, microwave at medium setting 10 to 15 minutes. Test for doneness: fillets should barely flake when pierced with fork. Remove fillets to serving platter, cover and set aside 10 minutes to finish cooking. Strain vegetables and arrange on top of fillets. Combine water and cornstarch, stir in poaching liquid. Microwave 3 minutes or until thick, stirring once or twice. Serve fillets topped with vegetables and sauce. Serves 6 to 8.

Tom Shelby, BS '33 MA '34
Tyler

The 1960s

Eggs, Grits
Crepes, Quiches, Rice

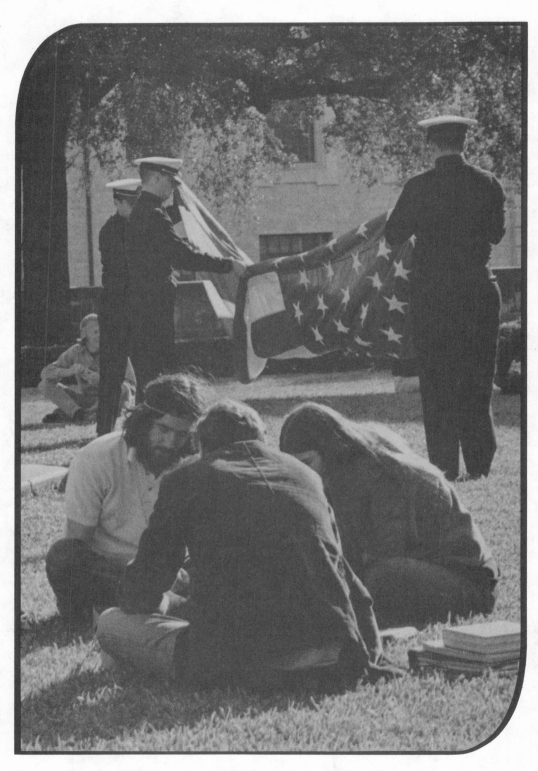

The new freedom of the late 1960s is somehow exemplified in this photograph. To each his own!

$\mathcal{D}$o your own thing! This slogan of the 1960s characterized the behavior of students at The University of Texas and across the nation. Not only were the young more numerous but they were more influential, healthier and wealthier, if not wiser, than their predecessors. The young taste-makers stamped a vigorous imprint on popular entertainment, popular fashion and popular behavior. They focused on institutional hypocrisy, racial discrimination and an unpopular war.

The early 1960s were not unlike the 1950s. Students at UT began to question the black-faced Cowboy minstrels; they also questioned a fraternity's actions of dressing as Mexican-Americans on March 2 and firing back, toward the Tower, when a traditional cannon salute was fired on the campus in commemoration of Texas independence from Mexico.

David Boroff, in a 1964 issue of the *Saturday Review*, called UT the "Cambridge on the Range." He continued, however:

> The University of Texas used to be a slum, but now it's a split-level suburb. It is like Austin itself where the University is located—a place where South and West meet. The many faces of UT are everywhere evident. The mystique of Big Football flourishes in fatuous splendor, and fraternity houses languish in segregated bliss. Texas is the scene of rambunctuous undergraduate play, but there is also a Socialist club and a brooding concern with integration.

When Boroff wrote these words, UT had a student population of 22,000 and a report to the Southern Association of Colleges and Schools declared that the University's enrollment would not go beyond 25,000. A year later, Regents decided to permit increasing numbers of the baby-boom generation to enter so that by 1969 more than 35,000 were enrolled. To accommodate this increasing enrollment, a building program, the Master Plan Development Report of 1964, plotted an expanding campus. New buildings in the 1960s included the Computation Center, West Mall Office Building, Business-Economics Building, Drama Building, Undergraduate Library, Art Building, Engineering-Science Building, Alumni Center, Calhoun Hall, Geology Building, Patterson Laboratory, Jester Center, and Music Building East (the new band hall).

UT students were not exactly the most sophisticated young college students in America. They reflected the Texas society of the 1960s; like Texas, the University was in painful transition. Campus politicians, not academicians, were "Big Men on Campus." Student life was unrelaxed and over-organized. Nowhere were election placards bigger or gaudier. One professor remarked, "Our students are interested in two things, football and social adjustment." Fraternity and sorority members comprised less than one-third of the student body during the first half of the decade, but they provided the leadership of planned frivolity.

Girls seldom thought of graduate study. Many majored in education. Their teased hairdoes (fluffheads) and short mini-skirts were uniforms of the period. Placards tacked on trees recommended that students learn "the Twist, the Jitterbug, and the Dallas Push."

The faculty in the 1960s was a representation of both old and new Texas. Harry Ransom, who served as both chancellor and president during part of the decade, had started a kind of inner brain trust of younger men that many referred to as "Harry's boys." He also was interested in creating an excellent library. He built the Academic Center, an open-shelf library for undergraduates, and began assembling one of the finest collections of Twentieth Century literature in existence. By the end of the 1960s, a number of programs at the University were ranked among the best in the country. In keeping with a major recommendation of the Committee of 75 in 1958, the University had strengthened its graduate program and was becoming a major research institution. Norman Hackerman served as president for three years before the decade ended. Frank C. Erwin, Jr., became chairman of the Board of Regents in 1966, and led the expansion and reorganization of the University System.

In the early and mid-1960s, students were generally polite. Most said "Sir" and "Ma'am." Round-Up was still a week-long rite that mirrored the University's many faces. It was a celebration in the spring that featured Texas Relays, a rollicking Western Dance, Moot Court finals, class reunions, honors day, an art show, and formal dances. In the fall, the big trek to Dallas to the Texas-Oklahoma football game during the Texas State Fair was a rite in itself. The pageantry of the Cotton Bowl included artifacts of the student culture: Bevo the mascot; Smokey the cannon; Bertha the drum; and the gigantic Texas flag, a gift from the University of Mississippi after the Cotton Bowl game in 1962. The rowdy pre-game celebration in downtown Dallas and its municipal auditorium resulted in front-page publicity about drunken brawls and celebrations, and each year broke the previous year's record of arrests.

Also characteristic of the 1960s were Sing-Song, water skiing, Varsity Carnival, weekly dances, formals, beer parties, and endless queen contests. A sign in front of the Texas Union in 1963 proclaimed, "Let's Have a UT Co-ed as Miss America!" One did become "Maid of Cotton" and another was "Miss Wool."

In loco parentis became a dead concept if only because University growth outstripped the growth of University housing. Regents permitted students to live where they pleased. They chose apartments and old houses with wooden floors and fenced backyards for their dogs. They decorated their rooms with bottles, burlap, papier-maché, fish nets, brightly colored tissue paper, and travel posters. Rock music blared from sophisticated stereo systems.

Only about 200 blacks were enrolled in any one semester during the 1960s. All but about one-tenth of the students were from Texas. The campus Students for a Democratic Society (SDS) chapter was small, but the group staged some large, noisy meetings on campus and produced leaders in the national movement against the Vietnam War.

Student leaders liked to say that University students did less partying and more learning in the 1960s, but approximately one-fourth were on scholastic probation. Most students were conservative, and a majority were lethargic. To avert protests occurring on other campuses across the country, UT students were given a greater voice in policy making.

The assassinations of John F. Kennedy, Robert Kennedy, and Martin Luther King had a sobering influence on the campus. The student sit-ins at the University of California at Berkeley also had an impact on Texas as on other campuses. The Vietnam War and the Kent State killings heavily influenced student thought and behavior. On August 2, 1966, Charles J. Whitman climbed to the top of the Tower and began firing with a high-powered rifle at students and passersby on and near the campus. He took the lives of 16 people and injured 31 others. The night before, the 25-year-old student had killed his mother and wife to save them from the embarassment he would cause. Whitman was killed by a police officer ninety minutes after the shooting began. The impact on the campus culture of these and other violent and forceful incidents produced change, and by the close of the 1960s, a different atmosphere pervaded the campus. Hangers-on and street people, often having no connection with the University, appeared in large numbers and used the Texas Union as a hangout. These "hippies" and "flower children" sold wares along the Drag. Stump speaking, Gentle Thursdays, and Flipped-Out Weeks became frequent, if unscheduled, events. Fraternity and sorority membership dropped, and to avoid criticism, members often stopped wearing their badges on campus. Sororities and a few fraternities no longer registered as official University organizations because they refused to say they did not discriminate.

The environment became an issue. Students spoke of protecting it while often leaving their demonstration area cluttered with fast food containers. They celebrated Earth Day and vocalized their opposition to cars and industry that polluted. They became "natural food freaks" and searched out the health food stores, did organic gardening in community gardens or on their patios.

The changing climate of the campus had a marked effect on interest groups and societies. Youth power, student activism, the hippie-Yippie movement, the black power movement, the women's movement, the "God is Dead" movement, and the pot culture produced big changes in student values, priorities, and goals. Drugs became a pervasive problem. Many students expressed a need to find their own "identity," to be more than a number on a campus that had computerized its records and its registration system. As the decade closed, University students pleaded for more freedom, more rights, and even more voice in University decision making. Despite all the noise, there was less actual violence at UT than on most major campuses.

Orange and White Weekend Brunches

Grandad's Pink Drink - p. 167
Bacon And Egg Casserole - p. 337
Spiced Fruit - p. 392
Orange-Nut Bread - p. 36

Happiness Punch - p. 168
Creamy Ricotta Cheese Crepes - p. 347
Hot Curried Fruit - p. 391
Orange Date Cake - p. 75

Toddy for Two - p. 167
Sausage Cheese Quiche - p. 351
Orange And Mint Salad - p. 395
Bertie's Cinnamon Rolls - p. 31

Orange Cow - p. 166
Huevos Poblanos - p. 341
Mama's Biscuits - p. 25
Cantaloupe Conserve - p. 52

King and Queen — from the Stanley Marcus Collection of Sicilian Marionettes, one of the collections housed in the Hoblitzelle Theatre Arts Library of the Humanities Research Center of The University of Texas at Austin.

This collection of marionettes was presented to The University of Texas by Mr. Stanley Marcus in 1965. Mr. Marcus purchased the marionettes in September 1960 in Palermo, the capital of Sicily. The collection, dealing with the legend of Charlemagne and his knights, contains forty-seven human characters, three magic devils, nine animals, and the enchanted flying hippogryph. It is representative of the many troupes of marionettes created in Sicily to perform the "Opera dei Pupi." Although the Sicilian marionette theatre reached the height of its popularity in the nineteenth century, a growing scholarly interest in its folkloric setting has helped to revive the tradition in recent years, even to the extent of renewing popular interest.

The Sicilian marionette in armor is much heavier than other puppets, weighing from seventeen to thirty-three pounds. It has only three strings, which move the left leg, the left arm and shield, and pull the sword. The right arm is equipped with a rigid iron bar instead of a string, which allows the puppeteer to produce the actions of jousting and sword fighting.

At the height of their popularity, the performances were always the same. The action was divided into episodes, one for each night through a period of thirteen months until the cycle was completed, after which it was begun again.

photo by Sherwood Inkley

Texas Scramble
Something delicious to crow about!

6 strips bacon
1 tablespoon butter
1 cup fresh corn, cut
    off cob or 1 can
    (12 oz.) whole
    kernel corn
½ cup finely chopped
    green pepper
¼ cup finely chopped
    pimiento
1½ teaspoons salt
    Pepper to taste
6 eggs

Fry bacon, drain and crumble. Reserve 3 tablespoons bacon drippings in skillet, add butter. Add corn, cook 1 or 2 minutes. Add green pepper, pimiento, salt and pepper. Cook 5 minutes, do not brown. Beat eggs, combine with bacon, add to skillet. Cook at low heat until eggs are set. Serves 4.

Jamina Ford, wife of Tommy Ford, BS '65
Waco

Bacon And Egg Casserole

3 tablespoons butter
4 tablespoons flour
1½ cups milk
1 teaspoon salt
¼ teaspoon pepper
1¼ teaspoons Worcester-
    shire sauce
¼ cup grated onion
8 hard-cooked eggs,
    sliced
12 strips crisp bacon or
    1½ cups cooked
    ham
¼ pound Cheddar
    cheese, grated

Melt butter; add flour, milk, salt, pepper, Worcestershire sauce and onion. Cook until mixture is thickened. In casserole arrange a layer of sauce, eggs, bacon or ham. Repeat until all ingredients are used. Top with grated cheese. Bake 25 minutes at 325°. Serves 6.

Ruth Ann Neves Powell, BS '72
Alvin

Egg Casserole

2 tablespoons butter
3 tablespoons flour
1 teaspoon salt
¼ teaspoon white pepper
2 cups milk
1 cup grated Cheddar
   cheese
16 eggs
3 tablespoons butter
1 can (3 oz.) sliced
   mushrooms
¼ cup chopped green
   onions
3 slices bread
3 tablespoons butter

Melt 2 tablespoons butter and mix in flour, salt, pepper, milk and cheese. Cook, stirring until bubbly. Set aside. Scramble eggs in 3 tablespoons butter. Stir in cheese sauce, mushrooms and onions. Pour egg mixture into buttered 3-quart casserole. Cover casserole and refrigerate at least 24 hours so flavors can "age." Top with bread crumbs. Bake 30 minutes at 350°. Serves 6. NOTE: To make bread crumbs, toast 3 slices bread and then crumble. Brown crumbs in 3 tablespoons butter.

Agnes Gloyna, wife of UT Dean Earnest F. Gloyna, MS '49
Austin

Ham And Egg Brunch
Great made ahead, very rich

8 hard-cooked eggs
½ teaspoon Worcester-
   shire sauce
1 teaspoon parsley
1 package (4 oz.) or ⅓
   cup finely chopped
   smoked ham
¼ cup butter or
   margarine, melted
½ teaspoon prepared
   mustard
1 tablespoon grated
   onion
1 cup grated Cheddar
   cheese
BÉCHAMEL SAUCE:
1 can (10¾ oz.) chicken
   broth
¾ cup milk
3 tablespoons butter
¼ cup flour
½ teaspoon salt
½ teaspoon pepper

Halve eggs lengthwise. Mix yolks with all ingredients except grated cheese. Stuff mixture into egg whites. Arrange in 7 x 11-inch casserole. Sprinkle with cheese.

SAUCE: Heat together broth and milk. Melt butter, add flour, cook as for cream sauce. Add hot broth mixture, ⅓ cup at a time, whisking until smooth. Season with salt and pepper. Pour sauce over eggs. Bake 20 minutes at 325°. Serves 6. To serve 8, use 12 eggs and the same amount of other ingredients.

W.J. (Billie) Stark, LLB '49 BBA '50
Englewood, Colorado

Cheese Egg Puff
An excellent plan-ahead recipe

¼ cup chopped green
   pepper
¼ cup chopped green
   onion
4 tablespoons (½ stick)
   butter or margarine
8 slices white bread,
   crusts trimmed
6 eggs
   Salt to taste
7½ 3 cups milk
½ teaspoon dry mustard
1 pound Cheddar
   cheese, grated

Saute green pepper and green onion in butter. Line 3-quart glass casserole with bread slices. Spread sauteed mixture over bread. Beat eggs with salt until fluffy, add milk and dry mustard. Mix well. Pour mixture over bread slices. Top with cheese. Cover and refrigerate 24 hours. Place uncovered in cold oven. Bake 1 hour at 350°. Recipe may be prepared 48 hours ahead and refrigerated until ready to bake. Serves 8 to 10.

Marilyn Atkins Biehl, BBA '71
Houston

Variation: *Omit green pepper and green onion. Add ½ pound browned sausage and ½ cup bacon bits.*

Roxie Potter, BS '75
New York, New York

Amy Lois Porter Oden, BA '21
Tyler

Charnita Justiss Spring, BA '73
Lufkin

Variation: *Omit bread. Use 2 cups frozen hash browns (thawed) sauteed with 1 pound sausage. Substitute Swiss cheese for Cheddar.*

Jamina Ford, wife of Tommy Ford, BS '65
Waco

BRUNCH HAM CHEESE . . . when you are tired of baking ham. Place sliced ham in shallow ovenproof dish. Top with 1 part prepared mustard and 2 parts tomato catsup. Repeat layers. Top with grated sharp Cheddar cheese. Bake 20 minutes at 350° or until heated and cheese has melted.

Matilda McCammon McFaddin, BA '18
Little Rock, Arkansas

Eggs

Kropsu
(Finnish Baked Pan Cake)
A fancy, puffy breakfast treat

¼ cup (½ stick) butter
　　or margarine
2 eggs
2 cups milk
1 cup flour, sifted
½ teaspoon salt
2 mangoes or 4 peaches
　Powdered sugar

Divide butter into 2 (9-inch) glass pans. Place in oven at 375° to melt butter. Remove before butter begins to brown. Beat eggs slightly. Add milk alternately with flour and salt, stirring after each addition. Press lumps against side of bowl to remove, do not beat. Add melted butter and stir into batter. Pour batter into buttered pans, bake 40 minutes at 375° or until puffy, set and lightly browned on top. Remove from oven, cut each cake in half. Place halves on 4 serving plates. Top each with sliced fruit, dust with powdered sugar. Serve warm. Serves 4.

Nancy Montgomery Winter, '63
San Antonio

Salzburger Nockerln
A souffled pancake for brunch, or for dessert with rum and fruit sauce

6 egg whites
5 tablespoons powdered
　　sugar
3 egg yolks, beaten
1 teaspoon flour
1 teaspoon grated
　　lemon rind
3 tablespoons sweet
　　butter
2 tablespoons milk
1 tablespoon sugar

Beat egg whites until stiff. Add powdered sugar and continue to beat until very thick. Fold in egg yolks, flour and lemon rind. In a 10-inch, deep-dish pie pan combine butter, milk and sugar. Heat until butter melts. Scoop 4 large mounds of egg white mixture onto butter mixture. Bake at 450° until peaks are golden, about 6 minutes. Sprinkle with powdered sugar. Serve immediately. Serves 4.

Gertrude Morris Neuhaus,
wife of V. F. (Doc) Neuhaus, '20
McAllen

340

Eggs

Huevos Rancheros De Amigos

A Sunday morning special to keep you from wanting to go back to sleep.

2 jiggers vodka
½ gallon V-8 cocktail
    vegetable juice,
    divided
1 large-sized onion,
    chopped
3 ribs celery, chopped
1 clove garlic, minced
1 large-sized green
    pepper, chopped
3 tablespoons olive oil
1 can (6 oz.) tomato
    paste
1 can (8 oz.) tomato
    sauce
1 can (10 oz.) tomatoes
    with green chile
    peppers
    Salt and pepper to
    taste
12 eggs
    Corn or flour tortillas

Before starting Huevos Rancheros de Amigos, make yourself a drink with the vodka and some V-8 juice. You will be better prepared to taste the recipe as you go. Saute onion, celery, garlic and green pepper in olive oil. Add tomato paste, tomato sauce, tomatoes and 1 cup V-8 juice to vegetables. Cook about 30 minutes at medium to low heat. Stir and taste occasionally, add V-8 juice, salt and pepper as needed. When vegetable mixture is cooked, drop eggs into mixture and poach, uncovered, about 5 minutes. Serve eggs with mixture on heated tortillas. Serves 6.

Shelley Friend, BJ '77
Austin

Huevos Poblanos

1 can (4 oz.) green chile
    peppers
2 cups half and half
    cream
½ cup chopped green
    onions
    Salt to taste
8 eggs
1 cup grated Monterrey
    Jack cheese

Puree in blender the chiles, cream, onions and salt. Pour into greased 3-quart shallow baking dish. Gently break eggs without breaking yolks into the liquid. Space the eggs evenly. Sprinkle with cheese. Bake 15 minutes at 350° or until eggs are set. Serve poached eggs on plates with sauce spooned over the top. Serves 4.

Betty Cook, '48
Dallas

341

John Wayne Casserole
A he-man breakfast—but pretty enough for his lady!

1 pound Monterrey Jack
cheese, grated
3 cans (4 oz. each) green
chile peppers, diced
1 pound Cheddar
cheese, grated
4 eggs, separated
1 tablespoon flour
½ teaspoon salt
¼ teaspoon pepper
1⅓ cups half and half
cream
2 tomatoes, halved and
cut into slices

Combine cheese and chiles, place in buttered 9 x 13-inch casserole. Mix egg yolks, flour, salt, pepper and cream. Fold in stiffly beaten egg whites. Pour over cheese mixture using a fork to help the egg mixture soak through the cheese mixture. Bake 1 hour at 300°. Remove from oven, arrange tomatoes decoratively over top of casserole. Bake 20 to 30 minutes more or until knife comes out clean when tested. Cut into squares. Serves 8.

Jim Jenkins, BBA '74 MPA '76
Dallas

Hash Brown Omelet
Crisp base, puffy souffle top, delicious

4 strips bacon
2 cups frozen hash
brown potatoes
¼ cup chopped onion
¼ cup chopped green
pepper
4 eggs
¼ cup milk
Salt to taste
Pepper to taste
1 cup grated American
cheese

In well-seasoned cast iron or teflon 10-inch skillet, fry bacon. Remove bacon from skillet, drain on paper towels. To drippings in skillet add potatoes, onion and green pepper. Saute over low heat until potatoes are almost done. Press mixture evenly over bottom of the skillet to form base for omelet. Combine eggs, milk, salt and pepper. Pour over potato mixture. Top with cheese and reserved bacon. Cover, cook at low heat 10 minutes. Loosen omelet. Serve in wedges. Serves 4.

Harriet Schmitt Livingston, BS '69
Fort Worth

Bacon Cheese Oven Omelet

12 strips bacon
6 slices (¾ oz. each)
   cheese
8 eggs, beaten
1 cup milk
   Salt and pepper to
   taste

Fry bacon. Curl 1 strip, chop 4 strips and cut the remaining strips in half. Cut cheese slices in half and arrange in buttered 9-inch pie pan. Combine milk and seasonings with eggs and whisk. Add chopped bacon. Pour mixture over cheese. Bake 30 minutes at 350°. Remove from oven. Place curled bacon strip in center of pie. Arrange half strips spoke-fashion over filling. Bake 10 minutes more. Cool 5 minutes before serving. Serves 5 or 6.

Terry Green, wife of Leonard F. Green, BA '79
Houston

TEX-MEX VEGETABLE OMELET. "Chop an onion and some shallots finely and saute slowly. Chop, finely, 2 or 3 lengths of celery, 2 fresh tomatoes, 2 jalapeños, a few mushrooms, and half a green pepper. Chop, also finely, two or three kinds of cheese, including Cheddar and Gruyère. Add in, mixed, say 6 or 8 or 10 eggs and a small dash of milk. Mix the mess together. In a covered pan, with corn oil, cook very slowly. Do not scramble, but as omelet hardens, lift edges (and perhaps punch holes in bottom) to let uncooked liquid cook. Serves up in pie-like wedges."

Ronnie Dugger, BA '50
San Antonio

Deviled Eggs

1 dozen eggs
1 teaspoon salt
2 medium-sized sweet
   pickles
1 rib celery
2 green onions
1 teaspoon dry mustard
2 tablespoons salad
   dressing
2 tablespoons tarragon
   vinegar
Paprika
Fresh parsley

Prepare eggs according to cookbook directions (See Index, Hard-Cooked Eggs). Separate yolks from whites. Mince pickles, celery and onion. Add mustard and salad dressing, combine with finely mashed egg yolks. Add vinegar slowly, beating to achieve firm mixture. All of the vinegar may not be needed. Pile filling into whites. Dust each egg with paprika, top with a parsley sprig. Chill at least 3 hours before serving. Serves 6.

Margaret Macha Kiefer, BA '69
Austin

Cheese Grits Casserole
Great way to use leftover meat; a complete meal with vegetable and salad.

1 teaspoon salt
1 cup hominy grits,
    non-instant
1 cup coarsely grated
    mild Cheddar,
    Muenster, Gouda
    or Swiss cheese
¼ teaspoon onion or
    garlic powder
2 tablespoons butter
1 can (4 oz.) chopped
    mushrooms, drained
1 cup cooked chicken,
    ham or beef, diced
1 cup thinly sliced
    celery
1 package (6 oz.) garlic
    cheese, sliced
    ¼-inch thick
½ cup potato or corn
    chips, crushed
    Paprika

In saucepan, bring 5 cups water and salt to boil. Slowly add grits, stirring. Cover. Simmer 25 to 30 minutes, stirring occasionally. Add shredded cheese and stir until melted. Season with onion or garlic powder. In skillet, melt butter and saute mushrooms and meat. In buttered 2-quart baking dish, layer half the grits. Add mushroom mixture. Sprinkle with celery. Cover with remaining grits. Arrange cheese slices on top in single layer. Sprinkle with crushed chips and paprika. Bake 20 to 25 minutes at 325°. Serves 6.

Twyla Lynn Tranfaglia, BA '73 MLS '74
El Paso

HARD-COOKED EGGS. Place room-temperature eggs in bowl of tepid water. Bring large pan of water to boil, add 1 teaspoon salt. Slowly lower wet eggs into water, immediately reduce heat to medium low. At beginning of cooking period, frequently stir eggs gently to center yolks. Cook 20 minutes, but do not boil. Drain, immediately submerge eggs into iced water. Peel eggs when cool. This method produces tender-cooked whites and no 5 o-clock shadow on yolks. Also, use eggs that are several days old.

DEVILED EGGS. For beautiful and easy deviled eggs, place tender-cooked white halves on serving tray (never place directly on silver). For variety, cut eggs crosswise rather than lengthwise. Cutting small slice from bottom of each white will help assure an upright stance. Fill pastry bag, fitted with large fluted tip, with smooth but firm yolk mixture. Pipe mixture into egg white cavities. Sprinkle with paprika, or decorate and garnish as desired. *Editor.*

Garlic Cheese Grits

1 cup grits, non-instant
4 cups boiling water
1 teaspoon salt
2 rolls (6 oz. each)
    garlic cheese, sliced
4 tablespoons (½ stick)
    butter
4 eggs, well beaten

Cook grits in water with salt until all water is absorbed, about 10 minutes. Add butter and cheese, stir until melted. Add eggs, stir thoroughly. Pour into 2-quart buttered baking dish. Bake 30 minutes at 400°. Excellent accompaniment for ham and barbecued meats. Serves 8.

Sandra Daniel Billingsley, '60
Greenville

Variation: *Substitute ¼ pound grated cheese for the 2 rolls garlic cheese. Add 1 clove garlic, minced, and 1 chopped jalapeño or ½ teaspoon red pepper or 1 teaspoon Tabasco or ½ can (4 oz. size) green chile peppers, chopped.*

Amy Purcell Powell, BS '55
Navasota

POLLY'S PIMIENTO CHEESE. Combine 1 pound grated Longhorn cheese; 1 onion, grated; 1 large-sized jar chopped pimiento, undrained; and enough salad dressing to make spreadable. Freezes well.

Jane Cornick Jamison, BS '66
Austin

Cheese Souffle

2 tablespoons butter
2 tablespoons flour
⅔ cup milk
1 cup grated cheese
3 eggs, separated

Melt butter, stir in flour. Add milk and cook over low heat until consistency of thick cream sauce. Remove from heat. Add grated cheese. Beat egg yolks, add to sauce and stir 3 minutes more. Beat egg whites until stiff but not dry. Incorporate ¼ of whites into sauce, stir to lighten sauce, then gently fold sauce into remaining egg whites. Pour into 1-quart straight-sided, buttered baking dish. Bake 30 minutes at 350°. Serves 2.

Nell Jones Herndon, BA '30
Bastrop

Pimiento Cheese

1 small-sized onion,
   minced
2 pounds sharp Cheddar
   cheese, grated
1 jar (7 oz.) chopped
   pimientos
3 hard-cooked eggs,
   finely chopped
2 teaspoons salt
2 tablespoons
   Worcestershire
   sauce
1 tablespoon prepared
   mustard
1 pint mayonnaise
   Pepper to taste
   Paprika to taste
   Garlic, onion and
      celery salts to taste

Combine all ingredients. Add seasonings to taste. Keep adding pepper, paprika, garlic salt, onion salt and celery salt to taste.
Yield: 6 cups.

Ann Clements, wife of Jamie Clements, BA '53 LLB '55
Temple

Crabmeat Crepes

12 crepes, 6-inch
   diameter
 1 can (6½ oz.) crabmeat
⅓ cup thinly sliced
   celery
 2 tablespoons finely
   chopped green
   onions
⅓ cup Girard's French
   Salad Dressing
 2 tablespoons diced
   pimiento
¼ teaspoon curry
   powder
 2 teaspoons lemon juice,
   divided
 1 can (10¾ oz.) cream
   of shrimp soup
½ cup half and half
   cream

Combine crabmeat, celery, onion, dressing, pimiento, curry and 1 teaspoon lemon juice. Lightly toss, divide mixture into 12 portions. Fill crepes. Place in 2-quart baking dish, cover tightly, bake 15 minutes at 350°. Combine remaining lemon juice, soup and cream. Cook at low heat, stirring constantly. Serve over baked crepes. Serves 6.

Sandy Lauer, wife of John Lauer, LLB '59
Kentfield, California

346

Creamy Ricotta Cheese Crepes

CREPE BATTER:

4 eggs
1 cup milk
1 cup flour
  Dash salt
1 tablespoon sugar
3 tablespoons butter,
  melted

FILLING:

1 pound Ricotta cheese
8 ounces cream cheese
¼ cup sugar
1 tablespoon cinnamon

TOPPING:

½ pound (2 sticks) butter
  or margarine,
  melted
10 eggs
1½ cups sour cream
1 tablespoon vanilla
1 teaspoon salt
2 tablespoons orange
  juice

In blender, combine eggs and milk. Add dry ingredients, blend quickly and strain. Set aside at least 1 hour at room temperature or refrigerate overnight. Add melted butter before cooking.

FILLING: Thoroughly combine ingredients. Spread each crepe with 1 heaping tablespoon mixture, roll jellyroll-fashion. Place, seam side down, in buttered 3-quart casserole. Arrange 15 crepes per casserole.

TOPPING: Combine ingredients and mix well. Pour mixture evenly over the 2 casseroles. Bake 40 minutes at 350°. These crepes are delicious served with fruit for brunch. Serves 15.

Iris Selber Nathan, '57
Beaumont

SWEETENED CONDENSED MILK. Place in blender 1 cup powdered milk, ¾ cup sugar, ⅓ cup boiling water and 1 tablespoon margarine. Blend at high speed until thickened and smooth, about 5 minutes. Store in refrigerator and use in recipes calling for Eagle Brand milk.

Spinach And Ham Crepes

CREPE:

3 eggs
1½ cups milk
1 cup flour
Salt
Red pepper
4 tablespoons butter, melted
Peanut oil

FILLING:

1 pound fresh spinach
1 cup finely chopped boiled ham, divided
3 tablespoons whipping cream
Salt
Nutmeg
Butter
1 tablespoon cornstarch (optional)
Mornay Sauce
1 tablespoon Parmesan cheese

CREPE: In blender, combine eggs and milk; add dry ingredients. Strain, set aside 1 or 2 hours at room temperature. Add cooled, melted butter just before beginning to cook crepes. Use peanut oil to grease crepe pans. Cook crepes on both sides.

FILLING: Remove stems and heavy veins from spinach leaves. Wash thoroughly. Cook in water 5 minutes, drain. Place half of ham in blender. Add spinach, cream, salt and nutmeg; blend until smooth. Pour mixture into saucepan, add remaining ham. Stir at low heat. If puree appears too thin, add 1 tablespoon cornstarch dissolved in 2 tablespoons cold water and stir until thickened. Spread 1 tablespoon ham puree on each crepe. Fold crepe into triangle, place in buttered casserole. Cover with Mornay Sauce, sprinkle with Parmesan cheese. Bake 15 minutes at 400°. Brown cheese slightly under broiler. Serves 10 to 12.

Paula Jo Black, BS '61
Dallas

Mornay Sauce

1 tablespoon butter
1 tablespoon flour
1 cup milk
3 tablespoons grated Swiss or Gruyère cheese
1 tablespoon grated Parmesan cheese
½ teaspoon Dijon mustard
Salt and pepper to taste

Melt butter, remove from heat. Add flour, stirring with wire whisk. Return to moderate heat. Gradually add milk, stirring constantly until sauce is thickened. Add remaining ingredients, salt and pepper to taste.

Paula Jo Black, BS '61
Dallas

Shrimp Quiche

PASTRY:
- ⅔ cup butter
- 2 cups flour
- 1 teaspoon salt
- 1 teaspoon sugar
- 3 tablespoons iced water

FILLING:
- ½ cup chopped yellow onion
- 2 tablespoons butter
- 1 pound boiled shrimp, peeled and deveined
- ½ cup grated Gruyère or Swiss cheese
- 4 eggs
- 1½ cups whipping cream
- ½ teaspoon salt
- ½ teaspoon white pepper
- 1 tablespoon chopped parsley

Cut butter into flour. Add salt and sugar and enough water to moisten dough. Refrigerate dough at least 30 minutes. Roll out dough, make a 10-inch shell and bake at 400° until shell begins to brown.

FILLING: Saute onions in butter until lightly colored. Add shrimp. Sprinkle cheese in bottom of baked shell. Top with shrimp mixture. Whisk eggs, cream, seasonings and parsley; pour over ingredients in shell. Bake 40 minutes at 375° or until top is lightly browned and custard is set. Cool 10 minutes before serving. Serves 8.

David M. Gould, BA '76
Houston

After The Game Quiche

- 1 unbaked 9-inch pie shell
- 6 eggs, beaten
- ½ cup chopped green onions
- 4 mushrooms, chopped
- 2 tablespoons butter
- ½ cup chopped cooked chicken, ham or turkey
- ½ cup grated Parmesan cheese
- 1 can (10¾ oz.) cream of celery soup
- ½ cup half and half cream
- 1 teaspoon salt
- ½ teaspoon pepper
- Dash garlic powder

Brush inside of pie shell with small amount of beaten egg. Using fork prick bottom and sides of shell. Bake shell 5 minutes at 450°. Cool. Reduce heat to 375°. Saute onions and mushrooms in butter. Combine with chicken and Parmesan. Spread mixture in pie shell. Combine eggs with remaining ingredients. Mix well. Pour over chicken mixture. Bake 30 to 35 minutes at 375° or until knife inserted into middle of pie comes out clean. Cool 5 minutes before serving. Serves 6.

Penny Porter Helms, BFA '66
Austin

Crab Supper Quiche

1 cup shredded Swiss
    cheese
1 unbaked 9-inch pie
    shell
1 can (6½ oz.)
    crabmeat, drained
2 green onions, chopped
3 eggs, beaten
1 cup cream
½ teaspoon salt
½ teaspoon grated lemon
    rind
¼ teaspoon dry mustard
    Dash mace
¼ cup sliced or slivered
    almonds

Sprinkle cheese over bottom of pie shell. Add crabmeat, then green onions. Combine remaining ingredients except almonds. Pour mixture in pie shell. Top with almonds. Bake 45 to 50 minutes at 350°. Remove from oven. Cool 10 minutes before cutting and serving. Serves 6 to 8.

Eleanor Ann Van Zandt Gerrard, BA '42
Victoria

HASTY HAMBURGER QUICHE. Brown ½ to 1 pound ground beef in skillet, drain and set aside. Mix ¼ cup mayonnaise, ½ cup milk, 3 eggs and ¾ cup biscuit mix until smooth. Stir into beef, 1 to 1½ cups grated Cheddar or Swiss cheese, ⅓ cup chopped green onion and dash pepper. Pour into greased 9-inch pie plate. Add ½ to 1 cup milk to fill pie plate after adding beef mixture (amount varies according to cheese and meat quantities). Bake 30 minutes at 400°. Serves 6.

Louise Harrell Mulkey, BA '61
Panhandle

Muenster 'N' Onion Quiche

1 unbaked 9-inch pie
    shell
1½ tablespoons Dijon
    mustard
½ cup chopped onion
2 tablespoons butter
1½ cups grated Muenster
    cheese
⅔ cup milk
1 egg, beaten
1 egg yolk, beaten
¼ teaspoon salt
    Pepper to taste

Bake pie shell 5 minutes at 375°. Cool. Spread cooled shell with mustard. Saute onion in butter. Layer cheese, onion, cheese in pie shell. Mix together remaining ingredients and pour over cheese. Bake 40 minutes at 350°. Serves 6 to 8.

Jane Lovett Wells, BFA '71
San Antonio

Sausage Cheese Quiche

1 pound sausage
½ cup onion
⅓ cup green pepper
1 cup grated Cheddar
   or Swiss cheese
2 cups milk
½ cup biscuit mix
4 eggs
¼ teaspoon salt
   Pinch of pepper

Saute sausage, onion and green pepper until sausage is browned. Mix with cheese in bottom of 10-inch, deep-dish pie pan. Blend milk, biscuit mix, eggs, salt and pepper in blender until smooth. Pour over sausage mixture. Bake 50 to 55 minutes at 350°. Serves 6 to 8.

Sara Catherine Collier, BBA '81
Austin

Spinach Quiche *quich - needs deep dish*

1 unbaked 10-inch pie
   shell
1 cup shredded Swiss
   cheese
3 eggs, slightly beaten
1 can (5.33 oz.)
   evaporated milk
2 teaspoons Worcester-
   shire sauce
½ teaspoon onion salt
½ teaspoon salt
   Pepper to taste
1 package (10 oz.)
   frozen spinach,
   cooked and drained
1 jar (2½ oz.) sliced
   mushrooms, drained
   or equivalent
   amount fresh
   mushrooms, sauteed
8 strips crisp bacon,
   crumbled, and
   divided
   Grated Parmesan
   cheese

Sprinkle Swiss cheese over pie shell. Combine eggs, milk, Worcestershire sauce and seasonings. Stir in spinach, mushrooms and half the bacon. Pour mixture into pie shell. Sprinkle with Parmesan. Bake 20 minutes at 350° remove from oven and sprinkle remaining bacon over top of quiche. Bake 20 minutes more. Serves 6 to 8.

Lynne Prater, wife of Harold G. Prater, BBA '55
Arlington

Tortilla Onion Quiche

4 flour tortillas
  (6-inch size)
4 ounces Monterrey
  Jack cheese with
  peppers, sliced
1 medium-sized onion,
  sliced into separate
  rings
5 eggs, beaten and
  divided
½ cup wheat germ
2 cups milk
½ teaspoon salt
½ teaspoon chile powder
¼ teaspoon dry mustard

Gently press a tortilla into each of 4 individual au gratin casseroles. Top with cheese slices. Dip onion rings into 1 beaten egg, coat liberally with wheat germ. Top cheese slices with about two-thirds of the coated onion rings; reserve remainder. In saucepan, heat milk until almost boiling. Gradually add milk to remaining eggs, beat well. Stir in salt, chile powder and mustard. Place casseroles in shallow baking pan on oven rack. Divide egg mixture among casseroles. Top with remaining coated onion rings. Bake 30 minutes at 350° or until knife inserted off-center comes out clean. Set aside at room temperature at least 10 minutes before serving. Serves 4.

Sara Avant, BS '78
New Orleans, Louisiana

Broccoli Quiche
Tasty—a meal in itself

2 packages (10 oz. each)
  frozen chopped
  broccoli, thawed
  and drained
1 medium-sized onion,
  finely chopped
1 cup Bisquick
4 eggs, lightly beaten
½ cup vegetable oil
½ cup grated extra
  sharp Cheddar
  cheese
1 tablespoon chopped
  fresh parsley
  Salt and pepper to
  taste

Combine all ingredients and mix well. Pour into buttered 10-inch pie pan. Bake 40 minutes at 350°. Serves 6 to 8.

Bessie Kilgore Merner, BA '30 MA '32
Faribault, Minnesota

Zucchini Quiche

4 cups thinly sliced
   zucchini
1 cup chopped onion
½ cup butter
½ cup chopped parsley
   or 2 tablespoons
   dried parsley flakes
½ teaspoon salt
½ teaspoon pepper
¼ teaspoon garlic
   powder
¼ teaspoon sweet basil
¼ teaspoon oregano
2 eggs, beaten
2 cups (8 oz.) grated
   Mozzarella or
   Muenster cheese or
   a mixture of both
   cheeses
1 can crescent rolls
2 teaspoons Dijon
   mustard

Saute zucchini and onion in butter 10 minutes. Drain well. Add parsley, salt, pepper, garlic powder, sweet basil and oregano. Combine eggs and cheese, stir into zucchini mixture. Unroll crescent rolls into 1 long, flat rectangle. Press over bottom and sides of 10-inch pie pan. (This uses about two-thirds of the rectangle; reserve remaining dough.) Spread crust with mustard. Pour in vegetable mixture. Cut remaining dough into strips and form a lattice on top of the pie, tucking ends under the crust edge. Bake 20 or 30 minutes at 375° or until center is firm. Cool 10 minutes before serving. Serves 8.

Ann Driscoll Hatchell, BS '65
Tyler

Artichoke Rice Salad
A very delicious, colorful cold salad

1 box (8 oz.) Chicken
   Rice-a-Roni
1 jar (6 oz.) marinated
   artichoke hearts
3 green onions, chopped
½ green pepper, chopped
1 can (6 oz.) chopped
   black olives
1 jar (4½ oz.)
   mushrooms,
   chopped
⅓ cup mayonnaise

Prepare Rice-a-Roni according to package directions. For this recipe the rice should be cooked until dry. Drain and reserve marinade from artichokes. Chop artichokes. Combine cooked rice with chopped vegetables. Combine reserved marinade with mayonnaise and pour over vegetable mixture. Chill. Serves 8 to 10.

Lynn Rosenfeld, BJ '72
Houston

Quick Rice Pudding
Great use for leftover rice

1 cup cooked rice
½ cup sugar
2 cups milk
1 teaspoon vanilla
2 eggs, slightly beaten
½ cup raisins
   Cinnamon or nutmeg

Combine all ingredients and pour into small casserole. Sprinkle with cinnamon or nutmeg. Bake 45 minutes at 350°. Serves 6.

Cindy Wilson Walker, BS '79
Houston

Rice Souffle
Marvelous way to use leftover rice

3 eggs
1 cup cooked and
   chilled rice
½ cup milk
2 tablespoons butter or
   margarine
4 ounces grated
   Cheddar cheese
   Salt to taste

Separate eggs, beat egg yolks and add to rice. Combine with milk, butter, cheese and salt. Stir well. Beat egg whites until stiff but not dry. Stir ⅓ of the whipped whites into rice mixture. Gently fold in remaining egg whites. Pour into buttered, 1-quart souffle dish. Bake 30 to 45 minutes at 300° until brown on top. Serves 4.

Myrtle Ligon, wife of Jack A. Ligon, BA '50
San Antonio

Water Chestnut Rice

¾ cup (1½ sticks) butter
1 can (6 oz.) sliced
   mushrooms
2 cups uncooked rice
2 cans (10¾ oz. each)
   cream of onion soup
1 soup can water
1 can (8 oz.) sliced
   water chestnuts

Melt butter in 3-quart casserole. Add remaining ingredients, stir, cover and bake 1½ hours at 350°. Serves 12.

Kay Rose Sims, BS '72
Mountain Home, Arkansas

Texas Rice Patties
Serve with a choice, Texas-sized steak

½ cup brown rice
½ cup diced tomato
½ cup grated carrot
½ cup finely chopped
    green pepper
½ cup diced onion
½ cup grated Mozzarella
    cheese
½ cup chopped pecans
½ cup wheat germ
1 teaspoon thyme
1 teaspoon salt
1 tablespoon butter or
    margarine
SAUCE:
1 can (8 oz.) tomato
    sauce
½ teaspoon garlic
    powder
1 teaspoon dried parsley
    flakes
  Grated Parmesan
    cheese to taste

Cook rice according to package directions. Prepare tomato, carrot, green pepper, onion, cheese and pecans using grinder or food processor if desired. When rice is cooked, combine with remaining ingredients. Mix thoroughly. If mixture seems dry, add a little milk. Shape into patties and place on greased baking sheet. Bake 30 to 45 minutes, depending on crispness desired.

SAUCE: Combine all ingredients and mix well. Heat until bubbly and pour over patties. Serves 4 to 6.

Jamie Carter Snell, BJ '73
Beaumont

Almond Fried Rice

¼ cup butter
1 large-sized onion,
    chopped
1 green pepper, chopped
3 smoked pork chops,
    thinly sliced
½ teaspoon pepper
¼ cup soy sauce
1 cup toasted slivered
    almonds
4 cups cooked rice
  Salt
1 tablespoon chopped
    pimiento

In heavy skillet melt butter and saute onion and green pepper until tender. Add pork, pepper, soy sauce, almonds, rice and salt to taste. Simmer until pork is cooked and flavors are well mixed. Add pimiento just before serving. Serves 6.

Ruth Ann Neves Powell, BS '72
Alvin

Chinese Fried Rice
Easy, fast, great for leftovers, or plan-overs!

¼ cup oil
3 green onions, thinly sliced
3 cups cooked and chilled rice
¾ teaspoon salt
¼ teaspoon pepper
1 tablespoon soy bean paste with garlic
½ cup julienne-cut cooked ham, pork, chicken or shrimp
3 eggs
1½ tablespoons soy sauce

Heat oil, add onions and saute until fragrant. Add rice gradually and fry gently 10 minutes or until oil is absorbed. Add salt, pepper, bean paste and cooked meat; stir well. Beat eggs until smooth and in a thin stream pour over the rice, stirring constantly. Heat gently, stirring until all egg is evenly distributed and set. Sprinkle with soy sauce. Serves 4 to 6.

Maurine Redfearn Bartos, BS '57
Waco

Variation: *Add 6 strips bacon, diced, and fry in wok. Use drippings to replace oil. Do not saute onion, add uncooked just before removing from heat. Increase meat to 1 cup.*

Sue Brooks Littlefield, BA '77 JD '80
Austin

Margarita's Arroz Mexicano
Mild to hot variations of an old favorite!

1 cup uncooked rice
2 tablespoons bacon grease or salad oil
1 fresh tomato, chopped
½ medium-sized onion, chopped
2 large-sized cloves garlic, minced
1 can (4 oz.) chopped green chile peppers
2 cups water
Salt to taste
Dash cumin

Saute rice in oil until golden brown. Remove rice and saute 1 minute, the tomato, onion, garlic and green chile peppers. Add rice, water, salt and cumin. Stir and cover, simmer 30 to 35 minutes or until tender. Serves 4 to 6.

Kay Jones Becker, BS '69
El Paso

Variation: "KINDA HOT". *Substitute chicken broth for water and ¼ cup picante sauce for green chile peppers. Omit tomato and garlic.*

Sandra Daniel Billingsley, '60
Greenville

Variation: HOT. *Use 1 onion, add 1 can (16 oz.) stewed tomatoes, 1 tablespoon picante sauce, 1 canned jalapeño, seeded and chopped. Drain liquid from tomatoes and add enough water to make 2¼ cups.*

Susan Fortson Magee, BA '76 MLS '78
Brownsville

Porky's Rice
And Green Chiles

Creamy, most delicious rice dish we have had

¾ cup uncooked rice
2 cups sour cream
  Salt and pepper to
    taste
1 pound Monterrey Jack
    cheese, divided
2 cans (4 oz. each)
    peeled green chile
    peppers
2 tablespoons butter

Cook rice according to package directions. Combine with sour cream and season to taste. Arrange half the mixture in bottom of buttered 9-inch square casserole. Cut ½ pound Monterrey Jack cheese into domino-sized pieces and wrap in strips of green chiles. Place on top of rice, add remaining rice mixture, dot with butter. Cover with remaining Monterrey Jack cheese, grated. Bake 30 minutes at 350°. Serves 4 to 6.

Richard A. Haberman, BA '61
Austin

Variation: *Use ¾ pound Monterrey Jack cheese in layers and top with ½ pound Cheddar cheese added during last 10 minutes of baking.*

Elaine Wiswell Guy, BA '75
Midland

Variation: *Substitute ½ cup Cheddar cheese for layering and top with ½ cup grated Parmesan cheese.*

Sylvia Cook, BA '65
Austin

Variation: *Reduce cheese to ½ pound and increase sour cream to 3 cups. Do not layer, use chopped chile peppers and mix together all ingredients. Bake 1 hour at 350°.*

Nancy Milburn Granaghan,
wife of John Thomas Granaghan, Jr., BA '73
San Angelo

Variation: *Substitute Cheddar cheese or 2 jars (8 oz. each) Cheese Whiz for Monterrey Jack. Substitute 4 to 6 canned jalapeños for green chile peppers. Stem, seed and chop jalapeños. Mix together with remaining ingredients.*

Agnes Warren Barnes, BS '57
Waco

Cheesy Jalapeño Rice

1 cup uncooked rice
1 onion, chopped
2 tablespoons oil
1 can (10¾ oz.) beef
    bouillon
1 to 3 jalapeño peppers,
    minced
3 cups grated Cheddar
    cheese
Half and half cream

Brown rice and onion in oil. Add bouillon and jalapeños. Cover and set aside. When rice has absorbed the liquid, layer rice and the cheese in 2-quart baking dish. Pour half and half cream to top of the rice. Cover tightly with foil, bake 45 minutes at 350°. Serves 6.

Sara Avant, BS '78
New Orleans, Louisiana

HOT AND SPICY RICE CASSEROLE. Combine 2 cups cooked rice with 1 can (10 oz.) tomatoes with green chile peppers; 1 small-sized onion, chopped; ¼ cup (½ stick) butter; 1 cup grated Cheddar cheese; salt and pepper to taste. Pour into buttered 8-inch square casserole. Top with ½ cup grated Cheddar cheese. Bake 30 minutes at 350°. Serves 4 to 6.

Sue and David L. Parsley, BBA '66
Nederland

Rice Frittato
Good for a main dish during Lent!

½ cup finely chopped
    onion
1 tablespoon butter
8 eggs
½ cup milk
1 teaspoon salt
1 teaspoon Worcester-
    shire sauce
2 dashes Tabasco
2 cups cooked rice
1 can (4 oz.) chopped
    green chile peppers,
    undrained
1 medium-sized tomato,
    chopped
½ cup grated Cheddar
    cheese

In 10-inch skillet over medium high heat, saute onions in butter until tender. Beat eggs with milk and seasonings. Stir in rice, chile peppers and tomato. Add to skillet. Reduce heat to medium low. Cover; cook until top is almost set, about 12 to 15 minutes. Sprinkle with cheese. Cover, remove from heat, set aside 10 minutes. Serves 4.

Sara Avant, BS '78
New Orleans, Louisiana

Sauce For Wild Rice
Add shrimp for a delicious gumbo-like entree

1 onion, finely chopped
2 tablespoons butter
2 cans (16 oz. each)
    tomatoes
1 can (10 oz.) tomatoes
    with green chile
    peppers
1 can (15 oz.) tomato
    sauce
1 can (8 oz.) sliced
    water chestnuts
1 can (6 oz.)
    mushrooms
1 cup water
¼ teaspoon cardamom
1 teaspoon oregano
1 bay leaf
  Cooked wild rice

Saute onions in butter until soft. Add remaining ingredients, simmer 1 hour. Serve over wild rice. This may be made ahead and frozen; this recipe also keeps refrigerated. Serves 12.

Jo Laynne Hill Boies, MM '72
Austin

Sausage-Wild Rice Casserole

2 packages (6 oz. each)
    wild rice mix
½ teaspoon poultry
    seasoning
1 pound sausage (bulk)
2 medium-sized onions,
    chopped
2 cans (4 oz. each)
    mushrooms
2 cups canned chicken
    broth
¼ cup flour
½ cup half and half
    cream
½ cup toasted slivered
    almonds

Cook rice according to package directions, adding poultry seasoning. Saute sausage, stirring to break meat into small-sized pieces until lightly browned. Remove sausage and drain on paper towel. Saute onion in sausage drippings. Add undrained mushrooms, cooked sausage, rice and broth. Combine flour and cream into smooth paste, stir into mixture. Pour mixture into 10-inch square oven-to-table casserole. Bake 25 to 30 minutes at 350°. Sprinkle with almonds when ready to serve. Serves 6 to 8.

Loraine McNeil Jackson, '46
Marble Falls

Fiesta Pilaf

½ cup (1 stick) butter or margarine
1 onion, thinly sliced
2 cups uncooked long-grain rice
4 teaspoons instant beef bouillon
4 cups water
2 cans (4 oz. each) mushroom pieces, undrained
1 cup raisins
1 cup grated carrots
1 package (2¼ oz.) cashew pieces

Melt butter in large-sized Dutch oven. Add onion and rice; cook over medium heat 8 minutes, stirring frequently. Dissolve bouillon in boiling water and add, with mushrooms, to rice mixture. Mix well. Cover and bake 50 minutes at 325°. Stir in raisins, carrots and cashews. (If rice mixture is dry, add 1 tablespoon butter and 1 cup boiling water.) Bake 10 minutes more or until liquid is absorbed. Serve with turkey in place of traditional dressing. Serves 6 to 8.

Helen Dixon Brown, MA '34
San Antonio

Holiday Rice
Delicious, great meat accompaniment with roast or chicken

½ cup coarsely chopped filberts
1 package (6 oz.) seasoned long grain and wild rice mix
1 can (14½ oz.) chicken broth
1 tablespoon lemon juice
½ teaspoon dried tarragon
¼ cup finely chopped mushrooms
4 tablespoons (½ stick) butter
Salt
Freshly ground pepper
¼ cup dry sherry
2 tablespoons chopped parsley

Toast filberts for 10 minutes at 350°, set aside. In small saucepan prepare rice mix according to package directions, substituting chicken broth for water and omitting butter. Add lemon juice and tarragon. Stir and bring to boil. Cover, simmer at low heat until liquid is absorbed and rice is tender. Saute mushrooms in butter. Add salt and freshly ground pepper to taste. Add sherry and parsley. With two forks toss mushroom mixture into cooked rice. Transfer to serving dish and top with roasted chopped filberts. Serves 6.

Tillie Fauntleroy, wife of O.W. Fauntleroy, BA '48
Tulsa, Oklahoma

Lone Star Red Beans And Rice

1 pound ground beef
¼ cup bacon grease
1½ cups chopped onion
½ cup chopped green pepper
1 clove garlic, minced
1 teaspoon chili powder
1 teaspoon salt
1 can (15 oz.) kidney beans, undrained
1 can (16 oz.) tomatoes, undrained
¾ cup uncooked rice
⅔ cup grated Cheddar cheese
½ cup chopped black olives

Brown beef in bacon grease. Add onion, pepper, garlic, chili powder and salt. Cook 5 minutes, remove from heat and add kidney beans, tomatoes and uncooked rice. Mix well, pour into a casserole. Sprinkle top with cheese and olives. Bake, covered, 1 hour at 350° or until rice is done. Serves 8.

Susan and Jim Kessler, Friends of UT
Austin

TEXAS HOT RICE (*Excellent with steak*). Cook 1 cup rice according to package directions. When cooked, add ½ pound grated Cheddar cheese, 2 to 4 canned jalapeños and 2 cups sour cream. Bake in buttered casserole 30 minutes at 350°. Serves 4.

Agnes Warren Barnes, BS '57
Waco

SWISS RICE. Toss 4 cups hot, cooked rice with 4 tablespoons butter. Add 3 eggs, beaten; 2 cups grated Swiss cheese; 1 cup whipping cream; ½ teaspoon salt; and a dash of pepper. Pour in buttered 2-quart casserole, bake 45 minutes at 375° or until center tests done. Serves 8 to 10.

Irene Reeb Meitzen, BA '65
San Angelo

HERB RICE. "Saute 1½ cups uncooked rice in 3 tablespoons olive oil, add ½ cup each chopped onion and celery, and ¼ cup chopped parsley. Cook 5 minutes, stirring constantly. Add 2 cups chicken bouillon, 1 cup dry white wine, a pinch each of oregano, thyme, rosemary, salt and pepper to taste and ½ teaspoon monosodium glutamate. Bring to boil, pour into 2-quart casserole. Cover, bake 30 minutes at 375°. Uncover and stir with fork, cover again and bake 10 minutes more. Serves 6 to 8."

Lena Pettit Hickman, BA '15
Austin

The 1970s

Salads
Salad Dressings

Most students remember standing in line at registration. One of the last long lines in front of Gregory Gymnasium is shown in this photograph. Students now register in the airconditioned Frank C. Erwin Special Events Center, and the process has been eased by data processing and preregistration.

*T*he social changes of the 1960s had a significant effect on the campus of the 1970s. Surges of change included the anti-war movement, widespread use of drugs, integration efforts, use of the pill, campus revolts, assassinations of John F. and Robert Kennedy and Martin Luther King, the "God-is-Dead" movement, and various anti-elitist movements. Demonstrations and protests became routine and commonplace at the University in the early 1970s. Students at the University protested the Vietnam War, the Kent State killings, the firing of Dean John Silber, the building of the Chancellor's house (Bauer House), the building of a wall around part of the campus, digging up the West Mall in preparation for new landscaping, the firing of President Stephen H. Spurr, the hiring of Lorene Rogers as president, cutting the trees on Waller Creek to make room for Bellmont Hall, Texas abortion laws, keeping nonstudents out of the Texas Union, and the possibility of being drafted. They also demonstrated for the rights of Chicanos, Blacks, women, the mobility impaired, married students, veterans, and foreign students.

Lowering the voting age from 21 to 18 in 1971 meant that most students were now adults. They could vote, drink alcoholic beverages, and make decisions that heretofore had been made for them. Politicians began trying to get the student vote in city, state, and national elections. The women's liberation movement had an impact on students at UT. More older women returned to classes to continue their educations. Consciousness-raising sessions and assertiveness training were "in" during the early 1970s. Federal legislation led honorary and service organizations to become co-ed, and women's athletics began to receive financial support. Alcohol was permitted on the campus in 1974: even the Texas Union began to sell beer, wine and mixed drinks! Co-ed floors became commonplace in the Jester Center dormitory complex that housed almost 3,000 students.

Incidents in the national life had their effects on student life. The Watergate scandals and the resignation of President Richard Nixon, the serious energy shortage, and spiraling inflation—all cast a gloomy shadow on the campus.

At the beginning of the decade, the UT System offices moved to some newly renovated government buildings in downtown Austin, and the Regents named Stephen H. Spurr as president following the short tenure of Bryce Jordan as president *ad interim*. The oversized College of Arts and Sciences had been split into four parts, and its dean, John Silber, was fired for protesting too much. In 1964 the Regents fired President Spurr and named Lorene L. Rogers acting president and later president over fierce objections from faculty and students to the method by which she was chosen. As she retired from the position in 1979, Peter T. Flawn became president to begin his "war on mediocrity." Before President Rogers left office, she created a College of Liberal Arts by putting back together three of the four units of the old College of Arts and Sciences, leaving independent a College of Natural Sciences.

Early in the 1970s, psychology was the most popular major. After the Vietnam War ended, changing economic conditions caused students to be more career oriented, and business administration became the most attractive field. Engineering and communications also drew large numbers. Enrollment in education and the humanities declined as overall enrollment climbed steadily from 39,000 in 1970 to more than 44,000 in 1979. More Merit Scholars registered, but grade inflation was an issue. Interest in continuing education increased and more older students attended classes.

The shuttle bus was extremely popular, and many students rode bicycles and mopeds. With increasing costs of rent and food, students moved back to the residence halls, which had been unpopular in the late 1960s, or to other less expensive places near the campus.

The Students' Association, after 76 years, was dumped by popular vote of the student body in 1978. Proclaiming it as a farce, serious student leaders urged its defeat. New centers of interest for students emerged in the Alumni Center, where a Student Involvement Committee became active and highly visible. The newly renovated Texas Union attracted student interest again, but the Union was plagued with financial problems and students in general grew tired of requests for fee increases. Fraternities and sororities increased in popularity again during the second half of the decade, but they had to combat continuing criticism for their nonintegrated memberships, their conservative life styles, their hazing, and their parties.

The Drag presented a different image. Drag vendors occupied so much sidewalk space on Guadalupe in the early 1970s that they were moved to 23rd Street where the city expanded the sidewalks and closed the street to traffic. Numerous fast food shops and more bookstores appeared while fashion shops almost disappeared. The Varsity and Texas theaters shifted from first-run films to increasingly risqué and finally X-rated pictures. Food vendors on The Drag and at other popular crosswalks sold sandwiches, egg rolls, fajitas, burritos, cookies, and homemade ice cream. The Schlotzsky, a wonderful, giant-size sandwich first made in the 1960s at a shop on South Congress, was a student favorite.

Discos drew big crowds. Students filled Valentine's, the Greenhouse, and the Keg any night of the week. Country western music and entertainment flourished. The Silver Dollar North and South were extremely popular on "student nights." Rock, hard rock, and rock-a-billy blared from stereos and loud speakers in the student neighborhoods. The West Austin Neighborhood Association complained about student behavior, but the University no longer assumed responsibility for off-campus activity. Students were full citizens, and they were subject to the laws of the community. The crowd that came to hear the ZZ Top rock band almost filled, and almost ruined, Memorial Stadium at a concert in September 1973. The Students' Association profited from the venture, but it took two years to get the stadium back into its former condition.

The Night Hawk on The Drag, Christi's on Town Lake, and El Mat on East Avenue closed as the decade ended. These popular restaurants for students were victims of the changing times. The manager of the Night Hawk claimed that few students wanted sit-down service anymore. The pace had changed, and fast food chains appealed to those in a hurry.

Jeans, T-shirts, and sandals dominated the fashion picture of the 1970s for both males and females. Skimpy bikinis and even topless swim suits were seen at Barton Springs, around apartment complex pools, and at Hippie Hollow on Lake Travis. Jogging shorts and warm-up suits were worn by increasing numbers of joggers on the stadium tracks, along Shoal Creek, at Town Lake, and even along streets in the campus neighborhood. Toward the end of the decade, however, fashions again began to change; students appeared neater as girls began to wear skirts and blouses, Mexican dresses, and sun dresses to class. More and more men also appeared neater in button-down collars and Izod shirts, and jeans and slacks began to replace cut-offs.

The University continued to expand to accommodate a growing student body. The 262 contiguous acres of 1970, became 316 acres by 1979. Building construction slowed down a bit by the end of the decade but not before 15 new buildings had been added and several others enlarged or renovated. Included among the new ones were the Harry Ransom Center, R.L. Moore and Ernest Cockrell Halls, the Communication Building, the grand new Perry-Castañeda Library, and some of the finest facilities for athletics in the country. The Tower burned orange twice during the decade to celebrate two national football championships. It also was turned orange to salute Nobel Prize winner, Ilya Prigogine, Heisman Trophy recipient Earl Campbell, and the UT Press's best-selling book, "The Book of Merlyn."

The surges of change that swept the campus in the 1970s affected society as a whole. Concerns on campus about the environment and energy, about drugs, values, and the nuclear family, and about making money all spilled over from the so-called outside world. The campus and the community became more closely related in the 1970s.

Bluebonnet Garden Luncheons

Persian Cucumber Soup - p. 212
Chicken Salad - p. 369
Cheese Biscuits - p. 26
Blueberry Mousse - p. 142

Mor's Salad - p. 372
Honey Whole Wheat Bread - p. 18
Orange Fruit Freeze - p. 394
Best-Ever Sugar Cookies - p. 99

Chilled Strawberry Soup - p. 213
Luncheon Salad - p. 375
Sausage Biscuits - p. 26
Louise's Luscious Lemon Layers - p. 101

Spinach Salad - p. 383
Broiled Bread Puffs - p. 174
Chocolate Crumble Balls - p. 133

Chicken Salad

4 chicken breasts
¾ cup celery, sliced
¼ to ½ cup green
  onion, sliced
2 teaspoons lemon juice
½ cup mayonnaise
  Seasoned salt
  Garlic salt
  Seasoned pepper

Bake chicken 1 hour at 350°. Cool. Remove skins. Place skins in pie plate and return to oven. Bake until all fat is rendered and skins are crisp and brown. Debone chicken and dice. Crumble crisp skins. Mix all ingredients and season to taste. Serves 4 to 6.

Deanna Cook Murphy, BA '59
Houston

Hot Chicken Salad
Crunchy casserole with a good combination of ingredients

4 cups diced cooked
  chicken
4 cups chopped celery
2 teaspoons salt
½ teaspoon tarragon
¼ cup grated onion
2 cups mayonnaise
2 ounces pimientos,
  chopped
1 tablespoon lemon
  juice
1 cup toasted almonds
¼ cup dry vermouth
TOPPING:
1 cup crushed corn-
  flakes
½ cup grated Parmesan
  cheese

Combine all ingredients except cornflakes and Parmesan. Set aside 1 hour. Place in buttered 2-quart casserole and refrigerate until baking time. Before baking, top with cornflakes and Parmesan. Bake 25 minutes at 350°. Serves 8.

Elizabeth Lynn Rosen, BBA '80
New Orleans, Louisiana

Variation: *Reduce almonds to ½ cup, add 1 can (8 oz.) chopped water chestnuts. Replace topping with 1 cup grated Cheddar cheese.*

Penny Porter Helms, BFA '66
Austin

Elizabeth's Chop Suey Salad

1 cup cooked chicken
¾ cup celery
1 can (16 oz.) bean
     sprouts
1 can (6 oz.) water
     chestnuts
1 cup sliced ripe olives
1 medium-sized green
     pepper, chopped
1 cup thinly sliced
     green onions and
     tops
4 cups shredded mixed
     salad greens

DRESSING:

1 tablespoon
     mayonnaise
2 tablespoons lemon
     juice
1 tablespoon peanut or
     salad oil
¼ cup soy sauce
4 strips cooked
     bacon, crumbled

Cut chicken into strips. String celery and cut diagonally. Drain and rinse bean sprouts. Drain and thinly slice water chestnuts. Combine all ingredients just before serving. Toss with dressing.

DRESSING: Combine mayonnaise, lemon juice and oil. Beat until smooth. Add soy sauce. Top dressed salad with crumbled bacon. Serves 8.

Sara May McCampbell Meriwether, BA '51
Austin

Gulf Coast Shrimp Salad

1½ pounds raw shrimp
1 large-sized avocado
     Lemon juice
3 hard-cooked eggs
2 medium-sized
     tomatoes, peeled
     and diced

SAUCE:

½ cup mayonnaise
½ teaspoon horseradish
2 teaspoons capers
1 teaspoon lemon juice
     Salt to taste

Boil shrimp. Cool, peel and devein. Dice avocado and brush with lemon juice. Combine ingredients and mix with sauce.

SAUCE: Chill 1 hour to allow flavors to blend. Spoon onto beds of lettuce. Serve with potato chips and French bread. Serves 4.

Lucile Nagle, BA '77
Nancy Nagle, MBA '78
Houston

Pickled Fish

1 dozen trout or white
    fish (about 4
    pounds total
    weight)
4 large-sized onions,
    sliced
2 lemons, thinly sliced
12 bay leaves
2 tablespoons mustard
    seed
2 tablespoons black
    peppercorns
1 cup water
2 cups vinegar
3 tablespoons sugar

Clean fish, removing skin and bones. Cut fillets into 1-inch slices. Cover with cold water and refrigerate overnight. Drain. In crock or plastic container (*Do not use metal*), layer fish, onions, lemons, bay leaves, mustard seed and peppercorns. Combine water, vinegar and sugar; bring to boil. Cool. When liquid is cooled pour over fish mixture. Cover container, refrigerate 6 to 10 days before serving. Keeps well, refrigerated, several weeks if you can keep hidden from the "nibblers." Serves 24 as first course, makes 48 Nicoise salads, or satisfies 96 nibblers.

Erika Reeb, Friend of UT
Corpus Christi

CHARLOTTE'S COTTAGE CHEESE SALAD. Combine 2 cups cottage cheese; 2 chopped avocados; 1 large-sized green pepper, chopped; 1 jar (2 oz.) chopped pimientos; ¼ cup mayonnaise; ½ can (4 oz. size) chopped green chile peppers; ¼ cup Italian Dressing; ¼ teaspoon seasoned salt; Tabasco to taste. Mix well and chill. Serves 4.

Sara May McCampbell Meriwether, BA '51
Austin

Shrimp Mousse
A good base for other seafood—crab, clam, lobster

1 packet unflavored
    gelatin
¼ cup water
1 can (10¾ oz.)
    condensed tomato
    soup
8 ounces cream cheese
½ cup chopped celery
¼ cup chopped onion
¼ cup chopped green
    pepper
1 cup mayonnaise
    Dash pepper
2 cans (4½ oz. each)
    shrimp

In a saucepan sprinkle gelatin into water, stir to dissolve. Heat until clear. Add soup and cream cheese. Over low heat, cook mixture until smooth. Remove from heat. Fold in remaining ingredients. Pour into lightly greased 6-cup mold. Chill. Serve as a spread for crackers, or mold in a loaf pan and slice for luncheon. Serves 6.

Brenda Brantley Croucher, BS '72
Houston

Mor's Salad

A Danish delight from a native of Denmark-turned-Texan

2 cans (4½ oz. each)
    shrimp
2 cans (6½ oz. each)
    crabmeat
2 jars (4½ oz. each)
    whole mushrooms
1 can (17 oz.) LeSueur
    peas
1 can (15 oz.) fancy
    asparagus spears
6 hard-cooked eggs,
    sliced
1 grapefruit, sectioned
    (reserve juice)
    Parsley for garnish

DRESSING:

1 cup Hellman's
    mayonnaise
6 tablespoons sugar
    Reserved juice from
      grapefruit
    Juice of 1 lemon
    Pepper to taste
    Salt to taste
¼ teaspoon dry mustard

Drain shrimp and crabmeat. Place on paper towel and check for cartilage and shell pieces. Drain all vegetables and reserve juices. Combine dressing ingredients. Use reserved vegetable juices to thin, if necessary, being careful not to make the dressing too soupy. Layer salad ingredients, pour dressing over mixture, and garnish with parsley and additional shrimp, if desired. Serves 10 to 12.

Kirsten Felker, wife of M.L. "Bud" Felker, Jr., '43
Longview

COLUMBUS EGG FLOWERS. Remove yolks from 6 hard-cooked eggs, combine with 1 tablespoon each Dijon mustard, salt, celery seed, sugar, and butter or margarine. Add 1 teaspoon each Worcestershire sauce and vinegar. Roll mixture into 6 balls. Cut egg whites into strips, arrange spoke-fashion on nasturtium leaves and center with egg ball. Yield: 6 salads.

Helen Dixon Brown, MA '34
San Antonio

Shrimp Rice Salad

1 package (10 oz.)
    frozen green peas
4 tablespoons water
½ teaspoon salt
½ teaspoon sugar
2 cups cooked rice,
    chilled
2 cans (4½ oz. each)
    medium-sized
    shrimp (cooked
    fresh shrimp may
    be used in
    equivalent amount)
1½ cups thinly sliced celery
½ cup sliced green onion
¼ cup toasted almonds
DRESSING:
½ cup salad oil
3 tablespoons cider
    vinegar
1 tablespoon soy sauce
2 teaspoons curry powder
1 teaspoon salt
½ teaspoon monosodium
    glutamate
½ teaspoon celery seed
½ teaspoon sugar

Cook peas in water with salt and sugar 4 minutes. Drain and chill. Rinse canned shrimp in cold water. Combine peas, rice, shrimp, celery, onion and almonds. Toss lightly.

DRESSING: Combine ingredients for salad dressing in blender or shake vigorously in a covered jar. Pour dressing over salad mixture. Refrigerate overnight, tossing and stirring occasionally. Serves 8.

Myrtle Ligon, wife of Jack A. Ligon, BA '50
San Antonio

Hot Lettuce Salad
A quick and easy one-dish meal for all seasons

1 pound ground beef
    Salt
    Freshly ground pepper
1 head iceburg lettuce
1 bottle (8 oz.) French
    dressing
1 can (16 oz.) green
    peas
    Dash Tabasco

Brown meat, stirring and separating lumps so that meat has mealy texture when cooked. Season with salt and pepper. Tear lettuce into bite-sized pieces and add to meat. Add dressing, mix thoroughly and cover. Simmer until lettuce is soft but still slightly firm. Drain peas and add to meat mixture. Season to taste with salt and pepper. Bring to a slow simmer, uncovered, stirring frequently. Serve in bowls with saltine crackers and Tabasco on the side. Serves 4.

Joe M. Coffield, BS '42
Shreveport, Louisiana

373

Niçoise Salad
Julia Child's recipe from the Gritti Palace

2 pounds new potatoes
2 tablespoons white
    wine
1 clove garlic
1 pound green beans
½ cup lemon juice
1½ cups olive oil or
    2 cups salad oil
2 tomatoes
1 onion, finely chopped
2 ounces (12) anchovie
    fillets
  Milk
½ cup pitted black olives
1 clove garlic, chopped
1 bunch leaf lettuce
1 can (7 oz.) albacore
    tuna, or 12 fillets of
    Pickled Fish
2 hard-cooked eggs*
2 tablespoons chopped
    parsley
2 green onions, chopped

Steam potatoes until tender, peel, slice ⅛ inch thick. Pour wine over potatoes while hot. Add garlic clove. Let marinate. Cook beans in large kettle of boiling water until al dente. Drain, immediately plunge into cold water. Let cool, drain and marinate in half of the dressing made of lemon juice and olive oil. Do not marinate for longer than 30 minutes or beans lose their fresh color. Slice tomatoes in wedges and marinate in ¼ of the dressing with onion. Soak anchovies in milk to cover. Marinate olives with chopped garlic in remaining dressing. Arrange lettuce leaves on platter, place drained potatoes in center with drained and dried anchovies laid across top. Arrange beans, tomatoes and tuna spoke fashion from center. Decorate with quartered egg wedges and olives around the edge. Sprinkle salad with parsley and green onions. Serves 8.

Dolores Simmons Snyder, BS '54
Irving

See Index, Hard-Cooked Eggs.

DIET ASPIC FOR SKINNIER LONGHORNS. Heat 1 can (15 oz.) tomato sauce. Add 1 package (⅝ oz.) each of lemon and orange Dezerta, stir to dissolve. Add 2¾ cups cold water and 3 tablespoons cider vinegar. Cool before pouring into buttered mold. Serves 8.

Frances Combest Rountree, BBA '38
Waco

Luncheon Salad
High protein, low calorie

1 cup cottage cheese
1½ cups alfalfa sprouts
½ cucumber, diced
2 small-sized carrots, grated
½ cup Cheddar cheese, diced
1 teaspoon basil
½ cup sunflower seeds
Prepared ranch-style salad dressing or your choice of dressing
Assorted salad greens

GARNISH:

2 tomatoes, cut into eighths
1 green pepper, sliced
3 hard-cooked eggs, sliced

Combine all ingredients except garnish. Arrange salad greens on plate, add salad atop the bed of leaves. Garnish with tomato wedges, green pepper and eggs. Serves 4 to 6.

Zula Thompson Vizard, BA '33 MA '35
San Antonio

Artichoke Salad

¾ cup rice, cooked
1 can (8 oz.) sliced water chestnuts
1 cup pitted black olives, sliced
¼ cup sliced onion
½ cup chopped parsley
¼ cup salad oil
¼ cup wine vinegar
½ package Good Seasons Italian dressing
¾ cup mayonnaise
1 can (14 oz.) artichoke hearts, chopped

Toss together all ingredients except artichokes, Fold in artichokes. Chill overnight to blend flavors. Serves 6.

Pat McCarty, BBA '49
Corpus Christi

Marinated Tomatoes And Artichokes

3 tomatoes, peeled and
  cubed
1 can (14 oz.) artichoke
  hearts
2 tablespoons chopped
  parsley
4 tablespoons garlic
  wine vinegar
½ teaspoon basil
½ teaspoon oregano
½ teaspoon salt
½ teaspoon sugar
¼ teaspoon thyme
  Dash pepper
  Dash dill weed
  Dash celery seed
½ red onion, chopped

Drain artichokes and cut into bite-sized pieces. Add to cubed tomatoes. Combine remaining ingredients. Pour over artichoke mixture. Marinate 12 to 24 hours in refrigerator. Serves 4 to 6.

Nancy Milburn Granaghan,
wife of John Thomas Granaghan, Jr., BA '73
San Angelo

Bean Salad

3 cans (16 oz. each)
  cut green beans
1 tablespoon anchovy
  paste
1 cup Hellman's
  mayonnaise
½ cup half and half
  cream
1 tablespoon fresh
  lemon juice
2 tablespoons tarragon
  vinegar
2 tablespoons garlic
  wine vinegar
¼ cup dried parsley
  flakes
¼ cup dried minced
  onion

Drain beans. Mix anchovy paste with small amount of mayonnaise, then add remaining mayonnaise and all other ingredients. Pour over green beans. Toss beans gently in mixture. Place in container with tightly fitting lid. Chill overnight. Turn beans several times to avoid crushing them. Serves 8 to 10.

Frances Combest Rountree, BBA '38
Waco

Marinated Green Beans
Keeps, refrigerated, 2 weeks

1 can (16 oz.) vertical
    packed green beans
1 cup corn oil
¾ cup tarragon vinegar
1 tablespoon sugar
½ teaspoon salt
    Pepper to taste
3 cloves garlic, whole

Drain beans and place in glass casserole. Mix remaining ingredients and pour over beans. Cover tightly. Marinate overnight. Before serving, remove garlic cloves and drain beans 1 hour. Serves 4.

Raye Virginia McCreary Allen, BA '51 MA '75
Temple

Variation: *Use 3 cans beans, reduce corn oil to ½ cup, add ½ cup sliced onion and dash celery salt.*

Deanna Cook Murphy, BA '59
Houston

Bermuda Salad Bowl

1 small-sized head
    cauliflower
½ large-sized onion
½ cup stuffed olives
⅔ cup French dressing
1 head lettuce
½ cup crumbled
    Roquefort or Bleu
    cheese

Wash cauliflower, separate into flowerets. Cut flowerets into thin lengthwise slices. Cut onion into crosswise slices, then separate into rings. Slice olives. Combine cauliflower, onion, olives and dressing. Chill. Wash lettuce, drain and shred. Toss with cheese and cauliflower mixture in salad bowl. Serves 4 to 6.

Irene Reeb Meitzen, BA '65
San Angelo

Cauliflower Salad

2 heads cauliflower
1 cup chopped celery
1 jar (4 oz.) green
    olives, sliced
1 jar (2 oz.) pimiento
    pieces
1 green pepper, chopped
4 ounces chopped
    Velveeta cheese
DRESSING:
6 ounces sour cream
4 ounces Caesar salad
    dressing

Separate cauliflower into flowerets. Add remaining vegetables and cheese.
DRESSING: Combine ingredients and pour over cauliflower. Chill overnight. Keeps 10 days, covered, in refrigerator. Serves 6 to 8.

Louise Harrell Mulkey, BA '61
Panhandle

Aunt Jeanne's Tomato Aspic

2 cups Snap-E-Tom
Tomato Cocktail
Juice
1 package (3 oz.)
lemon-flavored
gelatin
1 teaspoon horseradish
1 or 2 drops Tabasco
1 tablespoon dried
parsley flakes

OPTIONS:

Sliced artichoke hearts
Shrimp
Flaked crabmeat
Tuna

Heat Snap-E-Tom. In mixing bowl, pour hot liquid over gelatin. Stir until completely dissolved. Add remaining ingredients. For various flavors, add any of the options. Refrigerate until mold is firm. NOTE: To make the salad pretty, arrange avocado slices around the mold when placed on serving platter. If the aspic is used plain, add a dab of mayonnaise atop each serving. Serves 8 to 10.

Margaret Blair, BS '74
Phoenix, Arizona

Fresh Mushroom Salad

8 ounces fresh
mushrooms, sliced
½ bunch green onions,
chopped
½ bunch fresh parsley,
stems removed,
chopped
3 ounces Swiss cheese,
coarsely grated

DRESSING:

¼ cup oil
2 tablespoons tarragon
vinegar
1 tablespoon Worcester-
shire sauce
1½ teaspoons salt
⅛ teaspoon pepper
2 teaspoons dried
parsley flakes or 2
tablespoons
chopped fresh
parsley
1 clove garlic, halved

Combine salad ingredients.

DRESSING: Mix together all ingredients in blender or shake vigorously in screw-top jar. Pour dressing over salad 1 hour before serving, toss and refrigerate. Serves 4.

Brenda Thompson Kolinek, BBA '72
Uvalde

Jícama
Salad Of The Seasons
La Casita Speciality

½ pound jícama
2 large-sized green
    peppers
6 long slender carrots
2 bunches green onions
2 large-sized cucumbers
1 large-sized head
    Romaine lettuce
1 small-sized head
    red cabbage
4 tomatoes
½ bunch fresh cilantro
1 cup seasoned croutons

DRESSING:

½ cup cider vinegar
¼ cup lime juice
2 teaspoons salt
1 teaspoon pepper
1 teaspoon crushed red
    pepper flakes
1 teaspoon dry cilantro
2 teaspoons cumin
    powder
  Dash garlic powder
¾ cup salad oil
¼ cup olive oil

Peel and dice jícama. Dice green peppers. Scrub unpeeled carrots, thinly slice. Clean green onions, slice very thinly white and green parts. Scrub cucumber, do not peel, slice ¼-inch thick. Wash Romaine, do not break apart, slice ribs and leaves ½-inch thick to within 2 inches of base. Shred cabbage. Cut each tomato into 8 wedges. Finely chop cilantro. Combine prepared vegetables, cover and chill. To serve, toss with dressing, top with croutons. Serves 20 to 25.

DRESSING: Combine in blender the vinegar, lime juice and seasonings. With blender at medium speed, slowly pour ¼ cup oil into vortex until well blended. Add remaining oil. Yield: 2 cups.

Beverly Gibbs Harlan,
wife of Harris J. Harlan, BS '60
Tyler

Mustard Ring Mold

4 eggs
¾ cup sugar
1 tablespoon gelatin
1½ tablespoons dry
    mustard
½ teaspoon turmeric
¼ teaspoon salt
¼ cup water
½ cup vinegar
1 cup whipping cream,
    whipped

Beat eggs in top of double boiler. Thoroughly mix sugar, gelatin, mustard, turmeric and salt. Add water and vinegar to eggs. Stir in sugar mixture. Cook over boiling water until slightly thickened, stirring constantly. Cool to lukewarm. Fold in whipped cream. Pour into oiled 1½-quart ring mold. Chill overnight. Serve as accompaniment to baked ham or cold roast pork. Serves 6.

Fred Leisering, BBA '42
Lima, Peru

Sweet And Spicy "Orange" Marinated Carrots

Great as a side dish, salad, appetizer or snack!

2 pounds fresh carrots,
    scraped and sliced
1 medium-sized onion,
    chopped
1 small-sized green
    pepper, chopped
1 can (10¾ oz.) tomato
    soup, undiluted
½ cup oil
½ cup vinegar
¾ cup sugar
1 teaspoon dry mustard
    or 1 tablespoon
    prepared mustard
1 tablespoon Worcester-
    shire sauce
    Salt and pepper to
    taste

Cook carrots 20 minutes. Drain and cool. Add onion and green pepper. Mix remaining ingredients and simmer 5 minutes. Pour over carrots. Marinate 24 hours before serving. These carrots will keep, refrigerated, 2 weeks. Drain before serving. Serves 10.

Kay Appleman, BA '68
Bethesda, Maryland
Peggy Gross Lerner, BA '49
Dallas

Potato Salad

An old-fashioned special with new potatoes

1 pound new potatoes
¼ cup vinegar
1 onion, sliced
    Salt
1 teaspoon chopped
    pimiento
2 tablespoons chopped
    parsley
1 teaspoon salt
    Dash pepper
¾ cup salad dressing

Cook and drain potatoes; dice, and, while still warm, add vinegar. While potatoes are cooking, separate onion into rings, place in shallow pan and coat heavily with salt. Before adding onions to the potatoes, take onions in hand and rinse under running water. Drain. Combine with potatoes and remaining ingredients. Salad may be garnished with 2 hard-cooked eggs. Serves 4.

Mamie Strieber Shepperd, BJ '38
Odessa

380

Elsie Wagner's
Mashed Potato Salad
Reminiscent of Pennsylvania Dutch cooking!

3 large-sized
   potatoes
1 tablespoon butter
1 small-sized onion,
   chopped
3 tablespoons vinegar
1 tablespoon sugar
   Salt and pepper to
   taste
1 hard-cooked egg,
   chopped

Boil potatoes, peel and mash adding butter. Combine with remaining ingredients. Serve hot or chilled. Serves 6 to 8.

Ernest F. Smith, BA '40
Marshall

Papa's Potato Salad
Delicious warm or cold

6 medium-sized potatoes
½ cup celery
¼ cup white onion
3 medium-sized dill
   pickles
1 jar (2 oz.) pimiento
1 tablespoon dried
   parsley flakes
SAUCE:
1 large-sized egg
½ cup salad oil
1 teaspoon prepared
   mustard
1 or 2 tablespoons
   salad dressing
¼ cup dill pickle
   juice
   Salt and pepper to
   taste

Boil potatoes in lightly salted water. Cook until barely tender, not mushy. Cool. Remove skins and dice. Add chopped celery, onion, pickles, pimiento and parsley.

SAUCE: Beat egg until foamy. Add oil, beat well. Add mustard, salad dressing and pickle juice. Pour sauce over potatoes and mix well. Serves 8 to 10.

Denise Jaroszewski Chandler, BS '76
Houston

Raita
Mid-East Indian Salad

1 cup plain yogurt
½ cup sour cream
2 tomatoes, diced
1 cucumber, diced
¼ cup chopped green
    onion
1 teaspoon cumin
1 clove garlic, finely
    minced
½ teaspoon salt
¼ teaspoon pepper
¼ teaspoon red pepper
  Cilantro, coarsely
    chopped

Combine yogurt and sour cream. Add remaining ingredients, except cilantro. Chill. Garnish with cilantro. Serves 4 to 6.

Cindy Wilson Walker, BS '79
Houston

Sauerkraut Salad

1 jar (32 oz.)
    sauerkraut, drained
1 cup chopped celery
1 green pepper, chopped
  Red pepper or
  pimiento for color
1 onion, chopped
½ cup salad oil
½ cup sugar

Combine first 5 ingredients. Mix oil with sugar, pour over salad ingredients. Combine thoroughly. Refrigerate overnight before serving. Serves 8 to 10.

Bebe Canales Inkley, '57
San Antonio

Variation: *Drain sauerkraut thoroughly, rinse and drain thoroughly again. Substitute ¾ cup mayonnaise and ⅓ cup Dijon mustard for salad oil and sugar.*

Gem Meacham, BA '72
Odessa

Spaghetti Salad
A pasta substitute for potato salad

1¼ pounds spaghetti,
    broken
½ red onion, chopped
½ green pepper, chopped
1 cucumber, chopped
2 tomatoes, peeled and
    chopped
½ cup prepared Italian
    salad dressing
2 tablespoons Schilling
    Salad Seasonings

Cook spaghetti until al dente.* Drain. Combine spaghetti and chopped vegetables. Dribble Italian dressing over mixture and sprinkle with salad seasonings. Toss well, chill and serve. Keeps refrigerated 1 week. Serves 8.

Georgina Roach Lee, '62
Bastrop

*See Index, Pasta Al Dente.

SUPER SALAD. Combine 1 head each Romaine, bib and iceberg lettuce. Tear lettuce into bite-sized pieces. Make dressing of equal parts of La Martinique French and Bleu Cheese dressings. Pour over lettuce, toss and chill. Serve with Parmesan cheese sprinkled on top. Serves 8 to 10.

Pat Doney Holt, '48
Fort Worth

Spinach Salad

1 pound fresh spinach,
    torn into bite-sized
    pieces
1 can (16 oz.) bean
    sprouts, drained
    and rinsed
1 can (6 oz.) water
    chestnuts, drained
7 bacon strips, fried
    and crumbled
1 hard-cooked egg,
    sliced

DRESSING:
½ cup catsup
1 cup salad oil
½ cup sugar
1 onion, grated
⅓ cup vinegar
1 tablespoon Worcester-
    shire sauce
1 teaspoon salt

Combine spinach, sprouts, water chestnuts and bacon crumbles.

DRESSING: Combine in blender, or shake vigorously in a covered jar. Toss salad with ample amount of dressing. Garnish with egg slices. Serves 6 to 8.

Sandy Jennings Williams,
wife of Charles R. Williams, MBA '78
Fort Sill, Oklahoma

Seven Layer Salad
Presents a beautiful display in a tall, stemmed, glass serving container

1 head iceburg lettuce, torn into bite-sized pieces
8 hard-cooked eggs, chopped
1 bag (12 oz.) fresh spinach, torn into bite-sized pieces
1 pound bacon, fried crisp and crumbled
1 small-sized onion or 4 green onions, chopped
1 package (10 oz.) frozen English peas
Mayonnaise
Swiss cheese, grated

In glass container layer ingredients in order listed. Spread with thin layer of mayonnaise, garnish top with grated Swiss cheese. Cover with plastic wrap, refrigerate at least 12 hours before serving. Serves 10 to 12.

Louise Stromberg Bates, BS '34
Alice

Variation: *Combine torn spinach, thinly sliced eggs, and crumbled bacon in first layer, salt and pepper and sprinkle with 1 tablespoon sugar. Add finely sliced lettuce, peas, 3 bunches green onions (finely chopped). Use 1 cup each mayonnaise and salad dressing and 1 pound Swiss cheese.*

Peter S. Solito, '42
Houston

Zucchini Salad
An unusual way to serve zucchini

3 medium-sized zucchini, thinly sliced
½ cup minced green pepper
½ cup minced celery
½ cup minced onion
¾ cup red wine vinegar
¼ cup Burgundy wine
½ cup sugar
⅓ cup salad oil
1 teaspoon salt
½ teaspoon freshly ground pepper

Combine all ingredients in large bowl. Mix well. Cover and refrigerate at least 6 hours before serving. This salad will keep, refrigerated, 2 weeks—but it has never lasted that long! Serves 6.

Georgina Roach Lee, '62
Bastrop

Edward Larocque Tinker's zeal for a better understanding among the Americas finds a perfect visual setting in the Tinker Room on the fourth floor of the Academic Center, The University of Texas at Austin. Dr. Tinker focused his attention on the horseman as a common link between countries, since the gaucho in Argentina, the vaquero in Mexico, the huaso in Chile, the llanero in Venezuela, and the cowboy in the United States all originated in the horseback culture of Spain and created a legacy in literature and art as folk heroes. The South American saddle shown has elaborate tooling of eagles with arrows in claws over flags along with extensive silver ornamentation. Hanging on the saddle horn is a rawhide lariate.

photo by Sherwood Inkley

Vegetable Salad
Great with chicken or any meat, particularly barbecued chicken or beef

1 can (16 oz.) French-
    cut green beans
1 can (12 oz.) shoepeg
    corn
1 can (17 oz.) early peas
1 cup chopped celery
½ cup chopped green
    onions
1 jar (2 oz.) pimientos
DRESSING:
¼ cup vinegar
½ cup salad oil
½ cup sugar
    Salt and pepper to
    taste
    Dill and tarragon to
    taste

Drain beans, corn and peas. Combine all vegetables and mix thoroughly.

DRESSING: In blender, combine dressing ingredients. Pour over vegetables. Stir well. Refrigerate 24 hours before serving. Serves 12.

Eleanor Ann Van Zandt Gerrard, BA '42
Victoria

VEGETABLE PLATTER. Combine 1 cup salad oil, 1 cup garlic wine vinegar, 1 package Good Seasons Garlic Salad Dressing Mix. Pour dressing over 1 can (16 oz.) Blue Lake green beans (drained), add 1 onion (sliced), and 1 cucumber (sliced). Toss well and marinate 24 hours, refrigerated. Arrange on platter with cucumber and onion in middle and green beans around sides like spokes.

Virginia Calhoun McMordie, BS '46
Elgin

Tomato Vinaigrette
A prepare-ahead salad for summer patio cooking

4 large-sized tomatoes
1 cup olive oil
⅓ cup wine vinegar
2 teaspoons oregano
1 teaspoon salt
½ teaspoon pepper
½ teaspoon dry mustard
2 cloves garlic, crushed
6 lettuce leaves
    Minced green onion
    Minced parsley

Peel tomatoes by dipping quickly into boiling water. Slice only thick middle of tomato into 12 slices. Arrange slices in 8-inch dish. Combine oil, vinegar, oregano, salt, pepper, mustard and garlic; pour over tomatoes. Cover dish and chill 3 hours. Serve on lettuce leaf, sprinkle with onion and parsley. Serves 6.

Nancy Morris Wilson, MA '68
Dallas

Twelve Hour Vegetable Salad

Great for a party, easy to make ahead

1 head iceberg lettuce, shredded
1 package (10 oz.) frozen green peas
1 green pepper, chopped or sliced
1 medium-sized red onion, chopped or sliced
½ cup sliced water chestnuts
½ cup sliced celery
1½ cups sour cream
1½ cups mayonnaise
3 tablespoons sugar
Bacon bits
1 cup grated Cheddar cheese
½ cup Parmesan cheese
Cherry tomatoes, halved, (optional)

Layer lettuce, frozen uncooked peas, green pepper, onion, water chestnuts and celery in 9 x 13-inch dish. Mix sour cream, mayonnaise and sugar until sugar dissolves. Spread over salad. Top with bacon bits and cheeses. Garnish with cherry tomatoes. Cover, refrigerate 12 hours before serving. Serves 12 to 15.

Verna Sykes Farris, BS '74
Hurst

Variation: *Omit sour cream, bacon bits and Parmesan cheese. Add ½ cup more mayonnaise and reduce sugar to 2 tablespoons.*

Edith Royal,
wife of former UT Football Coach Darrell Royal
Austin

MAKE YOUR OWN FRENCH DRESSING. In blender, combine 1 can (10¾ oz.) condensed tomato soup, 1 tablespoon minced onion, 1½ tablespoons sugar, ¾ teaspoon salt, ¼ teaspoon pepper and ¾ teaspoon dry mustard. With blender, at low speed, add alternately ¼ cup cider vinegar and ¾ cup salad oil.

Charles R. Schneider, BBA '47
Austin

French Dressing

1 cup salad oil
⅓ cup vinegar
1½ teaspoons salt
2 teaspoons sugar
1½ teaspoons dry mustard
1 teaspoon paprika
Dash pepper

Combine all ingredients and beat with rotary beater until well mixed. Stir well before serving. Yield: 1½ cups.

Irene Reeb Meitzen, BA '65
San Angelo

Bleu Cheese Dressing

4 ounces Bleu cheese
1 cup mayonnaise
¼ cup salad oil
¼ cup sour cream
¼ cup buttermilk
1 tablespoon white
  vinegar
¼ teaspoon salt
¼ to ½ teaspoon garlic
  powder

Crumble cheese into mixing bowl. Add mayonnaise and salad oil, stir thoroughly. Add sour cream, stir again. Add buttermilk, vinegar, salt and garlic powder. Blend well and add more salt and pepper to taste if desired. Store, covered, in refrigerator. Yield: 2 cups.

Walter L. Geyer, BM '61
Dallas

A LIGHT AND SPECIAL SALAD DRESSING. In a jar with lid, combine 1 teaspoon salt, ½ teaspoon sugar, ¼ teaspoon pepper, ¼ teaspoon paprika, ¼ cup vinegar, ¾ cup salad oil and garlic powder to taste. Shake jar vigorously. Set aside a day or so before serving. Yield: 1 cup.

Walter L. Geyer, BM '61
Dallas

BLENDER SALAD DRESSING. In blender, combine 2 tablespoons lemon juice, 6 tablespoons salad oil, ¾ teaspoons salt, ¼ teaspoon pepper, ¼ teaspoon sugar, 1 clove garlic or 1 teaspoon garlic salt, 1 egg yolk and ½ teaspoon dry mustard. Blend until smooth. Yield: ½ cup.

Madeline Bynum Closmann, BJ '49
Houston

Ruth's Homemade Italian Dressing

1 cup olive oil
2 teaspoons chopped
  parsley
3 teaspoons chopped
  onion
4 cloves garlic, finely
  minced
2 teaspoons whole
  thyme
1 teaspoon salt
1 tablespoon vinegar
  Juice of 1 lemon
½ cup whipping cream

Put all ingredients in a jar with a tightly fitting lid and shake vigorously. Serve on quartered head lettuce. Yield: 2 cups.

Mitzi Nuhn Dreher, BS '54 MS '56
Austin

387

Thousand Island Dressing

1 cup mayonnaise
4 tablespoons chili
    sauce
3 tablespoons catsup
1 tablespoon chopped
    green pepper
1 tablespoon chopped
    red pepper
1 tablespoon chopped
    celery
1 tablespoon chopped
    green onion
1 teaspoon tarragon
    vinegar
1 teaspoon paprika
1 hard-cooked egg,
    chopped

Combine all ingredients and mix well. Add salt to taste. Keep refrigerated. Serve on salad greens, tomatoes or fresh vegetables. Serves 10 to 12.

Amalee Turek Jones, BA '26
Grand Rapids, Michigan

DRESSING FOR SPINACH SALAD. Combine 2½ teaspoons sugar, 1 teaspoon Worcestershire sauce, 1½ teaspoons onion salt, 2 tablespoons vinegar and ½ cup salad oil. Shake ingredients until well mixed. Yield: ¾ cup.

Suzanne Williams Nash, BA '67
Dallas

Mrs. Weldon's Coleslaw Dressing

1 cup white vinegar
½ cup water
½ cup sugar
1 egg, beaten
    Pinch of salt
    Dash pepper
2 tablespoons butter
2 tablespoons flour

Boil vinegar, water and sugar until sugar dissolves. Remove from heat, add 2 tablespoons mixture to egg and beat thoroughly. Add slowly to hot mixture, whisking constantly. Season with salt and pepper. Combine butter and flour, add a little of the hot mixture to make a smooth paste. Add to hot mixture, stir constantly until mixture has thickened. Cool. Keep refrigerated. Yield: 2 cups.

"This is a sweet-sour dressing, and makes wonderful coleslaw of plain shredded cabbage. To enhance the cabbage, add a fresh tomato, green pepper or crushed pineapple."

Doris Weldon Stokes, '29
Duncan, Oklahoma

Christmas Black Cherry Mold

A glistening wreath bedecked with magnolia leaves for the holiday buffet

2 cans (16 oz. each) pitted black bing cherries
1 can (20 oz.) crushed pineapple
3 packages (3 oz. each) black cherry gelatin
Seven-Up and fruit juices to make 4 cups liquid
1 cup chopped nuts
3 ounces cream cheese, softened

Drain cherries and pineapple, reserving juices. Add 2 cups boiling water to gelatin and stir until dissolved. Add Seven-Up to reserved juices to make 4 cups liquid, add to gelatin, stir and set aside to jell until consistency of egg whites. Stir nuts into softened cream cheese. Stuff the cherries with cream cheese mixture. Add pineapple to gelatin. Rinse a 2½-quart ring mold with cold water. Pour ⅓ of the partially set gelatin into mold. Add a layer of stuffed cherries, a layer of gelatin, a layer of cherries and top with remaining gelatin. Chill until firm. Unmold on a bed of washed magnolia leaves or Romaine or Bibb lettuce. Surround the mold with clusters of assorted grapes and place a bowl of Nellie's Salad Topping in center. Serves 16 to 18.

Idanell Brill Connally, '40
Houston

Nellie's Salad Topping

½ cup sugar
2 tablespoons flour
1 cup pineapple juice
1 egg, slightly beaten
2 tablespoons butter
1 cup cream, whipped
½ cup shredded American cheese
3 tablespoons Parmesan cheese

In saucepan, combine sugar and flour. Stir in pineapple juice and egg. Cook over low heat until mixture has thickened. Remove from heat. Add butter. Cool, and chill. Fold in whipped cream and half the American and Parmesan cheeses. Spoon into a bowl and sprinkle with remaining cheese. Serve with Christmas Black Cherry Mold. This topping is delicious with any molded salad.

Idanell Brill Connally, '40
Houston

Cranberry Sparkle Salad
Delicious with fowl or ham

1 package (6 oz.)
   raspberry-flavored
   gelatin
2 cups boiling water
1 can (16 oz.) whole
   cranberry sauce
1 can (15½ oz.) crushed
   pineapple,
   undrained
⅔ cup Burgundy wine
1 cup chopped pecans

Dissolve gelatin in boiling water. Fold in cranberry sauce and pineapple. Chill until gelatin has thickened. Stir in wine and pecans. Pour into large mold or individual molds.* Chill until firm. Serves 10 or 12.

*Edna Heflin Baker, BA '16
Houston*

*UNMOLDING GELATIN. To unmold gelatin, have ready a chilled plate moistened with water. This prevents gelatin from sticking upon being unmolded and allows you to center the mold more easily. Use a thin-bladed knife to carefully release gelatin from edge of mold. Then with finger on surface of gelatin, pull back gelatin until air reaches bottom of mold, releasing the vacuum. Turn mold over onto prepared plate. If necessary, place a warm damp towel over mold and shake the mold lightly. When gelatin releases, center on plate, wipe off any excessive moisture and garnish as desired.

Cranberry Salad

6 ounces cream cheese,
   softened
2 tablespoons
   mayonnaise
2 tablespoons sugar
1 can (16 oz.) whole
   cranberry sauce
1 cup crushed
   pineapple,
   undrained
½ cup pecans
1 cup whipping cream
1 teaspoon vanilla
½ cup powdered sugar

Combine mayonnaise and sugar into cream cheese. Add fruit and nuts. Whip cream. Add vanilla and powdered sugar. Fold gently into mixture. Pour into 9 x 12-inch glass pan. Freeze at least 6 hours. Cut into serving portions and serve on lettuce leaf. Serves 10 to 12.

*Ruby Crawford Pesek, BA '62
Lake Jackson*

Hot Curried Fruit

1 can (17 oz.) fruits
for salad
1 can (16 oz.) pitted
bing cherries
1 can (8 oz.) pineapple
tidbits
½ jar (6 oz. size)
maraschino cherries
2 bananas
1 teaspoon curry
powder
2 teaspoons cornstarch
¼ cup (½ stick) butter
or margarine,
melted

Drain fruit and cut all fruit into equal-sized pieces. Combine curry and cornstarch with melted butter. Stir into fruit. Place in buttered casserole. Bake 40 minutes at 350°. Serve hot as salad or side dish with ham, lamb or chicken. Serves 10 to 12.

Mary Ann Maley, BA '54
Smithville

CHARLOTTE'S CHEERFUL COMPOTE. *A good breakfast fruit dish.* Combine 1 can Mandarin oranges, drained, 1 package frozen peaches, 1 can partially drained pineapple chunks and 1 pint frozen strawberries. Refrigerate overnight. Add 3 to 5 bananas, sliced, just before serving.

Charlotte Plemmons Warren, BJ '76
Austin

Sherried Fruit Casserole

1 jar (8 oz.) spiced
apple rings
1 can (16 oz.) sliced
pineapple
1 can (16 oz.) peach
halves
1 can (16 oz.) pear
halves
1 can (16 oz.) apricot
halves
½ cup (1 stick) butter
or margarine
3 tablespoons flour
½ cup brown sugar,
firmly packed
1 cup sherry

Cut fruit into chunks. Arrange in 3-quart casserole. Melt butter, add flour and sugar, stir until smooth. Gradually add sherry, mixing well. Cook at medium heat until mixture thickens, stirring constantly. Pour over fruit, chill overnight. Bring to room temperature, bake 25 minutes at 350° or until bubbly. Serves 10 to 12.

Susan Collier Hanson, BS '78
Austin

Spiced Fruit

1 package (8 oz.) sliced
    peaches, drained
2 cans (16 oz. each)
    tart red cherries,
    undrained
1 cup brown sugar
1 lemon, grated rind
    and juice
1 orange, grated rind
    and juice
½ to 1 cup rum (either
    light or dark)

Combine all ingredients and cook in uncovered
saucepan, either on top of the stove until
liquid is thickened or in the oven 1 hour at
300°. Serve hot or cold with brown sugar and
sour cream as accompaniments. Serves
12 to 14.

Margaret Milam McDermott, '32
Dallas

24-Hour Fruit Salad

2 cans (15½ oz. each)
    pineapple tidbits or
    chunks, halved
1 can (17 oz.) Royal
    Anne cherries,
    pitted and halved
1 pound miniature
    marshmallows
DRESSING:
1 teaspoon salt
1 teaspoon dry mustard
1½ teaspoons flour
2 teaspoons sugar
1 teaspoon butter,
    melted
2 egg yolks
3 tablespoons cider
    vinegar
2 cups half and half
    cream
1 cup whipping cream,
    whipped

Drain canned fruits and combine with
marshmallows in 3-quart casserole. Set aside.
DRESSING: In saucepan, combine salt,
mustard, flour and sugar. Stir in butter, egg
yolks and vinegar. Cook at low heat, stirring
constantly, until mixture has thickened.
Remove from heat, slowly add half and half
cream, whisking constantly. Return to low
heat, cook until mixture thickens. Cool. Fold
in whipped cream, then fold dressing into fruit
mixture. Chill at least 4 hours before serving.
Serves 12.

Carol Pirrung Mann, MA '75 MLS '77
Mesquite

Fast Frozen Fruit Salad

1 cup sour cream
1 tablespoon lemon
    juice
½ cup sugar
    Pinch of salt
1 banana, diced
1 cup crushed
    pineapple, drained

Mix sour cream, lemon juice, sugar and salt thoroughly. Stir in banana and pineapple. Place paper liners in muffin tins. Fill each liner to the top. Freeze. Serve 2 salads on lettuce leaf with dollop of mayonnaise, a maraschino cherry and mint leaf decoration. Serves 4.

Becky Barlow Rivers, BS '71
and Steve Rivers, '68
Bastrop

Variation: *Add ½ cup pecans and ¼ cup chopped maraschino cherries.*

Marilyn Reneau, BS '70
Dallas

Variation: *Substitute 1 can (16 oz.) whole or jellied cranberries for bananas and lemon juice.*

Ruth Butler Hunt, '27
Fairfield, Iowa

CHERRY SURPRISE SALAD. Combine 1 can (14 oz.) sweetened condensed milk, 1 can (8 oz.) crushed pineapple (undrained), 1 can (21 oz.) cherry pie filling and 1 carton (8 oz.) Cool Whip. Chill overnight. Serves 6 to 8.

Phyllis Knowlton Schriever, '46
Pasadena

Jody's Dreamsicle Salad
Excellent as a salad or dessert

⅔ cup sugar
⅔ cup water
2 packages (3 oz. each)
    apricot gelatin
8 ounces cream cheese
1 can (20 oz.) crushed
    pineapple
2 jars (4½ oz. each)
    apricot baby food
8 ounces Cool Whip

Combine sugar and water and bring to boil. Add gelatin, set aside to cool. In blender, combine cream cheese with pineapple and baby food. Mix together gelatin and cream cheese mixtures. Fold in Cool Whip. Pour into salad mold and refrigerate. Serves 8 to 10.

Suzanne Williams Nash, BA '67
Dallas

Mincemeat Salad

1 package (3 oz.)
    orange-flavored
    gelatin
1 cup hot water
¾ cup orange juice
1 cup prepared
    mincemeat
1 cup chopped nuts

Dissolve gelatin in hot water. Add orange juice, mincemeat and nuts. Pour into lightly-greased 1-quart mold. Chill until set. Serves 8.

Sybil McKee Savage, BA '22
Sanderson

Orange Fruit Freeze
Different, very tart, but good

1 can (6 oz.) frozen
    orange juice
1 can (6 oz.) frozen
    lemonade
1 package (10 oz.)
    frozen strawberries
3 large-sized bananas,
    sliced
1 can (16 oz.) crushed
    pineapple

Thaw frozen juices and fruit. Do not dilute orange juice or lemonade. Mix together with bananas and pineapple. Freeze. Before serving, thaw to mushy consistency, about 2 hours. Serve as a salad or a dessert. Can be refrozen. Serves 6 to 8.

Nita Hixson Galloway, BJ '51
Wilmington, Delaware

Congealed Orange Salad
Use mandarin oranges for deeper "Longhorn color"

1 package (3 oz.)
    orange-flavored
    gelatin
1 cup hot water
1 cup fresh orange juice
1 cup crushed
    pineapple, drained
    or 1 cup mandarin
    oranges, drained
1 can (3½ oz.) flaked
    coconut
1 packet Dream Whip
1 cup milk
⅓ cup sugar

Combine gelatin with water and orange juice. Add pineapple or oranges and coconut. Refrigerate until of egg white consistency. Combine Dream Whip with milk and prepare according to package directions, adding ⅓ cup sugar. Combine with gelatin mixture. Chill in 1½-quart mold. Serves 6.

Frances Stanhiser Von Bieberstein, '31
Austin

Orange and Mint Salad

6 medium-sized oranges
2 tablespoons fresh
    mint, chopped
2 tablespoons salad oil
1 tablespoon lemon
    juice
1 tablespoon cognac

Peel oranges and slice into rounds. Arrange in serving dish. Sprinkle with mint. Combine oil, lemon juice and cognac; pour over oranges and mint. Chill. Serves 4.

Madeline Bynum Closmann, BJ '49
Houston

Pineapple Cream Cheese Salad

⅔ cup powdered sugar
8 ounces cream cheese
1 teaspoon vanilla
1 can (8 oz.) crushed
    pineapple, drained
¾ cup walnuts,
    cashews or pecans

Cream together sugar and cream cheese. Add vanilla, pineapple and nuts. Mix well. Freeze in ice cube tray (with cube sections removed) or large bread pan. Slice and serve on lettuce leaves. Serves 6.

Tommy Ford, BS '65
Waco

Red Hot Salad

1 cup red hots
    (cinnamon candy)
2 cups water
2 packages (3 oz. each)
    lemon-flavored
    gelatin
1 can (16 oz.)
    applesauce
8 ounces cream cheese
    Milk
¾ cup finely chopped
    pecans

Combine red hots with water, cook at low heat until red hots dissolve, stirring often. Remove from heat, add gelatin, stir until dissolved. Add applesauce, stir well. Pour mixture into lightly buttered 9-inch square pan. Refrigerate until set. Combine cream cheese with enough milk to make spreading consistency. Fold in pecans. Spread over congealed layer. Refrigerate at least 6 hours, covered, before serving. Good with ham or poultry. Serves 8.

Sarah Ragle Weddington, LLB '67
Washington, DC

Purple Plum Salad

2 eggs, beaten
2 tablespoons sugar
1 tablespoon gelatin
⅓ cup fresh lemon juice
Dash salt
¼ cup (½ stick) butter
  or margarine
1 cup miniature
  marshmallows
1 can (15¼ oz.)
  pineapple chunks,
  drained and halved
1 can (16 oz.) purple
  plums, drained,
  pitted and
  quartered
1 cup chopped pecans
1 cup whipping cream,
  whipped

Combine eggs, sugar, gelatin, lemon juice and salt in top of a double boiler. Cook over boiling water until mixture thickens and gelatin dissolves, stirring constantly. Remove from heat, add butter and marshmallows. Stir until marshmallows are almost melted. Cool until partially thickened. Fold in fruit, nuts and cream. Pour into greased 7 x 10-inch pan. Chill until firm. Cut into squares. Serves 8 to 10.

Margaret Benson Kennedy, BA '26
Arlington

Texas Union Fruit Salad
A fluffy frozen family treat

3 ounces cream cheese,
  softened
⅓ cup mayonnaise
1 teaspoon lemon juice
2 egg whites
⅓ cup sugar
1 cup whipping cream
6 large-sized
  marshmallows,
  diced
¼ cup mandarin orange
  slices, drained
1 can (16 oz.) fruit
  cocktail, drained
2 tablespoons chopped
  maraschino cherries
1 tablespoon chopped
  walnuts

Mix thoroughly, or blend in blender, the cream cheese, mayonnaise and lemon juice. Beat egg whites until foamy. Beat in sugar, a tablespoon at a time, until stiff peaks form. Whip cream until stiff. Fold cream into egg whites. Fold in cream cheese mixture and gently add remaining ingredients. Pour into 8-inch square pan and freeze. Serves 6 to 8.

Texas Union Dining Service
Austin

Wine Gelatin
Great with almost anything

2 envelopes unflavored
  gelatin
¾ cup sugar
¼ teaspoon salt
1 cup water
2½ cups rosé or red wine
2 tablespoons lemon
  juice
FROSTED GRAPES
(optional):
½ teaspoon water
1 egg white
¼ cup granulated sugar

Mix gelatin, sugar and salt in saucepan and stir in water. Heat slowly, stirring until gelatin dissolves. Remove from heat. Stir in wine and lemon juice. Pour into 4-cup tube mold and chill until firm.

GRAPES: Add water to egg whites, beat slightly. Brush mixture over grapes. Sprinkle with sugar until well coated. Unmold gelatin* onto wet serving platter, surround with sprigs of watercress and clusters of grapes. Serve as sorbet in sherbet glasses. Place clusters of grapes at base of each glass. Serves 6 to 8.

Pat Horton Maguire, BA '46
San Antonio

See Index, Unmolding Gelatin.

The 1980s

Folkloric Cuisine

The 27-story Tower of the Main Building is the identity symbol for U.T. Austin. As the University's first century ends, the Tower looms above a 316-acre campus and its 46,000 students.

$\mathcal{R}$eady or not, the 1980s are here! Whether or not Alvin Toffler, George Orwell, or even Aldous Huxley prepared us for this brave new world, we must accept the fact that their future is now.

Life today at the University of Texas is geared to a different beat, numbingly different from that at the turn of the century. The size and composition of the student body (more than 46,000 in 1981 from every state in the US and 90 countries), the size of the campus (316 acres with approximately 130 buildings), the quality of teaching, and the superb libraries and laboratories all combine to provide an enriched environment. The social revolution of the 1960s and '70s levels off in the 1980s as campus life styles become more reserved.

Students are more career-motivated than ever before. Almost one-fourth of the student body is registered in the College of Business Administration. Holding a job while getting a degree is a common practice. Large numbers of students work on campus, while more work in state and private offices and in businesses all over Austin. The high cost of living and the expense of an education have forced even those from middle-income families to look for part-time jobs. The proposed average budget for a single undergraduate Texas resident in 1981-1982 is $5,000 and for a nonresident single undergraduate is $6,000. An airconditioned room with board (20 meals per week) on campus costs almost $2,700, while a nonairconditioned room with board is slightly under $2,200. Small apartments rent for $300 per month and up. Expensive, privately-owned condominiums are "in," especially for upper-division students. Both men and women enjoy having a place in which to cook and to entertain friends and are willing to work and even postpone graduation a year or so to be able to afford sharing a condo.

The long registration lines of past decades are no more. The airconditioned Frank C. Erwin Special Events Center accommodates larger numbers more comfortably, while pre-registration and data processing simplify the process.

401

Students of the 1980's work hard and study hard and then play with the same enthusiasm. They dance at the Silver Dollar and drink at Scholz's, Beans, Raul's, the County Line, and Dry Creek. Their music may be a noisy mix of country western, rock, hard rock, and disco, but they also fill the new 3,000-seat Performing Arts Center Concert hall for an opera, a symphony, or a ballet and the 17,000-seat Special Events Center for an ice show or a circus. They enjoy the bars, night clubs, and restaurants on Sixth (Pecan) Street, and they participate enthusiastically in the University's excellent intramural sports program. Football is still the favorite intercollegiate sport, but basketball, baseball, and swimming draw crowds when the teams are highly competitive. Women's athletics, especially swimming and basketball, are becoming popular as teams win championships. Big all-University parties at Fiesta Gardens on Town Lake, several miles from the campus, attract as many as 5,000 or 6,000 students. Favorite local bands include "Little Bit of Texas," "Uncle Walt's" and "Beto y los Fairlanes."

A reversal of boy-girl roles is occurring as girls often ask boys for dates. Groups of students go out together and share expenses (dutch dates of the 1930's). Most fun of all, students today affirm, occurs when a big group gets together at somebody's condo or apartment to have a meal, watch Home Box Office (HBO) films on television, or enjoy an evening of conversation (the bull sessions of yesteryear students).

Barbeque and Mexican foods are still favorites. Austin has numerous fine restaurants that are popular among students. The County Line, whether on Bee Caves Road or on Bull Creek, is crowded with students, especially on weekends. Even the price of gasoline does not deter caravans from going 20 to 40 miles to Coupland or Camp Ben McCulloch for good barbecue. Cisco's Bakery and Coffee Shop, opened on East Sixth Street in 1949 by Rudy Cisneros, is still a favorite haunt. A lively group of student leaders that love the University call themselves "Cisco's Kids" and meet regularly at Cisco's for food, conversation, and fun. Huevos rancheros is a favorite breakfast item.

Unisex dress goes to class, to parties, and even to work. Both men and women wear jeans and shirts with button-down collars or polo shirts. Even though they tease about the "preppy-look," it is *the* fashion of the '80s.

"Pot smoking is accepted among students as a norm. Whether one smokes or not, however, is a personal choice, not a peer requirement," explains one who should know. Drinking is also a norm, as it has been through the decades. A new state law raises the drinking age from 18 to 19, but the average age of students is over 22. The more intimate personal relationships between the sexes publicized in the 1960s and continued through the 1970s still exist in the 1980s.

Students find time to travel while they study. A Mexican holiday in Puerta Vallarta, Acapulco, or Cancun, or a ski holiday on the slopes of Colorado or New Mexico are popular. A theater and museum trip to New York at Christmas, a summer tour of Europe, or a weekend on the beach at South Padre are not unusual in the 1980s. Students enjoy "shooting the rapids" on the Guadalupe River at New Braunfels today as they did at the turn of the century. They also like to go to San Antonio for a ride on the river and a meal at one of the river restaurants or to Laredo to visit the Cadillac Bar and shop in the markets for Mexican-made crafts.

In Austin, students find time to go out to "Hot Wheels," a miniature car drag strip in the north part of the city. They still enjoy Barton Springs, where the water is 68° year round, and jogging is even more popular now than in the 1970's. The fun-run sponsored by the Ex-Students' Association each fall and the Capital 10,000 each spring attract large numbers of students.

President Peter T. Flawn, is taking steps to tighten admission standards, improve teaching, recruit more minorities, and enhance the quality of life on campus. In March 1980, the United States Department of Energy chose the University as the site for the new national Institute for Fusion Studies, which will bring together the world's foremost physicists and energy researchers. The new Texas Experimental Tokamak (TEXT) was dedicated in May, 1981. University marine biologists at the Marine Science Institute on the Gulf Coast are probing the Gulf water just as its scientists at McDonald Observatory in the Davis Mountains are sending laser beams to the moon.

Students of the 1980s are moving into diverse spheres. They are more numerous, but they are better prepared, more affluent, more knowledgable, healthier, and more sophisticated than they have been in any previous decade of UT history. As in previous decades, however, they are still looking for approval from both peers and adults; they want to achieve; they need somebody to listen; they don't want advice; and they have confidence that their way will be better. They get discouraged but try to pretend they are not. They look for leadership but like to think of themselves as independent. As its first century closes, the University of Texas is better prepared than ever before to provide these bright students the exciting educational environment to nurture their development and self-fulfillment.

Menus

Hook 'em Horns Heritage

404

Lasagne

2 pounds ground beef
   chuck
1 tablespoon sweet
   basil leaves, crushed
1½ teaspoons salt
2 cans (6 oz. each)
   tomato paste
1 clove garlic, minced
1 tablespoon dried
   parsley flakes
1½ pounds fresh
   tomatoes, peeled
   and chopped
   or 1 can (20 oz.)
   whole tomatoes,
   undrained
10 ounces lasagne or
   wide noodles
3 cups creamy cottage
   cheese
2 eggs, beaten
1 teaspoon salt
½ teaspoon pepper
2 tablespoons dried
   parsley flakes
½ cup Parmesan cheese
1 pound Mozzarella
   cheese, sliced

Brown meat, skim fat. Add sweet basil, salt, tomato paste, garlic, parsley and tomatoes. Simmer, uncovered, until sauce has thickened, 45 minutes to 1 hour, stirring occasionally. Cook noodles, drain, rinse in cold water. Combine cottage cheese, eggs, seasonings and Parmesan cheese. Place half the noodles in buttered 3-quart baking dish, then add half the cottage cheese mixture, ½ pound Mozzarella slices and half the meat sauce. Repeat layers, ending with meat sauce on top. Bake 30 minutes at 325°. Set aside 15 minutes, then cut into squares and serve. Serves 10 to 12.

Dorothy Burwitz Doss, BA '40
Austin

Fettucine À La Joe

1 package (16 oz.) wide
    egg noodles
1 package (16 oz.) wide
    spinach egg noodles
Water
1 cup (2 sticks) butter
2 cups half and half
    cream
½ cup grated Parmesan
    cheese
1 cup grated
    Mozzarella cheese
2 tablespoons dried
    parsley flakes
¼ teaspoon garlic salt
¼ teaspoon pepper
½ cup diced proscuitto
    (Italian smoked
    ham)

In large stockpot, boil egg noodles in water until al dente*, drain and pat dry. Melt butter at low heat, add egg noodles, toss well and add remaining ingredients. Cook at medium to high heat, stirring constantly. The liquid will begin to boil and evaporate and noodles will absorb butter. Cover, reduce heat to low, cook 5 minutes more and serve soon. Serves 8 to 10.

Donna A. Lopiano,
Director, UT Intercollegiate Athletics for Women
Austin

*See Index, Al Dente.

Pseudo Pesto Sauce
A substitute for the wretchedly expensive Italian melange

2 cups each fresh
    spinach and fresh
    parsley or 2
    packages (10 oz.
    each) frozen
    chopped spinach
    and ¼ cup dried
    parsley flakes
3 cloves garlic
2 tablespoons dried
    basil
1 teaspoon salt
½ cup sunflower seeds
⅔ cup olive oil
1 cup grated Parmesan
    cheese

Clean greens and using only leaves (no stems), finely chop in food processor. If using frozen spinach, thaw slightly and chop, uncooked; add parsley flakes. Add remaining ingredients except cheese and process until mixture is a thick paste. Add cheese. Serve or store, covered, in refrigerator. The pesto will keep, refrigerated, about 2 weeks. *"The pesto is traditionally served on hot pasta, preferably green noodles. Also, the pesto is an excellent sauce for vegetables. Mix with an equal amount of mayonnaise to serve as a dip with fresh, sliced vegetables. Serves 6 as a pasta topping."*

Zula Thompson Vizard, BA '33 MA '35
San Antonio

Linguine With Clam Sauce
A recipe from Sicily—subtle and sophisticated

1 medium-sized onion,
   diced
2 cloves garlic, diced
3 tablespoons olive or
   corn oil
3 marinated artichoke
   hearts, sliced
12 stuffed green olives,
   sliced
3 sprigs parsley, finely
   chopped
6 fresh mushrooms,
   sliced
1 can (16 oz.) whole
   peeled tomatoes,
   drained and
   coarsely chopped
1 can (16 oz.) chopped
   clams with liquid
1 small-sized eggplant,
   peeled and cut into
   ½- to 1-inch cubes
1 box (12 oz.) linguine

Saute onion and garlic in oil. Add artichoke hearts and olives. Cook 2 minutes. Add parsley and mushrooms. Cook 2 minutes more. Add tomatoes, clams and eggplant. Cover and simmer 30 minutes. Prepare linguine according to package directions. Drain, portion onto 4 hot serving plates. Cover each portion generously with hot clam sauce. Serves 4.

John K. Dannelley, '73
Amarillo

Red Tomato
Italian Restaurant
Garlic Butter Sauce

2 cloves garlic, minced
1 pound butter
   Pasta
   Black olives
   Mushrooms
   Chopped parsley

Combine butter and garlic. Place a portion of pasta on serving plate, top with olives, mushrooms, and 2 ounces of hot butter garlic. Sprinkle with chopped fresh parsley. NOTE: Garlic butter combination also is used for garlic bread.

Red Tomato Restaurant
Austin

Manicotta À La Josephine

CREPE BATTER:

4 eggs
1 cup flour
1 teaspoon salt
Warm water

FILLING:

2 pounds Ricotta cheese
3 eggs
2 teaspoons dried
    parsley flakes
3 tablespoons Parmesan
    cheese
¼ teaspoon garlic salt
¼ teaspoon pepper
1 pound Mozzarella
    cheese, divided

SAUCE:

Use Zesty International
    Spaghetti Sauce or
    your favorite Italian
    tomato sauce recipe

CREPE BATTER: Unlike the pasta shell of most manicotti recipes, this version of manicotti utilizes a very light, paper thin crepe. Mix the eggs, flour and salt with an egg whisk. Gradually add warm water until you have an "egg nog"-consistency batter which is free of flour lumps. Strain. Lightly butter a 6- or 7-inch crepe pan. Make sure the crepe pan is hot before you pour the batter for each crepe. Pour 3 or 4 tablespoons batter into the pan and tilt it around so it spreads evenly. The crepe should be as thin as possible. You should see light through it if you hold it up. If the crepe is opaque, add water to thin. The crepe is cooked when the edges begin to curl and if you touch your finger to the center of the crepe, it is dry rather than sticky. Turn the crepe pan over and tap it gently on a dry cloth. The crepe should fall out easily, ready to be stuffed.

FILLING: Combine all ingredients except Mozzarella cheese. Mix Ricotta cheese, eggs, parsley flakes, garlic salt, pepper and Parmesan cheese. Cut Mozzarella into ½-inch square strips 3 to 4 inches long. Place 2 heaping tablespoons filling in center of each crepe, add 1 strip Mozzarella, envelope-fold crepe (i.e., the bottom of the crepe over the top of the filling, then the top of the crepe and then each side).

SAUCE: Use your favorite Italian tomato sauce recipe. Coat bottom of a large, square pan with about ¼-inch layer of sauce. Place the filled crepes side by side on top of the sauce. Pour the remaining sauce on top of the crepes until covered. Sprinkle grated Mozzarella cheese over top. Bake 30 minutes at 350° or until sauce starts bubbling. Serves 4 to 6.

"My family was in the restaurant business for more than 30 years. This recipe was a 'specialty of the house' created by my mother, Josephine Lopiano, who is, undoubtedly, the best cook I've ever known."

Donna A. Lopiano,
Director, UT Intercollegiate Athletics for Women
Austin

Beef Wine Spaghetti Sauce
Tastes like the sauce at Spaghetti Warehouse!

1 small-sized onion,
   finely chopped
2 cloves garlic, halved
¼ cup salad oil
2 cans (8 oz. each)
   tomato sauce
2 cans (6 oz. each)
   tomato paste
1 cup Burgundy wine
2 cups water
1 teaspoon basil
1 tablespoon sugar
¾ tablespoon salt
¼ teaspoon pepper
1 bay leaf
1 can (4 oz.) sliced
   mushrooms
1 pound lean ground
   beef
   Dash liquid smoke

Cook onion and garlic in heated oil until onion is limp. Add tomato sauce, paste, wine, water, spices and mushrooms. Cover, cook slowly 1 hour. Brown beef, drain, add to sauce. Cook slowly, stirring occasionally, two hours more or until mixture has thickened. Serve over favorite pasta. Serves 6.

Brenda Thompson Kolinek, BBA '72
Uvalde

Zesty International Spaghetti Sauce

1 cup chopped onion
1 clove garlic, minced
2 tablespoons butter
1 can (35 oz.) whole
   tomatoes, pureed
1 can (10 oz.) tomatoes
   with green chile
   peppers, pureed
2 cans (6 oz. each)
   tomato paste
¼ teaspoon dried
   oregano leaves,
   crushed
1 teaspoon salt
¼ teaspoon pepper
1 teaspoon dried basil
2 tablespoons chopped
   fresh parsley

Saute onion and garlic in butter. Add pureed whole tomatoes, pureed tomatoes with green chile peppers and tomato paste. Add all remaining ingredients, simmer 1 hour or until mixture has thickened. Serve with your favorite pasta. Serves 6 to 8.

Judith Morrison Martin, BA '77 BJ '77
Houston

Spacey Spaghetti Sauce

1 can (16 oz.) whole
    tomatoes
2 cans (6 oz. each)
    tomato paste
2 cans (15 oz. each)
    tomato sauce
Pinch baking soda
    (to remove acid)
2 onions, finely chopped
9 large-sized cloves
    garlic, minced
1 teaspoon Italian herb
    seasoning
1 teaspoon basil
½ teaspoon thyme
1 teaspoon oregano
¼ bunch fresh parsley,
    chopped
1 bay leaf
2 tablespoons pepper
2 tablespoons salt
2 green peppers,
    chopped
  Pork ribs and beef
    ribs, 1 or 2 per
    serving (wrapped in
    cheesecloth for easy
    removal)
  Mushrooms (optional)
3 teaspoons sugar
½ cup freshly grated
    Romano or
    Parmesan cheese

Into a large-sized crockpot (you really can make it better this way), pour tomatoes, tomato paste and sauce. Add baking soda, stir well. Add onion, garlic, herbs, seasonings, green pepper and meat. Cover, set at low temperature, simmer 8 to 12 hours. Add water as needed. Remove meat, add sugar and cheese. Cover, continue to simmer until sauce reaches consistency you like. Serves 12.

"I eat this sauce over spaghetti noodles several times each week. Sometimes I put it on top of leftover pizza I have brought home from the restaurant."

Alan Bean, BS '55
Houston

AL DENTE. *To achieve an al dente texture in pasta, cook the pasta in a large quantity of rapidly boiling salted, oiled water. A good ratio is 1 tablespoon salt and 1 tablespoon olive oil to 7 quarts water. Pasta should be added gradually so rolling boil is undisturbed. Using a long fork, stir the pasta only the first minute or two so that strands are constantly moving. This prevents the strands from glueing together or glueing to bottom of saucepan. Timing can be determined only by tasting, not once, but several times until no taste of raw flour remains and until pasta still offers slight resistance to the bite. The tiniest speck of white should still be present in the very center of solid round pastas.*

Spaghetti With Italian Sauce
A complete meal when served with salad, garlic bread and Zabaglione

1 tablespoon flour,
  browned
1 pound ground beef
1 pound ground pork
3 medium-sized onions,
  chopped
1 green pepper, chopped
4 cloves garlic, finely
  minced
1 can (10¾ oz.) tomato
  soup
1 can (6 oz.) tomato
  paste
1 can (16 oz.) tomatoes
1 can (4 oz.)
  mushrooms,
  chopped
1 bottle (4 oz.) stuffed
  olives
1 teaspoon salt
1 teaspoon Worcester-
  shire sauce
¼ teaspoon Tabasco
¼ teaspoon paprika
1 bay leaf
1 teaspoon sweet basil
  leaves, crushed
1 teaspoon chili powder
1 pound spaghetti,
  cooked
Romano cheese

Brown flour in heavy dry skillet over very low direct heat or in oven 30 minutes at 350° until golden brown, stirring frequently. Set aside. In large iron skillet, brown beef and pork; drain. Saute onion, pepper and garlic in olive oil. Add to meat. Add remaining ingredients, including browned flour, to meat mixture. Cook 2 hours, slowly, stirring often. Serve over cooked spaghetti. Top with Romano cheese. Serves 12.

Mitzi Nuhn Dreher, BS '54 MS '56
Austin

SCHEIHAGEN SLOPPY JOE SPAGHETTI SAUCE. Combing 1 pound ground beef; 2 medium-sized onions, chopped; 1 can (4 oz.) chopped mushrooms, well drained; and 1 teaspoon garlic powder. Cook until meat is browned; drain. Add 1 can (15 oz.) tomato sauce, 1 teaspoon oregano, 1 teaspoon brown sugar, and 1 tablespoon Dijon mustard. Simmer, uncovered, 30 minutes. Serve over cooked spaghetti or on hamburger buns for Sloppy Joes. Serves 4 as sauce, serves 8 as Sloppy Joes.

David R. Scheihagen, BS '77
Houston

Spaghetti Amore

1¼ pounds ground beef
½ cup chopped onion
¼ cup chopped green
    pepper
2 tablespoons salad oil
1 can (10¾ oz.) cream
    of mushroom soup
1 can (10¾ oz.) tomato
    soup
1 soup can water
1 large-sized clove
    garlic, minced
Salt to taste
1 cup shredded sharp
    processed cheese
½ pound cut spaghetti,
    cooked and drained

Lightly brown beef, onion and green pepper in oil, stirring occasionally. Add soups, water, garlic, and salt. Heat. Add ½ cup cheese and cooked spaghetti. Mix well. Place in 3-quart casserole, top with remaining cheese. Bake, uncovered, 30 minutes at 350° or until bubbly. Serves 8 to 10.

Agnes Henke Lundstedt, BS '53
Austin

Oven Spaghetti

3 tablespoons olive oil
½ cup chopped onion
1 tablespoon finely
    chopped celery
¼ teaspoon garlic
    powder
1 tablespoon finely
    chopped parsley
1 cup chopped fresh
    mushrooms
1 pound ground beef
1 teaspoon salt
⅛ teaspoon pepper
⅛ teaspoon paprika
1½ tablespoons Spice
    Islands Spaghetti
    Sauce Seasoning
2 cups canned tomatoes,
    chopped
2 cups canned tomato
    sauce
½ cup red wine
10 ounces spaghetti,
    cooked

Saute onion, celery, garlic powder, parsley and mushrooms in olive oil. Add beef. Add salt, pepper, paprika and spaghetti seasonings. Saute until beef is browned. Add tomatoes, tomato sauce and wine. Simmer 30 minutes, stirring occasionally. Add cooked spaghetti. Pour into greased 2-quart casserole. Cover, bake 30 minutes at 350°. Serves 5.

Jeannette Monnier Selway, BS '55
Dallas

Chicken Spaghetti

½ cup salad oil
1 large-sized onion, chopped
1 clove garlic, minced
1 large-sized green pepper, chopped
½ cup flour
1 hen (4 or 5 lbs.), boiled, deboned and diced
1 can (16 oz.) tomatoes
1 can (6 oz.) sliced mushrooms
3 cups grated American cheese, divided
1 package (16 oz.) spaghetti, uncooked
1 tablespoon Worcester-shire sauce
2 teaspoons curry powder
Dash Louisiana hot sauce
Salt and pepper to taste

In large saucepan, heat oil and saute onion, garlic and green pepper. Add flour. Add chicken, tomatoes, mushrooms, cheese and a little broth from the chicken. In remaining broth (add water to make 4 quarts) cook spaghetti al dente*, drain, add to chicken mixture and toss to coat well. Add seasonings and 1 more cup cheese. Use remaining cheese to sprinkle on each serving. Serves 12.

Jean Welhausen Kaspar, BA '52
Shiner

Variation: *MISS'S QUICKIE: To diced, boiled chicken, add 1½ cups chopped celery, 1 cup chopped green pepper, 1 small can pimiento, dash garlic salt, red pepper to taste and 1 teaspoon Worchestershire sauce. Combine with 1 package cooked spaghetti. Simmer 10 minutes.*

Jane Tulley Singleton, BJ '41
Houston

*See Index, Al Dente.

CHICKEN CHEESE SPAGHETTI. Cook spaghetti from 1 package (8 oz.) Italian Style Spaghetti Dinner according to package directions, drain. Saute 1 cup chopped green pepper in 2 tablespoons butter or margarine until tender. Stir in 1 can (16 oz.) stewed tomatoes, herb spice and Parmesan from packaged dinner. Add cooked spaghetti; 1½ cups cooked chicken, diced; and ½ pound pasteurized process cheese spread. Mix well. Spread in 2-quart casserole, bake 25 minutes at 350°. Top with remaining ½ pound cheese cut into triangles. Return to oven until cheese melts. This recipe may be prepared ahead and refrigerated or frozen until ready to use. Serves 6.

Louise Appleman, wife of Gordon Appleman, BA '59
Fort Worth

Spaghetti Alla Carbonara

1 pound bacon
1 onion, finely chopped
4 tablespoons olive oil
1 can (5.33 oz.)
    evaporated milk
½ cup grated Parmesan
    cheese
4 eggs
1 pound spaghetti,
    uncooked
6 quarts water
Salt and pepper to
    taste
Parsley

Dice bacon and cook until crisp but not burned. Drain. Saute onion in 3 tablespoons olive oil. Combine onion with milk, cheese and eggs. Mix together thoroughly. Cook spaghetti to al dente* with remaining 1 tablespoon oil added to cooking water. Drain, immediately return spaghetti to cooking pot. Add egg mixture and bacon, stirring rapidly to coat spaghetti. Do not allow eggs to cook! Season to taste with salt and pepper, sprinkle with chopped parsley. Serve immediately. Serves 6.

Kathleen Kenny Reily, BS '77
Vaihingen, Germany

See Index, Al dente.

Zotoni
A meal-in-one-round-up feast

4 large-sized onions,
    chopped
3 cloves garlic, minced
1 large-sized green
    pepper, chopped
1 cup salad oil
2 cans (10¾ oz.) tomato
    soup
1 can (15 oz.) tomato
    sauce
1 can (12 oz.) whole
    kernel corn
2 cans (6 oz. each)
    sliced broiled
    mushrooms,
    undrained
1½ pounds lean ground
    beef
1 package (16 oz.)
    spaghetti, cooked
1 pound grated
    American cheese
Salt and pepper
    to taste
Red pepper to taste

Saute onions, garlic and green pepper in hot oil. Add soup, tomato sauce and corn. Simmer meat in liquid from mushrooms. Add with mushrooms to tomato mixture. Prepare spaghetti according to package directions, drain and combine with tomato mixture. Add ½ pound cheese. This is a thick mixture. Divide into 2 buttered 3-quart casseroles. Sprinkle remaining cheese on top of each casserole. Cover, bake 35 to 45 minutes at 350°. Each casserole serves 8. Freezes nicely before baking.

Stella Jung Browning, BS '36
Fredericksburg

Mildred Rowntree, Friend of UT
Fredericksburg

Pizza Mia

CRUST:

1 packet dry yeast
1 cup warm water
   (110°)
1 tablespoon salad oil
3 to 4 cups flour (½
   whole wheat and ½
   white flour)
1 teaspoon salt

SAUCE:

1 small-sized onion,
   chopped
2 cloves garlic, minced
1 tablespoon olive oil
1 teaspoon sweet basil
1 teaspoon chopped
   parsley
1 teaspoon salt
½ teaspoon red pepper
1 tablespoon leaf
   oregano, crushed
1 can (9¼ oz.) tomatoes
1 can (8 oz.) tomato
   sauce
1 can (6 oz.) tomato
   paste

CRUST: Sprinkle yeast into warm water, stir, set aside 5 minutes to proof. Add oil. Combine flours with salt, add to yeast mixture, stir until dough is soft and pulls away from sides of bowl. Turn onto floured board and knead until smooth and elastic like bread dough. Put in greased bowl, let rise 30 minutes.

SAUCE: Saute onion and garlic in oil until soft. Add remaining ingredients, simmer 30 minutes. Put dough onto greased cookie sheet. Brush with olive oil, cover with sauce. Add any or all of suggested vegetables and meats, and at least 2 cheeses. Bake 10 to 15 minutes at 450°. Serves 4.

SUGGESTED VEGETABLES: Sliced mushrooms, chopped green peppers, sliced olives, chopped onion.

SUGGESTED MEATS: Sauteed and crumbled sausage, sliced pepperoni, sauteed and crumbled hamburger, diced Canadian bacon.

SUGGESTED CHEESES: Muenster, Brick, Parmesan, Romano, Cheddar.

"With a food processor to do the kneading and slicing, this pizza takes less than 1 hour to prepare."

Mary Burson, BS '75
Austin

Pizza Sauce
Great for do-it-yourself pizza party

1 can (8 oz.) tomato
   sauce
1 can (6 oz.) tomato
   paste
1 clove garlic, crushed
1 teaspoon sugar
1 teaspoon oregano
¾ teaspoon basil
   Dash red pepper
   Pita bread

Combine all ingredients. Spread on split pita bread. Garnish with your favorite toppings. Bake 20 minutes at 325°.

Peggy Jetton, wife of Bobby R. Jetton, BS '72
Spring

Mexican Casserole

1 pound ground beef
    or pork
1 medium-sized onion,
    chopped
2 teaspoons chili
    powder
2 teaspoons salt
1 can (4 oz.) green
    chile peppers,
    chopped
1 can (8 oz.) tomato
    sauce
1 cup water
8 ounces American
    cheese, sliced
6 tortillas

Brown meat and onion in a frying pan. Add chile powder, salt and green chile peppers. Combine tomato sauce and water. In buttered 2-quart casserole, layer half the meat mixture, half the tomato mixture, top with 3 tortillas cut into strips and half the cheese. Repeat layers, ending with cheese. Bake, uncovered, 40 minutes at 300°. Serves 4.

Agnes Henke Lundstedt, BS '53
Austin

Magee's Cabrito

6 tablespoons oil
3 to 4 pounds cabrito*,
    cut into serving
    pieces
1 medium-sized onion,
    chopped
½ green pepper, chopped
½ teaspoon salt
¼ teaspoon pepper
2 cloves garlic,
    chopped
½ teaspoon comino seed
½ jalapeño, chopped
¼ cup water
1 can (16 oz.) whole
    tomatoes, undrained

Place oil in large skillet and brown cabrito well on both sides. When browned, add onion. Cover, reduce heat and simmer 20 to 30 minutes (continue to turn meat while cooking). Add green pepper, salt and pepper. Cook, uncovered, 10 minutes. Add remaining ingredients, cover and simmer 45 minutes; do not allow meat to stick to skillet. Uncover, cook 10 minutes more. Serves 8.

Susan Fortson Magee, BA '76 MLS '78
Brownsville

In South Texas, cabrito (baby goat) is purchased packaged in assorted serving pieces. For T-Sips not living in the Valley, cabrito is generally a special-order item available as a whole carcass averaging 14 to 20 pounds. Editor.

Nopalapa

2 pounds lean beef
1 teaspoon pepper
1 teaspoon sugar
2 cloves garlic, minced
2 teaspoons oregano
4 tablespoons olive oil
4 tablespoons wine
    vinegar
1 jar (8½ oz.) pickled
    cactus (nopalitos),
    drained and
    chopped
2 cups chopped fresh
    tomatoes
½ to ¾ cup chopped
    onion to taste
16 flour tortillas

Cut meat into ½-inch cubes. Place meat into large-sized, zip-lock plastic bag. Combine next six ingredients, pour over meat, and lock bag. Turn bag upside down several times to coat meat with marinade. Refrigerate overnight, turning bag several times. Drain meat; brown; add cactus, tomatoes, onion and cook until onion is transparent and juice is almost reduced. Using slotted spoon serve onto warm tortillas. Serves 8.

Louise Hoehn, BA '59
Houston

Mexican Mush

A combination of Italian and Mexican flavors . . . great addition to potluck suppers!

2 cups medium-sized
    macaroni shells
1 pound ground beef
1 cup chopped onion
2 cloves garlic, minced
1 can (15 oz.) tomato
    sauce
½ cup water
1 teaspoon oregano,
    crushed
½ teaspoon salt
½ teaspoon ground
    cumin
¼ teaspoon pepper
2 bay leaves

Cook macaroni shells in boiling salted water, stirring constantly 3 minutes. Remove from heat, cover and set aside 10 minutes. Drain. In saucepan or flameproof casserole, cook beef, onion and garlic until beef is browned. Drain excess fat. Stir in remaining ingredients and bring to a boil. Add shells. Pour into 1½-quart casserole. Bake, covered, 30 minutes at 350°. Remove bay leaves. Stir mixture before serving. Serves 6.

Merle Tooke Lewis, BA '53 MLS '70
Waterville, Maine

Chilaquiles À Chavez
A spicy version of migas

8 strips bacon
8 corn tortillas (cut into
   1-inch squares)
4 green onions, chopped
8 eggs, beaten
1 medium-sized tomato,
   diced
2 to 4 jalapeños, minced
   Refried beans
   Salt and pepper to
   taste
   Additional tortillas
   Parmesan cheese,
   grated (optional)

Fry bacon, pat dry and set aside. Saute tortillas in bacon grease until barely crisp. Add green onion and saute. Drain excess grease. Combine eggs, tomato and jalapeños. Add to tortilla mixture. Scramble to desired doneness. Serve immediately with refried beans and warm tortillas (flour or corn). Bacon can be served as side dish, or crumbled into eggs. Sprinkle with Parmesan. Serves 4.

Adam Gene Chavez, BA '69
Austin

Fajitas
Made simple for Aggies

4 or 5 pounds skirt steak
   Lemon Pepper
      Seasoning
   Flour tortillas
   Refried beans
1 bunch green onions,
   chopped
1 bunch fresh cilantro
   leaves
   Avocados, sliced
   Sour cream
   Picante sauce

Prepare meat by cutting away all stringy membrane and fat. Season liberally on both sides with Lemon Pepper. Set aside 15 minutes. Grill quickly, over hot mesquite coals, turning frequently until grilled to medium rare. (Keep handy a bottle of water with spray attachment. Mist coals as needed to douse flames.) Cut diagonally into very thin slices. Fill a hot flour tortilla with a spoonful of refried beans, a sprinkle of onion and cilantro leaves, an avocado slice, a dollop of sour cream and a spoonful of picante sauce. Fold tortilla in half and savor that first fabulous bite. Exercise prerogative of "el jefe" (chief chef) to nibble, nibble, nibble. Serves 6.

Lloyd W. Jary, Jr. BArch '60
San Antonio

Chalupas

12 chalupa shells (flat,
   crisp fried tortillas)
4 cups warm refried
   pinto beans*
3 cups shredded iceberg
   lettuce
2 cups chopped fresh
   tomatoes
2 cups grated Longhorn
   cheese
1 cup chopped onion
   or green onion
3 cups cooked breast of
   chicken, chopped
1 cup sour cream
3 cups guacamole*
1½ cups picante sauce*

"People who live in San Antonio tend to have 'Fiestas' at the drop of a 'sombrero.' And I love the color, informality, and fun of the party and the preparation. My favorite food to serve is the chalupa. (To you non-aficionados of Mexican food, it is somewhat like a hero sandwich.) I serve it in lined baskets of various sizes as a 'build-your-own' buffet on a table ablaze with bright Mexican flowers. Mexican beer or Margaritas are the perfect beverages to accompany this meal. Although it is difficult to give exact amounts of the ingredients, I've given you approximate ones and, as you become better acquainted with the Chalupa Bar, you'll be able to adjust them according to the number of guests you will be entertaining. These ingredients will serve 6, allowing 2 chalupas per person.

Arrange your buffet table in the following manner: chalupa shells, hot beans, lettuce, tomatoes, cheese, onion, chicken, sour cream, guacamole and picante sauce.

Now you are ready to bring out the Margaritas and beer, turn on your favorite Mexican music and enjoy! *Viva La Fiesta!*"

*See Index

Bebe Canales Inkley, '57
San Antonio

Chilaquiles

2 medium-sized onions,
   chopped
1 clove garlic, minced
2 tablespoons salad oil
2 cans (16 oz. each)
   tomatoes
   Salt and pepper to
   taste
1 can (4 oz.) chopped
   green chile peppers,
   drained
12 corn tortillas
1 pound Monterrey Jack
   cheese, grated

Saute onions and garlic in oil until golden. Add tomatoes, salt and pepper to taste. Simmer until mixture is thickened, stirring frequently. Stir in green chile peppers. Cut tortillas into fourths and fry briefly in hot fat just until they are limp. Drain. In greased casserole, arrange in layers: tortillas, sauce, cheese. Repeat until ingredients are used, ending with cheese on top. Bake 15 minutes at 350° or until cheese is bubbly. Serves 8.

Shirley Coin Kleiman, BBA '47
Victoria

Paella

¼ cup salad oil
2 chicken breasts, boned
   and cubed
2 cups rice, uncooked
2 cans (10¾ oz. each)
   chicken broth
¼ teaspoon salt
⅛ teaspoon pepper
½ to 1 teaspoon saffron*
2 cloves garlic, minced
1 onion, chopped
1 can (16 oz.) tomatoes,
   chopped
2 uncooked sausage
   links, sliced
   into bite-sized pieces
1 pound raw shrimp,
   deveined
1 package (10 oz.)
   frozen green peas
3 carrots, sliced
½ green pepper, cut
   into strips

At medium heat saute chicken in oil until brown. Add rice, stirring constantly until rice is evenly browned. Bring chicken broth to boil; add salt, pepper, saffron and garlic. Add broth mixture to chicken and rice, add all remaining ingredients. Simmer, covered, 30 minutes or until all liquid is absorbed. Serves 6.

*More saffron may be needed depending on freshness.

Mary Canales Jary, '56
San Antonio

Pico de Gallo (Chile Macho)

1 to 3 whole jalapeños,
   as desired
½ cup finely chopped
   cilantro
8 to 10 green onions,
   minced
2 tomatoes, chopped
2 avocados, finely diced
Juice of 2 limes
Garlic salt, seasoned
   salt and seasoned
   pepper to taste

Stem and seed jalapeños and finely mince. Combine with remaining ingredients. Chill. Serve on small plates with tortilla chips, or serve on warm tortillas. Serves 8 to 10. NOTE: Show guests how to hold warm tortillas in palm of hand; spread tortilla with Pico de Gallo; fold and roll over, closing one end to keep mixture from dripping. Looks like an enchilada with one end tucked in.

Louise Hoehn, BA '59
Houston

Variation: *Omit jalapeños and cilantro. Use 3 tomatoes, 3 cans (4 oz. each) green chile peppers (chopped) and 1 clove garlic (finely minced).*

Louise Bates, BS '34
Alice

420

Turkey Sopa

Use left-over Thanksgiving turkey. Serve after we have left the Aggies behind!

4 tablespoons (½ stick) butter
2 cups chopped onion
1 can (16 oz.) tomatoes, chopped
3 cans (10 oz. each) tomatoes and green chile peppers
Salt to taste
5 cups cooked turkey, cut into bite-sized chunks
1 box (16 oz.) processed cheese spread, diced
1 package (16 oz.) nacho chips
1 can (13 oz.) evaporated milk

Saute onions in butter. Add chopped tomatoes and 3 cans tomatoes and green chile peppers. Drain whole chile peppers, cut lengthwise, remove seeds. Cut chile peppers into 2-inch strips, add to tomato mixture. Season lightly with salt, simmer at low heat 20 minutes. Butter 9 x 13-inch casserole, cover bottom with nacho chips using ⅓ of the package. Add half the turkey. Sprinkle ⅓ of the diced cheese over turkey, top with ⅓ of the sauce. Add a scant layer of nacho chips and repeat layers, ending with cheese. Pour evaporated milk over cheese, covering all of the mixture. Liquid should be half way up the sides of the 2½-inch depth and all nacho chips on top should be moistened. If more liquid is needed, add more evaporated milk. Cover with foil, bake 45 minutes at 350°. This casserole can be reheated and also will freeze. Serves 8 to 10.

Beverly Cottle, wife of J. Ted Cottle, BBA '32
El Paso

Pedernales Tacos

1 pound ground beef
Salt and pepper to taste
Salad oil
Flour
3 cloves garlic, minced
2 teaspoons oregano
1 teaspoon comino seeds
1 onion, finely chopped
12 taco shells
FILLING:
½ head lettuce, shredded
1 large-sized onion, chopped
2 fresh tomatoes, chopped

Boil meat with salt and pepper in enough water to cover meat. Drain and reserve broth. Place meat in skillet with shortening and a little flour, brown lightly. Add garlic, oregano, comino and onion. Keep adding broth until meat absorbs all moisture. Heat taco shells in oven. Place meat in taco shells. Add shredded lettuce, then onion, top with tomato. Serve immediately. Serves 12.

Stella Jung Browning, BS '36
Fredericksburg

Taco Salad

1 red or white onion,
   chopped
4 tomatoes, peeled and
   sliced
1 head lettuce, shredded
4 ounces sharp Cheddar
   cheese, grated
1 bottle (8 oz.) French
   dressing
   Dash Tabasco to taste
1 bag (6½ oz.) tortilla
   chips
1 large-sized avocado
1 pound ground beef
1 can (15 oz.) kidney
   beans, drained
½ teaspoon salt
   Chili powder to
   taste

Combine onion, tomatoes and lettuce. Add cheese, toss with dressing and Tabasco. Reserve 12 whole tortilla chips and crush remaining chips into small pieces. Add crushed chips to salad. Add avocado. Brown meat; drain; combine with beans, salt and chili powder. Simmer together briefly, add to salad. Use reserved whole chips as garnish. Serve immediately. Very tasty as main dish with hot buttered flour tortillas. Serves 6 as a main dish, serves 12 as a salad.

Rhonda Hodges, wife of Richard L. Hodges, BBA '74
Houston

Barbara White Stuart, '55
Dallas

Picante Sauce

HOT! It's good if your mouth can stand it!

1 pound jalapeños,
   stemmed and seeded
5 pounds fresh tomatoes
3 medium-sized onions
1 cup chopped celery
3 cloves garlic
   Juice of 1 lemon
2 tablespoons vinegar
   Dash dry mustard
   Dash cumin
   Dash oregano
1 teaspoon salt

Finely chop all vegetables in food processor or blender. Add lemon juice, vinegar and seasonings. Simmer, uncovered, at low heat 1 hour or until desired consistency. Yield: 18 half-pint jars. Store in freezer. Use as table sauce or for cooking.

Eugene Whiddon, BBA '47
Ruth Cotten Whiddon, BA '40
Beaumont

Mexican
Christmas Tree Salad

1 pound very lean
    ground beef
1 package taco
    seasoning mix
2 cans (15 oz. each)
    refried beans
3 avocados
    Juice of 1 lemon
    Garlic powder to taste
    Salt to taste
1 tablespoon picante
    sauce
1 carton (8 oz.) sour
    cream
4 green onions, finely
    chopped
1 can (4 oz.) chopped
    black olives
1 can (4 oz.) chopped
    green chile peppers
6 ounces Cheddar
    cheese, grated
6 ounces Mozzarella or
    Monterrey Jack
    cheese, grated
3 tomatoes, chopped
1 head iceberg lettuce,
    finely shredded
    Nacho chips

Brown meat, add taco seasoning mix and refried beans. Puree avocados with lemon juice; add garlic powder, salt and picante sauce. On a large serving platter or tray, spread warm meat and bean base, top with prepared avocado. Add ingredients, 1 at a time, in order given making each layer a bit smaller in size so that the salad tiers like a Christmas tree. Serve with nacho chips. No serving spoons or forks allowed. For dessert, serve pralines and strong coffee. Serves 4 to 6.

Joan Culver, wife of Joe Culver, BBA '53 MBA '58
Austin

Sopaipillas
(Cocina de Carlos)

4 cups flour
2 teaspoons baking
    powder
1 teaspoon salt
1 tablespoon lard
    Lukewarm water
    Oil for deep-frying
    Cinnamon sugar
    Honey

Sift flour, baking powder and salt. Work in lard and enough lukewarm water to make a stiff dough. Set aside 1 hour, then roll to ¼-inch thickness. Cut into 3-inch squares. Deep-fry in oil at 425°. Use slotted spoon to submerge each square in hot oil in order to have puffy sopaipillas. Fry until brown. Drain, sprinkle with cinnamon sugar and pass the honey! Serves 8 to 10.

Vergil Murphy, '28
Conroe

Folkloric Cuisine

Mexican Salad Bowl

½ head lettuce
1 package (12 oz.)
    fresh spinach
1 cucumber, peeled and
    sliced
5 green onions, sliced
¼ pound hard salami,
    sliced
2 tomatoes, chopped
1 avocado, sliced
1 cup grated Muenster
    cheese
8 black olives, sliced
6 mushrooms, sliced
3 tablespoons salad oil
1 tablespoon lemon
    juice
  Garlic salt
  Ground cumin

DRESSING:

½ cup oil
4 tablespoons fresh
    lemon juice
2 tablespoons sesame
    seeds, toasted
2 teaspoons salt
2 teaspoons sugar
½ teaspoon ground
    cumin
½ teaspoon pepper

Combine all ingredients except mushrooms, oil, lemon juice and seasonings. Chill. Marinate mushrooms in oil, lemon juice and seasonings.

DRESSING: Combine ingredients in a jar with a tightly fitting lid, shake vigorously and refrigerate. To serve, add mushrooms and dressing. Serves 12.

Susan Fortson Magee, BA '76 MLS '78
Brownsville

Flour Tortillas

2 cups flour
¼ tablespoon salt
¼ tablespoon baking
    powder
¼ cup shortening
  Warm water

Combine dry ingredients. Cut in shortening. Add enough water to make the pastry smooth and elastic. Divide dough into 12 pieces and roll each piece into a round shape. Remember, the thinner the dough is rolled, the better the tortilla. Cook at low heat in an ungreased iron skillet or on a griddle until the little bubbles are somewhat brown. Turn and cook other side. Serve warm with butter or keep refrigerated for later use. Yield: 12 tortillas.

Kimberly Fojtik, BBA '79
Greenwood, South Carolina

424

Aunt Martha's Tamale Pie

1½ pounds ground beef
1 onion, chopped
1 green pepper, cut into
  strips
1 clove garlic, minced
1 can (12 oz.) whole
  kernel corn,
  undrained
1 can (6 oz.) tomato
  paste
1 cup water
½ cup sliced ripe olives
2 tablespoons chili
  powder
1 teaspoon salt
1 cup grated Cheddar
  cheese

TOPPING:
¾ cup yellow cornmeal
½ teaspoon salt
2 cups water

Saute beef, onion, green pepper and garlic. Drain excess grease. Stir in corn, tomato paste, water, olives, chili powder and salt. Simmer 20 to 25 minutes. Stir in cheese until melted. Pour into 2-quart casserole.

TOPPING: Combine ingredients; cook at medium heat 15 minutes, stirring constantly until mixture thickens. Spoon over meat, bake 35 to 40 minutes at 375°. Serves 6.

Martha Francis Singleton, '40
Houston

Variation: *Omit cheese from base. Add ½ cup cornmeal mixed with ½ cup water during last 10 minutes of simmering the sauce. Substitute Spoon Bread Topping and use 3-quart casserole.*

Nita Hixson Galloway, BJ '51
Wilmington, Delaware

Spoon Bread Topping

1½ cups milk
1 teaspoon salt
2 tablespoons butter
  or margarine
½ cup cornmeal
1 cup grated Cheddar
  cheese
2 eggs, lightly beaten

Heat milk, salt and butter; slowly stir in cornmeal. Cook, stirring until thickened. Remove from heat, stir in cheese and eggs. Pour over meat mixture. Chill 1½ hours. Bake 35 to 40 minutes at 350°.

Nita Hixson Galloway, BJ '51
Wilmington, Delaware

First Lady Of Texas Chicken Enchiladas

3 large-sized chicken
 breasts
 Salt
1 cup chopped onion
1 clove garlic, minced
2 tablespoons butter or
 margarine
1 can (16 oz.) tomatoes,
 coarsely chopped
1 can (8 oz.) tomato
 sauce
¼ cup chopped green
 chile peppers
1 teaspoon sugar
1 teaspoon ground
 cumin
½ teaspoon salt
½ teaspoon dried
 oregano, crushed
½ teaspoon dried basil,
 crushed
12 corn tortillas
2½ cups shredded
 Monterrey Jack
 cheese
¾ cup sour cream

Simmer chicken breasts in water to cover until tender. Skin and debone. Sprinkle with salt, cut into 12 strips and set aside. Saute onion and garlic in butter until tender. Add tomatoes, tomato sauce, chile peppers, sugar, cumin, salt, oregano and basil. Bring to boil, reduce heat. Simmer, covered, 20 minutes. Remove from heat. Dip each tortilla in tomato mixture to soften. Place 1 piece of chicken and 2 tablespoons cheese on each tortilla, roll, place seam down in 2-quart baking dish. Mix sour cream into remaining sauce mixture, pour over tortillas, sprinkle with remaining cheese. Cover, bake at 350° until heated thoroughly. Serves 6.

Rita Crocker Clements, BA '53
Austin

Ripe Olive Enchiladas

12 corn tortillas
 Salad oil
2 cups sour cream
1½ pounds sharp Cheddar
 cheese, grated
1 can (6 oz.) chopped
 ripe olives
1 onion, finely chopped
2 cans El Paso Mild
 Enchilada Sauce

Using tongs dip tortillas in hot cooking oil 30 seconds; drain; then spoon sour cream, sprinkle cheese, olives and onion onto each tortilla and roll up. Place in baking dish, cover tortillas with enchilada sauce. Sprinkle remaining cheese, onions and ripe olives over enchiladas. Bake at 350° until bubbly. Serves 6.

William P. Fitch, III, BA '64
San Antonio

Chicken Enchilada Casserole
An after-game buffet treat for 20

2 chickens, 2½ to 3
   pounds each
8 ounces cream cheese
2 cans (10¾ oz. each)
   cream of mushroom
   soup
2 cans (10¾ oz. each)
   cream of celery
   soup
2 cans (10¾ oz. each)
   cream of chicken
   soup
1 carton (8 oz.) sour
   cream
1 onion, minced
2 cans (4 oz. each)
   chopped green chile
   peppers
24 corn tortillas
10 ounces Cheddar
   cheese, grated

Boil chicken, reserve broth. Debone and dice. In blender, combine cream cheese with 1 can of soup, blend until smooth. Remove from blender, add remaining soups, sour cream and onion. Mix well, add chicken and chile peppers. Heat reserved broth and dip tortillas until limp. Line one 5-quart or two 3-quart casseroles with tortillas. Add a layer of chicken, then a layer of tortillas; repeat layers using all ingredients. Top with grated cheese. Bake 45 minutes at 350°. Serves 20.

Eleanor Ann Van Zandt Gerrard, BA '42
Victoria

Green Enchiladas

1 chicken, about
   3 pounds
2 or 3 pounds green
   tomatoes or
   tomatillos
1 medium-sized onion,
   chopped
1 green pepper, chopped
   Green food coloring
   Salt and pepper to
   taste
15 tortillas
1 pound Monterrey
   Jack cheese, grated
1 carton (8 oz.) sour
   cream

Stew chicken, reserve broth. Peel green tomatoes by dipping into boiling water. Quarter tomatoes. In small amount of chicken broth, simmer tomatoes, onion and green pepper until tender. Cool. Blend mixture in blender until smooth. Add coloring until color of avocado pulp. Salt and pepper to taste. Debone and cut chicken into bite-sized chunks. Warm the green sauce, but do not boil. To assemble, in a second skillet, dip tortillas in hot fat to soften. Then dip tortillas in green sauce. Fill each tortilla with chicken seasoned with salt and pepper and 1 teaspoon cheese. Roll tortilla and place enchiladas side by side in baking dish. Cover tortillas with green sauce, add remaining cheese and dot with sour cream. Bake 15 minutes at 325°. The enchiladas may be prepared ahead, but do not cover with green sauce until ready to heat. Serves 8.

Mamie Strieber Shepperd, BJ '38
Odessa

1890 San Antonio Enchilada Sauce

3 tablespoons bacon
  grease
1 medium-sized onion,
  chopped
4 cloves garlic,
  chopped
1 can (28 oz.) whole
  tomatoes
1 can (14½ oz.) whole
  tomatoes and
  1 can water
2 teaspoons salt
¼ teaspoon pepper
1 dried chile Ancho
  pod, seeded
2½ teaspoons chili
  powder
1 teaspoon sugar

Saute onion and garlic in grease. Add tomatoes and water. Add salt and pepper; drop in chile pod (do not remove skin). Bring to a boil, lower heat and simmer until tomatoes and chile pod cook to a mush, approximately one hour. Sieve through a collander, or puree in blender (textures will differ accordingly). Return to saucepan. Add chili powder, sugar and more water to desired thickness. Bring slowly to a boil. Sauce makes enough for 2 dozen enchiladas.

To make enchiladas: Grate desired amount of Cheddar cheese and onion. Dip fresh corn tortillas in the sauce, fill with cheese and onion and roll. Arrange in baking dish. Cover with enchilada sauce and sprinkle with more cheese and onion. Bake at 300° until cheese is melted and sauce is bubbly. Serves 12.

Walter L. Geyer, BM '61
Dallas

Fiesta Enchilada Casserole

1 pound pork or beef,
  cubed
1 can (4 oz.) sliced
  mushroms,
  undrained
1 cup white wine
  Chopped green chile
  peppers to taste
1 cup sliced black olives
1 medium-sized onion,
  chopped
2 tablespoons butter
12 blue corn tortillas
1 avocado, cubed
1 cup grated Cheddar
  cheese
1 cup grated
  Monterrey Jack
  cheese

Brown meat and drain grease. Add mushrooms, mushroom liquid and wine. Simmer until meat is tender. Add green chile peppers and black olives. Simmer to blend flavors. Saute onion in butter. Soften tortillas by quickly dipping in hot water. Layer 6 tortillas in ungreased 10 x 13-inch baking dish. Spoon half of meat and chile mixture over tortillas. Follow with layer of avocado, onion and cheeses. Repeat layers. Heat 30 minutes at 350° or until cheese melts. Serves 6 to 8.

Sylvia Cook, BA '65
Austin

King Ranch Chicken Enchiladas

1 can (10¾ oz.) cream
   of mushroom soup,
   undiluted
1 can (10¾ oz.) cream
   of chicken soup,
   undiluted
1 can (10 oz. size)
   tomatoes with green
   chile peppers
12 corn tortillas, cut
   into triangles
½ pound (2 cups) grated
   American cheese
1 frying chicken (2½ to
   3 lbs.), cooked and
   reserve 1 cup broth
1 small-sized onion,
   chopped

Mix in saucepan soups, tomatoes and chile pepper and chicken broth. Heat. Cut chicken into bite-sized pieces. In buttered 3-quart casserole, layer chicken, tortillas, cheese, onion and soup mixture. Repeat layers. Bake 15 to 20 minutes at 350°. Serves 6.

Marilyn Marter, BS '74
Austin

Variation: *Add garlic salt; chili powder; and 1 large-sized green pepper, chopped, to soup mixture. Reserve tomatoes and combine with 1 can (8 oz.) tomato sauce and spread over top. Bake, covered, 30 minutes. Bake, uncovered, 30 minutes more.*

Gay Freeze Maguire, '71
Austin

Variation: *Use entire can of tomatoes and chile peppers. Substitute Cheddar cheese for American cheese.*

Nita Hixson Galloway, BJ '51
Wilmington, Delaware

Scholz's Rouladen

Veal cutlet
Pickles
Onion
Bacon
Egg
Flour
Bread crumbs
Brown gravy
Cream gravy

For each serving, flatten cutlet to thin 5-x 6-inch rectangle. Top with blanched bacon pieces, sliced hamburger pickles and chopped onion. Roll up on 5-inch side, dust with flour, dip in beaten egg, and roll in fine bread crumbs. Deep fry, drain. Place on plate, top with brown gravy and cream gravy. Serve with potato salad and sauerkraut.

Scholz's Restaurant
Austin

Pryor's Mexican Goulash
Live a little!

1 shaker salt
1 quart Sauza
    Conmemorativo
    tequila
2 Mexican limes,
    quartered
4 pats margarine or
    butter
1 large-sized onion,
    chopped
2 pounds ground chuck
    or ground round
2 cloves garlic, minced
½ teaspoon salt
1 teaspoon pepper
4 tablespoons chili
    powder
1 can (15 oz.) tomato
    sauce
2 cans (15 oz. each)
    red kidney beans

"First, lick top of left hand (at base of thumb), salt top of hand, lick off salt, drink one jigger of tequila slowly savoring the flavor and bite into 1 slice of lime squeezing slightly for juice. In a large frying pan saute chopped onion in margarine until rather clear. Repeat salt, tequila and lime routine. Add meat and brown lightly, breaking into fine pieces. (If ground chuck is used, drain most of fat off after browning.) Repeat salt, tequila and lime routine. Next add garlic, salt, pepper and chili powder and cook for 5 minutes more over medium heat, stirring often. Repeat salt, tequila and lime routine. Add tomato sauce and kidney beans (drain liquid from one can and give to your pet dog or goat). Cover and cook over low heat for 20 to 25 minutes more, stirring often. Repeat salt, tequila and lime routine two more times during this period.

To serve: (NOTE: It may be necessary to have someone who has not had any tequila do the serving for you.) Dish a good helping of goulash onto plate, topping with a slice of American cheese. Serve with a fresh salad of sliced avocados, green peppers and tomatoes along with whole kernel corn (be sure to unfreeze and heat before serving for better taste) or corn on the cob. Garlic toast or hot flour tortillas add a good touch. Serves 2 to 8 persons, depending on how hungry they are or what condition they are in. Ideal for after football game parties or sorority slumber parties. (Note: I would be available to attend either of these type parties to assure that the above preparation is done correctly.) The goulash actually tastes better if refrigerated and reheated the next day. Darn if I know why!

OPTION: If you do not like tequila, omit the shaker of salt and slices of limes and substitute 2 six-packs of Mexican beer for tequila (chill before drinking for best results.)"

Wally Pryor, BFA '51
Austin

Authentic Hungarian Gulyas
To be really festive, garnish with sliced dill pickles and dot with sour cream.

2 tablespoons shortening
1 large-sized onion, chopped
4 ounces paprika
1½ pounds stewing beef
Noodles or potatoes

Melt shortening in heavy skillet over low heat. Saute onion, stirring until translucent; do not brown. Add paprika, stir well. Add meat, stir until onion has coated the meat, pour hot water over mixture just to cover. Bring to boil, reduce to simmer, cover tightly and cook at least 1 hour. The gulyas will hold at warm heat until ready to serve. Add quartered potatoes during last 30 minutes of cooking, or serve over noodles. Serves 4 to 6.

"In Europe, paprika is bought in sharp, medium or sweet flavors and is bought by the kilo. Here I use half of an 8-ounce box for this amount of meat. I add hot sauce to taste for a sharper sauce. Sauce may be thickened with cornstarch if you prefer."

Eve Stein Kermacy, BFA '54 MEd '60
Austin

VEAL SCALLOPINE. Use 1½ pounds veal cutlet or tenderized beef round steak cut ¼-inch thick. Cut into serving pieces 3 x 3 inches. Place between sheets of waxed paper and pound with flat mallet or bottom of heavy skillet until thin. Combine 1 cup flour with salt and freshly ground pepper to taste. Heat 2 tablespoons butter and 2 tablespoons oil in large heavy skillet. Dredge steaks in flour mixture, add to hot oil. Brown thoroughly on both sides. Remove and keep warm. To skillet add 1 can (6 oz.) sliced broiled-in-butter mushrooms (undrained) and ½ cup white wine. Stir to incorporate particles in skillet. If sauce appears too thin, thicken with 1 tablespoon cornstarch mixed with ¼ cup cold water. Taste for seasonings, adjust accordingly, add a pinch of sugar if sauce is too tart. Serve with buttered egg noodles. Serves 4 to 6.

John D. Ryder, BBA '65
Seguin

VEAL SHANKS: Cut shanks into 2-inch thick pieces. Pat white pepper, salt and flour onto both ends. Saute 1 clove garlic in oil until browned. Add chopped carrots, celery, tomatoes, onions, 1 teaspoon fresh ginger root and 1 teaspoon grated orange peel. Add enough vermouth to cover. Cover, simmer slowly 2 hours. Remove meat and vegetables, boil remaining liquid at high flame to reduce and thicken, then pour over meat and vegetables. Serve hot with homemade noodles or brown rice.

Nancy Brown Negley, '58
San Antonio

431

Moussaka

1½ pounds finely ground
    lamb, veal or beef
1 medium-sized onion,
    thinly sliced
1 to 2 tablespoons
    butter or margarine
½ cup white wine
1 can (20 oz.) tomatoes,
    finely chopped
3 teaspoons chopped
    parsley
    Salt and pepper
1 large-sized eggplant
    Oil for frying
2 small-sized zucchini,
    sliced
7 or 8 teaspoons bread
    crumbs
2 egg whites, slightly
    beaten
    Béchamel Sauce
    Grated Parmesan
    cheese

Saute meat and onions in butter. Add wine, tomatoes, parsley, salt and pepper. Mix well and simmer, covered, 1 hour. Cut unpeeled eggplant into crosswise slices, saute in oil until golden brown. Saute sliced zucchini in oil or butter until tender crisp. When meat is cooked with very little liquid remaining, add 3 or 4 teaspoons bread crumbs and egg whites. Sprinkle ovenproof dish with a few breadcrumbs, add a layer of eggplant, then zucchini and half the meat. Repeat layers, ending with eggplant. Cover with Béchamel Sauce, sprinkle top with remaining cheese and bread crumbs and dot with butter. Bake 30 minutes at 225° or until lightly browned. Serves 6 to 8.

Evelyn Wilson Lindsay, '47
McAllen

Béchamel Sauce

3 tablespoons butter
3 tablespoons flour
2½ cups milk
½ teaspoon salt
    White pepper to taste
2 egg yolks

Make a "blonde" roux. Melt butter, add flour, cook 2 minutes, stirring constantly with a whisk or wooden spoon. Do not allow roux to brown even slightly. Add milk, whisking constantly. Bring just to boil, reduce heat, simmer 10 minutes or until sauce has reduced to 2 cups. Add salt and white pepper. Put egg yolks into a small mixing bowl, beat slightly, slowly beat in ½ cup of the hot sauce. When mixed, pour this mixture into the remaining sauce, whisking constantly. Do not boil after addition of egg yolks.

Evelyn Wilson Lindsay, '47
McAllen

Lamb Curry
Eat and enjoy!

2 pounds lean lamb,
(leg or shoulder
meat) or 2 pounds
round steak, cubed
1 small-sized onion,
chopped
2 tablespoons hot
salad oil
1 teaspoon curry
powder
¼ cup flour
Salt and pepper
4 cups steamed rice

CONDIMENTS:
Chutney
3 hard-cooked eggs,
mashed with a fork
4 strips crisp bacon,
crumbled
½ cup ground peanuts
½ cup grated coconut,
fresh if possible
Sweet pickle relish

Saute onion in hot oil until limp. Add meat
and cook until browned. Cover with water
and simmer until meat is tender. Make a paste
of flour, curry powder and 2 tablespoons
water. Stir paste into 2 cups stock from the
meat mixture. Return paste mixture to meat
and cook until gravy is thickened. Serves 4.

*"To serve, have each person take a helping of
steamed rice and spread it on his or her
warmed plate. The curried meat then goes on
top of the rice. Each person should place 1
tablespoon of each of the condiments on top
of the meat. A green salad and a fruit dessert
are a good combination with the curry.*

Dan C. Williams, BS '35
Dallas

Chicken Curry

3 tablespoons chopped
onion
3 tablespoons chopped
celery
½ cup butter
¾ teaspoon salt
1½ tablespoons curry
powder
¼ teaspoon ground
ginger
½ cup flour
4 cups milk
1 cup cream
4 cups cooked diced
chicken, or turkey,
duck, lamb or
shrimp
3 tablespoons sherry

Saute onion and celery in butter. Add salt,
curry, ginger and flour. Stir until smooth. Add
milk and cream. Whisk over medium heat
until sauce thickens. Add chicken. Just before
serving stir in sherry. Serves 10.

Jack S. Gray, BBA '35
Austin

MENU SUGGESTION: For 8-boy Curry serve
with cooked rice and condiments of chopped
peanuts, sieved hard-cooked egg yolks,
chopped cooked egg whites, chopped green
onion, crumbled cooked bacon, toasted
coconut, banana chips and chutney.

Indian Curry
Authentic "Embassy Row" curry

3 pounds stewing hen
1 quart milk, scalded
1 coconut (3 cups), grated
1 ginger root, chopped
1 tablespoon butter
2 teaspoons curry powder
1 slice onion
1 clove garlic, minced
Milk of 1 coconut
½ teaspoon brown sugar
1½ tablespoons cornstarch
1½ tablespoons flour
Cooked rice
Condiments

Simmer hen until tender. Skin, debone and cut into rather large pieces. Add grated coconut to hot milk. Cool 2 hours. Put ginger in hot water; peel and chop. Heat butter, add curry powder, heat 1 minute. Add onion, garlic and ginger. Stir constantly and add coconut milk. Cook 20 minutes. Add brown sugar. Add curry mixture to re-heated milk and grated coconut mixture. Cook, stirring constantly, until mixture comes to a boil. Cool. Strain through a cloth. Mix cornstarch and flour. Stir into liquid; bring to boil. Add prepared chicken; heat well. Serve over rice. Use any combination of condiments. Serves 6.

CONDIMENTS: Mango chutney, chopped salted peanuts, dried fresh coconut, stuffed olives marinated in French dressing, crushed crisp bacon, chopped hard-cooked eggs.

Dale Miller, MJ '32
Washington, DC

Lamb Anson

2 to 3 pounds saddle of lamb
Lemon halves
Rosemary
Fines Herbs
Salt
Freshly ground pepper
2 cloves garlic, peeled and quartered

Trim most of fat from lamb. Rub with lemon halves, rosemary, fines herbs, salt and tenderloin. Bake 15 minutes at 450° to brown. Reduce heat to 400°, bake 15 minutes per pound or until internal temperature reaches 140°. Remove and set aside 10 to 15 minutes before carving. Serves 4.

Thomas K. Anson, JD '80
Austin

MENU SUGGESTION: Serve with Marinated Tomatoes and Artichokes and Scalloped Eggplant.

Lamb Shish Kebab

2 pounds lamb

MARINADE:

¼ cup salad oil
2 tablespoons lemon
   juice
1 tablespoon grated
   onion
1 tablespoon chopped
   fresh parsley
1 teaspoon marjoram
1 teaspoon thyme
1 teaspoon salt
¼ teaspoon pepper

FOR SKEWERS:

1 large-sized green
   pepper, cubed
1 carton (1 pint) cherry
   tomatoes
½ pound small-sized
   onions
½ pound fresh
   mushrooms
12 skewers

Cut lamb into 2½-inch squares, ½-inch thick. Combine marinade ingredients and pour over lamb cubes. Marinate lamb at least 4 to 6 hours, preferably refrigerated overnight. Drain, assemble kebabs on skewers by alternating lamb, green pepper, cherry tomatoes, onions and mushrooms. Charcoal broil, basting with remaining marinade. Serves 4.

Shirley Coin Kleiman, BBA '47
Victoria

PORK CHOPS IN SOUR CREAM. Season 4 loin chops, (cut 1½-inches thick) with salt and pepper. Dredge with flour, brown in hot oil. Place in casserole. Combine ½ cup water, 2 tablespoons wine, 2 tablespoons brown sugar, ½ cup sour cream and 1 bay leaf. Pour over chops, cover, bake 1½ hours at 350°. Serves 4.

Joan Tompkins Hallmark, BFA '55
Tyler

Chorizo-Stuffed Pork Chops
For a cook-out after the Horns beat the Hogs

4 double-cut pork chops
with pockets

DRY MARINADE:

2 tablespoons lemon
pepper marinade
2 teaspoons garlic salt
1 tablespoon chili
powder
3 tablespoons paprika
1 teaspoon red pepper
1 teaspoon dry mustard
1 tablespoon sugar

STUFFING:

½ pound Chorizo
sausage
1 onion, finely chopped
1 rib celery, chopped
2 cloves garlic, minced
½ teaspoon red pepper
1 teaspoon pepper
⅓ cup seasoned bread
crumbs

Combine dry marinade ingredients and coat all surfaces, including inside pockets, of pork chops. Saute sausage and, when half cooked, add other stuffing ingredients except bread crumbs. Saute until sausage is browned, remove from heat, add crumbs. Stuff chops, close with toothpicks. Broil chops over medium hot charcoal fire, being careful that dripping grease does not flame up and burn. When cooked on all four sides, remove chops. Serves 4.

Wallace Pellerin, BBA '55
Austin

MENU SUGGESTION: Serve with Rice Souffle, Shoestring Carrots, Beer Bread, red wine and Bermuda Salad Bowl. Have Pineapple Nut Cake for dessert.

Tropical Ham Loaf

1 cup soft bread crumbs
¾ cup milk
2 eggs, beaten
1½ pounds ground ham
1 pound ground fresh
pork

TOPPING:

½ cup cider vinegar
½ cup water
½ cup brown sugar
1 teaspoon prepared
mustard

Soak bread crumbs in milk and gently fold in eggs. Carefully combine mixture with meats; do not pack or press. Form mixture into loaf in buttered 9 x 13-inch casserole. Combine topping ingredients and pour over loaf. Bake 2 hours at 325°. Baste often during baking. Serves 6 to 8.

Janiece Collier, wife of James E. Collier, BS '57
Hurst

Polynesian Sausage

1 pound Kulbassy
  sausage
1 cup onion, coarsely
  chopped
1 cup green pepper
  chunks
3 tablespoons cooking
  oil
1 can (16 oz.) whole
  peeled tomatoes,
  drained and
  quartered
1 can (20 oz.) pineapple
  chunks, drained
  (reserve liquid)
1 cup beef broth
1 tablespoon brown
  sugar, packed
¼ teaspoon garlic
  powder
¼ teaspoon pepper
2 tablespoons cornstarch
  Hot cooked rice

Cut sausage into ½-inch chunks. Cook in oil with onions and green pepper until onion is soft. Add tomatoes, pineapple, broth, brown sugar, garlic powder and pepper. Cover, simmer 5 minutes, stirring occasionally. Mix cornstarch with reserved pineapple liquid, add to sausage mixture. Stir until mixture is thickened, about 5 minutes. Serve over rice. Serves 6 to 8.

Cheryl Parsons Darnell, BJ '79
Austin

COUNTRY HAM WITH RED-EYE GRAVY. Slice country ham ¼-inch thick, leaving fat attached. Cook ham over low heat in heavy frying pan until browned on both sides. (A light sprinkle of sugar on each side before cooking intensifies flavor.) Remove ham from pan. Pour off excess fat, add ¼ cup brewed coffee to drippings. Bring to boil, pour over ham.

Gladys Bravenec Howard, BS '55
Tyler

FRIED APPLES. *(An old recipe from Bavaria).* Wash 6 medium-sized Jonathan or Winesap apples. Do not peel. Cut into quarters, removing core and seeds. Slice lengthwise, not too thin. Melt 2 tablespoons salad oil, butter or margarine in large skillet. Add apples and ¾ cup sugar to skillet, cover and cook over medium heat until there is a large amount of liquid and apples are a tiny bit tender. Watch carefully, stirring now and then. Remove lid to allow apples to finish cooking and the liquid to boil down some and thicken. Do not overcook the apples. Serves 6.

Frances McLean Van Horn, BA '70
Loveland, Colorado

Grilled Chops
À La Moutarde

2 tablespoons Dijon
    mustard
1 teaspoon dry mustard
1 teaspoon salt
    Freshly ground pepper
2 tablespoons butter,
    softened
4 to 6 large-sized chops
    (lamb, pork or
    veal)

HERB BUTTER:

2 tablespoons butter,
    softened
1 teaspoon finely
    chopped parsley
1 teaspoon finely
    chopped chives
2 teaspoons lemon juice
    Salt and freshly
    ground pepper

Make paste of Dijon mustard, dry mustard, salt, pepper and butter. Rub mustard mixture into both sides of each chop. Grill chops over a very hot charcoal fire 4 to 6 minutes on each side.
HERB BUTTER: Combine ingredients and mix well. Remove chops from fire and place each on a square of foil. Brush with Herb Butter. Seal each chop tightly by folding edges and return to charcoal grill for about 10 minutes more. Serve hot with Herb Butter from foil poured over chops. Serves 4 to 6.

Lloyd M. Bentsen, Jr., LLB '42
Washington, DC

Foie De Veau
À La Normandy
A Texas adaptation of a French favorite

1 firm, tart cooking
    apple
2 tablespoons butter
2 tablespoons oil
4 slices (½-inch thick)
    calf's liver, about
    ¾ pound
⅓ cup self-rising flour
    Seasoned salt to taste
    Freshly ground white
    pepper
¼ cup La Martinique
    French Dressing
¼ cup white wine
¼ cup Calvados

Slice unpeeled apples into rounds, core centers. Saute in butter until slightly tender, remove, add oil. Remove skin and veins from liver slices and wash slices. Dredge in flour seasoned with salt and pepper. Immediately place liver in hot oil and butter. Brown on both sides. Add dressing and wine, top liver with apple slices. Cover, cook at low heat 20 minutes, turning once. Liver should be glazed brown. Skim oil from pan, leaving browned particles. Heat Calvados, ignite, pour flaming over liver slices. Serve liver slices on bed of hot steamed rice, topped with apple slices and Calvados glaze. Serves 4.

Richard West, BJ '63 BA '63
New York, New York

MENU SUGGESTION: Serve with Texas Spinach Souffle, Grilled Tomato Cups and Edith Royal's Orange Custard.

Great Northern Bean Cassoulet

½ pound bacon
1 pound ground beef
1 medium-sized onion, chopped
1 can (31 oz.) pork and beans
1 can (17 oz.) lima beans, drained
1 can (15 oz.) large red kidney beans, drained
1 can (15 oz.) butter beans (optional)
6 ounces Canadian bacon, cubed
½ cup brown sugar
¼ cup catsup
1 tablespoon soy sauce
1 tablespoon Hickory Farms mustard
1 tablespoon brandy

Fry bacon, remove from skillet, drain and crumble. In drippings saute beef and onion, drain. Combine remaining ingredients with beef mixture and bacon. Bake in oven-to-table casserole, covered, 1 hour at 350°. Serves 8. Serves 8.

Ruth Butler Hunt, '27
Fairfield, Iowa

1980s Halloween Stew

1 medium-sized Arkansas sow's ear, sliced
1 level cup Rice Owl feathers
½ cup shredded SMU Mustang mane
½ cup chopped Houston Cougar fangs
2 pounds TCU Horned Frog legs
2 whole Baylor Bear claws, soaked overnight
1980 Texas-OU game ball
1 Texas Tech team captain
1 A&M Aggie quarterback

Brown meat, add 2 cups boiling water and remaining ingredients. Season to taste with Texas-OU game ball. Stir well with Red Raider (head first). Cover and simmer 2 hours, stirring occasionally. Remove game ball and bear claws, serve generous portion (in a bowl of cotton) to unsuspecting Aggie. Serves capacity crowd!

Beth Stephens Beck, BA '79
Austin

Committees

STEERING COMMITTEE

Bebe Canales Inkley, *Chairman and Graphics Editor*, '57

Gladys Bravenec Howard, *Recipe Editor*, BS '55

Dr. Margaret Berry, *Historical Editor*, BA '37

Nell Jones Herndon, *Testing Chairman*, BA '30

Charlotte Thornton, *Graphics Assistant*, BA '78

Gail Butzberger Chavez, *Head Proofreader*, BJ '71

Sylvia Cook, *Proofreader*, BA '65

Pauline Mills Edwards, *Proofreader*, MPA Candidate

Jerry Wilke English, *Proofreader*, '39

Penny Porter Helms, *Proofreader*, BFA '66

Mary Canales Jary, *Proofreader*, '56

Ruth Bownds Kershner, *Proofreader*, BJ '35

Edith Mae Sanders Livingston, *Proofreader*, BS '41

William S. Livingston, *Proofreader*, UT Vice President

Mary Lou Hopson Nuhn, *Proofreader*, '44

Nancy Fiske Pellerin, *Proofreader*, BS '57

Rose Marie Sharp, *Assistant Recipe Editor*, BJ '73

Loraine McNeil Jackson, *Staff Coordinator*, '46

Sheryn Jones, *Hart Graphics, Inc. Representative*

Sherwood W. Inkley, *Photographer*, BS '60

MARKETING COMMITTEE

Crockett English, *Chairman*, '36

Dr. Bob Witt, *UT Professor of Marketing*

Bob Hulan, *ESA Director of Operations*, BBA '77

Roy Vaughan, *ESA Executive Director*, '55

Cheryl Parsons Darnell, *Assistant Editor of Alcalde*, BJ '79

Charles R. Schneider, *ESA Records Manager*, BBA '47

ADVISORY COMMITTEE

Jean William Brown, *BJ '49*

Jean Kellner (Mrs. Bob) Durkee, *BS '53*

Priscilla (Mrs. Peter) Flawn

Hazel Harrod (Mrs. Harry) Ransom, *BA '42, MA '44*

Joan Hertz (Mrs. Glenn) Taylor, *BBA '57*

Steve Van, *BA '72*

Betty Brewer Chumney, *BA '53*

Acknowledgments

Acknowledging the many volunteers, staff and other friends who contributed to this cookbook is a very pleasant task. Our sincerest thanks and appreciation to John Stuart, who, during his presidency of the Ex-Students' Association, believed in the project and gave us his continual support; to Loraine Jackson, the staff coordinator, whose enthusiasm was contagious and without whom we couldn't have done it; to Susie Munson, who gave us the name for the cookbook (it was so obvious we didn't think of it); to Gladys Howard and Charlotte Thornton, who gave birth to the idea and put forth the effort to see the project to completion; to the efficient staff of the Ex-Students' Association, who were always available when we needed them; to Sheryn Jones, Hart Graphics representative, who held our hand and got us over the rough spots; to the ESA Executive Council, who provided us with the money for the project; to Nell Herndon, who blazed new trails between Bastrop and Austin while coordinating the testers; to the testers, who cooked till the book was "done"; to ESA Executive Director Roy Vaughan, who listened to every recipe each morning as they arrived and was not exhausted after he heard number 1700; to the hundreds of alumni who made the project happen and without whom there would not be a cookbook; to Jean Kaspar, the current Ex-Students' Association President, who inherited the project and predicted that it would sell more copies than Shiner sells six-packs; to Margaret Berry, one of the most knowledgable persons on the history of the University; to Rose Sharp, who lent us her journalism expertise; to the Barker Texas History Center and the University Writings Collection for the use of the historic photographs in the book; to Priscilla Flawn, whose knowledge of the University's treasures and collections was invaluable; to Bill Livingston, who read the historical manuscript while on the Flying Longhorn Alaskan trip; to all Texas Exes for their contributions to the campus culture; to Decherd Turner, Director of the Humanities Research Center, who gave us his valuable time and assistance in photographing the color plates, and last of all, to my family, Sherwood, Kim and Elise, who tolerated two years of cookbook talk and still promised to buy three copies.

Hook 'em and Cook 'em Horns!
Bebe Canales Inkley, '57
Cookbook Chairman

Testers

David Anson, Friend of UT
Tyler, Texas

Jo Laynne Hill Boies, MM '72
Austin, Texas

Martha Blair Allder, BJ '72
Kingwood, Texas

Susan Elkins Allen, BBA '75
Richardson, Texas

Whynell Aston, BBA '46
Mehlville, Missouri

Agnes Warren Barnes, BS '57
Waco, Texas

Maurine Redfearn Bartos, BS '57
Waco, Texas

Louise Stromberg Bates, BS '34
Alice, Texas

Beth Stephens Beck, BA '79
Austin, Texas

Sandra Daniel Billingsley, '60
Greenville, Texas

Marian Oldfather Boner, BA '30
    MA '31 LLB '55
Austin, Texas

Mary Boyles, wife of Jim Boyles,
    BBA '59
Dallas, Texas

Ann McCormick Byrd, '71
Austin, Texas

Ane Watson Casady, BA '70
Richardson, Texas

Denise Jaroszewski Chandler, BS '76
Houston, Texas

Dow Chapman, BBA '50
Austin, Texas

Joe M. Coffield, BS '42
Shreveport, Louisiana

Kathryn Lewis Colon, BBA '77
Corpus Christi, Texas

Sylvia Cook, BA '65
Austin, Texas

Sandra Lee Cooper, '75
San Antonio, Texas

Jose Correa, BS '48
Houston, Texas

Patsy Rucker Crowell, BA '43
Dallas, Texas

Deborah A. Devine, Friend of UT
Sanderson, Texas

Theo Smith Eichler, BS '38
Austin, Texas

Kathleen Tempel Elkins, '41
Shreveport, Louisiana

Roseanne Paul Elling, BS '75
San Antonio, Texas

Bess Powell Ezelle, '26
Sanderson, Texas

Jeanne Ferguson, wife of Paul Ferguson,
    BS '57
Tyler, Texas

Kathy Fife, BS '80
Austin, Texas

Jeanette Anne Fleming, BS '76
Pearland, Texas

442

Kimberly Fojtik, BBA '79
Guntersville, Alabama

Jamina Ford, wife of Tommy Ford,
   BS '65
Waco, Texas

Edmund P. Frank, Jr., BBA '74
Austin, Texas

Margaret Johnson Frazier, BM '42
Houston, Texas

Sharon L. Friedland, BA '75
New York, New York

Carol Gallman, wife of Jim Gallman,
   BS '74
Richardson, Texas

Juanita Hixson Galloway, BJ '51
Wilmington, Delaware

Lawana Geren, BS '71
Houston, Texas

Eleanor Ann Van Zandt Gerrard, BA '42
Victoria, Texas

Walter L. Geyer, BM '61
Dallas, Texas

Vera Lee Giles, wife of Rogan Giles,
   BBA '51 LLB '53
Austin, Texas

Jan Morrow Gray, BS '74
Austin, Texas

Marta Gray, BS '79
Houston, Texas

Carol Sue Hand, BS '72
Austin, Texas

Jo Shropshire Hannon, BBA '43
Austin, Texas

Susan Marie Palousek Harding, BA '69
Norristown, Pennsylvania

Tom Harlow, BBA '58
Austin, Texas

Carol Hebdon, wife of Jack Hebdon,
   BBA '77
San Antonio, Texas

Susie Hebert, Friend of UT
Houston, Texas

Penny Porter Helms, BFA '66
Austin, Texas

Ruth O'Hara Helms, BA '37
San Antonio, Texas

Ina Rue Herlocker, wife of Joe
   Herlocker, '51
San Antonio, Texas

Nell Jones Herndon, BA '30
Bastrop, Texas

Genevieve Toliver Houston, BBA '60
Dallas, Texas

Gladys Bravenec Howard, BS '55
Tyler, Texas

Joyce Jennings Hudnall, BS '53
Tyler, Texas

Jewell Huffines, Friend of UT
Big Sandy, Texas

Betty Allen Hurt, BA '54
Plainview, Texas

Bebe Canales Inkley, '57
San Antonio, Texas

Loraine McNeil Jackson, '46
Marble Falls, Texas

Caryl Nelson Jaeggli, BS '66
Dallas, Texas

Mary Barnes James, BA '71 BJ '71
Houston, Texas

Jane Cornick Jamison, BS '62
Austin, Texas

Mary Canales Jary, '56
San Antonio, Texas

Alice Gann Kaspar, '73
Ganado, Texas

Jennifer Kaufman, wife of Charles O.
   Kaufman, BJ '75
Little Rock, Arkansas

Eve Stein Kermacy, BFA '54 MEd '60
Austin, Texas

Susan Kessler, Membership Director of
The UT Ex-Students' Association
Austin, Texas

Elizabeth Ann Kibbe, BBA '78
Austin, Texas

Margaret Macha Kiefer, BA '69
Austin, Texas

Barbara Koy, wife of Ernie Koy, BA '66
Bellville, Texas

Joseph C. Kyle, Jr., BBA '73
Huntsville, Texas

Georgina Roach Lee, '62
Bastrop, Texas

Randolph H. Lewis, BA '41
Houston, Texas

Sue Brooks Littlefield, BA '77 JD '80
Austin, Texas

Susan Fortson Magee, BA '76 MLS '78
Brownsville, Texas

Judy Walker Mayo, BS '71
Dallas, Texas

Vicki McCanse, BBA '80
Austin, Texas

Vivienne L. McKitrick, BA '72 BS '75
Houston, Texas

Irene Reeb Meitzen, BA '65
San Angelo, Texas

Janis Dechman Modrall, BS '53
Houston, Texas

Eleanor Kennon Moore, BS '67
Austin, Texas

Nancy Gilmore Moyer, '50
Amarillo, Texas

Louise Harrell Mulkey, BA '61
Panhandle, Texas

Sharon E. Neeley, BBA '81
Austin, Texas

Patricia Maguire Nettles, BA '62
Bryan, Texas

Nancy Krause Nibling, BA '73
Lakewood, Colorado

John F. Owens, BS '55
Longview, Texas

Sandra Parks, wife of Fred Parks,
  BA '59
Euless, Texas

Glena Pfennig, BJ '64
Baytown, Texas

Carolyn Williams Pippin, BBA '48
Haskell, Texas

Roxie Potter, BS '75
New York, New York

Amy Purcell Powell, BS '55
Navasota, Texas

Lynne Prater, wife of Harold Glen
  Prater, BBA '55
Arlington, Texas

Marilyn Reneau, BS '70
Dallas, Texas

Patricia Morgan Richardson, BS '69
Arlington, Texas

Roberta Caffarelli Rife, BA '35
San Antonio, Texas

Becky Barlow Rivers, BS '71
Bastrop, Texas

Elizabeth Lynn Rosen, BBA '80
New Orleans, Louisiana

Opal Thomson Rosson, BA '27 MA '39
Houston, Texas

Phyllis Horn Rozen, BS '68
Corpus Christi, Texas

John D. Ryder, BBA '65
Seguin, Texas

Sybil McKee Savage, BA '22
Sanderson, Texas

Barbara Grant Schliebe, BS '68
Chapel Hill, North Carolina

Phyllis Knowlton Schriever, '46
Pasadena, Texas

Rose Marie Robinson Schwarzer,
  BBA '57
Austin, Texas

Nina Cook Segler, BBA '78
Dallas, Texas

Mary Lins Shetler, BA '79
Houston, Texas

Kay Rose Sims, BS '72
Mountain Home, Arkansas

Jinny Chappell Smith, BA '66
Dallas, Texas

Barbara Sneddon, Friend of UT
Sanderson, Texas

Peter S. Solito, LLB '42
Houston, Texas

Runelle Loyd Stembridge, BS '51
Gilmer, Texas

Renie Steves, wife of Sterling Steves,
  BA '50 LLB '54
The French Apron School of Cooking,
Fort Worth, Texas

Twyla Lynn Tranfaglia, BA '73
  MLS '74
El Paso, Texas

Everette L. Tucker, Jr., BA '58
Poquoson, Virginia

Zula Williams Vizard, BA '33 MA '35
San Antonio, Texas

Cindy Wilson Walker, BS '79
Houston, Texas

Ruth Cotten Whiddon, BA '40
Eugene Whiddon, BBA '47
Beaumont, Texas

Mary Fletcher White, BA '40
Oro Valley, Arizona

Virginia Stanberry Williams, '35
Austin, Texas

Margie Taylor Wilson, BS '70
Rockwall, Texas

Nancy Morris Wilson, MA '68
Dallas, Texas

Lois Fenske Wolff, BS '47
Kenedy, Texas

Donald D. Young, JD '77
Albuquerque, New Mexico

Contributors

Diane Akers, wife of UT Football Coach
  Fred Akers
Anna Pearl Alexander, BA '38
Bonnie Blades Allen, '51
Carol Ann Caldwell Allen, BS '74
Gladys Allen, wife of Tom Allen,
  BS '25 MS '27
Raye Virginia McCreary Allen,
  BA '51 MA '75
Susan Elkins Allen, BBA '75
Susan J. Allen, BJ '78
H. B. Amstead, BS '41 MS '49 PhD '55
Robert B. Anderson, LLB '32
Thomas K. Anson, JD '80
Kay Appleman, BA '68
Louise Appleman, wife of Gordon
  Appleman, BA '59
William R. Archer, Jr., BBA '50 LLB '51
Whynell Aston, BBA '46
Sara Avant, BS '78
Cynthia Henneberger Babel, BS '74
Edwin Argyle Bailey, '64
Edna Heflin Baker, BA '16
Rex Baker, Jr., BA '41 LLB '47
Dorothy Burr Banks, BA '23 MA '26
Brenda Wilson Barber, BS '68
Carolyn Row Barber, BS '46
Agnes Warren Barnes, BS '57
Nancy DeGraffenreid Barnes, BA '51
Carol Wueste Barrett, BS '69
June Barrett, BS '54

Betty Klutts Barton, BS '64
Maurine Redfearn Bartos, BS '57
Marie Blount Bassinger, BS '47
Louise Stromberg Bates, BS '34
Alan Bean, BS '55
Kay Jones Becker, BS '69
Beth Stephens Beck, BA '79
Eugenia Nash Belden, MA '36
Joe Belden, BJ '39
Nell Allen Bell, '48
Jan Bixler Bennett, BS '72
Lloyd M. Bentsen, Jr. LLB '42
Conrad Bering, '17
George J. Beto, MA '44 PhD '55
Peter Agnew Bickel, BA '66
Marilyn Atkins Biehl, BBA '71
Sandra Daniel Billingsley, '60
Susan Scott Birdwell, BS '69
William R. Birdwell, BA '69 DDS '73
Adele Houssels Black, BS '29
Paula Jo Black, BS '61
Margaret Blair, BS '74
J. S. Bleymaier, BBA '50
Theresa Bus Block, BS '77
Jane Weinert Blumberg, BA '37
Evelyn Cheatham Bochow, MBA '53
Jo Laynne Hill Boies, MM '72
John F. Bookout, BS '49 MA '50
Mary Katherine Welhausen Borchers,
  BBA '45
Mary Kay Borchers, BBA '73

446

Nannette Avant Borden, BM '76
Louise Farmer Boyer, BS '30
Mary Boyles, wife of J.G. Boyles,
   BBA '59
Ann Barber Brinkerhoff, BA '49
Ellen Brodnax, BA '41 MA '44
Joyce Kocurek Brooks, BS '69
Helen Dixon Brown, MA '34
Stella Jung Browning, BS '36
Margaret Otto Bryan, BS '76
Dorothy Hudson Burr, BBA '26
Mary Burson, BS '75
John W. Butler, Jr., BA '75
Aline Calhoun, '23
Earl Christian Campbell, BS '79
Betty Dupree Carpenter, BA '48
Connie Carpenter, BBA '80
Liz Carpenter, BJ '42
Mary Hall Carter, BJ '77
Ane Watson Casady, BA '70
Dorothea Gannaway Casberg, BFA '45
Steve Castlebury, BA '43
Denise Jaroszewski Chandler, BS '76
Don Chandler, BS '78
Adam Gene Chavez, BA '69
Katie Lewis Cheatham, '15
George Christian, BJ '71
Dixi Rhodes Clay, wife of Jerry H. Clay,
   BS '59
Beth Miller Clegg, '50
Ann Clements, wife of Jamie Clements,
   BA '53 LLB '55
Jamie H. Clements, BA '53, LLB '55
Rita Crocker Clements, BA '53
Madeline Bynum Closmann, BJ '49
Joe M. Coffield, BS '42
Robert Ellen Colbert, wife of Lester L.
   Colbert, BBA '25
Janiece McGraw Collier, wife of James E.
   Collier, BS '57
Sara Catherine Collier, BBA '81
Kathryn Lewis Colon, BBA '77
Judith Cody Colquitt, BS '60
Idanell Brill Connally, '40
Betty Cook, '48
Sylvia Cook, BA '65
Denton A. Cooley, BA '41
Dorothy Ann Cooley, BS '80

Audrey Fritz Cooper, wife of Richard
   Cooper, BBA '56
M. Julie Cooper, '12
Nancy Bell Cooper, BA '67
Jose Correa, BS '47
Beverly Cottle, wife of J. Ted Cottle,
   BBA '32
Carol A. Crabtree, BS '77
Diane Davis Cravens, BS '61
Tom Cravens, BBA '64
Carolyn Devault Crawford, wife of John
   Crawford, BBA '61
Gail Hayes Cromeens, BS '70
Fletcher Metcalfe Croom, '36
Walter Cronkite, '33
Brenda Brantley Croucher, BS '72
Julie Dryden Crow, BS '75
Joan Culver, wife of Joe Culver,
   BBA '53 MBA '58
Anna M. Curry, BS '68 MD '72
John K. Dannelley, '73
Cheryl Parsons Darnell, BJ '79
Jacqueline B. Davis, MLS '78
Dora Eleanor Good Dean, BBA '58
Patricia Lind Derx, '62
Sara Dobarganes, BS '79
Dana Humble Dodson, BS '77
Dwain Dodson, BS '76 MS '77
Bob R. Dorsey, BS '40
Dorothy Burwitz Doss, BA '40
Elaine M. Dove, MA '72
Mitzi Nuhn Dreher, BS '54 MS '56
Ronnie Dugger, BA '50
Willetta Albritton Eastland, BBA '76
Mary Zappalac Edwards, BFA '73
Theo Smith Eichler, BS '38
Louise Freedman Eiseman, BFA '51
El Rancho Restaurant
Kathleen Tempel Elkins, '41
Lee Elledge, '43
Sunny Iles Elledge, '43
Roseanne Paul Elling, '75
Crockett English, '42
Jerry Wilke English, '39
Glynda Harrell Eschle, BS '63
Bessie Evers, Friend of UT
Bess Powell Ezelle, '26
Chris Holley Fain, BS '75

Pam Farley, BS '79

Verna Sykes Farris, BS '74

Tillie Fauntleroy, wife of O.W. (Buzz)
Fauntleroy, BA '48

Kirsten Felker, wife of M. L. (Bud)
Felker, '43

M.L. (Bud) Felker, '43

Jeanne Ferguson, wife of Paul Ferguson,
BS '57

Wayne Ferguson, BBA '59 MBA '60

Kathy Fife, BS '80

William Bryan Finklea, LLB '50

Joe J. Fisher, BBA '63

Patty Jay Fiske, BBA '27

Wm. P. Fitch, III, BA '64

Priscilla Flawn, wife of UT President
Peter Flawn

Jeanette Anne Fleming, BS '76

Sharon Fleming, Friend of UT

Maria Luisa Flores, BA '77 JD '80

Mary Ann Flowers, BA '78

Bobbie Fly, wife of UT Regent Sterling
Fly, '43

Kimberly Fojtik, BBA '79

Carolyn Fonken, wife of UT Vice
President Gerhard Fonken

Jamina Ford, wife of Tommy Ford, BS '65

Steven R. Foy, BBA '79

Joe Frantz, BJ '38 MA '40 PhD '48

Margaret Johnson Frazier, BM '42

Shelley Friend, BJ '77

Carol Gallman, wife of Jim Gallman,
BS '74

Nita Hixson Galloway, BJ '51

T. Earnest Gammage, Jr., BA '39 LLB '39

Lawana Geren, '71

Eleanor Ann Van Zandt Gerrard, BA '42

Elizabeth Bailey Geyer, BM '57 MM '58

Walter L. Geyer, BM '61

Jeanne Schwarz Gilbert, '49

Vera Lee Knight Giles, wife of Rogan
Giles, BBA '51 LLB '53

Agnes Gloyna, wife of UT Dean Earnest
Gloyna, MS '49

J. A. Gooch, '29

David M. Gould, BA '76

Nancy Milburn Granaghan, '73

Elizabeth Howry Gray, '76

Jack S. Gray, BBA '35

Marta Gray, BS '79

Molly Moffett Gray, BFA '53

Sheila M. Gray, BBA '78

Lucy Green, BA '72

Terry Green, wife of Leonard F. Green,
BA '79

Marsha Newman Greiner, '64

Zuleika Stranger Griffin, BA '43

Elaine Wiswell Guy, BS '75

Mary Lu Ryan Haase, BS '57

Richard A. Haberman, BA '61

Joan Tompkins Hallmark, BFA '55

Carol Sue Hand, BS '72

I.B. Hand, BBA '40 LLB '40

Jo Shropshire Hannon, BBA '47

Susan Collier Hanson, BS '78

John P. Harbin, BBA '39

Mary Roberts Hardesty, MA '77

Susan Marie Palousek Harding, BA '69

Beverly Gibbs Harlan, wife of Harris J.
Harlan, BS '60

Tom Harlow, BBA '58

Ann Driscoll Hatchell, BS '65

Millie Haehnel, wife of Bill Haehnel '39

Carol Hebdon, wife of Jack C. Hebdon,
BBA '77

Penny Porter Helms, BFA '66

Charlotte Curtis Henderson, BS '37

G. P. Herndon, Jr., BBA '28

Nell Jones Herndon, BA '30

Robert L. Herndon, BS '66

Lena Pettit Hickman, BA '15

Elizabeth (Bitsy) Graham Hill, BA '44

Christine Sigmon Hines, BS '73

Rhonda Hodges, wife of R. L. Hodges,
BBA '74

Louise Hoehn, BA '59

Becky Burns Hoffman, BS '68

Sally Baumgardner Hoffman, BS '75

Murph Holley, BBA '50

Pat Biel Holley, BBA '50

James T. Holman, BJ '59

Pat Doney Holt, '48

Burt C. Hooton, '68

Anthony E. F. Howard, BS '57

Gladys Bravenec Howard, BS '55

Pat Howard, wife of Henry Howard, BS '59

Jewel Hudler, BA '22 MA '26
Alicia Hudnall, '81
John F. Hudnall, BA '58 MD '61
Joyce Jennings Hudnall, BS '57
Ruth Butler Hunt, '27
Catherine Baumstark Hurd, BS '69
Bebe Canales Inkley, '57
Walther John Ives, MA '51
Jennifer McNeil Jackson, BS '70 MEd '75
Loraine McNeil Jackson, '46
Mary Barnes James, BA '75 BJ '75
Jane Cornick Jamison, BS '66
Mary Canales Jary, '56
Jim Jenkins, BBA '74 MPA '76
John H. Jenkins, '63
Stephanie Jackson Jenkins, BS '68
Peggy R. Jetton, wife of Bobby R. Jetton,
    BS '72
Kittie Fae Robison Jinkins, BS '19
Claudia Taylor (Lady Bird) Johnson,
    BA '33 BJ '34
Amalee Turek Jones, BA '26
Bess Harris Jones, BJ '34
Helen Johnson Jones, BA '39 MLS '51
Susan Chafin Jones, MA '76
Jonelle Thornberry Jordan, BM '48
Robert E. Joseph, '54
Carmen G. Kanapi, PhD '67
Alice Gann Kaspar, '73
Jean Welhausen Kaspar, BA '52
Carolyn Frost Keenan, BS '76 MA '78
Margaret Benson Kennedy, BA '26
Eve Stein Kermacy, BFA 54 MEd 60
Susan and Jim Kessler, Friends of UT
Elizabeth Ann Kibbe, BBA '78
Margaret Macha Kiefer, BA '69
Joe M. Kilgore, '39
Patsy Aliece Kirby, wife of Clarence
    Kirby, BA '58
Sharen Ann Kirksey, BS '76
Shirley Coin Kleiman, BBA '48
Trudy Iverson Kokernot, BS '71
Brenda Thompson Kolinek, BBA '72
Samuel L. Kone, CE '12
Barbara Koy, wife of Ernie Koy, BA '66
Ronya Kozmetsky, wife of UT Dean
    George Kozmetsky
Billie Krausse, wife of Dan Krausse, BS '47

Joe Kyle, Jr., BBA '73
Tom Landry, BBA '49
Sandra Lauer, wife of John Lauer,
    LLB '59
Jo Ann Nelson Law, '43
Harding Lawrence, BBA '42
Lowell Lebermann, Jr., '57
Georgina Roach Lee, '62
Doris Robinson Legg, BA '26
Fred Leisering, BBA '42
Peggy Gross Lerner, BA '49
Merle Tooke Lewis, BA '53 MLS '70
Randolph H. Lewis, '40
Grace Lewis Ley, BS '23
Myrtle Ligon, wife of Jack A. Ligon,
    BA '50
Evelyn Wilson Lindsay, '47
Rebecca Linkous, BJ '81
Sue Brooks Littlefield, BA '77 JD '80
Edith Mae Sanders Livingston, BBA '41
Harriet Schmitt Livingston, BS '69
Patti W. Livingston, BA '75
Donna A. Lopiano, UT Director of
    Athletics for Women
Johnnye Jean Weinert Lovett, BA '48
Agnes Henke Lundstedt, BS '53
Jane H. Macon, BA '67 JD '70
Wales Madden, Jr., BA '50 LLB '52
Mauricio B. Madero, '33
Susan Fortson Magee, BA '76 MLS '78
Gay Freeze Maguire, '71
Pat Horton Maguire, BA '46
Mary Ann Maley, BA '54
Sylva Fant Maley, '26
Humboldt C. Mandell, Jr., BS '57
Carol Pirrung Mann, MA '75 MLS '77
Edward F. Manning, JD '72
Betty Lou Wenger Marburger, '55
Carolyn Williams Marks, BS '60
Sammie Farrier Marshall, '47
Marilyn Marter, BS '74
Judith Morrison Martin, BA '77 BJ '77
Martin's Kum Bak Place (Dirty's)
Charles D. Mathews, LLB '37
Harriett Kidder Matlock, '47
Martha Maynard, BS '80
Judy Walker Mayo, BS '71
Pat McCarty, BBA '49

Margaret Milam McDermott, '32
Matilda McCammon McFaddin, BA '18
Sharon Duncan McFarland, BA '74
   MLS '76
Vivienne L. McKitrick, BA '72 BS '75
Joe McMordie, husband of Virginia
Calhoun McMordie, BS '46
Virginia Calhoun McMordie, BS '46
T. N. McNabb, Friend of UT
Gem Meacham, BA '72
Maxine Kubela Mebane, BS '35
Irene Reeb Meitzen, BA '65
Sara May McCampbell Meriwether,
   BA '51
Dale Merlo, BS '75
Bessie Kilgore Merner, BA '30 MA '32
Nancy Mitchell Meyers, BS '75
Louise Buckner Milburn, BBA '48
Dale Miller, MJ '32
William Kay Miller, BA '34 LLB '34
Janie Dechman Modrall, BA '53
Bernice Milburn Moore, BJ '24 MA '32
Janette McIntyre Morrow, BA '45
Hudson Moyer, BBA '54, LLB '57
Nancy Gilmore Moyer, '50
Louise Harrell Mulkey, BA '61
Susan Weber Munson, BFA '67
William B. Munson, IV, LLB '67
Jewel Morris Murchison, '26
Patricia Reichenbach Murray, BA '72
Deanna Cook Murphy, BA '59
Vergil Murphy, '28
Lucy Nagle, BA '77
Nancy Nagle, MBA '78
Suzanne Williams Nash, BA '67
Iris Selber Nathan, '57
Nancy Brown Negley, '58
Gertrude Neuhaus, wife of V.F. (Doc)
   Neuhaus, '20
Judy Newton, wife of Regent Jon
   Newton, BA '63 LLB '65
Nancy Krause Nibling, BA '73
Carol Reeb Nietenhoefer, BS '66
Tommy Nobis, '62
Arno Nowotny, BA '22 LLB '25 MA '32
LaVerne Stugard Nowotny, BS '29
Ken Nuhn, BArch '49
Mary Lou Hopson Nuhn, '44

Karen McBride O'Brien, BS '72
Amy Lois Porter Oden, BA '21
Betty Cunningham Olguin, '60
Judith Lott Oliver, '30
Debbie Deering Owen, BS '79
Dorothy M. Owens, Friend of UT
John F. Owens, BS '55
Shirlee McCulley Page, BBA '65
Virginia Nalle Page, BJ '33 MJ '35
Cissy McDaniel Parker, BS '44
Fred Parks, BBA '59
David L. Parsley, BBA '66
Sue Armintor Parsley, wife of David
   Parsley, BBA '66
Harriet Williams Peavy, BA '63
Nancy Fiske Pellerin, BS '57
Wallace Pellerin, BBA '55
Bobbie Sloan Peltier, wife of Al E.
   Peltier, BS '51
Judy Perrone, wife of UT Systems
   Operations Officer Charles Perrone
Betty Sugg Person, Friend of UT
Ruby Crawford Pesek, BA '62
Theresa Valenta Pesek, '49
Anthony Petrick, BBA '65
H. C. Pfannkuche, '22
Glena Russell Pfennig, BJ '64
Rosemary Fanning Pinson, wife of Robert
   M. Pinson, BA '41
Carolyn Williams Pippin, BBA '48
Annette Plemmons, wife of John L.
   Plemmons, '65
Sara Armstrong Post, BS '67
Roxie Potter, BS '75
Amy Purcell Powell, BS '55
Ruth Ann Neves Powell, BS '72
Lynne Prater, wife of Harold G. Prater,
   BBA '55
Marjorie Price, wife of Meredith Wayne
   Price, BBA '70
Cactus Pryor, '41
Wally Pryor, BFA '51
Catherine M. Ragel, Friend of UT
Fred Ramsey, '57
Adelle Neely Rannefeld, BA '42
Red Tomato Restaurant
James Reddy, BS '56
Ruth Reddy, wife of James Reddy, BS '56

Erika Reeb, Friend of UT
John P. Reeves, BA '51
Kathleen Kenny Reily, BS '77
Marilyn Reneau, BS '70
Henry Renfert, MD, Friend of UT
Patricia Morgan Richardson, BS '69
Glynis Kirchhof Richter, BS '79
Roberta Caffarelli Rife, BA '35
Steve Rivers, '68
Becky Barlow Rivers, BS '71
Ruth Roach, wife of Lloyd Roach,
    LLB '50
Lynda Johnson Robb, BA '66
Ray Roberts, '33
Dick Rolle, '35
Elizabeth Lynn Rosen, BBA '80
Lynn Rosenfeld, BJ '72
Opal Thomson Rosson, BA '27 MA '39
Frances Combest Rountree, BBA '38
Mae Caller Rowland, BBA '32
Mildred Rowntree, Friend of UT
Edith Royal, wife of former UT Coach
    Darrell Royal
Phyllis Horn Rozen, BS '68
John D. Ryder, BBA '65
John T. Ryder, BA '68
Barefoot Sanders, BA '49 LLB '50
Sybil McKee Savage, BA '22
David R. Scheihagen, BS '77
Patrice McCullen Schexnayder, BA '70
Caroline Hunt Schoelkopf, BA '43
Scholz's Restaurant
Tex Schramm, BJ '47
Charles R. Schneider, BBA '47
Charles Schreiner, III, BA '47
Phyllis Knowlton Schriever, '46
Scottish Rite Dormitory
Nina Cook Segler, BBA '78
Jeannette Monnier Selway, BS '55
Linda Hughes Sharkey, BS '71 MEd '73
Rose Marie Sharp, BJ '73
Dorothy Shepperd Shelby, BA '32
Tom Shelby, BS '33 MA '34
Gillett Sheppard, LLB '56
Mamie Strieber Shepperd, BJ '38
Mary Lins Shetler, BA '79
Michael G. Shirley, BA '70 JD '72
Sue A. Lebel Shirley, BS '64

Marialice Shivers, wife of Allan Shivers,
    BA '31, LLB '33
Robin N. Siewert, BS '79
Kay Rose Sims, BS '72
Jane Tully Singleton, BJ '42
Martha Francis Singleton, '40
Ernest F. Smith, BA '40
Liz Smith, BJ '50
Jinny Chappell Smith, BA '66
R. J. Smith, '50
Jamie Carter Snell, BJ '73
Dolores Simmons Snyder, BS '54
Peter S. Solito, '42
Ralph Spence, BBA '42
Charnita Spring, BA '73
Evelyn Brown Squyres, BA '51
Stagecoach Inn
W. J. (Billie) Stark, LLB '49 BBA '50
Joan Ortloff Steinhoff, BS '70
Runelle Loyd Stembridge, BS '51
Ruth Sterling, wife of former UT Regent
    Walter Sterling, LLB '25
Doris Weldon Stokes, '29
Lisa Evans Strickhausen, BS '77
Barbara White Stuart, '55
Bobbie Rainey Sublett, '31
Suzanne Adele Tausend, '79
Ruth Brooks Teague, '39
Texas Union Dining Service
Joe C. Thompson, Jr., BBA '62
Theresa Velten Thompson, BS '78
Eloise Engle Thornberry, BA '42
Charlotte Thornton, BA '78 MA '81
Sunshine Neely Thurmond, BA '37
Esther Knudson Tipps, MS '56
Carolyn Braselton Townsend, BA '66
Twyla Lynn Tranfaglia, BA '73 MLS '74
Minifred Boyles Trigg, '56
Susan Dillon Tschudi, BA '71
Everett Tucker, Jr., BA '58
Clydine Wagner Tweedy, BS '46
Dale Sandgarten Udashen, BA '75
Carolyn Kongabel Vance, BS '55
Frances McLean VanHorn, BA '70
Billie Gault Vaughan, BS '71
Zula Thompson Vizard, BA '33 MA '35
Florence Stanhiser Von Bieberstein, '31
Sylvia Bone Waldrop, BS '56

Cindy Wilson Walker, BS '79
Harvey "Chick" Wallender, '36
Charlotte Plemmons Warren, BJ '76
Emma Stullken Webb, '23
Sarah Ragle Weddington, LLB '67
Sharon Wehner, BA '67
C.T. Wells, BS '37 MS '37 PhD '39
Jane Lovett Wells, BFA 71
Richard West, BJ '63 BA '63
Marsha Herndon Wheless, BBA '76
Eugene Whiddon, BBA '47
Ruth Cotten Whiddon, BA '40
Mary Fletcher White, BA '40
Sandy Jennings Williams, wife of Charles
    R. Williams, MBA '78
Dan C. Williams, BS '35
Virginia Stanberry Williams, '35
Charles M. Wilson, III, BBA '70 JD '74
Nancy Morris Wilson, MA '68

Pauline McAnnelly Wilson, BS '40
Nancy Montgomery Winter, '63
Lois Fenske Wolff, BA '47
Carol Hall Wood, BS '54
Carol A. Woodlock, BS '79
Bonita Granville Wrather, wife of Jack
    Wrather, BA '39
Jack Wrather, BA '39
Betty Wright, wife of Jim Wright, '41
Emrys Ann Ryder Wuest, '60
Gladys Riskind Wueste, BS '38 MEd '50
Marietta (Bitsy) Watson Wynne, BS '54
Jim Young, BA '48
Katherine Young, MS '44
Pat Martin Younts, BS '53
Louy Younts, '51
Oscar G. Zuniga, '54

Index

454

455

458

460

462

COOK 'EM HORNS, Texas Exes Cookbook
P.O. Box 7278
Austin, Texas 78712

Please send_____copies of *Cook 'em Horns.* $16.95 each _____

Postage and handling $ 2.00 each _____

Texas residents add 5% tax   .85 each _____

     Total amount enclosed: $ _____

Name _____

Street _____

City _____ State_____ Zip_____

- -

COOK 'EM HORNS, Texas Exes Cookbook
P.O. Box 7278
Austin, Texas 78712

Please send_____copies of *Cook 'em Horns.* $16.95 each _____

Postage and handling $ 2.00 each _____

Texas residents add 5% tax   .85 each _____

     Total amount enclosed: $ _____

Name _____

Street _____

City _____ State_____ Zip_____

- -

COOK 'EM HORNS, Texas Exes Cookbook
P.O. Box 7278
Austin, Texas 78712

Please send_____copies of *Cook 'em Horns.* $16.95 each _____

Postage and handling $ 2.00 each _____

Texas residents add 5% tax   .85 each _____

     Total amount enclosed: $ _____

Name _____

Street _____

City _____ State_____ Zip_____